Independent Belarus

UKRAINIAN RESEARCH INSTITUTE
DAVIS CENTER FOR RUSSIAN STUDIES
HARVARD UNIVERSITY

Cambridge, Massachusetts

INDEPENDENT BELARUS
DOMESTIC DETERMINANTS,
REGIONAL DYNAMICS, AND
IMPLICATIONS FOR THE WEST

edited by

Margarita M. Balmaceda
James I. Clem
Lisbeth L. Tarlow

Distributed by Harvard University Press for the
Ukrainian Research Institute and Davis Center for Russian Studies,
Harvard University

Publication of this book has been supported by the
Smith Richardson Foundation

Library of Congress Cataloging-in-Publication Data

Independent Belarus : domestic determinants, regional dynamics, and
implications for the West / edited by Margarita M. Balmaceda, James I.
Clem, Lisbeth L. Tarlow.
    p. cm.
English and Belarusian.
Includes index.
  ISBN 0-916458-94-6 (alk. paper)
  1. Belarus--Politics and government--1991- 2. Belarus--Foreign
relations. I. Balmaceda, Margarita Mercedes, 1965- II. Clem, James I.
III. Tarlow, Lisbeth L.
  DK507.817 .I54 2002
  320.9478'09'049--dc21
                                    2002003837

ISBN 0-916458-94-6 (softcover)

Contents

Acknowledgments

We are indebted to the help of many people and institutions who made this project possible.

Our largest debt is to the Smith-Richardson Foundation, which provided us with a grant that made possible the organization of this conference, a fact-finding trip to Belarus in September 1999, and the publication of this book. We would like to thank the Davis Center for Russian Studies and the Ukrainian Research Institute, both at Harvard University, for their institutional support of this project. We are grateful to their directors, Timothy Colton and Roman Szporluk, for their guidance as we set off in this project. We are indebted to Prof. Jan Zaprudnik for his help and advice throughout the project, and for his willingness to look over the first draft of the book. We would like to thank Olga Klimanovitch of the Minsk office of the USIS for her tremendous help in the organization of the fact-finding trip to Belarus. We are indebted to Donna Griesenbeck and Melissa Griggs provided invaluable organizational support, and to Alex Bulanov and Philip Nikolaev for their research assistance.

We would like to thank those who contributed to this book, either as authors or as other participants in the April 1999 conference. In addition to the authors in this volume, these are Uladzimir Snapkoŭski, Alexandra Gujon, Aleksandr Lukashuk, Mikk Titma, and Amb. Daniel Speckhart. In addition, we are indebted to Hannes Adomeit, Kelly McMann, Rawi Abdelal, Sarah Mendelson, William Zimmerman, Coit Blecker, Oles Smolansky, Timothy Snyder, and Alexander Pivovarsky for their comments on specific chapters.

The transformation of our manuscript into a book would not have been possible without the indefatigable work of Robert De Lossa and Daria Yurchuk at the Ukrainian Research Institute. Mikhail Volodin provided timely and important insights on issues of language and politics. His help at various stages of this project is much appreciated.

Finally, Margarita Balmaceda would like to thank Dr. Muriel Joffe of the Institute of International Education and the Fulbright Program for making possible a Fulbright lectureship that was pivotal for her work on the project. She is also greatly indebted to Dr. Marian Glenn and Amb. Clay Constantinou of the School of Diplomacy and International Relations at Seton Hall University for their support for this project. Last but not least, she would like to thank Dr. Marianne Sághy and Dr. Maren Jochimsen for their companionship, help, and support through two winters of fieldwork in Belarus.

Technical Note

The presentation of Belarusian personal names and place names is problematic. The use of Belarusian or Russian is taken by many as a political statement. However, the use of Belarusian itself is difficult, since there are competing orthographies that claim centrality and authenticity. For the present volume, the editors have made the decision to utilize Belarusian forms for all individuals of Belarusian citizenry and for all toponyms within Belarus proper. The Library of Congress transliteration system is used with one modification—the absence of ligatures. Where there are competing "Belarusian" forms for a place name, we have chosen the one that seems to us more widespread in academic Belarusian usage. Thus, Minsk, *not* Miensk; and Polatsk, *not* Polatsak. When a Belarusian form differs so radically from its Russian variant that it would impede recognition by scholars accustomed to the Russian form, the Russian form is given in brackets following first usage of the Belarusian. Thus, Lukashenka is given alone, while Liavonaŭ has "[Leonov]" following its first usage. The index has equivalent forms for all Belarusian names in order to facilitate searching for the names in other resources. The only exception to this rule is in the authors' names, where their form of preference has been used. As well, Belarusian authors with well-established English-language forms of their names are given in that form.

All dollar-denominated figures are in US currency, unless otherwise noted.

Queries regarding content should be directed to:

Belarus Project
Davis Center for Russian Studies
Harvard University
Cambridge, MA 02138 USA

Queries regarding distribution or promotion should be directed to:

HURI Publications
Harvard Ukrainian Research Institute
1583 Massachusetts Ave.
Cambridge, MA 02138 USA

List of Contributors

Margarita M. Balmaceda received a doctorate in politics from Princeton University in 1996. She is an assistant professor at the School of Diplomacy and International Relations at Seton Hall University and an associate of Harvard University's Ukrainian Research Institute, where she also is co-director of the "Belarus Factor" project. She spent fall 1997 and spring 1999 as a Fulbright lecturer at the Belarusian State University in Minsk. Among her publications are *On the Edge: the Ukrainian- Central European-Russian Security Triangle* (Budapest, 2000) and "Myth and Reality in the Belarusian-Russian Relationship: Implications for the West," *Problems of Post Communism* 46 (May/ June 1999). She currently is working on a book on pipelines and foreign policies in Central-East Europe, with grants from IREX and other foundations.

Between 1995 and 1999, **Patricia Brukoff** served as an international economist in the Office of the Assistant Secretary for International Affairs at the U.S. Department of the Treasury, where she worked on the Russia Desk following Russian, Belarusian, and Moldovan macroeconomic, trade and tax policy developments. Dr. Brukoff is currently working at the International Monetary Fund in Washington, DC. She holds a BA from Princeton University in Politics and Russian Studies, and a doctorate in Policy Analysis and Post-Soviet Studies from the RAND Graduate School.

James I. Clem is executive director of the Ukrainian Research Institute at Harvard University. He received his doctorate from the University of Michigan in 1995, where his dissertation topic was on the development of political party organizations in western and eastern Ukraine. He received a Post-Doctoral Fellowship at Harvard's Davis Center for Russian Studies, and has taught at the College of the Holy Cross and the Harvard University Summer School. He co-edited, with Nancy Popson, *Ukraine and Central Europe: Multi-level Networks and International Relations* (Washington, DC, 2000) and co-wrote, with Peter Craumer, an article entitled "Ukraine's Emerging Electoral Geography: A Regional Analysis of the 1998 Parliamentary Elections," *Post-Soviet Geography and Economics* January–February 1999.

Timothy J. Colton is director of the Davis Center for Russian Studies and Morris and Anna Feldberg Professor of Government and Russian Studies at Harvard University. Dr. Colton received his doctorate in government in 1974 from Harvard University. He has written and edited several books, including a lengthy study of urban politics in Soviet Russia, *Moscow: Governing the Socialist Metropolis* (Cambridge, Mass., 1995). In 1998, he co-edited a volume on the 1993 elections entitled *Growing Pains: Russian Democracy and the Election of 1993* (Washington, DC, 1998). Professor Colton is also the author of "Understanding Iurii Luzhkov," *Problems of Post-Communism* September-October 1999; and *Transitional Citizens: Voters and What Influences Them in the New Russia* (Cambridge, Mass., 2000). His current research focuses on electoral patterns in post-Soviet Russia. Prof. Colton is the winner of award for best scholarly book in government and political science, Association of American Publishers, for *Moscow: Governing the Socialist Metropolis* (Cambridge, Mass., 1995). He currently is working on a book about Russia's former president, Boris Yeltsin.

Elaine M. Conkievich is currently deputy head of the Organization of Security and Cooperation in Europe (OSCE) Office in Yerevan, Armenia. Prior to this, she was for three years the senior mission program officer on Central Asia with the Conflict Prevention Centre in the Secretariat of the OSCE in Vienna. Before that, she worked with OSCE missions in Belarus, Bosnia and Herzegovina, and Latvia, primarily in the areas of human rights and democratization. In addition, she has worked with UNITAR in Geneva on training and research in the areas of peacemaking and preventive diplomacy. Ms. Conkievich's area of specialty is preventive diplomacy, focusing especially on Eastern Europe and the former Soviet Union.

Yuri Drakokhrust is an editor at the Belarusian Service of Radio Liberty in Prague, Czech Republic, where he also worked as a correspondent from 1996 to 2000. He received his degree in mathematics from Belarusian State University. Between 1982 and 1993, Mr. Drakokhrust worked at The Institute of Math and Economics of the Belarusian National Academy of Sciences.

Dmitri Furman is the director of the Commonwealth of Independent States Research Center at the Russian Academy of Sciences' Institute of Europe. He received his doctorate in history from Moscow State

University. Professor Furman is an expert on the issues of national determination, territorial division, European history and culture, and the role of religion in societies. Among Professor Furman's publications are *Towards The Islamic Reformation* (Moscow, 1999), *Belorussiia i Rossiia: Obshchestva i gosudarstva*, ed. (Moscow, 1998), *Chechnia i Rossiia: Obshchestva i gosudarstva* (Moscow 1999), and *Ukraina i Rossiia: Obshchestva i gosudarstva* (Moscow, 1997).

Sherman Garnett is professor and dean of the James Madison College at Michigan State University. From 1994 to July 1999 he was a Senior Associate at the Carnegie Endowment for International Peace in Washington, DC, where he specialized in the foreign and security policies of Russia, Ukraine, and the states of the former USSR. At Carnegie, Dr. Garnett also directed the project on Security and National Identity in the Endowment's Russian and Eurasian Program. Before joining the Endowment, Dr. Garnett served at the U.S. Department of Defense as the acting deputy assistant secretary of defense for Russia, Ukraine, and Eurasia. He also was director for European security negotiations and representative to the CSCE for the Defense Department. Dr. Garnett received his doctorate in Russian literature from the University of Michigan. He has published widely. His recent publications include *Rapprochement or Rivalry? Russian-China Relations in a Changing Asia* (Washington, DC, 2000), *Belarus At The Crossroads*, S. Garnett and R. Legvold, eds. (Washington, DC, 1999), *Getting It Wrong: Regional Cooperation And The Commonwealth of Independent States*, M. Olcott, A. Åslund and S. Garnett, eds. (Washington, DC, 1999), *Keystone in the Arch: Ukraine in the Emerging Security Environment of Central and Eastern Europe* (Washington, DC, 1997).

Algirdas Gricius is an adviser on European cooperation to the Ministry of Foreign Affairs, Lithuania, and associate professor of Political Science at the Institute of International Relations and Political Science at Vilnius University, where he focuses on Baltic Sea area politics. His publications include "Russia's Enclave in the Baltic Region: A Source of Stability or Tension?" in *Kaliningrad: The European Amber Region*, P. Jonnieme and J. Prawitz, eds. (Brookfield, Vt., 1998); "Lithuania and its Belarusan policy," *Lithuanian Foreign Policy Review* 1999(3) (Vilnius: Foreign Policy Research Center); "Vliianie, Beloruskogo faktora na vneshniuiu politiku Litvy i stabil'nost' v Baltiiskom regione," in *Belorussiia na pereputie v poiskakh mezhdunarodnoi identichnosti,*

Sherman Garnett and Robert Legvold, eds. (Moscow, 1998); and "Enlargement of the European Union and Security of the Baltic States," *Politologiia* 1997(2).

Rainer Lindner is a researcher and lecturer at the Department of History and Sociology (East European Desk) at the University of Konstanz in Germany. In 1996 he was a research fellow at the Ukrainian Research Institute at Harvard University. He received his doctorate from the Eberhard-Karls-University of Tübingen. Until 1998 he was a researcher at the Stiftung Wissenschaft und Politik (SWP), where he took part in the project "Post-Soviet Puzzles: Mapping the Political Economy of the Former Soviet Union." In 1997 he founded the annual "Minsk Forum: International Conferences on Belarus– Politics, Economy, and Foreign Affairs." His recent works on Belarus include: *Historiker und Herrschaft. Nationsbildung und Geschichtspolitik in Weißrußland im 19. und 20. Jahrhundert* (Munich, 1999) [=Ordnungssysteme. Studien zur Ideegeschichte der Neuzeit, Bd. 5]; *Die Ukraine und Belarus in der Transformation. Eine Zwischenbilanz,* Rainer Lindner and Boris Meissner, eds. (Cologne, 2001); *Handbuch der Geschichte Weißrußlands,* Dietrich Beyrau and Rainer Lindner, eds. (Göttingen, 2001). He also has authored numerous articles on history and contemporary politics in Russia, Ukraine, Belarus, and Moldova.

David R. Marples is professor of history at the University of Alberta. He is the author of eight books, including *Lenin's Revolution: Russia 1917–1921* (London, 2000) and *Belarus: A Denationalized Nation* (Amsterdam, 1999). In 1999 he was awarded the Faculty of Arts Research Prize for Full Professors by the University of Alberta. His recent articles include: "The Parliamentary Elections in Belarus: Lukashenka's Dress Rehearsal?" *The Harriman Review* 14(1) January 2001 (co-authored with Uladzimir Padhol); "International Nuclear Safety: The Case of the Chernobyl Nuclear Power Plant," *Vermont Law Review* 24(4) Summer 2000 (co-authored with Tatyana E. Cerullo); "The Demographic Crisis in Belarus," *Problems of Post-Communism* 47(1) January–February 2000; and, "National Awakening and National Consciousness in Belarus," *Nationalities Papers* 27(4) 1999.

Arkadii Moshes has been a researcher at the Institute of Europe (Military and Political Studies Section, European Policy Department) since 1992. In May 1996 he was appointed head of section, European Security and Arms Control. Mr. Moshes is a specialist on Ukraine's domestic and foreign policy and on Russia's relations with Ukraine, Belarus, the Baltic States, and Northern Europe. He has published over 70 articles and papers, including *Overcoming Unfriendly Stability: Russian-Latvian Relations at the End of 1990s* (Bonn–Kauhava, Finland, 1999), "Ukraine and Russia: A Chronic Crisis," in *Between Russia and the West: Foreign and Security Policy of Independent Ukraine,* K. Spillman, A. Wenger and D. Muller, eds. (Bern–New York, 1999), "Changing Security Environment in the Baltic Sea Region and Russia," in *Baltic Security: Looking towards the 21st Century,* G. Arteus and A. Lejins, eds. (Latvian Institute of International Affairs, 1997). He also has co-authored a report on Russian-Belarusian relations that was commissioned by the Council on Foreign and Defense Policy.

Uladzimir Padhol is a professor of philosophy at the Belarusian People's University in Minsk. A former employee of the Belarusian branch of Radio Liberty (1994–96), he currently provides expert analysis on the Belarusian media for the OSCE Advisory and Monitoring Group in Minsk. He has authored over 200 articles in Belarusian journals and newspapers, and is the author of a book entitled *Osnovy politicheskoi psikhologii* (Minsk, 2000). His main research interests lie in the area of political psychology and the strategy and tactics of the oppositionists in post-totalitarian countries. He recently published "The Parliamentary Elections in Belarus: Lukashenka's Dress Rehearsal?" *The Harriman Review* 13(1–2) April 2001 (co-authored with David R. Marples).

Hrihoriy Perepelytsia is Head of the Military Department of the National Institute for Strategic Studies (Ukraine) and associate professor of the Institute of International Relations at Taras Shevchenko National University in Kyiv. He studied at the Military Political Academy and the author of more than 50 publications.

John C. Reppert is executive director for research at the Belfer Center for Science and International Affairs, John F. Kennedy School of Government, Harvard University. He joined the Center in October 1998 after retiring as a brigadier general from the U.S. Army, following nearly 33 years of active service. He has specialized in areas of international arms control and military affairs of the states of the former Soviet Union. He has published on Russian/Soviet national security issues and arms control policy and prospects. He received a doctorate from The George Washington University in International Affairs and an MA from the University of Kansas in Soviet and East European Studies. Dr. Reppert's recent publications include "Ten Years of Arms Control Inspections," in *New Horizons and new Strategies in Arms Control,* James Brown, ed. (Sandia National Laboratories, 1998); and "The Politics of Russian Military Reform," in *The Russian Armed Forces at the Dawn of the Millennium,* Michael Crutcher, ed. (Carlisle Barracks, Penn., 2000).

Astrid Sahm received her doctorate from Frankfurt University in 1998. From 1999 to 2001 she was a Fellow at the Center for European Social Research at Mannheim University, Germany. She is the author of *Transformation im Schatten von Tschernobyl. Umwelt- und Energiepolitik im gesellschaftlichen Wandel von Belarus und der Ukraine* (Münster, 1999) and the editor of the *Belarus-News* quarterly newsletter. She currently is an assistant professor at the Department of Social Science, Mannheim University.

Andrei Sannikov is a member of the Coordinating Council of Democratic Forces of Belarus and of the National Executive Council (a "shadow cabinet"). He graduated from the Minsk Linguistic University in 1977 and, after working at the UN Secretariat office, from the Diplomatic Academy in Moscow in 1989. In 1995 he was appointed deputy foreign minister of Belarus, responsible for security and disarmament issues and bilateral relations between Belarus and the West. In November 1996 he resigned in protest of President Lukashenka's policies. In November 1997, Mr. Sannikov co-founded a civic initiative called Charter'97 and became its international coordinator.

Lisbeth L. Tarlow is associate director of the Davis Center for Russian Studies at Harvard University. She received a doctorate in international relations in 1997 from the Fletcher School of Law and Diplomacy at Tufts University. Her dissertation was on the intersection of Soviet domestic and foreign policymaking in Soviet-Japanese relations during the Gorbachev period. An article based on her dissertation, "Russian Decision-Making on Japan in the Gorbachev Era," appeared in *Japan and Russia: The Tortuous Path to Normalization, 1949–1999,* Gilbert Rozman, ed. (St. Martin's Press, 2000).

Kirsten Westphal received her doctorate from Giessen University in 1999. She currently is a fellow at the Institute of Politics at the Justus Liebig University in Giessen, Germany. She is the author of *Russische Energiepolitik, Ent- oder Neuverflechtung von Staat und Wirtschaft* (Baden-Baden, 2000) and several other publications on Russian energy politics and Gazprom.

Hans-Georg Wieck was the head of the OSCE Advisory and Monitoring Group in Belarus from December 1997 until December 2001. He served in the Foreign Service of the Federal Republic of Germany, 1954–1993, including postings as ambassador to Iran, the Soviet Union, and India. From 1970–1974 Dr. Wieck was the director of Politico-Military Planning in the German Ministry of Defense. From 1985 until 1990 he was the president of the Federal German Foreign Intelligence Agency (BND). Dr. Wieck served as an adviser to President Eduard Shevardnadze from 1993 to 1996. He received his doctorate from Hamburg University.

Caryn Wilde is a native of Minnesota and an International Development Specialist. She lived in Belarus from 1994 to April 2001, and continues to consult there intermittantly. She has worked primarily with Belarusian third sector organizations and small businesses. Ms. Wilde also works as an independent contractor to facilitate projects for Western Development Agencies. She currently is a Democracy Fellow advising USAID/Russia on strengthening Russian NGOs and engaging the citizenry in participatory civil society.

A native of Homel, Belarus, **Leonid Zlotnikov** received an MA in economics at Moscow University and a Kandidat Nauk degree at the Economics of Civil Works Research Institute in Moscow in 1978. A frequent contributor to the weekly *Belaruskii rynok,* he has published extensively in this and many other venues on issues economic projection, problems of transition economies, and small business development. He was assistant professor at the European Humanities University (1996–1999), has worked as a policy expert for a number of research centers and as an expert of the Committee on Economic Policy and Reforms of the Supreme Soviet of the 13th Session. He currently is an economic consultant at the International Finance Corporation's Minsk office.

Abbreviations

ABA–CEELI	American Bar Association–Central and Eastern Europe Legal Initiative
ACDI-VOCA	Agricultural Cooperative Development International–Volunteers in Overseas Cooperative Assistance
AMG	Advisory and Monitoring Group (of OSCE)
BPF	Belarusian Popular Front
BSSR	Belorussian Soviet Socialist Republic
BWEE	Belarusian Women's Economic Empowerment Project
CEE	Central and Eastern Europe
CFE	Conventional Forces in Europe
CIS	Commonwealth of Independent States
CSCE	Conference on Security and Cooperation in Europe
EBRD	European Bank for Reconstruction and Development
EU	European Union
EWI	East West Institute
GONGO	"Government" NGO
IISEPS	*See* NISEPI
IMF	International Monetary Fund
MID	Ministry of Foreign Affairs of the Russian Federation
MoU	Memorandum of Understanding
NATO	North Atlantic Treaty Organization
NGO Assembly	The Assembly of Belarusian Pro-Democratic Nongovernmental Organizations
NGO	Nongovernmental Organization
NIS	Newly Independent States

NISEPI	Nezavisimyi institut sotsiaľno-ėkonomicheskikh i politicheskikh issledovanii [Independent Institute for Socioeconomic and Political Studies; IISEPS]
NKVD	Narodnyi komissariat vnutrennikh del [People's Commissariat of Internal Affairs; Soviet Secret Police]
NTV	Nezavisimoe televidenie [Russian Independent Television Channel]
ODIHR (OSCE)	Office for Democratic Institutions and Human Rights of the OSCE
ORT	Obshchestvennoe rossiiskoe televidenie [Public Russian Television]
OSCE	Organization for Security and Cooperation in Europe
OSCE AMG	OSCE Advisory and Monitoring Group
"Parliamentary Troika"	European Parliament, Parliamentary Assemblies of the Council of Europe, OSCE
Radio Svaboda	Radio Liberty (Belarusian Service)
RFE/RL	Radio Free Europe/Radio Liberty
RTR	Rossiiskoe teleradio [Russian Teleradio Television Channel]
SCAF	Support Center for Associations and Foundations
SME	Small and Medium Enterprise
SMI	*Rus.* Sredstva massovoi informatsii [(Russian-language) Mass Media]
TACIS	European Union's Technical Assistance for the Commonwealth of Independent States
UNDP	United Nations Development Program
UNO	United Nations Organization
USAID	United States Agency for International Development
USIS	United States Information Service
USSR	Union of Soviet Socialist Republics
UWB	United Way Belarus

Independent Belarus

Map of Belarus, showing political divisions. Prepared by the Central Intelligence Agency, U.S. Government, 1997.

Introduction
Margarita M. Balmaceda,
James Clem,
and Lisbeth L. Tarlow

The fall of the Berlin Wall in 1989 ushered in a period of democratization and market reform extending across the East-Central European region, with one important exception: Belarus. Its fledgling attempts at democracy, ironically, have produced a leader who has suspended the post-Soviet constitution and its institutions, and created a personal dictatorship. Of all the countries in the region, Belarus alone has failed to be accepted into the Council of Europe.[1] Located in the center of the European continent, Belarus lies at the crossroads of an expanded NATO and the Russian "near abroad." This fact underlines the importance for European security as a whole of the future of the Belarusian-Russian relationship, as well as Belarus' relations with its Central European neighbors.

The fact that Belarus has increasingly strengthened its ties with Russia since 1995 has important implications for current plans to forge new regional security structures. The series of agreements between Russia and Belarus that began in May 1995 and have evolved to the present day includes not only the long-term stationing of 25,000 Russian soldiers on Belarus' territory, but also the eventual abolition of official borders between the two countries. In fact, Belarus has been so closely identified with the building of a new post-Soviet security sphere that some authors have started to call the Russian-led CIS

---

[1]   Kathleen J. Mihalisko, "Belarus: Retreat to Authoritarianism," in *Democratic Changes and Authoritarian Reactions in Russia, Ukraine, Belarus, and Moldova,* Karen Dawisha and Bruce Parrot, eds. (Cambridge, 1997), p. 224.

collective security agreements the "Minsk Treaty Organization."[2] In a 1998 interview, Belarusian President Aliaksandr Lukashenka called the reunification of Russia, Ukraine, and Belarus "inevitable . . . and no opponent will be able to prevent it."[3] These agreements, which signaled the beginning of recent Russian attempts to reconstruct a single post-Soviet economic, political and military space, have an important impact on Central European security perceptions.

For example, Belarus' considerable military power has been a concern for Poland since 1991.[4] Belarusian-Russian integration has a de-stabilizing effect on Poland because it raises the prospect of a de facto 563 mile-long Polish-Russian border. It also raises questions about the impact that a possible loss of Belarusian sovereignty could have on Poland's own sovereignty, questions that exacerbate the domestic Polish security debate.[5] A closer relationship with Belarus may also affect Russian perceptions of Poland's strategic role within NATO. Given the potential abolition of borders between Russia and Belarus—resulting in the abolition of the Belarusian buffer between two historical enemies—the existence of NATO front-line troops along the Polish border might be too provocative for the Russians to accept.[6]

Developments in Belarus can also have important consequences for Ukraine. Many Russian politicians and policymakers would like the next step to be the "Belarusification" of Ukraine, preventing its incorporation into European structures. Another important way in which Ukrainian national security—and European security in general—is dependent on developments in Belarus lies in the energy sphere. The Russian Federation is in the process of building a massive pipeline—the Yamal Pipeline—running from northwestern Siberia through Belarus to Germany. Such a pipeline will change the future of

---

2   Arkady Dubnov, "Lukashenko's 'Initiative,'" *New Times* April 1995: 43.

3   RFE/RL Newsline 2(147) 3 August 1998: paragraph 2.

4   See Roman Kuzniar, "A Map of Security," *Polish Western Affairs* 35 (January 1994): 35.

5   See Sokrat Janowicz in *Gazeta Wyborcza*, 16–17 May 1995, translated in *Transition* 1(10) 23 June 1995: 398.

6   Miranda Anichkina, "Russia Revives the Corpse of the Soviet Union," *The European* 26 May–11 June 1995: 11.

energy supplies to Western Europe, making those countries more dependent on Russian gas. Moreover, the existence of an alternative transit route through Belarus changes the balance of power between Russia and Ukraine, which is Russia's current gas transit partner. The completion of the Yamal Pipeline will considerably reduce Ukrainian transit revenues and reduce the leverage such a transit position offers Ukraine vis-à-vis its more powerful neighbor.

The Belarusian experience as an exception to the broader regional trend toward reform offers a valuable opportunity to analyze how democracy can fail in a post-Soviet context. By putting the Belarusian experience in comparative perspective, the relative importance of such factors as the weakness of Belarusian national identity and the individual role of its president, Aliaksandr Lukashenka, can be evaluated. An understanding of the degree of Belarusian exceptionalism is vital to calculating the probability of developments in Belarus being repeated in neighboring countries.

This question of the "exportability" of the Belarusian experience to other countries in the region is one of several crucial policy questions relating to the country. Far from being a strictly academic question for political scientists, the future of Belarusian political and economic development has far-reaching implications beyond its borders. Indeed, Lukashenka's ability to *portray* a functioning neo-socialist economy is exploited by conservative forces throughout a region marked by chronic declines in production and wage arrears. If in Russia Lukashenka is a symbol of the "success" of anti-reform policies, in other, more economically troubled former republics his role is potentially more explosive. In Ukraine, for example, deep rifts in society over the pace of economic reform and ties with Russia can be exacerbated by the Belarusian example. Nostalgia for the Soviet Union, combined with the perception that Lukashenka represents a return to a golden Soviet past, undermines democratic and market reforms in East-Central Europe and the Newly Independent States. The reality facing policymakers is that a strategic geopolitical space is under the firm control of an unpredictable, undemocratic leader. Far from being a small, neo-communist backwater, Belarus is emerging as a country the West can no longer afford to ignore.

Background

Belarus was the setting for the historic Belavezhskaia Pushcha Agreements of December 1991, but there was little evidence in the preceding years that Belarus would become a sovereign state. The relative weakness of Belarusian national identity, and the determination of an entrenched Communist elite, prevented the growth of a broad-based nationalist independence movement which could foster the development of civil society. Instead, the opposition Belarusian Popular Front (BPF) remained a small group of intellectuals, and the Belarusian state was formed and led by those same Communist leaders who had opposed independence only a year earlier.

In the early years of independence the Belarusian government was split between maintaining neutrality and aligning with the Russian Federation. Former Chairman of the Supreme Soviet Stanislaŭ Shushkevich placed a high priority on protecting Belarusian sovereignty, especially vis-à-vis Russia, and thus facilitated Belarusian membership in several European and international organizations, including the Conference on Security and Cooperation in Europe (CSCE, now OSCE), European Bank for Reconstruction and Development (EBRD), International Monetary Fund (IMF), and the World Bank. It is also important to note that in May 1992 the Belarusian government made the monumental decision to give up its inherited nuclear weapons, according to the START-I Treaty, and to accede to the Non-Proliferation Treaty. Shushkevich was instrumental in pushing these moves through, and Belarus was rewarded by the U.S. with an increase in aid from $8.3 million to $65 million.[7]

The other tendency in Belarusian foreign policy—towards closer integration with Russia—was represented by former Prime Minister Viachaslaŭ Kebich. Early on, Kebich believed that the only solution to Belarus' immediate financial difficulties was closer integration with Russia, and an aggressive Russian foreign policy in those early years helped Kebich's view to win out over Shushkevich. After the CIS summit in Tashkent in May 1992, where Shushkevich refused to sign a collective security agreement with Moscow, Kebich went to

---

[7]   Jan Zaprudnik and Michael Urban, "Belarus: From Statehood to Empire," in *New States, New Politics: Building the Post-Soviet Nations*, Ian Bremmer and Ray Taras, eds. (Cambridge, 1997), p. 303.

Moscow and signed a broad bilateral agreement creating a "common economic, political and social space," and also ceded command of 30,000 Belarus-based strategic troops to Russia.[8] Russian pressure, stemming from Belarus' economic, and especially energy, dependence on Russia, helped to cement this foreign policy direction. In 1994, it helped to oust Shushkevich, as well. It thus is important to note that the trend towards a re-integration with Russia originated before Lukashenka's rise to power.

In domestic political terms, the clear turning point in Belarusian political development was Lukashenka's election as president of Belarus in July 1994. The Constitution of 1994 created a presidential republic, with a balance of power between executive, legislative, and judicial branches of government. Soon after taking power, however, Lukashenka's authoritarian tendencies emerged. In April of 1995, riot police, acting on Lukashenka's orders, beat up BPF deputies inside the building of the Supreme Soviet. By the following year, the number of personnel within the internal security forces had risen to double the size of the armed forces.[9] Later in that year, Lukashenka subverted the elections to the Belarusian parliament, and then completely marginalized that institution in November 1996 through a nation-wide referendum on direct presidential rule.

That critical referendum has left Lukashenka unopposed in his drive to create a personal dictatorship, based on a classic combination of naked force and a cult of personality. His increasingly erratic behavior, however, has complicated on-going plans for any kind of merger between Belarus and Russia. The union agreements between the two countries, signed since 1997, are nevertheless nowhere near the point of implementation. Even monetary union is complicated by the anti-reform Belarusian economy and the hidden and not-so-hidden costs it is steadily incurring. The existing customs union works to the distinct disadvantage of Russia, which loses in trade with an unliberalized Belarusian economy. Politically, association with Lukashenka is becoming more of an embarrassment than an asset for an avowedly democratic Russian leadership. Nevertheless, under a recent defense pact, Russia operates forward-warning, air-defense

---

[8] Mihalisko, "Belarus: Retreat to Authoritarianism," p. 248.

[9] Ibid., p. 257.

systems on the Polish border. In sum, it is an uneasy relationship and that uneasiness is a source of instability in the region.

Despite the urgency of the situation in Belarus and its relations with neighboring countries, there is little in the English-language, scholarly, and other professional literatures on Belarus to guide policymakers. Although two important books in English on Belarus have been published since 1991, important gaps remain. Written by a leading expert on Belarus, Jan Zaprudnik, *Belarus: At a Crossroads in History* provides an excellent account of Belarusian nation and state-building and covers events up to 1993, but it is now eight years out of date, and obviously does not include the Lukashenka era.[10] The other major contribution has been the book *Belarus at a Crossroads,* edited by Sherman Garnett and Robert Legvold.[11] With its focus on security issues, the book understandably discusses domestic political and economic issues to a much lesser degree. Despite the respective strengths of these contributions, this small body of literature is insufficient for the policy challenges which Belarus presents now, and will undoubtedly continue to pose to its European neighbors, the United States, and Russia.

For these reasons, an international group of scholars, policymakers, and members of nongovernmental organizations gathered at Harvard University in May of 1999 to discuss developments in Belarus, covering a broad spectrum of issues: domestic politics and economics, trade, bilateral relations with neighboring countries, integration with Russia, and regional security. As the organizers of the conference, we sought to bring multiple perspectives to our collective analysis of Belarus; in addition, we tried to move beyond widely-held assumptions about Belarus toward a more nuanced view of developments there. For example, we confronted the idea that Lukashenka rules by force alone, without real popular support, as well as the myth that Belarus is moving smoothly down a road toward integration with Russia. Members of international organizations, foreign policy analysts and diplomats, and academics all shared their unique experiences and perspectives for the overarching goal of providing a realistic assessment of the situation in Belarus for policymakers.

---

[10]   Jan Zaprudnik, *Belarus: At a Crossroads in History* (Boulder, 1993).

[11]   Washington: Carnegie Endowment for International Peace, 1999.

This book is our attempt to share the collective knowledge and experience represented at that Harvard conference with the broader—and growing—audience interested in Belarus. The book accurately reflects the diversity of opinion and perspective that was present at the conference. The approaches employed by our contributors vary from analytical think pieces to advanced quantitative and deconstructionist methodologies. In all cases, however, contributors were asked to examine their respective policy issues with the policymaking community in mind. Each of the resulting sections of the book present differing perspectives clustered around a common issue-area.

Part One of the book focuses on the internal dynamics of political development in Belarus—how they affect the chances for the country's return to a more democratic path of development (in contrast with the present trend towards further authoritarianism) and how this situation affects the country's relations with neighbors and major powers alike. In order to have a sense of the relative feasibility of various policy alternatives, it is essential to gain a realistic view of what is actually happening at the level of the Belarusian leadership, the opposition, organized civil society, and at the popular level. In other words, it would be tempting to adopt a comforting picture of a long-suffering Belarusian society oppressed by an authoritarian despot lacking popular support—and of a popular and united opposition. This picture, however, would not reflect reality in an accurate way, and policies based on romanticized assessments of developments in Belarus run the risk of missing their target and being ineffectual.

By focusing on regime consolidation and sources for regime change, the chapters in this section pay attention to those factors that have fostered Belarus' move toward authoritarian rule, as well as those elements which could provide the basis for democratic-oriented changes. Given the fact that most countries in Belarus' neighborhood have chosen (although not necessarily implemented successfully) the path of market liberalization and political democratization, the question of why Belarus has "deviated" from this model has important comparative political and policy implications.

Each of the chapters in Part One of the book addresses the issue of Belarus' domestic political "anomaly" from a different perspective, and provides important clues for its understanding. Rainer Lindner examines the "phenomenon" of Belarusian president Aliaksandr Lukashenka's rise to power and the subsequent consolidation of his regime. Lindner attributes Lukashenka's unlikely rise from former collective farm director to the Belarusian presidency to a variety of factors: the frustration of Belarusian society in the early 1990s with failed economic reform; Lukashenka's manipulation of the weakly institutionalized Belarusian political system; the lack of a strong Belarusian elite; and the resonance of Lukashenka's populist appeals. Lindner deconstructs Lukashenka's brand of populism, "Lukashism," into a shrewd mixture of economic pragmatism (prompt payment of wages and pensions), anti-Westernism, and rejection of ethnic Belarusian symbols in favor of Soviet ones. Reinforcing this populist strategy is an all-embracing presidential administration, a "state within a state," that, while often inefficient, props up the regime. Lindner concludes by identifying "cracks in the monolith" of the Lukashenka regime that may be widened through Western engagement.

In their chapter, David Marples and Uladzimir Padhol look more in depth at the challenges facing the Belarusian opposition. Marples and Padhol divide the opposition into "hard-line" and "soft-line" camps, defined by the degree to which they will cooperate with the Lukashenka regime. In their examination of groups such as the Belarusian Popular Front, Charter 97, and others, Marples and Padhol paint a pessimistic picture of an opposition plagued by internal rifts and alienation from Belarusian society. The authors nevertheless hope that the limited opportunities for political contestation available in the Belarusian political system will serve as a mechanism for the opposition to mount a credible challenge to the regime.

Timothy Colton next examines what is often an overlooked factor in the Belarusian political system: the role of mass public opinion. Drawing on survey data from 1998 and 1999, Colton uncovers a complex structure of attitudes toward one of the most pressing foreign policy issues facing Belarus: the question of integration with the Russian Federation. Regression analyses show some surprising patterns, or lack thereof, in support for integration: education and use of the Belarusian language, for example, are not useful explanatory variables. Evidence is found, however, to support widely-held views that younger and urban (especially residents of western Belarusian cities) residents are more in favor of Belarusian independence. The most powerful predictors of attitudes toward integration—perhaps unsurprisingly—are overarching attitudes toward Belarusian independence and the Russian Federation. What emerges in the end is a complex picture of a society interested in integration to a certain extent, but also in favor of Belarusian sovereignty. Colton concludes that these attitudes will likely constrain the integration process.

Part Two of the book focuses on the Belarusian economy. Understanding the actual state of the Belarusian economy is important for two reasons. First, it is important to understand whether the relative stability of the Belarusian economy is likely to be maintained in the near future, since any disruption in this stability could usher in a period of heightened social and political tensions. No less important are the regional implications of the Belarusian economic path as a "model." Lukashenka's ability to maintain a modicum of economic stability has become something akin to a model in a region marked by continuing declines in production and chronic wage arrears.

Patricia Brukoff's paper, "The Belarusian Economy: Is It Sustainable?" looks at the domestic dynamics of the Belarusian economy to seek clues to the question of how long Lukashenka's brand of non-reform can continue to keep the economy afloat—or at least to provide dependable heat and small, but regular, paychecks to the population. She identifies the factors that led to a period of economic growth in 1996–1998, the limits inherent to this approach, and the domestic and international factors that have led to a comparatively slow but steady decline since 1998. Brukoff reaches the conclusion that without continued high levels of support from Russia living standards will continue to deteriorate at an even faster rate. As continuation of such support is not guaranteed, Belarus has sought a rapprochement with international financial institutions.

Leonid Zlotnikov's chapter looks at the growth (or lack thereof) of private enterprise and private economic networks in Belarus in the first years after independence. He also examines Lukashenka's attempts to limit, control, or coopt these new entrepreneurs. This has important policy implications, since private economic networks and the growth of small and medium enterprises can provide an indicator of the strength of civil society, as well as of possible alternative sources of power. Much Western assistance to democratization processes in Belarus has been based on the assumption that, although it is oppressed, there exists the basis of a middle class that could act as the nucleus of political opposition to Lukashenka. Zlotnikov concludes that few of the preconditions necessary for the middle class to develop as a political alternative to Lukashenka are present in Belarus. At the same time, divisions within the state bureaucracy, state enterprise directors and Lukashenka's entourage itself might actually open a window to political change.

Margarita Balmaceda's chapter analyzes the domestic and international consequences of Belarus' important role as a transit route for fuel and consumer goods between Western Europe and Russia. The issue of transit has important foreign policy implications, since it is one of the keys to the country's importance for Russia and its Central European neighbors. Moreover, income from transit has been one of the most important sources keeping the "Belarusian model" (and, more specifically, Lukashenka's power itself) alive. At the same time, the issue of transit reflects many of the tensions and contradictions in the Belarusian-Russian relationship.

Part Three of the book looks at the variety of interactions between Belarus and Russia in order to identify future scenarios for this vital relationship. In his chapter on "Lukashenka's Role in Russian Politics," Arkady Moshes argues that it is very difficult to assess Lukashenka's role vis-à-vis Russia, since his position remains contra-dictory. It seems that the Belarusian leader uses integrationist movements to strengthen his present political power within Belarus and to guarantee a prominent political role in the union between Russia and Belarus. However, after a detailed analysis of the development of the closer Russian-Belarusian relations, the author notes that Lukashenka's role should not be exaggerated, inasmuch as he remains only a marginal player on the Russian political arena and does not enjoy any popularity among either Russia's Right or Left. Lukashenka currently pursues the twin goals of staying in power in Belarus and preserving the Belarusian economic model, based on post-Soviet economic inertia and control. He uses his popularity among Russians and Belarusians as a main supporter of integration to achieve those goals. Moshes also argues that, despite Lukashenka's relative popularity among Russia's regional governors—popularity that is based primarily on economic pragmatism—he will not become a major political player in Russia without the support of Russia's Left, which considers him to be a rival in the integration process, and the Right, which views him as undemocratic, authoritative, and a threat to Russia's political climate. Russia, on the other hand, uses its rapprochement with Belarus to strengthen its economic situation, to gain political support among Russians who support the union with Belarus, to counterbalance its Left opposition, and to strengthen its domestic and international standing as a strong state. There is nothing, though, that indicates Russia's readiness to grant Belarus special status or to accept it into the union on equal terms.

Andrei Sannikov shows that the regime's ineptitude in conducting successful economic reforms, its reluctance to part with the Soviet past, its dependence on energy and raw material supplies, and the presence of the authoritarian regime of Lukashenka—all have made the country an important and convenient target for Russia's strategic game of expansion and strengthening, both within the CIS and in the international arena. Sannikov outlines three distinct areas where Russian and Belarusian interests unequally converge and where Russia uses Belarus to its strategic advantage. One such area is the military: Belarus' proximity to Western Europe allows Russia to counterbalance NATO and to conveniently deploy its military troops on Belarus' territory. Another factor is the economy, where Russia uses Belarus' territory as the shortest and most efficient economic passage to Europe. Russia also profits from Belarus' energy dependence and lack of mineral resources. The final factor is political. Russia uses integration with Belarus to reinforce Russia's position both within the CIS and internationally.

Several chapters of this book point to the elements of tension and conflict lying beneath the surface of the Russian-Belarusian Union that was established in 1997, but is still far from realization. Yuri Drakokhrust and Dmitri Furman's piece on "The Game of 'Virtual Integration'" analyzes this question in detail by examining the history of Russian-Belarusian "integration initiatives" and showing that the major aim of these initiatives has not been integration itself—which would curtail Lukashenka's power and impose serious costs on Moscow—but the *struggle* for integration (as a political "game"). Drakokhrust and Furman also discuss the prospects for the political game of integration continuing into the Putin era.

Part Four of the book looks at the implications of Belarus' current situation, as well as its future prospects, for the evolving European security environment in the wake of the first wave of NATO eastward enlargement.

John Reppert analyzes the defense relationship between Belarus and Russia. Although the various agreements of integration signed by the two states since 1991 have included terms pertaining to security issues, the events of 1999, including NATO enlargement to the Belarus border, NATO's decision to intervene militarily in Kosovo, and the renewal of Russian warfare in Chechnya, make the defense relationship between Russia and Belarus more important than at any time since the collapse of the Soviet Union. In his chapter, Reppert reviews the evolution of this defense relationship, and addresses the prospects and security consequences of full integration of the two defense establishments. He concludes that powerful forces, such as Belarus' own troubled history and NATO enlargement, may well push Belarus to finally conclude a meaningful security arrangement with Russia and thus transform regional security in the center of Europe.

In their chapter on "Power and the Yamal Pipeline" Astrid Sahm and Kirsten Westphal discuss the interplay between political and economic power in the Yamal gas pipeline currently being built by Russia's Gazprom from northwestern Siberia to Germany, through Belarus. They analyze Yamal's strategic implications from the perspective of Gazprom's relationship with the Russian state and its international strategy as a budding Russian multinational corporation. They also look at the likely effect of the pipeline in terms of the power relationship between Russia and Lukashenka's Belarus. Sahm and Westphal conclude that, although the pipeline increases Belarus' bargaining power vis-à-vis Gazprom, Lukashenka's hopes may be exaggerated, since only one part of Russia's gas sales abroad will be exported through Belarus and the country will not be in a position to play the role of monopolist "gatekeeper" of Russia's gas exports, a role played until recently by Ukraine.

The next three papers in this section focus on the "Belarus policies" of Poland, Lithuania, and Ukraine. Echoing the same kinds of challenges faced by the West, these three "frontline states" faced the question of how best to react to events in Belarus and how and to what extent to engage the Belarusian leadership. Indeed, the Belarusian situation has acted as a catalyst for cooperation between these countries, which held summits in 1996 and 1997 specifically to discuss this issue.

Agnieszka Magdziak-Miszewska examines the obstacles and possibilities faced by Poland in seeking to establish a constructive policy towards Belarus. According to Magdziak-Miszewska, in the pre-Lukashenka era of the early 1990s, Poland lost an important opportunity to become fully involved in Belarus and thus prevent its slipping back into a Russian sphere of influence. The inability to do this had to do not only with the Polish elite's own over-concentration on relations with the West at the expense of building relations with its eastern neighbors, but also with the anti-Polish stereotypes adopted by many Belarusian political movements at the time. Today, the Belarusian opposition has abandoned those anti-Polish stereotypes, but Poland is again limited in its policy options by the existence of a large Polish minority in Belarus, which has become a de facto hostage of the Lukashenka regime. In this context, the author believes that cooperation between democratically-minded nongovernmental groups on both sides of the Belarus-Poland border may be one of the most realistic and fruitful policy options.

Algirdas Gricius shows that despite tensions between the Lithuanian and Belarusian governments, economic trade and energy transfers have preserved ties between the two countries. While trade and transit serve to link them, they also have created a problem in the form of border security. For the time being, the advantages of continued economic interaction serve to smooth over political differences between the countries and their differing geopolitical orientations. Gricius emphasizes that the Lithuanian strategy of a dialogue with the Belarusian regime, as opposed to a strategy of isolation, is the only realistic method for change.

Hryhoriy Perepelytsia contrasts the different paths taken by Belarus and neighboring Ukraine in the post-Soviet period. Both in terms of economic reform, and especially foreign policy, the two countries have employed different strategies. While both countries lie between the Russian Federation and the enlarging European Union, Belarus has turned to Russia for support, while Ukraine attempts to serve as a "bridge" between Russia and the rest of Europe. Perepelytsia shows how Belarus represents a different alternative to Ukraine—threatening to sovereignty-oriented elites in Ukraine, but also appealing to Leftists and much of the Ukrainian mass public. Belarusian integration with Russia is a destabilizing force in the region, he argues, but other alignments, such as a north-south Baltic-Black Sea axis, are also possible. More likely, Perepelytsia argues, is the possibility of joint Ukrainian-Belarusian-Russian integration on the basis of a common Slavic union.

The last section of the book builds on the insights provided by the previous chapters in order to draw a clear picture of the dilemmas presented by the Belarusian situation for the West, identify Western (and especially American) interests, and the various available policy alternatives and instruments, including engagement through various international organizations and nongovernmental actors.

Sherman Garnett sets the themes of the Belarusian policy dilemma faced by the West. Much of this dilemma, according to Garnett, consists of Belarus' strategic importance, as it stands as a vital crossroads where the post-Soviet space meets an expanding Europe, combined with the Western view that Belarus is a stagnant place, a kind of socialist theme park. The West has largely placed Belarus in the category of states to be neglected and isolated. Yet Belarus could play a significant—and largely destabilizing—role in the region and in Europe as a whole. An increase in the destabilizing potential of the "Belarus factor" might occur through the country's integration with the Russian military or through the growth of the internal instabilities that then spread into Lithuania, Poland, Ukraine, and Russia. Garnett considers that ignoring Belarus is a short-sighted approach. He argues instead that long-term stability and successful democratic reforms in the region do not depend solely on balancing the policies of Moscow, Brussels, or Washington with tendencies towards isolating the area. Rather, they also rest on seeking to foster an interaction of these capitals with Minsk, Warsaw, Kyiv, Vilnius, and other small- and medium-sized states that can make their influence felt because they have "breathing space" with Belarus. Garnett also recommends ending Belarusian security isolation, strengthening the dialogue between the Belarusian and Western militaries, encouraging regional initiatives with Belarus, creating incentives in favor of Europe, supporting internal democratic reforms, and engaging Russia into the West's pro-active diplomacy with Belarus.

Hans-Georg Wieck describes the role of international organizations in the process of democratization in Belarus. He discusses a number of concrete recommendations by the EU Council to the Belarus government, the realization of which were made preconditions for further technical and financial assistance to Belarus. Recommendations included: the establishment of a dialogue between the president and the Supreme Soviet of the 13th Session, establishment of a dialogue between the president and the opposition forces, restoration of the principles of the separation of power and the freedom of press, the guarantee of free elections, and the implementation of market reforms. As the proposed measures have not received proper response from the Belarus leadership, the country has found itself in an international vacuum. Despite these frustrating results, the dialogue between the Belarus government and international organizations continues. One such example is the work of the OSCE Advisory and Monitoring Group that focuses on developing democratic institutions in Belarus, monitors human rights and freedom of the press, engages in a dialogue with the opposition, and continues to advocate democratic values and ideas in the country. Despite the difficulties involved, there is no alternative to continuing this dialogue, since the failure to do so may push Belarus into an even closer relationship with Russia and farther from democratic reforms.

In her chapter, Elaine Conkievich focuses on the situation of Belarusian nongovernmental organizations (NGOs) under Lukashenka. Despite harassment and other difficulties, the number of such NGOs is growing. The political situation in Belarus has pushed groups pursuing democratic reforms into the so-called "opposition" along with political parties, trade unions, and the independent media. Conkievich sketches in her paper both the political and legal difficulties that NGOs face in Belarus, as well as some examples of their successful work in the country. Despite the fact that NGOs and other public groups are legal and protected by the 1994 Law On Public Associations, the government of Belarus (and some parts of the law) make the existence and functioning of NGOs in Belarus very difficult. In fact, government officials in Belarus have a right to fully control and monitor the work of local NGOs. They also have full rights to harass existing NGOs by denying or delaying the registration that is required of them by the new re-registration law. In addition to administrative pressure from the government, Belarusian NGOs suffer from a poor administrative and communication skill base, lack of a nurturing climate for NGOs in the country (where the role and purposes of NGOs are not understood), and strong competition among local NGOs. Conkievich, looking at the interaction between the Belarusian NGOs and international organizations that provide assistance to them, concludes that investing and supporting Belarusian NGOs is the best and most efficient way to make an impact on Belarus, since NGOs directly deal with, and have an influence on, citizens and society in general. They independently promote democracy, market economy, and the rule of law.

Caryn Wilde draws on her experience as an NGO consultant to present a different perspective on the challenges facing NGOs in Belarus as they embark on a strategy of engagement. She argues that how the West faces those challenges most likely will influence the success of the overall reform process in Belarus. She outlines four important challenges: (1) the absence of a pre-existing infrastructure for the third sector, and the lack of support among the Belarusian people for the concept of a third sector; (2) the Belarusian administration's belief that only governmental structures should provide services to the people, and its ability to obstruct those who believe otherwise; (3) the likelihood that progress, by Western standards, will be slow because many of the philosophies proposed may first require acceptance and adaptation to the Belarusian culture; and (4) the importance of balancing the interests of Belarus and the West. Despite these challenges, Wilde affirms that much progress has already been made, as hundreds of NGOs are already serving their constituencies well.

Policy Implications and Suggestions

Bringing any edited volume to press necessitates time for the publications process. Faced with that simple reality, we have sought to keep this volume current, while carefully editing it and including a scholarly apparatus. All of the authors have revised their contributions to take into account events through 2000, and in certain cases they have incorporated material from well into 2001. Although this means that the volume is not technically "aware" of the fact that Lukashenka handily won the August–September 2001 presidential election and heavily manipulated the October 2001 parliamentary elections to install his supporters, the studies herein have, quite remarkably, retained their full relevance to the present situation in Belarus. This is a testament both to the perspicacity of our authors and the lack of change in Belarus. Indeed, even events with implications as dramatic as those of 11 September 2001 have yet to alter substantially the dynamics of power within Belarus and the surrounding region.

Although the authors gathered in this book present differing perspectives, some policy implications and suggestions emerge naturally from them. The first and most clear policy recommendation has to do with the need for a more nuanced view of Belarus, of the sources of support for Lukashenka, and of the nature of the various social actors on which a democratization agenda may rely. Because of his flamboyant leadership style and unpredictability, the West has become fixated on Lukashenka as the embodiment of the Belarusian "anomaly." Western policymakers would benefit from paying closer attention to the sources of Lukashenka's support and the structural factors (in great part stemming from Belarus' Soviet legacies) that have made the rise of such a leader possible. This is important in the medium-term horizon as such conditions could lead to the emergence of a similar leader in the future.

Despite the bleakness of the general picture, there do exist important areas where the West can become effectively engaged in Belarus without supporting Lukashenka's regime. Formulating such policies requires identifying and taking advantage of a number of "cracks in the monolith" identified by the authors in this book. Some of these "cracks" that could be exploited through creative Western engagement are the tensions between various groups within the political elite currently in power, in particular tensions between Lukashenka and state enterprise managers and between Lukashenka and "nomenklatura entrepreneurs" in his own presidential administration. The "increasingly closer" relationship with Russia is plagued with differences and contradictions, which could be used by the West as the basis for a policy of constructive engagement in Belarus.[12] As support from Russia becomes less of a foregone

---

[12]   On this topic, see Margarita M. Balmaceda, "Myth and Reality in the Belarusian-Russian Relationship: What the West Must Know," *Problems of Post-Communism* 46(3) May–June 1999: 3–14.

conclusion, Belarus is being increasingly forced to seek accommodation with international financial institutions. This is another crack that Western policies could use as a means to engage the Belarusian government in a dialogue on democratization.

It may turn out that Lukashenka's authoritarian rule stands in the way of any real reforms. If that is the case, then the real long-term challenge will come once he leaves office and a more or less divided opposition comes to power. At that moment Belarus' new leadership will be afforded a brief "window of opportunity" in its dealings with the West, without whose help Belarus stands little chance to implement long-overdue structural reforms at a moderate social cost. Part of the tragedy of the Belarusian situation lies in the fact that, in its current shape—bitterly divided and with little contact with the population as a whole—the Belarusian opposition is in no condition to take up this challenge. Given this situation, Western engagement, including, most importantly, engagement by Belarus' regional neighbors, should work to promote forces for change within the current regime in the short run, and the development of a more unified, pro-democracy opposition for a future regime transition.

1

Timothy J. Colton
*Belarusian Public Opinion and the Union with Russia**

A missing ingredient in commentary on Belarusian-Russian diplomacy since the collapse of the Soviet Union is Belarusian society. The oversight goes back to wrongheaded assumptions. Discussion in the West commonly takes it for granted that (1) the essence of the relationship is a giant and imperialistic Russia dictating to a helpless Belarus, and (2) inasmuch as Belarus has a voice, it embodies the aspirations of no one but the government of Aliaksandr Lukashenka, so that ordinary people there can safely be ignored or marginalized as unwilling victims of the authorities. Anchored though they may be in background realities deserving of our attention, and congruous though they may be with our human sympathy for the underdog, these twin premises are in their usual guise so overstated as to cloud sober judgment. The power asymmetry between the two nations and Moscow's ambitions to recoup its losses, constants across the entire post-Soviet space, are insufficient to account for the emergence of a distinctive Russian-Belarusian "union." Belarusian perspectives and choices must be brought into the picture.[1] Moreover,

* The author thanks Rawi Abdelal, Margarita Balmaceda, and Keith Darden for their detailed comments on a draft of the chapter and Melissa Griggs for her research assistance.

[1] The contrast with Belarus' neighbors along the Baltic coast (Lithuania and Latvia, which border directly on it, and Estonia) is instructive. All three of these small nations have wrested complete independence from Russia. To the south, post-Soviet Ukraine, a former union republic with five times Belarus' population, is also far freer

despite escalating authoritarianism in Belarus, it would be myopic to limit the search for understanding of its Russia policy to the presidential palace, the Belarusian political elite, or, for that matter, the Minsk-centered political opposition. The Lukashenka phenomenon did not arise in a social vacuum; he and his regime do not operate in one today.

This chapter investigates the state-society nexus in Belarus as it bears on the desirability and terms of consolidation with the Russian Federation. Concretely, I will map the structure of mass opinion on the issue, explore its distribution and determinants, and ponder some policy lessons. I rely on data from a large-scale monitoring survey of a probability sample of the adult Belarusian population conducted by IISEPS (the Independent Institute of Socioeconomic and Political Studies), one of Belarus' most expert polling firms.[2] The survey took place in November of 1999, several years into the tortuous bargaining over the bilateral union and weeks before Presidents Lukashenka and Boris Yeltsin, at a summit on the eve of Yeltsin's retirement, initialed the pact launching the union and blueprinting its first five years. Altogether, IISEPS field workers questioned 1,507 citizens in every one of Belarus' six oblasts (regions). Ninety-seven percent of the respondents were of voting age, eighteen and older. Three percent were sixteen- and seventeen-year-olds, nearly all of whom will have the franchise in the Belarusian presidential election scheduled for 2001.[3]

---

of Moscow. An exhaustive analysis of Belarusian-Russian relations would go into the nuances on the Russian side, which are outside the scope of this paper.

2   The data were kindly made available by Oleg Manaev, the director of the institute, which uses the initials NISEPI (Nezavisimyi Institut sotsial'no-ėkonomicheskikh i politicheskikh issledovanii) in its Russian-language materials. I am grateful to members of his staff who reviewed tendencies in Belarusian public opinion with me in a visit to the institute's offices in Minsk in September 1999 and to Oleg Veremeichik of the institute for his stalwart help with technical questions. Andrei Vardomatski, the head of Market and Opinion Research Belarus, another very professional Minsk firm, was also generous with his time and knowledge.

3   The questionnaire was in the Russian language and was entitled "Life in Our Time." Field workers handed it to respondents, who then filled it out alone or in the presence of the worker. The sample is a two-stage probability sample of the population aged sixteen and over. IISEPS chose primary sampling units after stratification by oblast, rural/urban place of residence, and, for urban settlements,

To claim hyperbolically that public opinion has been *the* mainspring of Belarus' foreign and domestic policies is not my purpose here. My point of departure is the observation that public opinion has carried *some* weight and is capable of doing so for the foreseeable future. There is no denying that the popular mood in many quarters was amenable to the turning back of the political clock in Belarus soon after the extinction of the USSR in 1991. Lukashenka rocketed from collective-farm chairman and amateur politician to president in 1994 by triumphing in a competitive election in which, along with denouncing corruption and betrayal of the achievements of socialism, he "campaigned unflaggingly for Russian-Belarusian integration."[4] Lukashenka took over 80 percent of the popular vote in the runoff on 10 July 1994. The runner-up, Prime Minister Viacheslaŭ Kebich, was scarcely less enamored of closer relations with Moscow than Lukashenka, and had presided over an attempt at a currency union with Russia which was only thwarted by the reluctance of Russian leaders to foot the bill.[5] As president, Lukashenka has repeatedly capitalized on mass sentiment to leapfrog procedural

---

community size. Urban settlements were selected by probability proportional to population, except for the six oblast centers, which were selected with certainty, and rural settlements were chosen with equal probability. The 46 primary sampling units include all 6 oblast centers, 7 other cities with populations of 50,000 or more, 12 smaller towns, and 21 rural districts. Respondents were selected randomly from the official register of inhabitants. For individuals who could not be reached, research supervisors were allowed to make substitutions from a reserve list for up to 10 percent of the target group. Sixteen percent of respondents were in the city of Minsk, 13 percent in the rest of Minsk Oblast, 13 percent in Mahilioŭ [Mogilev] Oblast, 13 percent in Vitsebsk [Vitebsk] Oblast, 16 percent in Homel [Gomel] Oblast, 15 percent in Brest Oblast, and 14 percent in Hrodna [Grodno] Oblast.

[4] Martha Brill Olcott, Anders Åslund, and Sherman W. Garnett, *Getting It Wrong: Regional Cooperation and the Commonwealth of Independent States* (Washington, D.C., 1999), p. 173.

[5] Kebich had engineered the downfall of the pro-independence chairman of the Supreme Soviet, Stanislaŭ Shushkevich. He was vulnerable, though, to Lukashenka's charge of complicity, as head of the Belarusian government at the time, in the dissolution of the USSR in 1991. One of Lukashenka's favorite statements on the campaign trail was that independence "has given nothing to Belarus." Quoted in Rawi Abdelal, *National Purpose in the World Economy: Post-Soviet States in Comparative Perspective* (Ithaca, 2001), chap. 6. This valuable new study notes the popularity in Belarus in the mid-1990s of measures to tighten relations with Russia.

obstacles and subdue his adversaries. In 1995 he prevailed by huge majorities in a referendum authorizing negotiations with Moscow over economic harmonization, reinstating Soviet-era heraldry, and revoking the statutory privileges for the Belarusian language enacted during the upheaval of the late 1980s. In an ensuing referendum in 1996, he persuaded the electorate to acquiesce to presidential decrees peremptorily substituting a more pliant legislature for the sitting Belarusian supreme soviet and lengthening his term from five to seven years. As time wears on, compliance on the part of the populace will continue to be vital to the flamboyant and crafty populist's efforts on all fronts—curbing unrest on the streets, winning elections and any plebiscite on a new deal with Russia, and fending off West European and American pressure. Perceptions and preferences at the grassroots, in short, are and will remain a constraint on the actions of the Belarusian administration, if not a font of inspiration for them.

What the People Want

National independence is on the face of it an elementary thing. Either a geographic unit stands on its own feet in the international community or it does not. The legal and ceremonial trappings of sovereignty—national political institutions, flag and anthem, embassies, a seat in the United Nations—would normally be a definitive guide, legible to citizens and foreigners alike.

Belarusians as a rule are comfortable with their country having the formal accouterments of statehood. About two respondents in three, of those consulted in the 1999 IISEPS survey, agreed with the principle that Belarus "should be a sovereign and independent state" (in Russian, *chtoby Belarus' byla suverennym, nezavisimym gosudarstvom*), with a desultory one in ten respondents turning thumbs down (see Table 1). Even on so cut-and-dried a question, though, some dissonance is audible, in the form of the one-quarter of the members of the survey sample who were unable to give an answer to it.[6]

---

6   "Don't know" responses, as excerpted in this article, cover responses coded "Hard to say" and, much rarer, refusals to answer the question.

Table 1

Popular Support for the Principle of Belarusian Independence[a]

Response[b]	Percent
Yes	67
No	9
Don't know	23

a.   N = 1,507.
b.   *Question reads:* "Do you want Belarus to be a sovereign and independent state?"

The murmur of uncertainty surrounding what the citizenry really wants swells to a drumbeat if we inspect responses to questions posed in the very same survey that take aim at the disputed connection with Russia. When three putative models for the arrangement were submitted to respondents in 1999, opinion split three ways (see Table 2). The most palatable option was that of "good-neighborly relations between independent states" *(dobrososedskie otnosheniia dvukh nezavisimykh gosudarstv),* followed in order by "a union of independent states" *(soiuz nezavisimykh gosudarstv)* and "unification into a single state" *(ob"edinenie v odno gosudarstvo).* Belarusians' impressive solidarity on territorial integrity in the abstract thus melts into dissension over the application of the principle in practice. The most pro-independence position has the largest number of apostles (around 40 percent)[7] and the most pro-unification position the smallest (around 20 percent). Individuals in the intermediate category, about one-third of the whole sample, advocate a so-called union of independent states, the course of action that coincides with the proclaimed objective of the Belarusian and Russian governments. One way to visualize this constituency is as a swing group. Contingent on circumstances, it could merge with either of the two polar groups into

[7]   This figure may overestimate support for total independence, since "good-neighborly relations" already implies some warmth in ties with Russia. Unfortunately, the survey did not also pose the question in alternative terms that would let us probe for wording effects. Nor did it ask about details of a possible unification, such as a common currency or a common legislature. These are points that could be probed in future research.

a majority coalition congenial to a relatively distant or, conversely, a relatively intimate association with Russia.

Table 2
Preferences for the Relationship between Belarus and Russia[a]

Response[b]	Percent
Good-neighborly relations between two independent states	42
Union of independent states	34
Unification into a single state	22
Don't know	2

a.　N = 1,507.
b.　*Question reads:* "What kind of relationship between Belarus and Russia do you think would be best?"

The lay of the land looks rather different in Table 3. It recaps citizens' intended decisions in a national referendum on amalgamation with Russia where the proposed change is phrased as a voluntary "unification" *(ob"edinenie)* of the countries, without stipulating one state or two. The vague wording is very much in the spirit of the referendum question Belarusian voters are apt to see so long as Lukashenka and his loyalists are the ones in charge of drafting the ballot. When unification is couched this way, as a dichotomous choice, a plurality (48 percent) of all Belarusians, and a majority (about 60 percent) of all who say they would cast a vote, tip their hand for unification.

Table 3
Voting Intention in Possible Referendum on Unification with Russia[a]

Response[b]	Percent
For unification	48
Against unification	34
Would not vote	15
Don't know	3

a.　N = 1,507.
b.　*Question reads:* "If there were a referendum today about the unification of Belarus and Russia, how would you vote?"

How should we reconcile this encouraging result, from Lukashenka's and the unionists' vantage point, with the apparent reverence of Belarusians for sovereignty and the frosty reception they give to wholesale absorption into Russia? Tables 4 and 5 shed some light on the contradiction by breaking down respondents' position on the mock referendum by type of response to the foregoing questions. True to form, an overwhelming proportion (about 85 percent) of those who discount Belarusian independence rally to the unification choice on the referendum (see Table 4). But note that the champions of independence in principle would in the referendum declare for unification at a rate of almost 40 percent, while those lacking any stated position on the principle of independence would vote for unification at a rate of more than 60 percent. In Table 5, reporting on the more commodious three-way question, we again see those who take the unqualified pro-Russian position fixing with virtual unanimity to endorse a referendum resolution on union. More intriguing, almost two-thirds of those who relish a partial union of two juridically independent states are willing to concur in unification in a referendum; a plurality of the Lilliputian "Don't know" category would follow suit. By this yardstick, the swing group in the Belarusian electorate leans *towards,* not away from, a tighter embrace of Russia.

Table 4

Percentages Intending to Vote in a Referendum for or Against Unification with Russia, by Support for the Principle of Belarusian Independence[a]

Voting intention on unification	Support for principle of independence		
	Yes	*No*	*Don't know*
For	37	86	63
Against	45	6	14
Abstain	14	6	19
Don't know	3	1	4

a.   N = 1,507.

What the polling data in their totality advise is the presence of more than a little confusion and discord in Belarusian society about policy vis-à-vis Russia, and at the same time of certain intelligible patterns in the blend. Some Belarusians think coherently about the subject; others come close to wanting to square the circle. We will find these mental gymnastics strange only if we forget the intricacies of the subject and the fuzziness that has suffused public discourse over it.[8] The union and "union state" hailed in the rhetoric of Lukashenka and his Kremlin partners lend themselves to a medley of interpretations, running from a supranational alliance through a loose confederation and onward to the outright swallowing of Belarus, in one bite or in morsels, by the Russian Federation. To deepen the enigma, the Belarusian and Russian politicos who most ardently salute the marriage—including Lukashenka—not infrequently seem to harbor hidden qualms about it.[9]

Table 5

Percentages Intending to Vote in a Referendum for or against Unification with Russia, by Preference for the Relationship between Belarus and Russia[a]

Voting intention on unification	Preferred relationship			
	Two independent states	Union of independent states	Single state	Don't know
For	13	62	93	39
Against	63	19	3	19
Abstain	20	15	3	31
Don't know	4	4	1	11

a.   N = 1,507.

---

[8]   This fuzziness stretches back into the Soviet period, when the Belorussian Soviet Socialist Republic was, after all, a charter member of the United Nations. In the closing years of Soviet rule, Belarusian leaders articulated positions on relations with the central government and with the other members of the Soviet federation that were often distinguished—as elsewhere in the USSR—by their circumlocution and verbal excess.

[9]   One American study concludes that, "Lukashenko's personal political power depends on his continued ability to deliver political and economic benefits to his supporters, which means that he could not permit a union that would pass the important positions of Belarus' political or economic life to Russian control." Olcott, Åslund, and Garnett, *Getting It Wrong,* p. 177.

The manifest attitude of rank-and-file Belarusians toward a re-affiliation with Russia depends to a sizable extent on how the question is phrased. There exists no unambiguous consensus to be mobilized, no compromise to be hit upon that will please everybody. Belarusians seldom quarrel with the tenet of sovereignty, and those who would elect to preserve Belarus as a completely separate state do make up a plurality of the population. And yet, transitivity of preferences appears to be engendering a majority, albeit a tenuous majority, prepared to move one way or another into the Russian orbit. The consent of so many Belarusians to dependence upon Russia, without them always abandoning faith in the ideals of independence and national dignity, suggests that considerations in addition to the intrinsic merit of sovereignty enter into the shaping of their preferences. We shall now delve into what the overall array of inputs might be.

How to Explain Public Opinion

Where does Belarusian mass opinion governing the interplay with Russia originate? Why are millions of people cheerful about a rapprochement with the successor to the Soviet entity from which Belarus exited a decade ago, whereas others staunchly resist it and still others are mired in indecision? I restrict myself to three broad lines of inquiry well elaborated in the theoretical and applied literature on political behavior, and in those confines to a series of more fine-grained propositions. The triad of conceptual categories I employ ascribe the genesis of attitudes pertaining to Russia to sociological, mass media, and political variables. All are dealt with as heuristic devices, giving rise to various hypotheses which are not by definition mutually exclusive. None has an ounce of proven explanatory power until calibrated with the empirical evidence.

Sociology

One approach to elucidating public opinion in any country links it to the country's social morphology and dynamics. Citizens' preferences on a political issue, in this reading, are an extension of attitudes they acquire in the nonpolitical domains of their lives or internalize in a process of socialization densely structured by social group.

What in Belarus' social makeup could lie behind viewpoints on unification with Russia? Our familiarity with the Soviet and post-

Soviet societies generally and of Belarus specifically puts forward several possibilities.

Identity. A core area to scrutinize anywhere in Eastern Europe or Eurasia is feelings of national identity. A creditable guess would be that Belarusian citizens who empathize first and foremost with the Belarusian nation and its sustaining myths will be more insistent than others on independence from Russia. The IISEPS questionnaire did not ask straightaway about individuals' passport ethnicity or nationality *(natsional'nost',* in Soviet parlance). This is not a crippling defect, as a towering majority of the citizens of Belarus (roughly 80 percent) are ethnic Belarusians (their fellow East Slavs, the Russians, are just over 10 percent).[10] The issue of relations with the Russian Federation will ultimately be settled inside the titular group.

The 1999 data do furnish two telling measures of identity. The first is language use. Survey respondents were asked which language they spoke most often from day to day.[11] Stunningly few of our subjects (4 percent) said they habitually spoke Belarusian. Forty-one percent mentioned conversing in Russian, 24 percent in both Russian and Belarusian, 31 percent in a compound *(smeshannyi)* Belarusian-Russian dialect, and less than 1 percent in another tongue. Monolingual Belarusian speakers are scarce in all portions of the population; rural and older people tend to get by in the hybrid dialect, and urban dwellers and the young in Russian.[12] The evidence is very much in keeping with the lament of nationalist intellectuals about the linguistic russification of Belarus under Soviet auspices and the dearth of Belarusian-language instruction in the schools. Linguistic assimilation was pushed much further in Belarus than in neighboring

---

[10]   The most recent inter-census data places ethnic Belarusians at 80 percent, Russians at 11 percent, and all others at 8 percent. In the 1989 Soviet census, Belarusians were 78 percent, Russians—13 percent, Poles—4 percent, and others—5 percent.

[11]   "Which language do you mostly *(v osnovnom)* use in everyday communication?"

[12]   In our sample, prevalent use of Russian rises from 21 percent in villages to 60 percent in Minsk; use of the joint dialect declines from 51 percent in villages to 12 percent in Minsk. By age group, 57 percent of sixteen-to-nineteen-year-olds speak mainly Russian, but 21 percent of persons of age sixty or over; the joint dialect is favored by 24 percent of sixteen-to-nineteen-year-olds and by 54 percent of those sixty or older.

Ukraine, despite the considerably smaller share of the population accounted for by ethnic Russians.[13]

The second kind of identity measure taps into religious convictions. Sixty-five percent of survey respondents purported to be religious believers and 35 percent to be secular. Although, regrettably, there was no question item on religious creed, believers in Belarus by and large would profess Orthodox Christianity, the mother faith of most Russians and Belarusians, with a smaller group being Belarusian Greek Catholics (Uniates) or Roman Catholics, a fair-sized portion among the latter of Polish heritage.[14] The survey also asked about indulgence in prayer and worship. While the median Belarusian citizen does not do a lot of either, there are gradations of apathy and fervor. Around two-thirds of survey informants in 1999 said they attend church services from time to time and around 55 percent that they pray sometimes.[15] Religious belief and observance vary less by

[13]   See the excellent background discussion in Roman Szporluk, "West Ukraine and West Belorussia: Historical Tradition, Social Communication, and Linguistic Assimilation," *Soviet Studies* 31 (January 1979): 76–98. See also Steven L. Guthier, "The Belorussians: National Identification and Assimilation, 1897–1970," *Soviet Studies* 29 (January 1977): 37–61, and Abdelal, *National Purpose in the World Economy,* chap. 6. Ethnic Russians came to 22 percent of the population of Ukraine in 1989, 9 percentage points more than their share in Belarus.

[14]   In medieval times, the forerunners of today's Belarusians, like the forerunners of today's Russians and Ukrainians, were predominantly Orthodox. Many subsequently converted to Roman Catholicism or to the Uniate Church (which is a Catholic church under the jurisdiction of the Vatican, but uses the Byzantine rite) while under Polish-Lithuanian rule. (Russia took over the region in the late eighteenth century.) The tide ran in the diametrically opposite direction under Russian imperial control. IISEPS surveys in the late 1990s consistently found about 10 percent of Belarusian citizens aged sixteen or over to be professed Roman Catholics and about 1 percent of them Greek Catholics. As many as 40 percent of the Catholics are probably ethnic Poles. The Greek Catholic Church was forced underground in both Belarus and Ukraine by Soviet repression from 1946 to 1987. For a succinct summary, see Stephen K. Batalden and Sandra L. Batalden, *The Newly Independent States of Eurasia: Handbook of Former Soviet Republics,* 2nd ed. (Phoenix, 1997), pp. 59–60. Further historical detail is available in Nicholas P. Vakar, *Belorussia: The Making of a Nation* (Cambridge, Mass., 1956), chaps. 3–5.

[15]   Even some nonbelievers in Belarus partake of religious rituals. Twenty-eight percent of the secular said that they attend church some of the time (vs. 88 percent of believers), and 11 percent of nonbelievers said they pray some (vs. 81 percent of believers).

community size and age group than language use does, but there is a clear regional pattern, with elevated levels of religiosity in western regions of Belarus, adjoining the Polish, Lithuanian, and Ukrainian borders.[16]

One can easily envisage identity variables exerting an effect on Belarusian folk attitudes toward the axis with Russia. For language use, a plausible prediction is that monolingual Russian speakers will be predisposed to prefer integration with Russia and persons who speak some Belarusian to prefer separation. Religion, by contrast, could slice either way. Catholicism would assuredly bias adherents against a compact with Orthodox Russia, just as it has stoked anti-Russian passions in Poland and Lithuania. Were the ancestral bonds of Eastern Orthodoxy to be decisive, they would bind the typical Belarusian to his or her co-religionists in Russia (and in Belarus). But bitter memories of church closings and persecution of the clergy in the Soviet period, should they linger in people's consciousness, could hammer a wedge between Orthodox Belarusians and Russians by fueling misgivings in Belarus about reunion with the homeland of "scientific atheism."

Social status. Political sociologists frequently trace systematic connections between behavior and the individual's niche in the status hierarchy of society. Many nationalist movements (those, for example, of the Basques in Spain, the Tamils in Sri Lanka, and the Scots in the United Kingdom) are rooted in the higher-status social strata in the group, from which their leaders are recruited and where engagement with the cultural objectives of the nationalist project is greatest. Is this the case in Belarus? The most discriminating indicator of socioeconomic standing in the 1999 polling data is of the respondent's educational level. Approximately 60 percent of our informants possessed the secondary- and vocational-school diplomas that were the gateway into blue-collar employment in the Soviet Union. Practically equal minorities had less or more schooling than that.[17]

---

[16]   Eighty percent of survey respondents in Brest and Hrodna, the two regions abutting Poland, said they were believers. Levels of church attendance and private prayer were also much above average there.

[17]   Four percent of respondents had an elementary education, 16 percent an incomplete secondary education, 37 percent a secondary education, 25 percent a

Generation. Another fault line along which attitudes toward policy may cleave is generational. This is especially liable to occur in countries undergoing rapid social change. Survey research in other Soviet successor states has turned up stiff age-related discrepancies in public opinion and voting behavior. The issue of Belarus' independence from Russia ought to evoke instincts ingrained in citizens over the decades. It would be reasonable for Belarusians in the senior cohorts, molded psychologically in the Soviet period—and for the oldest of them in the most tyrannical years of it—to be more pro-Russian and more pro-unification than the middle-aged and the youthful, reared in a less oppressive moral climate.[18]

Spatial location. Geography gives us yet another subset of conjectural influences. Residents of the big cities in most countries—whatever their linguistic, generational, or other traits—are as a group more liberally inclined than people who live in villages and small towns. In Belarus, this correspondence would as likely as not nudge urbanites toward the independence banner and rural dwellers toward an accord with Russia.[19] Regional location might also be a hefty stimulus, given the conspicuously different historical experience of different sections of Belarus. Of keen interest are the two western oblasts of Belarus, Brest, and Hrodna [Grodno]. They were, in marked contrast to the westernmost parts of Ukraine, fully incorporated into the Russian Empire along with the rest of the Belarusian lands during the eighteenth-century partitions of Poland. From 1921 until the Nazi-Soviet Pact of 1939, however, Brest and Hrodna were provinces of the interwar Polish state. Their rich traditional ties to Poland, their proximity to Lithuania and Ukraine, and their relative ease of westward trade and travel raise the possibility that the local populace will have more reservations than in other areas of Belarus about the

---

specialized secondary (vocational) education, and 18 percent a complete or incomplete higher education. There is also some occupational information in the IISEPS data. I have found it less helpful than the information about education.

[18] Twenty-six percent of respondents were younger than thirty, 18 percent were in their thirties, 35 percent in their forties and fifties, and 21 percent sixty or older.

[19] Thirty-three percent of the IISEPS respondents lived in oblast centers (about half of them in Minsk), 13 percent in other cities with populations of 50,000 or more, 20 percent in smaller towns, and 34 percent in villages.

scheme for the union with Russia.[20] Minsk, a seat of government whose role would be downgraded if Belarus were to forfeit its autonomy, is a third locality where reunification with Russia could be costly to many.

Economic position. The last prominent place where we can sift for society-based influences on political attitudes is the economic realm. In the post-Soviet context, Belarus is of course a laggard in economic reform, Lukashenka having frozen most of it in the mid-1990s, but private enterprise and the accompanying differentiation of reward have been tolerated in scant doses, chiefly in urban trade and services. Ten percent of the IISEPS survey sample were self-employed, proprietors of a business, or workers in a private company. In all likelihood more pertinent than participation in the stunted private sector, the 1999 poll registers how well Belarusians think they are faring in the current economic environment. Asked how things had gone financially for them in the past year, 61 percent of respondents said they had worsened, dwarfing the 8 percent who detected an improvement; between the poles, a tidy minority (31 percent) recounted that there had been no change. It is not readily evident how these economic indicators might impinge upon attitudes toward Russia. So far as privatization goes, one could deduce a case for Belarusians in the non-state sector either welcoming the union with Russia (because that country's government has pushed economic reform much further than theirs) or spurning it (because it would hinder collaboration with, and assistance from, the affluent capitalist economies of the West). With regard to current economic welfare, it would be common sense to infer that prosperous Belarusians will be warmer than their countrymen to Lukashenka's government and by the same token more hospitable to its prized Russia démarche.

[20] Brest, adjacent to Ukraine as well as Poland, was badly affected by the Chernobyl nuclear disaster of 1986. Hrodna borders on Lithuania and Poland. Urban centers in Brest and, especially, the Hrodna region were also home in their day to very large Jewish communities. They were decimated by the Holocaust, and most survivors emigrated in the 1970s, 1980s, and 1990s.

Mass Media

A completely different tack would be to nest the analysis of Belarusian opinion in the web of communication about public issues in which citizens, their demographic characteristics notwithstanding, are enmeshed. The focus here would be not on where individuals are in the social structure but on how they learn about the political world.

Long-term upbringing aside, in the short term Belarusians, like their counterparts elsewhere in the former Soviet Union, glean the preponderance of their information about politics and government from the mass media—television, radio, and the printed press. Crucial media outlets, and television stations and studios without exception, have stayed on the state's books, and their management and content are in the firm grip of the Lukashenka machine. The *official media* accordingly reach more Belarusians than any other wellhead of political news. In the 1999 survey, 64 percent of respondents said they were regular recipients of news from the state-controlled media.[21]

This is not to say that the Belarusian leadership enjoys a monopoly on the dissemination and manipulation of political information. As is poorly comprehended abroad, just as many Belarusians (63 percent in November 1999) routinely draw on other purveyors of information as on the state-run media. Some 20 percent of those interrogated by IISEPS said they regularly patronized the *non-state Belarusian media,* mostly newspapers and ephemera published by civil-society organizations and dissident groups. Seven percent frequented *Western media sources,* mostly radio stations.[22] And more than half of Belarusians (52 percent) tuned in with regularity to the *Russian mass media* in 1999. Belarus is more saturated with media signals from Russia than any other ex-Soviet republic, owing to physical and cultural propinquity and near-

---

[21] The question reads: "From which sources do you most often *(chashche vsego)* receive information about life in Belarus?" Multiple positive responses were permitted, so they sum to more than 100 percent.

[22] The survey question gives as examples of Western media Radio Liberty, Voice of America, and the BBC, but also Polish television. Poland joined NATO in March 1999. Some Belarusians in the western part of the country are able to receive Polish television on their home sets. Regular use of the Western media was highest in the IISEPS survey in Hrodna Oblast and the city of Minsk.

universal fluency in Russian. Russia's major national television networks (ORT [Obshchestvennoe rossiiskoe televidenie], RTR [Rossiiskoe teleradio], and the commercial channel NTV [Nezavisimoe televidenie]) all broadcast in Belarus, with local advertising clips and announcements dubbed in, and have bureaus in Minsk; leading daily newspapers (such as *Izvestiia, Komsomol'skaia pravda,* and *Sovetskaia Rossiia*) can be purchased by subscription or at street kiosks; a few Russian magazines can also be found.[23] The Russian media are riveted on Russian stories, but report Belarusian (and Belarusian-Russian) news frequently in their daily bulletins and weekly roundups. Though hardly immune to official duress at home, Russian editors and correspondents have had stouter defenses against it than their Belarusian mates, and their work on Belarus passes muster with the rulers of what is still a foreign country, whose slant on the Belarus problem has not been identical to Lukashenka's. This superior balance is acknowledged in many circles in Belarus itself and has been a recurrent thorn in relations between Minsk and Moscow.[24] A telltale sign is that when IISEPS asked survey informants in November 1999 who in the news media had been most forthright in covering the anti-Lukashenka "Freedom March" in downtown Minsk the previous month, Russian television was cited more than any other source (by 30 percent of all respondents).[25] That Russian TV was most esteemed by big-city, well-educated, and younger Belarusians is another factor in its favor.

[23]   The range of Russian newspapers available at kiosks is narrow, and they tend to sell out quickly. The only Russian weekly newsmagazine available is *Itogi,* and that only in a few kiosks in Minsk. Most of the available magazines are about women's fashion, automobiles, or sexual hijinks. I owe these detailed observations to Margarita Balmaceda.

[24]   The most notorious incident involved the arrest of two ORT correspondents in the summer of 1997. President Yeltsin intervened on their behalf, and they were later released, tried, and handed suspended sentences by a Belarusian court.

[25]   Next in order were Belarusian state television (26 percent), Belarusian official newspapers (13 percent), unofficial Belarusian newspapers (11 percent), and Belarusian state radio (9 percent). Russian television was the most trusted source on the Freedom March for 44 percent of all regular consumers of the Russian media and 14 percent of others. Respondents were allowed to give more than one positive answer.

Aggregating what we know about exposure to official news organs and other sources, we come up with a portrait of the Belarusian media audience which, far from being homogeneous, is composed of quite disparate segments. As Table 6 shows, the population subdivides into almost exactly equal thirds: one group (in the bottom left quadrant of the table) is hostage to the government's in-house media; a second (on the upper right) banks solely on alternatives to the official media (the alternatives are not denoted in the table); and a third group (on the upper left of Table 6) obtains information from the official media and at least one countersource. The merest handful (3 percent in our sample, on the bottom right of the table) cull no information about current events from the media.

Table 6
Media Exposure in Belarus (Percentages of Total Adult Population)[a]

Regular information from some medium other than Belarusian state media	Regular information from Belarusian state media	
	Yes	No
Yes	30	33
No	34	3

a.   N = 1,507.

In any industrial country, contact with the mass media bathes citizens in a stream of fresh facts, updates on previous knowledge, and prescriptive advice, all of which may serve as action cues. While some repetition and mutual reinforcement across media types are inescapable, the variety in the media flow in post-Soviet Belarus is adequate to offer somewhat differentiated cues to the citizen seeking to form or revise a political opinion. The domestic and foreign media brief Belarusians on the state of affairs in Belarus and on the repercussions of changing it. All other things being equal, one would expect that a steady diet of the bowdlerized output of the official state media would prejudice Belarusians in favor of the union with Russia and that exposure to the unofficial Belarusian media and the Western media would prejudice them against it. For the Russian media, we are required to entertain rival predictions. Broadcasts and newspaper articles of Russian parentage, if they acquaint consumers with the

Russian headlines and remind them of Moscow's pro-union philosophy, ought to advance the cause of unification. But the relative candor of the Russian press makes it a double-edged sword. Either by accosting Belarusians with bad news about their own government (news which in Belarus would not slip through the censors' net) or by bringing them up against ugly features of Russian life, the Russian media, oddly enough, may subvert the very integrationist sentiments in Belarus which the Russian government is counting on to prop up the union treaty.

Political Considerations

My third paradigm concentrates on a proximate target, namely, normative attitudes on other public issues and choices which may entwine with attitudes about the Russian-Belarusian union. Attitudes on cognate issues could spring from the same primal values, or individuals could see strides toward or away from one policy goal as likely to have an instrumental impact on fulfillment of another. Either way, citizens' thinking, in our case about the pros and cons of unifying with Russia, would be shaded by, if never rigidly compelled by, their likes and dislikes on the rest of the political agenda.

The 1999 IISEPS questionnaire contained an ample battery of questions about contested issues in Belarusian politics. They are diverse in their substance, scope, and ideological and affective overtones. Most germane to relations with Russia are those touching on the spheres of sovereignty, possible revival of the Soviet Union, the economic transformation of Belarus, Russia's domestic problems, relations with the West, and support of President Lukashenka.

Belarusian sovereignty. The question on whether Belarus should be "a sovereign and independent state" (see the summary in Table 1) ought to be as determinative as any of views about affinity with Russia. Nonetheless, as addressed above (see Table 4), it is mystifying that so many individuals who laud sovereignty say they would vote for unification in a referendum. Other stakes, therefore, are necessarily involved.

Restoration of the USSR. The Soviet Union is dead and buried, and yet numerous erstwhile subjects still grieve for it. Belarusians wanting to fortify ties with Russia may wittingly or unwittingly be acting out nostalgia for the multinational socialist state that both nations inhabited until 1991. Although most outsiders would dismiss resurrection of the USSR as a chimera, a fondness for the past or an inchoate hope for rollback of the fatal decisions of a decade ago might creep into Belarusians' (and Russians') assessments of their mutual relations. The 1999 survey asked respondents if they took a positive or a negative attitude toward "the restoration *(vosstanovlenie)* of the USSR," without any prompting on the odds of a restoration coming about. Positives led negatives 38 percent to 31 percent; "Don't knows" were an unusually high 31 percent.

Economic reform. As with individuals' standard of living, Belarusians' principled opinions on the virtues of market vs. planned economics may color their foreign-policy stance. Given Lukashenka's penchant for administrative remedies to economic problems, enhanced interaction with either the Western powers or with Russia ought to be of some appeal to local proponents of a market economy, as either would lead away from the neo-Soviet status quo in Belarus. All the same, one suspects that of the two tracks it is speedy integration with the West—as taken in the 1990s by Poland and the three Baltic states next door—that will have the approval of pro-market Belarusians, with those who are for state control favoring the hookup with Russia. Asked in a closed-ended question in the IISEPS poll what kind of economic system they would recommend for Belarus, 41 percent supported a market economy "with insignificant state regulation," 32 percent supported a market economy with significant regulation, and 24 percent supported a planned economy.

Russia's Time of Troubles. A motif that surfaces spontaneously in conversations with Belarusians about their eastern neighbor is how disconcerted they are by Russia's internal turmoil. It is not too much of a leap for them to wonder what this disorder would do to them and their compatriots if the interstate frontier were to be dismantled overnight. Two items on the IISEPS questionnaire probed sensibilities on the issue. The first asked if "in the case of the unification of Belarus and Russia, Belarusians will have to fight in Russian 'hot spots' like Chechnya"; the second asked if "terrorists will be able to extend their activity into Belarus" after the union is sealed. These were timely queries, as the pollsters went into the field in the autumn of 1999, in the aftermath of the unsolved bombings of apartment houses in Moscow and other Russian cities and the revival of the war in the Russian North Caucasus. Fifty-three percent of respondents expressed the fear that in a Belarusian-Russian union Belarusian boys would see combat duty in Chechnya-like conflicts and 65 percent that Belarus would be more prone to terrorist attacks.[26]

Relations with the West. Maybe Belarusians' attitudes toward tying the knot with Moscow are a function of their preconceptions of the West, and not of Russia per se. Two useful formulations of their ideas are imbedded in the IISEPS poll. One question audits for admiration of or aversion toward foreign societies. Respondents were asked if they wanted "life in Belarus to be like life" in any of eight countries named or, as a ninth eventuality, to stay like it now is in Belarus. Seventy-five percent designated one of the foreign lands, of whom the lion's share wished to imitate the two Western nations on the roll, Germany (41 percent) or the United States (21 percent). Poland finished a distant third at 6 percent,[27] with China ticked off by 1 percent, Russia by fewer than 1 percent, and the three other post-Soviet countries on the ledger (Ukraine, Lithuania, and Latvia) by several percent.[28] The second question that piques interest is cloaked in the vocabulary of the Cold War, with which Belarusians over the age of thirty-five spent all their adult lives, and alludes to security and military issues. It asks baldly which if any countries "present a threat to Belarus." Sixty-two percent invoked a threat and, similar to the question on imitation of other societies, most references elicited were to individual Western countries or to NATO as a whole, which was a

---

[26]   Asked to appraise the Russian intervention in Chechnya, 46 percent of participants in the IISEPS survey took a positive attitude and 26 percent a negative attitude, with the remainder undecided or unable to answer.

[27]   There is a regional spread in opinion here, as respondents in the two oblasts adjoining Poland were the only two to have above-average enthusiasm for Poland—Brest (7 percent of respondents) and Hrodna (17 percent, or just 1 percent less than those who wanted Belarus to be like the United States).

[28]   Leaving things as they are in Belarus was preferred by 16 percent; the balance gave no answer or volunteered one of a smattering of other countries.

permitted response on this question.[29] Belarusians' positions on either emulation or threat could in theory have an impact on opinions about the union with Russia. Interestingly, these ruminations on the West are orthogonal attitudes, thoroughly disassociated one from the other. For example, the portion of IISEPS survey respondents who wanted to imitate a Western country was almost precisely the same among persons who worried about a Western threat to Belarus as for those who saw no such danger.[30]

Voting Intention. We cannot overlook one final, straightforward political posture we may well imagine molding preferences on Belarusian-Russian relations. Since the dalliance with Moscow commenced in 1995–1996, President Lukashenka has been an evangelist for progress toward some kind of union, tirelessly promoting it in Belarus and on his periodic tours of Siberia and European Russia. His government is a one-man show. So what would be more natural than for the unification crusade to be wedded in the public's sight to the personage and authority of Aliaksandr Lukashenka? Popular perspectives on the union might be nothing more or less than a proxy for evaluations of Lukashenka. Were this to be so, intended vote in the next Belarusian presidential election would be an accurate predictor of the voter's stance on Russia. IISEPS's poll, like all reputable polls in recent years, recorded wide support for Lukashenka. Forty-four percent of respondents said in reply to an open-ended question that they would vote for him if a presidential election were held tomorrow, 29 percent that they would vote for some other candidate, and 28 percent that they did not know or would abstain.

[29] Twenty-seven percent of respondents cited the United States, 3 percent Germany, and 42 percent NATO. Russia was defined as a threat by 8 percent. The question allowed multiple responses.

[30] The converse, of course, is also true. Forty-six percent of respondents who wanted the country to emulate the West saw a Western threat to Belarus, indistinguishable from the 48 percent among respondents who did not want to emulate the West.

Estimating Effects on Opinions

Enumeration of the manifold possible influences on mass preferences for Belarus' relations with Russia gets us only so far. To proceed to the cardinal task of establishing which if any of them actually have an effect, statistical tools are indispensable. Cracking open the toolbox and revisiting the IISEPS data, we would not gain from examining the potential catalysts of Belarusian opinion one by one. The panoply of causal factors, and the overlaps among them, call for a multivariate method which will test explanatory variables simultaneously for association with the outcome and pinpoint their discrete effects. For the sake of ease of interpretation and accessibility to nonspecialist readers, I have estimated the associations by means of linear (ordinary least squares) regression.

The results of the regression are displayed in Table 7. The dependent variable throughout (see note "a" beneath the table) is the three-way measure of opinions about a compact with Russia encapsulated in Table 2 above, rendered into an equal-interval index with unification into a single state as its highest value. The values of all independent variables in the regression are described in notes "b" through "o." Each parameter in the body of the table is an estimate of the mean change in the value of the dependent variable, up or down, associated with a unit change in the independent variable referred to in the table cell. To facilitate comparisons between variables, I have recoded the dependent variable and each of the independent variables to bound them numerically at 0 and 1. For any explanatory variable of interest, a regression coefficient of, say, .50 would indicate that a change from the minimum to the maximum value of that variable would on average be accompanied by a shift of .50 (50 percentage points) in the measure of the opinion outcome, in other words a change from preference for good-neighborly relations between independent states to one for a union of independent states or, equivalently, from preference for a union of independent states to fusion into a single state.[31]

---

[31]   One of the several by now well-known shortcomings of ordinary least squares in such a context is that it may yield predicted values of the dependent variable that are, strictly speaking, absurd. In the OLS regression utilizing all the independent variables, summarized in the third column of Table 7, predicted values for 29 cases stray below

Table 7
Influences on Preference for Close Relationship with Russia (Regression Coefficients)[a]

Explanatory variables[b]	Model 1: Sociological variables only	Model 2: Sociological + mass media variables	Model 3: Sociological + mass media + political variables
Sociological variables			
Identity			
Monolingual Russian[c]	.01	.01	.02
Religious believer[c]	.03	.03	.01
Religious observance[d]	-.16**	-.17**	-.11**
Education level[e]	-.07	-.03	.03
Age group[f]	.27**	.21**	.09**
Spatial			
Community size[g]	.02	.04	.04
Minsk[c]	-.14**	-.10**	-.07*
Western Oblasts[c]	-.13**	-.12**	-.07**
Economic			
Work in private sector[c]	-.03	-.00	.00
Family finances[h]	.08**	.04	.00

(con't next page)

0 and for 18 cases they go higher than 1. This makes a total of 47 out-of-range predictions out of 1,466 observations, or 3 percent. Truer estimates can be arrived at through more complex nonlinear algorithms based on a logistic transformation of the dependent variable. Experimentation with one such technique, ordered probit, produced results that are substantively little different from those given in Table 7.

Explanatory variables[b]	Model 1: Sociological variables only	Model 2: Sociological + mass media variables	Model 3: Sociological + mass media + political variables
Mass media variables			
Official Belarusian[i]		.15**	.03
Unofficial Belarusian[i]		-.11**	-.05
Russian[i]		-.12**	-.07**
Western[i]		-.05	.05
Political variables			
Belarusian sovereignty[j]			-.34**
Restore USSR[k]			.20**
Market economy[l]			-.07**
Russian disorder[m]			-.16*
Relations with the West			
Emulate[n]			-.01
Threats[o]			.07*
Intent to vote for Lukashenka[c]			.07**
Constant	.36	.35	.66
Adjusted R^2	.09	.15	.34

** $p \leq .01$
* $p \leq .05$

a.   Dependent variable a three-point index with values for responses to question about preferred relationship with Russia, as summarized in Table 2. Values from lowest to highest are for "good-neighborly relations between two independent states," "a union of independent states," and "unification into a single state." Numerical range compressed to the unit interval (0, 1). Sample N = 1,466. Omits thirty-six respondents who could not answer the question and five for whom data on one sociological characteristic was missing.

b.   Values of all independent variables compressed to the unit interval.

c.   Binary measure.

d. Five-point index (base zero, one point awarded for occasional church attendance and for occasional prayer, two points awarded for regular church attendance and for daily prayer).

e. Five-point index (values for elementary education, incomplete secondary, secondary, specialized secondary, and some higher).

f. Six-point index (values for ages sixteen to nineteen, twenties, thirties, forties, fifties, sixties and older).

g. Four-point index (values for village, city of less than 50,000, city of 50,000 or more, regional center).

h. Three-point index (values for worsening over past year, no change or don't know, improvement).

i. Three-point index (base zero, one point awarded for regular exposure to the media, one for assessment of fair coverage of Freedom March in October 1999).

j. Binary measure (values for disagreement and agreement with principle that Belarus should be a sovereign and independent state). Don't knows coded at mean of the distribution.

k. Binary measure (values for negative attitude toward restoration of USSR, positive attitude). Don't knows coded at mean of the distribution.

l. Three-point index (values for preference for planned economy, market economy with significant state regulation, market economy with insignificant state regulation). Don't knows coded at mean of the distribution.

m. Three-point index (base zero, one point awarded for fear that Belarusians will have to serve in Russian wars, one for fear of terrorism).

n. Binary measure (positive if respondent wants Belarus to be like Germany or the United States).

o. Binary measure (positive if respondent sees threat to Belarus from Germany, the United States, or NATO).

A key to deciphering the table is to appreciate the combinations in which explanatory variables have been folded into the analysis. The explanatory variables are grouped by generic category—sociological, mass media, and political. They are injected into the equation in blocs, a device which for any one variable makes allowance for the impact of related variables whose statistical effects on the outcome might otherwise be attributed spuriously to that variable. These controls are imposed between as well as inside blocs, on the basis of what to me are tenable assumptions about causal ordering among the blocs. I assume that the sociological variables condition (are causally prior to) the mass media variables and they and the mass media variables in turn condition the political variables. And so, while estimations of the effects of sociological variables on individuals' opinions are made only with due regard for the other sociological variables (Model 1 in Table 7), measures of the effects of media variables control statistically for the prior and confounding sociological variables as well as for one another (in Model 2), and measures of the effects of the political variables control for the effects of the sociological, media, and other political variables (in Model 3). In the idiom of electoral analysis, coefficients like these gauge the "total effect" of a variable, net of the effects of other explanatory terms that are causally antecedent to or collateral with the variable under review.[32] Total effects on preferences for the Belarusian-Russian relationship are set forth in the gray-shaded areas in Table 7.

Sociological Variables

As the table lays out plainly, no single factor or group of factors, once rigorously analyzed in the nested regression, fully explicates the situation. Many of the potential causes we have rehearsed do come into play in complementary fashion. Their effects on Belarusians' opinions are not uniform but run an expansive gamut in size. The regressions also disconfirm a number of our hunches, the variable proving not to bear consistently on the attitudinal outcome.

Five out of ten of our sociological variables (see Model 1) are vindicated as meaningful predictors of citizen preferences, in that their coefficients, subject again to the proper statistical controls, clear the conventional threshold of statistical significance (a chance of 95 percent or more that they differ from zero). We can say in sum that they wield a modest influence on Belarusian attitudes toward Russia. Taken together, as the coefficient of determination (adjusted R^2) at the bottom of the table's first column conveys, the socio-demographic indicators explain approximately one-tenth (.09) of the variation in individuals' opinions. Their residual effects as the blocs of mass media and political variables join the nested regression may be found in the top bar of the second and third columns. For the most part, those effects are less than the total effects, since some or much of their influence on the dependent variable is transmitted by the mass media and political variables.

The most potent social-structural influence by far on attitude toward Russia is the citizen's age. All other social characteristics held constant, the oldest Belarusians were about one-quarter more likely

---

[32]   For discussion, with applications to post-communist countries, see Timothy J. Colton, *Transitional Citizens: Voters and What Influences Them in the New Russia* (Cambridge, Mass., 2000). That study owes a heavy methodological debt to Warren E. Miller and J. Merrill Shanks, *The New American Voter* (Cambridge, Mass., 1996).

(.27, in the point estimate) than the youngest to prefer unification into a single state as against maintenance of two independent states. Decades of assimilation of Soviet mores and norms and the stresses and opportunities of different biographical trajectories have truly done their work, endowing Belarusians from successive generations with pronouncedly different notions about their country's ties to Russia.[33] Of the five sociological indicators with some impact, the least derives from the measure of family finances. Private economic welfare is positively related to a pro-unity position, but faintly (the coefficient is .08). Two of the other social factors with a confirmed effect on popular opinion are spatial—residency in Belarus' capital, Minsk, or in its western oblasts, Brest and Hrodna. The quantitative evidence of the survey on this score neatly corroborates the qualitative testimony of scholars and frequent travelers to Belarus. And, although belief in God as such does not budge attitudes toward Russia, religious observance decidedly does, and in an expressly detrimental direction. The total effect of observance on citizen acceptance of a union (-.16) is second in absolute magnitude only to age group among the sociological variables. The precise origins of this effect—be they implanted in the Orthodox majority, in the Roman and Greek Catholic minorities, or, as I would surmise, in both—cannot be made out from the IISEPS survey and should be a priority in future research.[34]

According to the data, four social indicators besides religious belief—those for a job in the private sector, education level, community size, and monolingual Russian speakers—do not work as explanations of public opinion. The curtailment of economic reform in

[33] The raw proportions show a precipitate gradation. Support for "good-neighborly relations," as opposed to tighter ties with Russia, declines from 58 percent among sixteen-to-nineteen-year-olds to 29 percent among those sixty and older.

[34] One tantalizing tip comes from splitting the sample regionally, between the west and the rest, and running the regression with the social variables separately in the two segments. For respondents polled in Brest and Hrodna oblasts, where Roman Catholic and Belarusian Greek Catholic believers are relatively plentiful, the coefficient for the effect of religious observance is larger than average (its magnitude is -.21). For other respondents, the coefficient is about one-third lower than in Brest and Hrodna (its magnitude is -.14), but its sign is the same and it is still significant at the .01 level. The burden of this indirect evidence is that religious observance has a negative effect on support for the union with Russia in all the religious confessions in Belarus, and it is stronger for persons of Catholic and Uniate faith than for the Orthodox.

Belarus makes the irrelevance of work in private business explicable. The irrelevance of education and urbanization, both of them classic indicators of modernization, comes as a mild shock. The better-educated classes and the big cities may be fertile soil for nationalist political movements in many other countries, yet not in current-day Belarus, where neither variable has a serious effect one way or the other.[35] The dramatic novelty the analysis discloses is the debunking of any explanatory role for language. It is remarkable to a comparative social scientist that the Belarusian language does not provide the platform for national self-assertion and self-determination that the etymologically similar Ukrainian tongue offers the titular group in nearby Ukraine. Nor—the flip side of the coin—have those Belarusians who speak Russian, the two languages equally, or a cross-bred dialect nurtured idiosyncratic attitudes on relations with the Russian metropole.[36] The explanation for this nonfinding presumably lies in the ubiquity of the imperial language, Russian, the historically-conditioned fragility of language-maintaining and language-enriching institutions (the press, schools, book publishing, the theater and cinema, and so forth) in the Belarusian-speaking community, and the interweaving of language use and other aspects of private and public life in Soviet and post-Soviet Belarus. Detailed study of this anomaly is a topic best left for another day.

Mass Media Variables

The mass media variables in our rundown perform just about as well as predictors of Belarusian public opinion concerning Russia as the social variables do. The variables are constructed as additive indexes of measures of frequency of recourse to the four media sources and trust in the fairness of their coverage of events. Incorporation of them into the estimation in tandem with the sociological variables (see Model 2 in Table 7) boosts the fraction of the variation explained to 15 percent (.15). A regression using the media variables alone—an

---

[35]   For parallel discussion of the urbanization factor from an earlier period, using aggregate data and contrasting Belarus with Ukraine, see Szporluk, "West Ukraine and West Belorussia," pp. 91–92.

[36]   The language variable used in the regression (see note "c" in Table 7) is a binary variable with monolingual Russian speakers coded 1 and all others 0. Alternative codings were also fruitless.

artificial test, since it would omit controls for confounding sociological variables—would explain 9 percent.

Of the four media variables, one, for uptake of Western mass communication, turns out to have no perceptible stimulus on opinions of the Belarusian-Russian union. The measures of immersion in the official and the unofficial Belarusian media do have independent effects, in the predicted direction and at roughly the same modest level (the coefficient is .15 for the official media and -.11 for the unofficial media). The more Belarusians cull information from state-owned television, radio, and newspapers, the more likely they are to endorse some version of the closer camaraderie with Russia which is ceaselessly touted in those outlets. The more they ingest from unofficial publications, the less sold they tend to be on integration.[37] The most peculiar media effect stems from the Russian mass media. Here the data validate the one of the pair of hypotheses we adduced above that is least conducive to success of the policy enunciated by Russia itself. How ironic it is, and how perverse it has to seem to the Russian and Belarusian governments, to witness exposure to the Russian media dampening enthusiasm for the union *with Russia*. We may speculate, as earlier in the chapter, that the reasons have to do with greater frankness in reporting on both Belarus and the Russian Federation, but the available information lets us take the argument no further.

Political Variables

The political variables that comprise our third generic category of explanation supply the best clues of all to the puzzle. Augmenting the sociological and mass media variables with the political variables (see Model 3 in Table 7) raises the fraction of the variation explained to a healthy one-third (.34). So securely yoked are the political indicators to the outcome that a regression harnessing only them as explanatory variables would do almost as good a job of predicting Belarusian

---

[37] There is probably some element of circularity to this relationship, as is often so when media effects are studied in the politics of any country. In addition to revising their political opinions because of what they watch on television or read in the newspaper, Belarusians could fit their viewing and reading habits to political opinions. Only well-aimed time-series survey research would enable us to tell how important this reciprocity is.

preferences on Russia policy (adjusted R^2 = .32) as the regression encompassing the entire suite of explanatory variables.

Personal standpoints on the connection with Russia resonate significantly to six of our seven political variables. Tops on the list, and not illogically so, is the fundamental opinion on the value of Belarusian sovereignty. It brandishes the highest total-effect coefficient (-.34) of any variable in any category, although, to repeat, even so lofty a value leaves it miles short of explaining everything about what Belarusians make of the issue. Two other opinions have total effects of more than .10: position on the phantom dream of reinstating the USSR (total effect .20, the third highest of any variable) and angst over the spread of Russian-style disorder into Belarus after unification (total effect -.16). One of these assessments is largely emotional and backward-looking; the other is hard-nosed and forward-looking. Like the evaluation of the worthiness of national independence, neither is much removed thematically from the decision at hand, about whether and how to overhaul Belarus' relationship with Russia.

When we venture farther afield on the issue docket, the conceptual link with Belarusian-Russian relations attenuates, and so, the statistical modeling certifies, does the observed link in attitudes. Contrary to prediction, the wish to have Belarus emulate or not emulate the leading Western countries does not have the slightest echo in attitudes toward the union with Russia. Anxiety about alleged threats from NATO and preferences on the transition to the market economy are statistically significant predictors, and in the anticipated direction—those agitated by a hostile West and those who propound a planned economy in Belarus are more pro-unification than their peers—but both times the total effect is anemic, with a magnitude below .10. It is more of a surprise to see our last political variable, support of Lukashenka, also have so minor an effect. It made perfect intuitive sense to hypothesize that Belarusians would displace assessments of their autocratic president onto the cause he has pursued exuberantly from the day he took the oath of office. I have had Belarusian political activists several times lecture me on this coupling, in effect reducing the overture to Russia to the hobby horse of one man. There is indeed a statistically significant connection between intent to vote for the incumbent and position on the unity program. All told, though, with appropriate statistical controls in place the Lukashenka factor makes an unspectacular difference to the likelihood of a Belarusian citizen going all out for the union with Russia. The total effect is .07, or about one-fifth the parameter for position on Belarusian sovereignty and one-third the parameter for approval of bringing back the USSR.[38]

Conclusions and Policy Implications

Belarus is a small country. A perpetual temptation for the representatives of a big country is to suppose that the problems of such a place are in ratio to its physical bulk and have simple causes and simple solutions. Few people in the shrunken superpower to Belarus' east know or care that much about Belarus. If it can be done at low cost and risk, and if nothing else changes in the interim, the Russian elite and population will in the end buy into some formula or other for reunification.[39] Americans and most West Europeans, it goes without saying, know and care incomparably less about Belarus. Unless it sinks into Bosnia-like pandemonium, it will never be a preoccupation of the Atlantic alliance. The gist of Western policy to date—that the bilateral union is a bad idea, yet when all is said and done one for the Belarusians to sort out for themselves in uncoerced dialogue with the Russians—is sound enough. With all that has happened in their environs, ten million Belarusians will be happier as

---

[38]   In bivariate analysis, without controls for other causal variables, the connection appears much stronger. Of survey respondents who intended to vote for Lukashenka in the next presidential election, 33 percent favored unification into a single state, 41 percent a union of two independent states, and 26 percent maintenance of two separate states; among persons not intending to vote for Lukashenka, those percentages are 14, 29, and 57. Even these data, though, do show many anti-Lukashenka Belarusians acquiescing in some kind of new arrangement with Russia. Forty-three percent of them favor either a union of independent states or full-fledged unification.

[39]   In a survey of the Russian electorate supervised by Michael McFaul, Polina Kozyreva, Mikhail Kosolapov, and myself in November–December 1999, 70 percent of voters agreed with the statement that Russia and Belarus "should unite in a single state." Sixty-three percent approved of unification with Ukraine. The two attitudes are highly correlated. In Moscow governing circles, one hope for the union with Belarus—rarely stated in public but often glimpsed in private discussion—is that it can later be broadened to admit Ukraine.

an autonomous society, at liberty to build cooperative bridges to its east and west, than as an appendage of the new Russia. One hundred and forty-five million Russians, for their part, have more pressing things to which to devote their energies than a territorial enlargement that caters to some of the most escapist intellectual tendencies in their midst and promises to insert yet another complication into their already convoluted federal system. Reunification with Belarus would be an expensive distraction from the act of national reconstruction without which Russia cannot lift itself out of its chronic morass. By canceling out Belarus as a trade and cultural pathway to the thriving societies beyond it, it would also abet isolationism and protectionism in Russia, at a juncture of growing interdependence in Europe and the world.

The West will need to supplement the policy cornerstones it now has in place with dozens of tangible decisions, making many of them on the fly in reaction to the initiatives and provocations of the governments immediately affected. There are points on which Western and Russian interests may in the end clash, but there also are others where, if they are creatively construed, synergy is within grasp. One basic interest Russia and the Western countries share is in any formal consultation with the Belarusian public about the union with Moscow being transparent and not an insult to the intelligence of the electorate. The survey data are unequivocal on Belarusians' expressed attitudes toward a union with Russia—that they pivot substantially on how the choice about the union is framed. That being the case, the campaign and the ballot must spell out for Belarusians in plain language what a union will entail and what avenues it will foreclose. Russia's interests would be as ill served by a farcical referendum as the West's. Any realist in the Kremlin will realize that an illegitimate Russian-Belarusian union is an incomparably greater evil than no union at all and would conjure up endless rancor with Belarusian patriots, debates about precedent-setting referendums on annulment, and maybe violence. It is a horizon on which the stability of the Russian Federation could conceivably be in jeopardy.

A prerequisite of responsible decision-making in the West is discerning analysis of Belarus, its history, and the motives for its flirtation with Russia. The beginning of wisdom is to admit that the political landscape of Belarus, cramped though the scale may be, is complex in organization, not simple. And complexity does not imply shapelessness. The opinions about Belarusian-Russian accord dissected in this essay, and the causal factors underpinning them, have a structure that reveals its contours to the patient investigator. That structure is multidimensional. Attitudes toward rapport with Moscow are driven by a mix of social-structural, mass media, and political variables, all of them with their own inner logic and dynamics. The preeminent sociological factors are generation, religious practices, and geographic location. The Belarusian communications media, official and unofficial, have demonstrable effects on mass attitudes consonant with the intentions of those who steer them. The Russian media, in a curious twist, turn out to bolster the message of the anti-unification forces that hold sway in the unofficial Belarusian media. Of the explicitly political variables we canvassed, Belarusians' position on dealings with Russia is most sensitive to the premium they place on national sovereignty, to their outlook on revival of the USSR, and to nervousness about Russian disorder engulfing peaceful Belarus. In sifting the evidence, we also have thrown cold water on several ostensibly credible explanations of opinions about the union with Russia. For instance, Belarusians' preferences, flouting expectation, are not at all influenced by language spoken, and they are but weakly influenced by appraisals of President Lukashenka.

Grassroots opinion in Belarus and, to insofar as it constrains policy, the fate of Belarusian-Russian relations will hinge on developments in the two countries and, to a lesser but not a trivial degree, on Western behavior. Within Belarus, many integral influences on mass attitudes, among them all of the sociological influences, stand to change at a glacial pace at best. Generational replacement should eventually have a profound effect on the distribution of opinion, but it will take far longer to work itself out than the politicians' timetable is likely to allow. Crises in Vladimir Putin's Russia, if they gave freer rein to cynics about Belarus and critics of Lukashenka, could drain unification of its momentum during the five-year trial period. A more critical line in the Russian mass media could, our data hint, help sour Belarusian opinion on persevering with unification. So, too, could a radical deterioration of law and order in Russia or the eruption of more Chechnyas. Of the political variables we perused, the most volatile and unpredictable is the Lukashenka factor. Regardless of what I have said about the paucity of direct influence of attitudes toward him upon attitudes toward Belarusian-Russian relations, his overthrow or withdrawal from the political stage in disgrace could have indirect effects on popular thinking. Among other things, Aliaksandr Lukashenka's elimination could pave the way for a purge of his confederates and the makings of a new elite consensus in Belarus against him and all his works. So salient in the inventory of the latter is the entente with Russia that it would be a leading candidate for the axe.[40] Even if pro-union groups triggered a referendum or a climactic election to adjudicate the issue, the official Belarusian media would have wheeled against the unity project, a change sure to amend some citizens' opinions.

Short of so abrupt a reversal of course, Western leverage in the battle over the minds of Belarusians is limited. Remember from Table 7 how meager an effect all variables associated with the West have on Belarusian mass preferences. Exposure to the Western news media is skimpy and neither contributes to nor detracts from the desire to unify with Russia. The widespread yearning for emulation of the West's prosperity likewise has no palpable effect. The only West-related variable significantly correlated with opinions of Belarusian-Russian relations (and not at a high level at that) is the icon of the West as a *menace* to Belarus. That image will without a doubt loom taller in Belarus, as it will in Russia, if and when NATO presses ahead with its contemplated expansion in the Baltic zone. It is perhaps no great challenge for officials in Western capitals to make the decisions needed to ratchet up the volume of Western radio broadcasts to Belarus, give them a friendlier face, and improve their linguistic accessibility. But confronting the tradeoffs in the security arena will be no easy thing. As policymakers start doing so, it is their obligation to be awake to the fact that nations with markedly dissimilar pasts and presents are pawns in the game, that their populations at large matter in the reckoning, and that ordinary people in even semi-democratized countries do not think in unison.

---

[40]   Russia might be out of sync with Belarus here, as the eviction of Lukashenka would erode resistance among liberal and centrist forces to consummating the union. Russian Communists and nationalists will back it under almost any circumstances.

2

David R. Marples and Uladzimir Padhol
*The Opposition in Belarus: History, Potential, and Perspectives**

The term "opposition" has been applied to the various political parties and groups in Belarus that have turned against the presidential regime of Aliaksandr Lukashenka. This chapter seeks to answer the following questions concerning the Belarusian opposition: What is the main source of its power and can this be used to change the regime? Why is there a gap between the opposition and Belarusian society? How has the dialogue between the two sides, held under the auspices of the Advisory Monitoring Group (AMG) of the Organization for Security and Co-operation in Europe (OSCE) in Minsk, influenced the opposition? What role has the West played in the events in Belarus? Can one predict the likely outcome of the present conflict?

Sources of Power and Influence for Change

Understanding the source of the opposition's power and its influence for change demands a comprehension of the origins of the present-day opposition and an analysis of its composition and structure. The structure of the opposition defines its functions and allows the exposure of new functions that both strengthen and weaken it, including its primary function: the removal of Lukashenka from the political arena and its own emergence as the leadership of the country.

* The authors express their thanks to Liuba V. Pervushina, Ph.D. candidate at the Minsk State Linguistic University, Belarus, and Elena Krevsky, Ph.D. candidate, Department of History and Classics, University of Alberta, for their assistance with this paper.

In order for the opposition to come to power, its political parameters must correspond with the following ideal model. First, the opposition must have one or more political leaders who are able to acquire, in a short time, an electoral rating surpassing that of Lukashenka. Second, the leader of the opposition must have the support of an absolute majority of the nomenklatura. This person must enjoy a high international support, not only from Moscow, but also from the West in a measure surpassing Moscow's support of Lukashenka. Third, the opposition must have a united ideological platform during the period of culmination in the struggle for power, along with united and coordinating organizations and a single leader. Fourth, it needs financial backing surpassing that of the Belarusian president. Finally, the opposition requires full access to the mass media, including support from the Russian media, such as the television stations ORT [Obshchestvennoe rossiiskoe televidenie] and RTR [Rossiiskoe teleradio]. Bringing the opposition to power requires the construction of alternative power structures or the opportunity to win over Lukashenka's power structures within a short time. All the above-mentioned indicators must reach a critical stage at the same moment as an abrupt fall in the standard of living.

One characteristic of the opposition in Belarus, thus far, has been the weakness of its leaders. Another is the divergence in approaches to opposition—there are both hard-line and soft-line groups. Hard-line opposition groups adhere to a number of critical issues on which they maintain there can be no compromise: Belarus as an independent state free from Russian influences or any alliance with the Russian Federation; the division of powers; market reform; respect for human rights and the priority of the law; and reinstitution of Belarusian national symbols, such as the white-red-white national flag, the national emblem, and Belarusian as the sole state language. Probably most important are recognition that Lukashenka has been ruling illegally since 20 July 1999, when, according to the original 1994 Constitution of Belarus, his mandate ended, and the restoration of the former Supreme Soviet (referred to as the "Supreme Soviet of the 13th session"), which was dissolved by Lukashenka after the referendum of November 1996.

The "soft" or consensus opposition groups, on the other hand, are prepared to reach an accommodation with the government on a number of issues, but still stand firm on others: the division of powers, respect for human rights and the sanctity of the law, the declaration that Lukashenka has been an illegal ruler since 20 July 1999, the declaration of the authority of the former supreme soviet, and an alliance or close friendship with Russia according to legal processes.

The priorities of the opposition have changed constantly in the independence period. As the Soviet Union began to disintegrate, the primary goal was to create an independent and democratic state, with priority given to the national idea. In 1991, the aim was to build this state with a market economy and respect for human rights. From late 1996, however, the opposition has sought to defend independence and restore democracy in Belarus.

The opposition is divided into various parties and groups. The major political parties are the Belarusian Popular Front (BPF), the Conservative Christian Party of the BPF, the United Civic Party (UCP), the Social Democratic Party (Narodnaia Hramada), the rival Social Democratic Party (Hramada), the Women's Party, the Labor Party, the Liberal Democratic Party, and the Communist Party. There are also a number of public organizations, such as centers for human rights, including the Helsinki Committee, Viasna, and Charter-'97, formed to focus international and national attention on the abuses of human rights in Belarus. The Free and Official Trade Unions can also be counted on the side of the opposition, as can the Belarusian Congress of Officers, formed in November 1999. In addition, there are legitimate assemblies in opposition to the president, particularly the Supreme Soviet of the 13th session, the Coordinating Consultative Council of the opposition, and the more recently formed National Executive Committee, or "Shadow Cabinet."

International observers have frequently commented that no individual opposition leader has emerged capable of posing a threat to the popularity of Lukashenka. However, a number of prominent political leaders have become well known to the Belarusian public. These leaders include Mykhail Chyhir [Chygir], the prime minister under Lukashenka prior to November 1996; Miacheslaŭ Hryb [Mecheslav Grib], the chairman of the Supreme Soviet of the 12th session; Siamion [Semen] Sharetski, his counterpart in the assembly of the 13th session; Mikalai Statkevich, the leader of the Social Democratic Party; Zianon Pazniak [Zenon Pozniak], head of the

Conservative Christian Party of the BPF; Vintsuk Viachorka [Vechor-ka], leader of the BPF; Stanislaŭ Bahdankevich [Stanislav Bogdan-kevich], the former chairman of the National Bank of Belarus; Anatol Liabedzka [Lebedko], the Deputy Chairman of the Supreme Soviet of the 13th session; Siarhei Haidukevich [Sergei Gaidukevich], the leader of the Liberal Democratic Party; and Siamion Domash, the former leader of Hrodna [Grodno] Oblast in western Belarus.

Although the official media has remained under the close control of the government, there are several outlets for the opposition. The most effective opposition newspapers in Belarus today are *Narodnaia volia*, *Belorusskaia delovaia gazeta*, and the workers' newspaper *Rabochii*. The journal *Grazhdanskaia alternativa* caters to the national intelligentsia. Several regional newspapers have successfully sus-tained an independent line, including *Vitebskii kur'er*, *Brestskii kur'er*, and *Borisovskie novosti*, which are supplied in turn by BelaPAN, the information agency based in Minsk. Other newspapers that operate outside the government or presidential dictum are *Belorusskii rynok*, *Svobodnye novosti*, and *Belorusskaia molodezhnaia*. Two radio stations also broadcast in Belarus, Svaboda (Svoboda; Radio Liberty) and Racja (Ratsia), although their influence is rather limited.

We shall focus in more depth on four of the opposition movements. The progress or lack thereof of each has been crucial to the development of the political impasse that exists in Belarus today.

The Belarusian Popular Front—"Adradzhennie"

The Belarusian Popular Front (BPF) was formed in 1988 as the first opposition party to emerge in the republic. It supported the establish-ment of an independent sovereign state. Over the past decade, the BPF membership has dwindled to about 40 percent of its original figure. In 1999, a split occurred within the BPF, and the membership divided into two almost equal parties: the BPF Conservative Christian Party, led by Pazniak, with about 1,000 members; and the BPF "Adrad-zhennie" Party (about 1,300 members), under Viachorka. This divi-sion followed two years of conflict within various parts of the party.

Viachorka began his political career in 1979 (at age 18) when he helped form the Belarusian Workshop, the first informal Belarusian youth organization. It became a cover for an underground national liberation group that organized actions, published literature, and established international contacts. In its second stage, the organization was called Talaka ('Joint Work'). In 1987, it was transformed into the Confederation of Belarusian Organizations, with more than 50 affiliated members. In the following year, these organizations became the basis for the formation of the BPF. Viachorka and others advocated the view that the most important factor in the creation of an independent Belarusian state is the impact of the national idea on the consciousness of the people. The national ideology, from the outset, was offered as an alternative to the dogma of Marxism-Leninism.

Political leaders such as Pazniak, who heralded from an older generation of national activists, felt that political methods should predominate in the quest to create an independent national state. Pazniak himself entered politics in a psychological state of fear and hatred. In the Kurapaty Forest, just outside Minsk, he had exhumed graves of the victims of the mass executions conducted by NKVD, Stalin's secret police, in the 1930s. After the discovery of the remains, he began to live in fear for his life. His career was motivated by his unmitigated antagonism toward Stalin and the Communist (Russian) authorities. During the Soviet period, he often remained jobless and isolated, developing an ascetic existence. Under Pazniak's leadership, the BPF developed as a defender of the population against Communist repression, against those who concealed the magnitude of the 1986 nuclear accident at the Chernobyl power station in Ukraine, and against Communist corruption.

Belarus' initial period was a difficult one. The Communist majority in the Supreme Soviet, through the vehicle of the media, sought to portray BPF members as fascists. Their campaign was quite successful. Even Pazniak himself suffered from this image, despite the fact that he was only one year old at war's end and his own father had perished during the German occupation. The myth persisted until 1994. In 1989, the BPF captured about 30 seats in the legislature, despite a slanderous campaign waged against it in the national media. However, it appears that Pazniak, fresh from this triumph against the odds, severely overestimated the national consciousness of the electorate. Their vote for the opposition deputies was a vote of protest against the government. Once it became evident that the 30 BPF deputies could do little to change the nature of the Supreme Soviet, electoral support for them dissipated; indeed, the BPF became equated with the problems of the government.

Pazniak's faith in a future national Belarusian state, which had been an integral part of his thinking for several years, appeared to be justified by the declaration of independence on 25 August 1991, following the failure of the putsch in Moscow. In fact, the political leadership of Belarus had little choice but to declare independence. All the former Soviet republics were officially leaving the Soviet Union, and Belarus had either to follow suit or remain within a USSR that clearly had no future. There was one other, seemingly improbable alternative: Belarus, in alliance with Russia, could leave the USSR without a formal declaration of independence. However, this became infeasible once Boris Yeltsin had clearly embarked upon the construction of an independent, democratic Russia, without any manifestation of its imperial past. Those Belarusian Communists who voted for independence within the Supreme Soviet of the 12th session did so with their own livelihood in view—within an independent Belarus, they would not have to share their relative wealth with the corrupt leaders in Moscow. Pazniak saw the issues differently: he perceived the independence vote as a remarkable victory for the policies of the BPF and his own leadership.

The Supreme Soviet perpetuated this perspective for some time by passing laws that supported the development of national culture and market reforms. Pazniak frequently noted that the 30 opposition deputies were dictating the policies of the 300 others. The electorate saw matters differently: in their view, the BPF was deeply immersed in the corruption that had spread throughout the legislative body. At first, matters seemed to be progressing on course. In 1992, the BPF collected signatures to dissolve the legislature of the 12th session and organize new elections. Altogether, some 450,000 signatures were collected, but only the BPF advocated new elections. Other centrist parties, such as the United Democratic Party, opposed the dissolution of the supreme soviet. Both Communists and Democrats denounced what they perceived as the "politics of the restoration of national culture." The Supreme Soviet decided not to hold a referendum, after which Pazniak claimed that the body was no longer legitimate. Despite that, the BPF deputies remained in the legislature.

In this same period, 1992–1993, the public perceived a new, more contemporary enemy than the wartime fascists and their alleged collaborators. The new enemy was corruption within the ruling bodies of the republic. Corruption on a large scale was first uncovered in the town of Barysaŭ [Borisov] (population 150,000), 50 miles northeast of Minsk, where several local leaders were accused of corrupt activities. When the local authorities tried to prevent an inquiry, the local deputies of the town soviet appealed to Stanislaŭ Shushkevich, the chairman of the Supreme Soviet. Other cases followed, and thus Shushkevich, who was identified with the non-Communists in the legislature, had overall charge of the anti-corruption campaign. In the winter of 1993, a conference of public prosecutors and judges was held in Minsk, and Shushkevich had an opportunity to expose in full the degree of corruption in the republic, a move that implicated even the prime minister, Viachaslaŭ Kebich. However, Shushkevich elected to mention only a small portion of the cases discovered. In the summer of 1993, the deputies from Barysaŭ were prosecuted. They had hoped that Shushkevich would appear as a witness on their behalf; however, he did not attend the hearing, ostensibly because he wished to maintain good relations with the government hierarchy.

These events played a role in the removal of Shushkevich as chairman of the Supreme Soviet (this time on the grounds that he himself was involved in corruption), and in the conflict between Shushkevich and Pazniak that led them to run against each other in the presidential elections of 1994. Both were defeated ignominiously when Lukashenka won the election as a result of his position as chairman of a parliamentary commission to investigate corruption. Subsequently, the divided opposition was heavily defeated in the elections to the Supreme Soviet of the 13th session the following year. At the same time, Lukashenka held a referendum on the abolition of the national flag and symbols, the elevation of Russian as the state language, and the institution of the right of the president to dissolve the supreme soviet. Despite holding a hunger strike, the depleted and demoralized opposition was unable to counter such a move.

The period 1994–1995 can be seen as the low point of the BPF, a time when the party had clearly failed to attract the electorate to the causes it espoused. Thereafter, it revived, however, for two reasons. First, Belarusian youth were generally alienated by the abrupt elimination of national symbols, an issue confronted by the BPF. Second, the BPF found a new source of activity in public demonstrations and protests, which were bolstered by the youthful element. The most successful of these protests was the Charnobyl Shliakh (Chernobyl Way) of 26 April 1996, in which 50,000 people took part and resulted in vicious clashes with the militia. The BPF enjoyed a revival in popularity in part because Russia's involvement in a war in Chechnya, linked with Lukashenka's avowed policy of union with Russia, suggested to young Belarusians that they might be obliged to participate in military conflicts outside the borders of their republic. The revival was limited in scope, however, as long as the BPF, under Pazniak, refused to cooperate with other parties. In the summer of 1996, Pazniak left Belarus, initially as a refugee to the United States, but eventually settling with other dissidents (and his family) in Warsaw, Poland. Only in 1999, after the rift in the BPF leadership and the formation of the two divisions, did the Belarus-based faction of BPF under Viachorka offer peace feelers to other groups in the opposition. Despite its decline from its heyday in the late 1980s, the BPF remains the best organized of all the Belarusian opposition groups, maintaining branches in all major towns and districts of the republic.

Charter-'97

Charter-'97, a movement launched by Belarusian democratic activists in November 1997 specifically to oppose Lukashenka's authoritarian policies, caused a significant stir in the West when it was first established. It brought with it the idea of uniting the opposition around the popular aspiration of respect for human rights. Its charter was created by Deputy of the Supreme Soviet of the 13th session Liudmila Hraznova [Graznova], former Deputy Foreign Minister Andrei Sannikaŭ [Sannikov], and several political activists, the best known of whom was Zmitser (Dzmitrii) Bandarenka [Dmitrii Bondarenko]. The text of the charter was edited by Viachorka and BPF member Liavon Barshcheŭski [Lev Barshchevski], and the first to sign the declaration was the renowned Belarusian writer, Vasil Bykaŭ [Vasilii Bykov]. The text was published in the opposition newspapers, and citizens were invited to sign it.[1]

---

1   For the full text of the Charter, see Appendix I, pp. 459ff.

The initial signatories of Charter-'97 decided that the group would have no official framework or political leadership. In reality, however, Bandarenka and his associates presented themselves to the media as representatives of the organizational committee of the Charter, and in meetings with foreign diplomats, as strong political leaders behind whom stood the organization's 100,000 signatories. With these moves, an apolitical movement took on political dimensions.

The self-appointed leaders of Charter-'97 created still another schism in the opposition movement. Political leaders, such as Pazniak and Shushkevich, resented the manipulation of the public's perspective and began to allude to Charter-'97 as an organization created by the intelligence service of the Russian Federation. Shushkevich followed up by writing a critical letter to the media. The Bandarenka group, however, began to appeal to foreign organizations, particularly in the United States, for funding to support a mass movement, receiving as much as $20,000. Sannikaŭ spoke at international conferences, maintaining that the Charter was the only force capable of bringing about a change of regime in Belarus. Critics claimed that Sannikaŭ was employed by the KGB and was merely following its orders. Bandarenka, in particular, has been the most successful of the Charter-'97 leaders in attracting support and funding from foreign sources. Whatever the truth behind the organization and development of Charter-'97—and it is a murky and difficult story to fathom—it has certainly failed as a united opposition movement.

The Workers' Movement

A working-class movement developed in Belarus toward the end of the Soviet period, reaching its peak in March–April 1991. About 120,000 workers gathered on 4 April in Minsk's Independence Square, and most factories in Belarus went on strike. Among the workers who played a prominent role in this strike were Siarhei Antonchyk, Heorhy Mukhin, and Henadz Bykaŭ. Antonchyk had already earned a reputation as a skillful propagandist. A man with a versatile mind and a persuasive manner, he had been elected as a deputy to the Supreme Soviet of the 12th session. In response to the strike, Prime Minister Kebich felt obliged to raise workers' salaries, after which the strikes tapered off.

The First Congress of the Free Trade Unions was held at the end of November 1991, and at Antonchyk's behest, Bykaŭ was elected chairman. At the start of 1992, the Free Trade Union had 12,000 members, but by the end of 1999, the number had declined to around 6,000. The trade union movement has also been plagued with corruption and internal leadership struggles, and public support has likewise declined. Antonchik himself left the movement in 1994, but returned to political activity in 1998 during the preparation of the Congress of Belarusian Democratic Forces.

Opposition to the Lukashenka Presidency

Lukashenka's election as the first president of Belarus led to the formation of a new stage in the contemporary opposition movement. It began with several political leaders leaving the presidential team, including Iuri Zakharanka, Viktar Hanchar, and Mikhail Chyhir. In addition, new political leaders, such as Viachorka and Statkevich, emerged from the opposition. The creation of a new opposition structure began with the elections to the Supreme Soviet of the 13th session in 1995 and 1996. During these elections, a particularly malevolent campaign was launched against the BPF. At this time, there were two conflicting factions of the opposition: first, the street opposition, the nucleus of which was formed by members of the BPF under the leadership of Pazniak; second, the opposition to Lukashenka in the Supreme Soviet, led by Sharetski. The latter began the process of impeachment of the president in the late summer of 1996 but were unsuccessful in this campaign.

After the contentious referendum of November 1996 and the dissolution of the Supreme Soviet of the 13th session by the government, several deputies of that legislature appeared in the opposition campaign, including Sharetski, Hryb, and Domash. From the beginning, there were significant differences on issues between these deputies and the BPF members, and the former were seen in some quarters as weak leaders who had forced Sharetski to sign a compromise agreement with Lukashenka prior to the referendum under the auspices of then-Russian Prime Minister Viktor Chernomyrdin. However, the BPF members within Belarus, led by Deputy Chairman Iuri Khadyka, began to work with Sharetski.

The Communist Party was divided after the November 1996 referendum, with one faction supporting Lukashenka and the other moving closer to an accommodation with the BPF. Once Viachorka took over from Pazniak as BPF leader, close cooperation between the two parties that had once been bitter enemies became plausible.

The political opposition, on the other hand, is united on only one issue: the need to remove Lukashenka from office. Just as Belarus is situated between countries now moving into NATO and the European Union (EU) to the west and Russia to the east, so there are politicians who look to the West and others who turn to Russia. The two orientations offer very different visions of the direction in which Belarus should move in the future. As for the Russian Federation itself, some forces (Communists or pro-Communists) would like to maintain Lukashenka in power. Others support Lukashenka in the hope that Belarus will join the Russian Federation. A third group supports the democratic part of the opposition and wishes to establish a democratic regime in Belarus that will then unite with democratic forces in Russia, as represented by Anatoly Chubais and Grigorii Yavlinsky. Finally, it is significant that there are potentially recalcitrant elements currently within the Lukashenka government that might conceivably join the opposition at some point.

The Rift between Opposition and Society

There are a number of reasons why an impasse between the opposition and the different parts of the electorate has remained. Citizens of Belarus, in general, have yet to adhere to democratic values, and in some sectors, the mentality of the former Soviet period still prevails. The opposition, as noted, has never had a leader acceptable to the population as a whole, and some of its leaders are former, disillusioned members of the Lukashenka team. Others have held positions that are hardly calculated to have mass appeal. Bahdankevich, for example, is a banker, and in the minds of the electorate, banks are frequently equated with corruption. The opposition lacks access to the mass media: government newspapers, such as *Sovetskaia Belorussiia*, have regularly denounced opposition figures. Some leaders have misused financial support from the West. Finally, the structure of the opposition never remains constant; it changes each year and the electorate cannot keep pace with the bewildering political scene. A political figure needs to emerge who represents certain values in order for the opposition to receive public support.

In one sense, because the backing of the electorate is limited, each individual leader clashes with his fellow leaders to secure the available support for himself. The source of support is largely restricted to the national-conscious intellectual elite and to the youth and worker movements. An illustration of the outlook of Belarusians is reflected in national holidays, all of which listed in the official calendar are commemorations of events that occurred during the Soviet period.[2] The national holiday is 3 July (the date on which Minsk was freed from German occupation in 1944). The opposition holds marches and demonstrations on other dates that are deemed significant, but there is no consensus on which dates should take precedence. Thus, the nationalists observe 8 September, the day in 1514 when an army of the Grand Duchy of Lithuania (with Belarusians in its ranks) defeated an army of Muscovy, and 25 March, the anniversary of the founding of the short-lived Belarusian National Republic in 1918. Other groups observe 15 March, the day of the adoption of the 1994 Constitution, and hold protests on 24 November, the date of the 1996 referendum, and 2 April, the date when the first Russia-Belarus confederation was announced in 1996. All sides agree on the significance of 26 April, the anniversary of the Chernobyl accident. This date has less significance as the years pass by, although it received significant commemoration on the 10th and the 15th anniversaries of the accident.

The role of the media in consolidating the Lukashenka regime was noted earlier. There is one Belarusian TV channel and three Russian-based TV channels. Though there is a considerable difference in outlook, all these channels have in common support for Russian-Belarusian integration. In the past, the Russian stations often have upset Lukashenka, particularly through their graphic portrayals of militia brutality in breaking up demonstrations in Minsk. The opposition media operates under duress. Insofar as it is effective at all,

---

[2]   See, for example, Astrid Sahm, "Political Culture and National Symbols: Their Impact on Belarusian Nation-Building Process," *Nationalities Papers* 27(4) December 1999: 656–67.

it is effective only in the capital city of Minsk. Elsewhere, these newspapers are not widely distributed and have little impact. The BPF newspaper *Svaboda* has experienced a number of transformations and name changes, none of which have allowed for a strong voice and wide distribution. The president, on the other hand, appears on TV nightly, and his speeches are printed in full on the pages of high-circulation government newspapers. The media is thus a critical factor in the failure of the opposition to obtain widespread recognition in Belarusian society, particularly among the elderly, the military, and those living in rural areas.

The gap between the opposition and society is hardly an abyss, but it clearly exists. Sociological surveys conducted in November 1999 indicated that 37 percent of Belarusian citizens oppose a union with Russia, while 35 percent support it. The opposition is firmly against the union, while Lukashenka is its chief advocate. These figures may be somewhat misleading, because Lukashenka personally is far more popular than any individual rival leader. The president has skillfully manipulated public opinion. When former Prime Minister Chyhir was released from prison, for example, but before his trial had begun, Belarusian television announced that he had already cost the state some $4 million, thus creating ill feeling toward him among the public. The president, in this and other cases, has been adept at creating enemies of the state. The chief bugbear is NATO, and internal opponents are frequently identified as allies of NATO who are working against the interests of Belarus.

The OSCE Dialogue

The dialogue held under the guidance of the OSCE AMG, and in particular its leader, the German diplomat Hans-Georg Wieck, initially had a positive impact on the opposition. Its leaders had an opportunity to meet regularly and to coordinate their positions. They began to seek compromises. This coordination allowed the opposition to prepare effectively for the parliamentary elections scheduled for 2000, in order to divide up electoral districts among respective members, and to avoid futile competition between the different parties. The start of consultations with the Lukashenka government gave rise to optimism in the West that the Belarusian opposition had formed a united front. This opinion was bolstered by the creation of a unified platform among the opposition leaders, which included access to the official media, the release of political prisoners, and the preservation of an independent Belarusian state.

The role of the Western states vis-à-vis Belarus has changed considerably in recent years. In 1998 and the first half of 1999, the politics of the United States predominated and was manifested in the departure of 11 ambassadors from Belarus following their eviction from the Drazdy complex. In the absence of the U.S. ambassador for a protracted period, Germany began to play the leading role among the Western states. Indeed, the organization of talks between Lukashenka and the opposition was a German strategy, devised in part by Wieck and in part by the German embassy under Ambassador Horst Winkelmann. To put policy differences simply, the United States supported more radical means to influence the Belarusian president, whereas Germany followed a policy of appeasement, of satiating Lukashenka. Western influence has been defined by political competition between NATO and the OSCE, the two major Western organs dealing with Belarus on behalf of the Western powers. Since the OSCE summit in Istanbul in 1999, Germany has been the leading force in Belarusian politics.

The dialogue thus far has failed to bridge the gap between the Belarusian government and the opposition. According to Viachorka, OSCE efforts have succeeded in two things: achieving a dialogue between the OSCE and the government, and between the OSCE and the opposition. They have not attained their main objective, a dialogue between the government and the opposition.[3] Moreover, the process has frequently been marred by further infighting among opposition leaders, particularly between Statkevich, the leader of the Social Democratic Party who enjoys significant public support, and Shushkevich, the founder of a rival movement (with the same name) that has little support. Once again, the opposition leaders have focused on the weaknesses and failings of their fellows rather than on the Lukashenka government. As a result, the process of creating a dialogue has been a source of significant support to and consolidation of the Lukashenka regime. Simply by appointing a spokesman,

---

[3]   Authors' interview with Vintsuk Viachorka, Minsk, Belarus, 21 December 1999.

Mikhail Sazonaŭ, to take part in the dialogue, Lukashenka has appeared to be cooperating with the OSCE. He has, however, made no compromises and has failed to live up to his promises to give the opposition access to the media prior to new parliamentary elections in the year 2000.

The Political Year 1999: A Retrospective

The "Presidential Election" of 16 May

The year 1999 brought an abundance of opportunities for both Lukashenka and the opposition. The date 21 July hung over the head of the president like the sword of Damocles. According to the 1994 Constitution (amended drastically by Lukashenka after the 1996 referendum), presidential elections should have been held in Belarus in 1999. Members of the opposition as well as the United States and major European powers stand by the inviolability of the 1994 Constitution and do not recognize the changes incorporated in November 1996. Lukashenka, on the other hand, maintains that his presidency expires in November 2001.

The leaders of the opposition had a solid social and political platform from which to attack Lukashenka. It was based on three positions: (1) During Lukashenka's five years in power, the standard of living has decreased significantly; (2) Lukashenka's legitimate term as president ended on 20 July 1999; (3) The opposition suggested holding an election in which Lukashenka could also take part. This was an indicator that it adhered to the democratic process rather than seeking to overthrow the president by illegitimate means.

At this time, there were five potential alternative candidates for president from the ranks of the opposition: Sharetski, Hanchar, Chyhir, Pazniak, and Henadz Karpenka, the leader of the United Civic Party. Their goals were often contradictory and each considered his rivals as a larger obstacle than the president himself. Sharetski's position seemed more secure than the others in that if the president's term expired, then, according to the 1994 Constitution, he would automatically become the interim president. Hanchar had taken on the role of organizer of the 1999 presidential elections, but without declaring himself a potential candidate. His popularity rose accordingly, because the electorate considered him to be working for selfless motives. At the outset of the campaign, he was arrested and detained by the KGB and went on a hunger strike, which further enhanced his standing. Indeed, Hanchar, in the early spring of 1999, appeared as a credible opponent to Lukashenka. By contrast, Chyhir, the imprisoned former prime minister, had difficulty obtaining the 100,000 signatures required for nomination.

Ultimately, there were only two candidates for the election: Pazniak and Chyhir. The untimely death of Karpenka on 6 April was a devastating blow to the opposition, because the UCP leader was one of the few politicians with broad appeal and, concomitantly, the ability to unite several competing factions in a common cause. Hanchar closely controlled the May elections, ingeniously finding solutions to problems, but hardly in ways that endeared him to the major candidates. Chyhir conducted the election campaign from his prison cell. In reality, his wife Iulia took over his campaign, along with a journalist friend, Tatsiana Vanina. Both were members of the BPF, which aroused the anger of Pazniak, who tried to remove them from the party. Pazniak withdrew from the campaign in its closing stages, in protest at Hanchar's decision to take ballot boxes around to apartment buildings to circumvent the lack of suitable polling stations. Ultimately, Hanchar announced that over 53 percent of the electorate had taken part in the election,[4] but the results were in dispute and no official verdict was ever issued. Few believed the figure of 53 percent. Indeed, the election served to discredit further the opposition and significantly reduced Hanchar's personal standing.[5]

Attempts to Establish Dual Power

The date 20 July 1999 represented an obvious opportunity for the opposition. Lukashenka would no longer have international recognition after that date. Once again, however, there was no consensus on what action should be taken. Two schools of thought prevailed in two distinct political centers. Pazniak, who was increasingly detached from events in Belarus, hoped that the BPF

---

[4]   Cited in *Belorusskaia gazeta*, 24 May 1999.

[5]   For a detailed discussion of this election, see Uladzimir Padhol and David R. Marples, "Belarus: The Opposition and the Presidency," *The Harriman Review* 12(1) Fall 1999: 11–18.

would create a civic parliament that would take power by 21 July. However, many of Pazniak's supporters realized that such a parliament would not receive international recognition in Europe or elsewhere because foreign powers would focus instead on the legitimacy of the Supreme Soviet of the 13th session. A civic parliament would be illegitimate and encumbered from the start by its lack of authentic power. Pazniak has maintained, on the other hand, that the Supreme Soviet of the 13th session is a pro-Russian body that has received backing from the authorities in Moscow as a useful counter to Lukashenka. A large rally took place on Oktiabrskaia Square in Minsk, but for the most part, Pazniak's supporters were absent.[6]

The Supreme Soviet of the 13th session planned to hold a formal meeting to declare Sharetski the acting president. The indefatigable Hanchar was once again the organizer of the event, intending to gather together some 100,000 people as an expression of overwhelming public support for a change of regime. The gathering was billed as a "Farewell to Lukashenka," with promises to workers in the outlying regions that their transport costs would be covered and beer and sausages would be provided upon their arrival in October Square in Minsk. In order to summon the workforce, Hanchar depended on the services of Antonchyk, who offered payments to the workers through a newly created body called the Alternative Labor Exchange. However, only about 5,000 attended the rally, and most people dispersed once they discovered that neither food nor drink had been provided. Though the rally did not take place as planned, a significant rally took place in Hrodna, attended by 3,000 people. It appeared that there was some momentum for a change of government, but effecting it would require decisive action on the part of Sharetski.

Sharetski, however, acted tentatively and was clearly afraid that his elevation would lead to his sudden demise. For several days, he took refuge in the German hotel that quartered the OSCE AMG. On 21 July, when his bodyguards came to escort him to the decisive meeting of the Supreme Soviet, they found the new leader reluctant to leave his apartment. Eventually, he was persuaded to attend the meeting, held at the Faculty of Philology building at the Belarusian

---

6   Uladzimir Padhol was present at this rally.

State University. About 1,000 people were present, but Sharetski declined to proclaim himself president. He maintained initially that he would make this proclamation from Lithuania once he had crossed the border and that he would become acting president if a provisional government were established. However, a significant portion of those gathered could not agree on the choice of Cabinet members. Subsequently, Sharetski crossed the border into Lithuania. By this action, he effectively abdicated his position as de jure interim leader of the country.

Lukashenka may no longer have been legitimate in the eyes of foreign powers, but he was the only leader in Belarus and, as such, the various embassies continued to deal with him. Though Sharetski dallied with the idea of declaring a new government-in-exile, it was clear that foreign recognition would not be forthcoming.

Hanchar now emerged as the clear leader of the effort to unseat Lukashenka. He calculated that after the poor harvest of 1999, popular discontent could be channeled into political protests and lead to a revival of the idea of dual power.[7] Hanchar's strategy anticipated that some members of the Lukashenka government would turn on their leader. This notion was not far-fetched, because it was well known that the president was seeking scapegoats for the poor harvest. Hanchar evidently felt that the head of the presidential administration, Mikhail Miasnikovich, might not remain loyal to Lukashenka. Hanchar had, by this time, effectively taken over the leadership of the Supreme Soviet in the absence of Sharetski. On the night of 16 September, however, Hanchar and a colleague, Anatol Krasnoŭski, disappeared in a suspected kidnapping close to Hanchar's apartment in Minsk. At the time of writing, there has been no indication of his whereabouts despite increasing international concern. Whether the kidnapping was undertaken on behalf of the government or was unrelated to the events of the summer, Hanchar, the most active

[7] *Belorusskaia gazeta* 2 August 1999. In this article, Hanchar advocated that the West should withhold credits from Russia until the Belarusian question was resolved and all citizens of Belarus were mobilized under the leadership of a revived Supreme Soviet of the 13th session.

(though highly controversial) member of the opposition movement, was suddenly removed.[8]

As a result of this event, the focus of the opposition once again devolved on the Belarusian Popular Front. On 1 August, the VIth Congress of the Belarusian Popular Front conducted an election for the chairmanship of the party. Prior to the Congress, the leadership of Pazniak, which had endured for ten years, was undisputed. He was challenged, however, by Viachorka. Pazniak received 156 votes in favor and 156 opposed; Viachorka received 152 in favor and 160 opposed. In response to this surprising result, Pazniak sent a letter to BPF members on 8 August, stating:

> The unity of the organization can no longer be maintained. Artificial restrictions can lead only to a catastrophe. It is necessary to proceed from what unity remains—the unity of the Belarusian national idea, the principles and the goals of rebirth. It is necessary to strengthen this unity in a new systematically structured BPF organization.

Pazniak continued by declaring that there must be two structures of the BPF: one devoted to public activity (Viachorka), and the other focused on the national question and based on a position of conservatism. The reality, however, was that Pazniak and many of his main supporters were now based outside the country. The task of reorienting the BPF toward the existing political situation and opportunities fell to Viachorka, who was later confirmed as the new chairman of the BPF once the Congress continued in October. Viachorka opposed the idea of dividing the BPF and opted instead to maintain the organization in its present form. His election as chairman was supported, 228 votes to 11. The emergence of Viachorka has strengthened the BPF and provided new links to the other opposition parties that hitherto had been restricted by Pazniak's more narrow approach. Thus, potentially, the opposition, by the end of 1999, had renewed opportunities for cooperation both inside and outside the confines of the Supreme Soviet of the 13th session.

---

[8]   Hanchar had other schemes. One was to declare Chyhir the prime minister of Belarus, with Sharetski as acting president. This bizarre idea would likely have extended Chyhir's prison sentence, for conspiring against the Lukashenka government, and removed him as a potential rival to Hanchar himself. See *Belorusskaia delovaia gazeta* 1 September 1999.

Perspectives

During the negotiations with the OSCE, Lukashenka agreed to hold parliamentary elections in 2000 and a presidential election in 2001. This agreement represents a diplomatic triumph for Lukashenka in that a presidential election in 2001 signifies implicit recognition of the changes he has made to the 1994 Constitution. The parliamentary election, on the other hand, is likely to be boycotted by the major opposition parties because of the government's lack of compromise on access to the media and the release of political prisoners. The opposition has been denied an allotted time slot on national television and a column in the two most widely circulated national daily newspapers, *Sovetskaia Belorussiia* and *Narodnaia hazeta*.

Can the opposition have a significant impact on the elections and on government policy in general? At present, there are insufficient unifying factors in place, and there is a notable lack of coordination of efforts within the international community. Indeed, the authority and longevity of the Lukashenka presidency have been facilitated by the divisions among the opposition and the reaction to these of the electorate, particularly in Minsk, where all politics are centered.

Several issues will determine the future of the opposition. First, there is the issue of Belarus' integration with Russia. Since the financial collapse of Russia in mid-August 1998, this policy has received mixed reaction in Belarus. It is no longer perceived as a solution to economic and social problems in Belarus: the revelation that Russia, the provider, is in reality a country dependent on continual loans and credits from the West has bolstered Lukashenka's position as a leader only insofar as he has pursued policies independently of Russia. Belarus continues to subsidize its obsolete factories and collective farms,[9] pursuing a path of economic backwardness. Yet, it is this policy that endears the president to sections of the public, particularly those in rural areas and those nostalgic for the Soviet era. Though integration with Russia has reached a critical point, particularly in the areas of military-security and currency merger, Lukashenka must tread a fine line between

[9]   See, for example, *RFE/RL Poland, Belarus, and Ukraine Report* 2(10) 14 March 2000.

cooperation and a full-scale merger that would render Belarus the status of a western province of Russia. Integration has occurred in several stages with painfully slow progress, but it is taking place nonetheless.

Second, the Western powers have adopted varied approaches. In generalized terms, the United States has been more critical of violations of human rights and has been more willing to hear the opposition case while carefully limiting its contacts with the Lukashenka administration.[10] The OSCE, the OSCE AMG, and the German Embassy, on the other hand, have adopted a more tolerant, though critical approach, which has sought to keep the dialogue in place despite a notable lack of progress on all fronts. In the long term, the OSCE mission in Belarus is unlikely to succeed. The government has made some mileage out of its willingness to hear the OSCE viewpoint, but it has conceded very little. The presidential elections of 2001 will mark the decisive stage in the process, but only if the elections take place on a democratic basis, with equal access of all candidates to the media and substantial financial support for any candidate who chooses to oppose Lukashenka.

Where does this leave the opposition in the year 2000? Key figures have been nullified by government repression or unexplained disappearances—Hanchar, Iuri Zakharanka (founder of the Belarusian Congress of Officers), and Chyhir (now out of prison but in the middle of what is likely to be a lengthy trial). Pazniak, the scourge of the pro-Communist factions for a decade, is now on the periphery of Belarusian politics and unlikely to play a key role in the future. Statkevich is a popular figure among the Germans and has a higher standing among the electorate than either Sharetski, the acting president in exile, or Shushkevich, the effective leader of the country at the time of independence. Anatol Liabedzka, deputy chairman of the United Civic Party, would likely be the candidate favored by the United States. Former Speaker Miacheslaŭ Hryb has served as

---

[10] On 9 March, for example, both Sharetski and Shushkevich spoke at a U.S. Congressional hearing on Belarus held in Washington, D.C. At the OSCE summit in Istanbul in summer 1999, U.S. President Bill Clinton was approached directly by Lukashenka and was unable to avoid the Belarusian president. The brief meeting, which was insignificant and clearly not planned by Clinton, was widely publicized on Belarusian television.

chairman of panels of the Shadow Cabinet and may be a compromise candidate for the various political factions that oppose Lukashenka. Finally, Viachorka, a young, European-style politician with an excellent command of several languages, including English, will clearly play an important role for the opposition in the future. Viachorka's immediate task is to convince the electorate that the BPF is a party of the center rather than the Right or extreme Right, and that the meaning of *"narodnyi"* in the name of the party signifies popular, rather than national.

The various parties and individual candidates to date have proved unable to collaborate effectively. There are, however, some precedents for such cooperation. The Congress of Democratic Forces, which met in January 1999 and supported the unofficial presidential elections the following May, is a case in point. Charter-'97, in its initial stages, was another example of a number of groups working together toward a united goal. The opposition thus far has been unable to avert the government's linking them to a period of unprecedented corruption and economic decline that occurred immediately after independence. Events, such as NATO's attack on Serbia in April 1999, have also enabled the government to portray the opposition as pro-Western and simultaneously anti-Belarusian. Thus, the opposition needs more than just unity—it must present a different image among the electorate of an entity that is patriotic but not anti-Western, that supports independence and nation-building without being seen as Russophobic, and that advocates privatization and economic reform without endangering the living standards of the population. To fulfill these goals is impossible without an alternative perspective to that of the government, and access to media to voice it. It also requires the careful and overt use of funds supplied by foreign supporters and foreign governments.

Thus far, the opposition has proved unequal to such formidable tasks, but, at the same time, the next few years will provide a number of significant opportunities to change the political outlook and provide an authentic challenge to the presidency of Aliaksandr Lukashenka.

3

Rainer Lindner
The Lukashenka Phenomenon

> The same as in the times of the notorious stagnation
> and the regime of the Soviet 'gerontocracy' quietly
> going mad in the beginning of 80s, the suffocating
> atmosphere of all-round suspicion, spy mania, anti-
> Western bellicosity, lack of freedom and police
> control prevail in the Belarusian official policy.[1]
>
> Anatol Maisenya (1995)

When the famous journalist and ambitious politician Anatol Maisenya
died in a car crash in 1996, there already were indications that
Belarus, the "land of unrealized hopes," would present a problem to
the international community of states when Poland became a member
of NATO, causing Belarus, an increasingly unsettled region, to border
on the North Atlantic bloc. Now that future has become reality.
Relations between Minsk and the United States, the European Union,
and Germany are tense.

In the course of my analysis of the Lukashenka phenomenon, I
will cover the failed process of elite building in Belarus as well as
Aliaksandr Lukashenka's path to power. I will then describe the
regime's consolidation of Belarusian institutions and society. "Cracks
in the monolith" within the presidential administration will be
investigated. Finally, I will conclude with three recommendations for
Western policymakers about what action should be taken. The

---

[1]   Anatol Maisenya, "Chronicle of a Crashing Country or Is there an Alternative to
the Authoritarian Regime in Belarus?" (1995), in *The Land of Unrealised Hopes: A
Portrait of Time and a Portrait of Man,* ed. Anatol Maisenya et al. (Minsk, 1997),
p. 216.

questions on which I intend to focus have been formulated by Timothy Colton and Robert Tucker in their *Patterns of Post-Soviet Leadership:* individual character and values, leadership roles and institutions, the state and cultural framework, and the effectiveness of political leadership.[2]

For the last ten years, societies on the territory of the former Soviet Union have been in transition. The history of such societies in transition during the 20th century—like those in South America or Asia—indicates that this long period is by no means unusual. Change requires time, and possibly the passing of the older generation, particularly in cases in which, along with its economy and its social relations, a society's intellectual structures are undergoing a fundamental conversion. What can be observed of the entire region is valid also for Belarus: the economy, politics, and society are burdened with deficits. On the other hand, whereas Russia, Ukraine, the Baltic States, and Azerbaijan have Western advocates of their interests, Belarus under Lukashenka is in danger of falling into an economic and political abyss located at the western periphery of a malfunctioning CIS and the eastern border of a relatively prosperous zone of NATO (and EU) enlargement without such advocates. From a Western perspective, the country continues to demonstrate one of the slowest rates of transformation among the societies of the former Communist world and is having a difficult time developing viable ties with the European network of states and other international organizations. In contrast to Russia and Ukraine, where Presidents Putin and Kuchma are pursuing dialogue with Western institutions, Belarus, under President Lukashenka, poses a threat to fragile East European stability. A number of recent events seem to signal that Belarus is on its way to becoming a failing state, with little potential to mobilize against this failing.

We are not speaking of Milošević or Saddam Hussein, to whom future historians will one day attribute the inability of the world during the last decade of the 20th century to establish more peaceful conditions after the end of the East-West conflict. We are speaking

---

[2]   Timothy J. Colton and Robert C. Tucker, eds., *Patterns in Post-Soviet Leadership* (Boulder, 1995).

not of an aggressive troublemaker, but of a noisy critic of Western politics within Eastern Europe and of a post-Soviet leader who embodies the particular heritage of his republic. Each post-Soviet republic has brought forth leaders (mostly presidents) with regionally determined patterns of political behavior: the Russian head of state has taken up the heritage of imperial claims with the war in Chechnya; the leaders of the traditional societies in Uzbekistan, Azerbaijan, and Kazakhstan have remained autocratic clan politicians; and the Baltic states have continued to rely on links to Western Europe. Lukashenka, in turn, attained a type of power that embodies the essence of the Belarusian state—a power based on a subjugated elite but that nevertheless results in minimal state sovereignty. The element connecting these post-Soviet leaders is to be found in the infallibility that the Communist elite claims for itself. To this extent, Lukashenka is no exception within the context of post-Soviet leadership structures; however, in 1994, the West was confronted with a Lukashenka who lacked the polish of the upper Soviet state elite, not to mention the qualifications of a trained politician. This fact has made dealing with him increasingly difficult. It is this deficiency of political provenance, this absence of the classical characteristics of a member of an elite, and this particular situation of a transformational period that impede dealings with the type of post-Soviet non-politician he represents.

Aliaksandr Lukashenka's Path to Power and the Non-Elite of Post-Soviet Belarus

In Belarus, as in similar countries, the dissolution of the Soviet Union presented a challenge to existing power structures, which sought to preserve their positions. Those who retained them demonstrated their adaptability and profited from the slow and often stagnant process of transformation within administrative structures. Many of the patronage clientele of the 1980s are still in office at both the central and local level. With the term "party of power," sociologists and political scientists have attempted to describe a phenomenon which is difficult, if not impossible, to define clearly. Very generally, this "invisible power" has been described as a bloc composed of the pragmatically oriented and more or less de-ideologized upper strata of the old establishment, the representatives of the state apparatus, the mass media, and managers in the traditional sectors of industry and agriculture. Nevertheless, many new interest groups, power structures, and political actors have emerged during the last half decade. In all the post-Soviet transforming societies we see a struggle for distribution of resources and "administrative currency" (G. Sapov) on the "administrative market" (S. Kordonskii).

For Belarus in particular, it might be a great impediment to the emergence of a newly formed national elite that a state with a well-ordered administrative structure, a real separation of powers, and constitutional institutions does not yet exist. On the other hand, the instability and fuzziness of political and economic development within a very vague legal order challenge the emergence of a specific elite with the potential to have a real impact on these weak structures of governance.[3] After the dissolution of the Soviet Union, Belarusian political society was preserved without any significant changes; many of the former party staff belonged to the mobile strata of the population, capable of switching their attitudes and their functional utility. In the top echelons, something strange happened: non-elite representatives captured the posts of prime minister, chairman of the Supreme Soviet (Viarkhoŭnyi Savet), and president one by one. Whereas Premier Viacheslaŭ [Viacheslav] Kebich (1990–1994) still belonged to the late Soviet leading groups, with a life-long party and economic career in the capacity of Moscow's man in Minsk, chairman of the Supreme Soviet Stanislaŭ [Stanislav] Shushkevich (1991–1994), as a university professor, did not represent any influential interest groups beyond the politicized post-Chernobyl society of

---

[3]   For an overview, see Rainer Lindner, "Leading Groups in Belarus in Past and Present," *Vector* 1997 (2): 11–15. For a more detailed analysis of the current elite structure in Belarus see the contributions of Leonid Zaiko, "Elite Groups in the Republic of Belarus," pp. 243–302; Olga Zagorul'skaia, "The System of Interest Representation in the Republic of Belarus," pp. 657–84; and Irina Bugrova, "Political Actors and Channels of Interest Articulation in the Republic of Belarus," pp. 685–708, all in *Post-Soviet Puzzles: Mapping the Political Economy of the Former Soviet Union,* eds. Klaus Segbers and Stephan De Spiegeleire, 4 vols. (Baden-Baden, 1995) vol. 3, *Emerging Societal Actors—Economic, Social and Political Interests: Theories, Methods and Case Studies.* See also Rainer Lindner, "Domestic and Foreign Policy Conditions behind Structural Changes in the Ukraine and Belarus," *Aussenpolitik/German Foreign Affairs Review* 46 (1995): 365–75.

Belarusian intelligentsia and concerned citizens.

In mid-1994, when the newly elected president, Aliaksandr Lukashenka, unexpectedly found himself at the head of an independent European state in rapid economic and financial decline, he started his journey back to the familiar Soviet-designed society within the new union. Whereas his rival in the presidential elections, Prime Minister Kebich, whose close connections to both party and industrial structures also extended across the inner CIS borders, represented the late Soviet functional elite, Lukashenka became the embodiment of this great retreat after a disappointing period of being non-Soviet and independent. He had been part of the low-level Soviet elite, which performed the most frustrating party jobs at the grassroots, in the Army, the *sovkhozes*, the enterprises, etc. People like Lukashenka had internalized most methods of Communist Party work, with its controlling functions and its conception of the class enemy. The Belarusian president's political capital is his ability to speak the language of the masses rather than of the intellectuals. As a nonintellectual and a representative of a specific post-Soviet non-elite, he was, and more than likely still is, able to mobilize the electorate for a future in a familiar setting.[4]

The similarity between modern history and recent developments in Belarus has led to familiar behavior by the new dominant political groups. For five years they tried to redefine the political and economic interests of their state. At present, the formal high-level Belarusian political actors and economic elites of the transformation period and the bilateral Russian-Belarusian structures, in fact little more than a substitute quasi-Soviet apparatus dominated by a capillary system of Russian interest groups, seem to represent the old and new organizational and "psychological" security system. This indicates that the building of a new state and a new national elite in Belarus can only take place within this historically determined framework. The first concrete steps in this direction were already taken in April 1996 and April 1997, when the Russian-Belarusian contracts were signed and unification was not much more than a question of time. From the

---

[4] See Dmitri [Dmitrii] Furman and Oleg Bukhovets, "Belorusskoe samosoznanie i belorusskaia politika," *Svobodnaia mysl'* 1 (1996): 70.

very beginning, the Belarusian presidential non-elite was ready to strike against the Constitution by playing a part in Yeltsin's pre-electoral and anti-NATO extension campaign. As in its earlier history, Belarus was reduced to the role of a pawn in the power game between East and West. In the meantime, Lukashenka is stepping out of the role of observer into one of actor to the same extent that Boris Yeltsin is disappearing from the political stage. With his opposition to an eastward extension of NATO, Lukashenka lays claim to the position of advocate for the transformation losers, whose numbers are much larger than those of the winners; however, here too Lukashenka is able to profit from the fact that in this anti-Western attitude he need not adjust to new, more complex constellations, but can continue uninterrupted within his own "text."

If we assume a qualitative term for "elite," then:

> . . . today, being an "elite" implies to supervise main channels and currents of "resources." It implies being able to purposefully include these resources in various national and international processes, thus ultimately achieving efficient use and augmentation of resource bases. To be able to do this, one should possess up-to-date techniques of thought and be trained to use the existing range of semiotic machines and synergistic capabilities held within the spectrum of human activity (capabilities of signs, expertise, cultural norms, ideology, those of joint, group and collective psychological activity).[5]

The post-Soviet leadership seems to be another nomenklatura rather than an "elite." Its members lack the requisite norms, skills, and values of elites in other countries. "In particular, this manifests itself in their inability to work with mass political processes under conditions of inter-professional communication, incomplete information, uncertainty and collective action, under conditions of innovation, crisis, accidents, extreme conditions and calamities. The existing nomenklatura are unfortunately not able to operate systems of intelligence and reflection. Roughly speaking, it (in its bulk) is simply

---

[5]   This definition in Petr Shchedrovitskii, "In Search of Form," in *Post Soviet Puzzles*, eds. Segbers and De Spiegleire, vol. 1, *Against the Background of the Former Soviet Union* (Baden-Baden, 1996), p. 149.

illiterate in social and human terms."[6] This is particularly true in Lukashenka's case.

The gradual erosion of independence—symbolically started by Lukashenka when he shredded the Belarusian white-red-white banner after a first referendum in 1995—of the judiciary, the media, the Supreme Soviet, and even private business and the step-by-step removal (through individual terror and imprisonment) of a potential new elite causes the young state to suffer once more from lack of capable leadership and increases its international isolation, although it needs help in almost every way. In the end, Belarus is not ailing because of its president, but rather because of the lack of a genuine functional elite that, with its economic and political knowledge, could free the state from the psychological and structural shackles of the past. Lukashenka's election as president can, in retrospect, be regarded as the logical consequence of the society's lack of elites.

The biography of the Belarusian president confirms the conjectures we have made thus far. Aliaksandr Lukashenka was born on 30 August 1954, a year after Stalin's death, in Aliaksandryia, in the Shkloŭ district. A Belarusian by nationality, Lukashenka, who grew up fatherless, received an average education in the province and graduated in 1975 from the Pedagogical Institute of Mahilioŭ [Mogilev]. Following that, he completed his two years of national service (1975–1977) with the border troops of the Soviet Union's KGB. After one year (1977–1978) as secretary of the Komsomol Committee of Shkloŭ's State Grain Trade and two years (1978–1980) as Secretary of the Shkloŭ District Organization of the "Knowledge" Society, Lukashenka completed two years of service as a political officer in a unit of the Soviet Army. In 1979, at the age of 25, Lukashenka was granted party membership.

He left the Army in 1982 and worked as the deputy director of Shkloŭ's Construction Supply Combine until 1985. During this time, the rhetorically gifted Lukashenka honed his persuasive powers as a history teacher and economist at the Agricultural Academy. In the same year, the 30-year-old joined the Shkloŭ district Lenin Kolkhoz as party secretary; two years later he took over the direction of the

6   Ibid.

"Haradets" Sovkhoz. His political career began a year before the
dissolution of the Soviet Union, when he was elected as a People's
Deputy to the Supreme Soviet of the BSSR and soon thereafter of the
Belarus Republic. In 1993, he took over the chair of the Anti-
Corruption Committee. On 10 July of that year, 39-year-old
Aliaksandr Lukashenka was elected the country's president in a run-
off. Since then, he has been the recipient of further honors. He is a
Member of Honor of the Russian Academy of Social Sciences,
President of the National Olympic Committee of Belarus, and was
awarded the International Sholokhov Prize.

This biographical sketch serves to outline the elements that form
the scope of the president's experience, in which his basic political
convictions, his language and its employ as a means of persuasion,
and his conceptual universe in its entirety have developed. The
Enlightenment and European modern and civil society belong as little
to the major subjects of his educational canon as do the efforts made
by the traditional party nomenklatura to maintain a diplomatic two-
facedness. Even after his entry into the world of politics, Lukashenka
has been reliant upon not having to take leave of the microcosm from
which he originates. To meet the new terminological and intellectual
demands facing him, he has asserted the validity of the Russian
village's sense of justice in his work as a member of the Supreme
Soviet and—incidentally at Shushkevich's suggestion—the head of
the Anti-Corruption Committee. With this he has laid the cornerstone
for his interregional reputation as an upright actor in a corrupt
environment.

It was above all his sole dissenting ballot in the Supreme Soviet
against the Belavezhskaia Pushcha Agreements of December 1991
and the dissolution of the Soviet Union that Lukashenka laid bare his
absolute trust in the basic ideological values of his youth.[7] As

---

[7] This is not without controversy, however. Although Lukashenka himself has
claimed that he cast the lone dissenting vote, others claim that it was, in fact, cast by
the chairman of the Constitutional Court, Valeri Tikhinia, who stated on the eve of
Lukashenka's constitutional referenda in 1996 that he had done so. The vote itself was
by secret ballot and Lukashenka's claim was made much later. See Valeri Tikhinia,
"Ia ne khotel by, chtoby kto-to segodnia pytalsia prisvoit' moi golos," *Narodnaia volia*
96 (October) 1996: 1.

Maisenya put it, "Ideological dogmata, which got stuck in the memory of Lukashenka from the times of his stormy Komsomol youth, acted like a stone dragging the country back into the bright Soviet past." The presidential election of 1994 took place in a time of disappointed expectations. With an agenda touting the preservation of existing structures and the replacement of "corrupt cadre" ("It's all a matter of cadre!"), Lukashenka managed to shatter the few remaining hopes of a population that had not only hit economic bottom, but was not even able to extract from a range of national values the energy stemming from an identity. In the language of the village, which is not familiar with the term "cadre," these were "dishonest people who get rich at the cost of the commune." In this way, Lukashenka won the election as the advocate of the little people who had had enough of the party elite and the old faces. Nonetheless, in Lukashenka they consciously opted for a familiar terminological system of coordinates, within which there was from the outset additional available space for a newly emergent Soviet Union. Looking back, it is striking that, after Lukashenka's takeover of power, even his later critics—the term "enemies" also applies—such as Valeri Karbalevich, cherished hopes and admired the "revolution in the forms and methods of (his) dealings with the people."[8] In his "young crew" he included people like Viktar Hanchar [Viktor Gonchar], who later became one of his opponents and who disappeared in 2000 together with other critics of the Lukashenka regime.[9]

From the beginning of his presidency, Lukashenka has not had a self-contained world-view at his disposal, let alone an ideology of his own. With the set pieces gathered along his narrow educational path, from the quarry of Soviet ideology and in reliance on Panslavic elements from the 19th century and the Stalinist era, Lukashenka and his closest advisors have filled out the terminological space denoted by "Lukashism."[10] Since then, the opposition has accused him of

---

[8] Valerii Karbalevich, "Vnutripoliticheskie protsessy," in *Belarus-Monitor, Spetsial'nyi vypusk,* ed. NCSI Vostok-Zapad (Minsk, 1995), p. 8.

[9] Rainer Lindner and Astrid Sahm, "'Dialog' ohne Dialog vor 'Wahlen' ohne Wahl: Belarus' vor den Parlamentswahlen," *Osteuropa* 50 (2000): 991–1003.

[10] This somewhat hapless designation has been coined by Belarusian oppositional

"slavofascism," and the U.S. complains of his antidemocratic stance
and willingness to enter into an alliance with Serbia's Milošević;
others reprimand Lukashenka's populism as a dangerous strategy set
on restoring East-West antipathy. Lukashenka shares with Milošević,
and with Saddam, a socialist/communist past and the new conjuring
up of traditional myths of integration. In this fashion, he takes into
account Milošević's greater Serbian nationalism and Saddam's
interpretation of Oriental myths as a "new Saladin."

Lukashenka's political actions are directed overwhelmingly
against the West, while favoring contacts with Russia and the CIS,
India, China, Iraq, Iran, and others. At the Plenary Meeting of the
Millennium Summit of the United Nations in New York on 6 September 2000, Lukashenka made harsh and unwelcome comments on U.S.
foreign policy without naming the Clinton administration: "Having
fully experienced the horrors of devastating wars, Belarus cannot
watch idly the attempts to break the stability of the established world
order, to disrupt geopolitical equilibrium in the world and bring back
the times when the states were divided into first and second-rate
countries . . . Unfortunately, we are facing more frequent attempts in
international relations of the bigger powers to treat all alike and reject
any national and regional specifics that do not fall into the customary
framework of the 'Western way of life.'"[11]

Lukashenka's Regime:
Consolidation over Belarusian Institutions and Society

The process of regime consolidation over institutions and society has
passed through three phases. We set the first turning point at the
national referendum taken on 14 May 1995. It was at this point that
the Lukashenka system was installed, in a step that was as much
factual as it was symbolic. Its primary characteristics consisted of the

---

intelligentsia for the governmental system.

[11] Statement by his Excellency Mr. Aliaksandr Lukashenka, President of the
Republic of Belarus at the Plenary Meeting of the Millennium Summit of the United
Nations, New York, 6 September 2000. See <http://www.un.org/ga/webcast/
statements/belarus.htm>.

departure from moderate-national and constitutional (on 15 May) state politics, the return to the symbols of the "Belarusian Soviet Republic" and to a legally based Belarusian-Russian bilingualism. At the same time, this date constitutes the end of an appreciable rapprochement with Western institutions, which was distinguished by participation in the Partnership for Peace proceedings, the March 1995 general agreement with the EU concerning partnership and cooperation, and observer status in the European Council. With the new election of its Supreme Soviet, which opened on 14–28 May 1995, and completed its second round on 29 November, the new Belarusian Republic had for the time being fulfilled the basic criteria for membership in the European Parliament. On the occasion of Lukashenka's visit to Brussels in the spring of 1995 there was talk of a "deepening of European integration" and a "continuation of our reforms and strengthening of our integrative relationships." In addition, Lukashenka came out in favor of a "definitive inclusion of his country in the European region by means of acceptance into the EU." The "bridge function of Belarus between East and West due to its favorable geopolitical situation" was said to constitute a good prerequisite for this. In addition, the Belarusian president recommended that "his country's wide range of political and economic options be regarded as a decisive advantage." He claimed to operate under the assumption that "the extension of NATO would contribute in no way to the destabilization of the situation in this region" and that "the Belarusian people (would) never (pursue) belligerent ends."[12]

Nonetheless, the increasing debate concerning the enlargement of NATO meant the end for Lukashenka's world view. On 23 February 1995, he referred for the first time to the need for a new security doctrine because of the expected NATO extension to Poland's and the Baltic States' eastern borders. He perceived this enlargement of NATO up to Belarus' western border as an alarming sign: "NATO is nearing our borders." The balance of power would be in danger if Poland were to enter into the Western alliance, he stated.[13] The

---

[12] *Zviazda* 10 March 1995: 1, 3.

[13] *Svaboda* 10 March 1995: 5.

principle of neutrality, to which Belarus had to that point subscribed, and which Ural Latypaŭ, at that time a colonel in the Belarusian KGB and subsequently minister of foreign affairs, had loquaciously justified for the Sandhurst Institute in February 1994, started to become just as untenable as the attempts that Belarus had undertaken under Lukashenka since October 1991 to create a nuclear-weapon-free zone in Eastern Central Europe.[14] The plans for NATO enlargement brought forth a harsh reaction from the Belarusian leader. Whereas Ukraine signed a Charter on a Distinctive Partnership with NATO in July 1997 and has advocated closer relations with the alliance, Lukashenka's opposition to cooperation with NATO remains unaltered. The president has repeatedly pointed out that the security needs of the European states should not be met through the strengthening of new blocs, but through a demilitarization of Central Europe and an increase in European integration. He fears that, following NATO enlargement, Belarus will once more find itself between two political and military blocs, and that the projected NATO membership of neighboring Poland must be perceived as a potential military threat. The shooting down of a U.S. balloon over Belarusian territory in September 1995 was, despite the regret expressed later, an almost symbolic act of political transformation. The pressure of foreign policy, the resulting fixation on Russia, and a growing individual struggle for power, implemented not least as a means of distancing himself from the opposition, made 1995 possibly the most decisive year in the emergence of Lukashenka's system.

The second phase begins with the so-called national referendum on 24 November 1996, which equipped the president with further authority and to a certain extent confirmed, through the voice of the people, his chosen course of consolidating the regime and using primarily economic means to slow change within the system.[15] In

---

[14] Ural Latypov [Latypaŭ], "Neutrality as a Factor in Belarusian Security Policy" (Working paper for the Conflict Studies Research Center, The Royal Military Academy Sandhurst), February 1994; Virginia Rosa, "Safeguarding the de facto Nuclear-Weapon-Free zone in Central and Eastern Europe," thesis, Free University Berlin, 1999.

[15] OMRI, Daily Digest, Part II, 26 November 1996. See Astrid Sahm, "Schleichender Staatsstreich in Belarus. Hintergründe und Konsequenzen des

accordance with the new constitutional text, a Chamber of Representatives (*Palata pradstaйnikoй*) of the new Belarusian parliament, the National Assembly (*Natsyianal'nyi skhod*), consisting of 110 deputies, had already been constituted on 26 November 1999.[16] To perfect the new legislative body, an additional upper house was created, termed the "Republican Council," whose 66 seats were occupied mainly by the president's allies. In November 2000, the elections to the new parliament were accompanied by harsh violations of OSCE principles and overshadowed by the disappearance of several opposition politicians. The election law was partly changed by the president after strong interventions by European organizations; however, neither the OSCE, nor the European Council, nor the EU recognized the results of the elections. Thus, by means of a "conservative revolution," the contours of which were set by the part of the ruling elite already in 1996, the entire political system was transformed into a presidential dictatorship, in the process of which the parties and the two houses of the parliament sank into irrelevance.[17]

Among the most important consequences that the November referendum has had for constitutional politics relevant to current policy are the following: The president appoints and dismisses the members of the government and holds the right of veto; however, he does not have the right to alter the responsibilities of the council of ministers. Presidential decrees can, "under special circumstances," take on the form of laws; only with a two-thirds majority can the parliament obstruct or withdraw these bills or laws (Art. 85, 101). Should the government's Chamber of Representatives issue a vote of no confidence or refuse to confirm the ministerial presidents suggested by the president, the president may dissolve the lower house. Similarly, in the case of gross offenses against the Constitution,

---

Verfassungsreferendums im November 1996," *Osteuropa* 5 (1997): 475–87.

[16] Kanstytutsyia Riespubliki Belarus. "Praekt (Sa zmeianniami i dapaйnenniami)," *Holas Radzimy* 19 September 1996: 3–7.

[17] Natsional'nyi tsentr strategicheskikh initsiativ (NCSI) "Itogi konstitutsionno-politicheskogo krizisa v Belarusi: uroki i posledstviia," in *Belarus Monitor* 1997 [=Spetsial'nyi vypusk po materialam "kruglogo stola" 17 December 1996].

designated as such by the Constitutional Court, both chambers of parliament can also be dissolved. The president can be removed from office only in the case of grave illness prohibiting him from carrying out his official duties or in the case of a political crime (Art. 88). Amendments to the Constitution can be instituted at the initiative of the president or as a result of a national petition for a referendum or of a referendum. In the first two cases, the parliament may vote over the respective recommendations; however, it may not initiate any constitutional amendments of its own (Art. 138, 140). The president alone can initiate referenda. The president can designate half of the judges for the Constitutional Court (Art. 116) and of the Central Election Commission. The president also designates the respective chairs of these bodies, but the Republican Council must confirm them. The president's term of office was extended indirectly by two years, until 2001, because his five-year term has been calculated anew from when the new constitution was adopted (Art. 142).[18]

The president's coup d'état was directed not only against the democratically elected parliament, the Supreme Soviet of the 13th Session, but also against all independent governmental and non-governmental institutions. The Constitutional Court, the national bank, the nongovernmental organizations operating in Belarus, and the media were the groups most immediately affected, with the intention of disciplining and keeping watch over them. The president of the Constitutional Court was dismissed, as were the director of the national bank and his successor. Early in 1997, nongovernmental organizations were forced to undergo an extensive official financial investigation, as a result of which the Belarusian branch of the Soros Foundation had to temporarily discontinue its work as of May 1997. Other organizations, such as the research center "Vostok-Zapad" or the "Chernobyl Children's Fund" association were levied minor fines. Similarly, Lukashenka called in 1996 for the re-registration of all private enterprises, as a result of which 70 percent of businesses and small stores ceased to exist. It was in particular after the referendum of 24 November 1996, that the parties lost further influence on the course of politics. It may be regarded as a curious result of the

---

[18] Sahm, "Schleichender Staatsstreich in Belarus," p. 477.

referendum that most of the parties once again found themselves together in the role of the opposition. Despite the wide range of the oppositional spectrum, repeated calls for an "antidictatorial coalition" proved unrealizable;[19] the groups' respective positions were too widely spread. Alone, the remaining representatives of the Supreme Soviet of the 13th Session dissolved by Lukashenka formed a bracket of interparty opposition during this phase of the regime's consolidation. What has been lacking since then, and since the sudden death of figures like Anatol Maisenya and Hienadz Karpenka, is a charismatic figure who could challenge the president in forthcoming elections in the fall of 2001.

The third phase is the consolidation of power that began in 1997 with an illusory economic stability, which was propagated externally and internally and seemed to justify completely Lukashenka's model of conservative transformation.[20] While announcing unrealistic economic growth figures, Lukashenka also took measures meant to demonstrate his power, such as the expulsion of the U.S. ambassador to Minsk, Kenneth Yalovitz, in late March 1997; the failed talks of 18 June 1997, with representatives of the European Council and the EU on the subject of determining the constitutionality of the new parliament, the arrest of the ORT [Obshchestvennoe rossiiskoe televidenie] team on 26 July 1997, and the invitation of the Russian governors to the historically symbolic and semiotically significant Brest fortress. Finally, with the impounding of the ambassadors' residences in June 1998, Lukashenka was building himself up to appear in his own country, and in parts of the former Soviet Union, as a dervish battling against Western strategies of expansion. Lukashenka has loudly criticized NATO's power to determine the destiny of entire peoples and states. He has claimed that this expansion demands heightened defensiveness of his country and

---

[19] L. V. Krivitskii and S. N. Nosov, "Belorusskaia demokratiia: uroki porazhenii" NCSI "Demokraticheskie protsessy v Belarusi: osnovnye tendentsii i protivorechiia" *Belarus Monitor* February 1997 [=Spetsial'nyi vypusk]: 12–18.

[20] Rainer Lindner, "Belarus 1997/98: Krise der Transformation und Transformation der Krise," in *Minskij Forum I: Belarus-Germaniia 28–30 November 1997,* eds. Rainer Lindner and Leonid Zaiko, pp. 3–6 [=*Belarus Monitor* 1998].

heightened readiness and ability to do battle of its army. Within this context and especially after Kosovo, he has more than once expressed regret regarding the elimination of nuclear weapons: "The 1992 decision of the Belarusian leadership to allow the withdrawal of nuclear weapons from the country was a crude mistake, if not a crime."[21]

All this indicates, particularly in the current phase of the consolidation of his regime and in the face of NATO bombs in Kosovo, that plans for foreign policy have taken on special meaning for Lukashenka. After having settled the country's domestic matters in an authoritarian-dictatorial fashion, he has come to see new options for action and impact in foreign policy. Encouraged by the predominately positive reception of his propagandistic one-man show in the streets and squares of the former Soviet Union, Lukashenka's model has come to define itself primarily in terms of foreign policy. Here we should mention its pillars, which reach nearly equivalent height: Panslavism, anti-Americanism, and neo-Soviet aspirations. Meanwhile, the Belarusian opposition is not alone in warning of the transition from a local to a global "Lukashism," which could threaten to reprogram a gigantic nuclear power. Like a weakling trying to pick a schoolyard fight, Lukashenka keeps trying to provoke the West. For this reason, one must raise the question of the "exportability" of the Belarusian experience to other countries.

Moreover, while "Russia and Ukraine go begging to the West," Lukashenka promotes the image that little Belarus is defying the U.S. and Western Europe. He means to build up the alliance that he called for between Russia, Belarus, Iran, India, and China in late February 1999, as a "counterweight to a one-poled world." Although the semantic incongruity of his coinage concerning the world's "monopolarity" may remain hidden to Lukashenka, the term itself is symptomatic: first, Lukashenka's thoughts remain stalled at the level of a bipolar constellation of political power, and, second, he has been able to adapt seamlessly his anti-Americanism from the material taught during his own school days and that he himself disseminated as a propagandist. In this context, he has spoken out in favor of creating

---

[21] Quoted in *Belarusian Review* Fall 1998: 29.

a "powerful center" that would serve to counteract NATO's and the U.S.'s world domination. In Kyiv, on 12 March 1999, in response to the entry of the Czech Republic, Hungary, and Poland into NATO, Lukashenka said that Belarus would reinforce its armed forces. "We are conducting very serious consultations with Russia, and I think Ukraine will be interested, too."[22] To reduce tensions on NATO's new eastern borders, Western political advisors face the challenge of recommending unconventional paths to resolution that take into consideration Lukashenka's cultural coordinates. After all, Lukashenka wrote a letter to President Clinton in late November 1998 in which he admitted having made mistakes in his dealings with the West. Even though this appeal cannot lead to Lukashenka yielding on the question of NATO's eastward expansion or to him giving up his politics of rapprochement with Russia, the letter indicates the existence of a new realism in Lukashenka's foreign policy.[23] After 25 March 1999, and the beginning of NATO strikes against Yugoslavia, Lukashenka and his views on the West were prevalent in the post-Soviet space, even among the editors and readers of the liberal *Belorusskaia delovaia gazeta.* As quoted by Radio Free Europe/Radio Liberty, Lukashenka said, "the Americans, along with NATO and their allies—like the Fascists in their own time—have committed an act of aggression" against Yugoslavia.[24] Undoubtedly, the Kosovo affair stimulated massive support for consolidation of the Lukashenka regime within Belarus and in the former Soviet Union. After its decline over the past two years, the CIS framework within the Tashkent Treaty has gained new impetus, not from within, but from the outside.

Authoritarianism and integration, characteristics of a social utopia of post-Soviet political thought, have deeply split society into supporters and opponents of Lukashenka's policies. On one side we find the great majority of those who support his political course and

---

[22] RFE/RL Newsline 3(51) Part II, 15 March 1999.

[23] Werner Adam, "Weißrußland gesteht Fehler im Umgang mit dem Westen ein," *Frankfurter Allgemeine Zeitung* 30 November 1998: 5. The issue of religious solidarity is important here.

[24] RFE/RL Newsline 3(60) Part II, 26 March 1999.

his person. As the country's leading politician, Lukashenka is still more popular than all his adversaries combined. As long as the oppositional spectrum between the People's Front and the moderate Communists, whose basic opposition to Lukashenka is essentially identical, is not able to attain a unified voice, Lukashenka will be able to lead the population to believe that the country has no political opposition at its disposal. The extent to which he enjoys an advantage over the political forces pursuing him was demonstrated by polls on the "Sunday issue" at the end of 1998, according to which Lukashenka, with 49.8 percent of the vote, was ahead of Stanislaŭ Shushkevich, with 12 percent;[25] however, Lukashenka's popularity has been in decline since 1999. In late 2000, a rating of the "National Institute of Socioeconomic and Political Studies" was published in which Lukashenka received the support of only 32 percent of potential voters. To the question: "Who should be elected as the new president of Belarus?" 22.3 percent supported "an independent candidate" (not specified), 8.5 percent supported candidates of the democratic opposition, 2.2 percent supported candidates of other parties, and 31.9 percent could not answer the question.[26]

On the other side, we find the disappointed intelligentsia of the capital, which has, not without sarcasm, designated the Belarusian government as the "only one in the whole world" that strives with all its might to do away with state sovereignty while the Belarusian people simultaneously reject its national language and symbols. Along with the physical consequences of Chernobyl, Belarus has developed clear indications of a "psychological and legal" Chernobyl, as not only the national attributes of Belarusian sovereignty, but also the beginnings of democracy and a rule of law, have been given up.[27] Intellectuals in Minsk, who for the most part reject Lukashenka's

---

[25] Andrej Wardomazkij, "Popularität Lukaschenkos steigt trotz Krise," *Belarus News* 4 (1998): 11–12.

[26] See *Belarus News* 12 (2000): 10.

[27] V. A. Rovdo, "Natsional'naia ideia kak forma artikuliatsii grazhdanskogo obshchestva Belarusi," in"Demokraticheskie protsessy v Belarusi," *Belarus Monitor* February 1997 [Spetsial'nyi vypusk] ed. NCSI, pp. 39–47; Vladimir Nistiuk, "Belorusskaia vesna: pozhar na torfianike," *Narodnaia volia* 15 March 1997: 1,3.

course, have turned to searching for medical-pathological reasons for the president's policies. They claim that a head of state who "is a traitor to the country's interests" and negates its independence (along with its symbols and language) can only be "insane." Lukashenka is said to have a "maniacal thirst for power" and show symptoms of a "chronic complaining complex."[28]

In his person, Lukashenka unites above all the voices of those strata of society removed from educated spheres, the village people and the late- and post-communist elite, who, embittered at the collapse of the Soviet Union and disappointed with perestroika and glasnost, have longed for a new "strong man." The "Lukashenka phenomenon" is simultaneously the product and the expression of crisis. It has been said that the president can exist only in a permanent crisis, under the conditions of mass hysteria and a societal "psychological state of emergency." His myth is based on a constant "endangering" of the country or his person by an "Public Enemy Number 1" whose identity is subject to change. Lukashenka has stigmatized all his political adversaries from Shushkevich to Stanislaŭ Bahdankievich (chairman of the National Bank) as "enemies of the people."[29] Therefore, it was only a logical consequence that, in October 1997, Lukashenka caused a law concerning "injury to the honor and dignity of the Republic and the president" to be passed to protect himself from public attacks. Since then all criticism of the president's governance and person can officially be punished with high fines. And with that we have touched on what is certainly a final fundamental factor in his consolidation of power.

For the moment, though, Lukashenka's leadership remains unchallenged, while the population has almost completely abandoned any trust in the political parties and a multiparty system. In late 1999, the majority saw the solution of the present economic crisis in a

---

[28] Aleksandr Potupa [Aliaksandr Patupa], "Belarus '97: The Present Situation and its Prospects," in *Prism* (The Jamestown Foundation), June 1997, Part 2; Zbigniew Wilkiewicz, "Zur politischen Entwicklung Weißrußlands. Oppositionelle Stimmen, veröffentlicht in Polen," *Osteuropa-Archiv* June 1997: A235–45.

[29] Anatol Maisenya, "Belarus in the Shadows: The Sad Results of the Two-years' Rule of President Lukashenko," in *The Land of Unrealised Hopes,* p. 326.

stronger integration with Russia and the CIS countries. In the opinion of most of society, molded as it has been by the president's mass media, the Supreme Soviet elected in 1995 and the opposition that has arisen from it are to blame for this crisis.[30] Institutions of a democratic political system are far from being regarded as "effective instruments" of policy in the political understanding of the majority of the population. In fact, the policy pursued by Lukashenka in 1999 led to a situation in which parliament and parties no longer play a decisive role either by law or in the people's consciousness. With the founding of his "People's Patriotic Union," the presidential party, Lukashenka did not, as is sometimes suspected, legitimize political disputes in a system of differing political interests; rather he had merely gained the insight that even in an authoritarian state, a political *Hausmacht* (power base) can be of significant meaning. This applies above all in the case in which the appearance of a democratic organization should be preserved for the benefit of outside observers.

At present, the electoral campaign is in full swing in Belarus, although from the outset neither of the two envisaged trips to the polls has had or will have a chance of being implemented legally under the current conditions. The democratic parties are boycotting the elections that the president has scheduled for April. The president is boycotting the presidential election prepared for 16 May by the democratic parties. In its most recent resolution on Belarus, the European Parliament reports on occurrences that demonstrate Lukashenka's battle against the electoral preparations and the persons and newspapers concerned, the severity of which seems to be increasing as the day draws closer. The Europeans are convinced of the necessity of carrying out elections in Belarus before Lukashenka's regular term of office has expired. In the meantime, after having previously refused categorically to agree to the election of a new head of state, which the opposition had arranged for 16 May, the opposition no longer rules out the possibility of participating in the elections, for which the president himself has called, should they come to pass. Admittedly, the opposition would only cooperate with Lukashenka in such an

---

[30] Igor' Kotliarov, "Belarus mezhdu proshlym i budushchim. Sotsiologicheskii analiz," *Narodnaia gazeta* 25 March 1997: 1,4.

election if the nongoverning forces were allowed free access to the media.

Playing the Populist Game:
Lukashenka and the Belarusian Population

At the core of Lukashenka's system of rule is the mobilization of the greater part of the population. In this, the Belarusian president has continued on a national level what he learned as a rural propagandist and is now limited to passing on. Wages, salaries, fellowships, and pensions, kept at the lowest possible level but paid out promptly, have attained a nearly mythical status in the post-Soviet world. Even though by the winter of 1998–1999 these punctual wage payments, particularly in the production sector (e.g., Tsvetotron in Brest), were increasingly becoming a thing of legend and not reality, Lukashenka was until very recently able to amass support with this strategy, especially in the "near abroad." This mobilization has occasionally had contradictory characteristics, combining old-style Stakhanovite exhortations with capitalist enducements. The harvest of 1998 was brought in under conditions of increased competition, such as had been tested during the collectivization of the 1930s. Peak workers received bonuses that were distributed from the presidential budget. Lukashenka has skillfully implemented such strategically important bonuses to ease social unrest and to simulate a consistent and successful economic strategy. Even more important than these bonuses in kind and in cash is the rhetoric of mobilization, which perpetuates the symbolic terminology of earlier decades. There is talk of the "battle for harvest yields." "All forces" are to be deployed in this "battle for bread." If in earlier days (above all in the postwar decade), the struggle to feed the population was propagated as a patriotic duty in defense of the fatherland in the battle of ideological systems, Lukashenka now employs it to strengthen his position within the country and with his closest neighbors. Having enough bread at one's disposal, which has an almost mythical symbolic content in the history of Slavic culture, should be a matter of course in Belarus, announced Lukashenka during a television address. At a time in which Belarus "is being attacked all over the world," the country should demonstrate that it does not have to rely on anyone else.

While remarks like these are directed not least at the West, it is with respect to Russian society that Lukashenka has emphasized that he keeps his household in good order and that the people of his country have enough to eat. When he designates himself as "father," he is taking this mode into account. Once again, we note the presence of the family unit of the Russian village. He, the president of Belarus, does not go begging for money in the West, but instead takes care of matters at hand. In early 1998, Lukashenka started a major campaign to improve discipline in the workplace. Working teams (collectives) in concerns and cooperatives were to return to mutual surveillance and to the discipline of old. Here, too, the force behind the scenes was the Soviet concern system and party surveillance of the work collectives. Colleagues who repeatedly came late to work were to be punished, as were those who wasted or misappropriated material or refused loyalty in any other form to the concern or the collective. Workers were encouraged to use "trouble telephones" to inform on offenses they had observed their colleagues committing against norms and rules. Criticism and self-criticism, that disciplinary ritual from the Stalinist era, was in this way to be rehabilitated as a form of social interaction.

A further means of consolidating a regime that had been put to the test under Stalin and remains legitimate within the realm of experience of the population's majority, molded as it is by Soviet history, is the public settling of scores with opponents of the regime or with unreliable elements from among one's own numbers. During the past three years, arrests of politicians of the ruling party have been repeatedly shown live on Belarusian state television. Similar to the case of the Minister of Agriculture Vasil Liavonaŭ [Leonov] (whom Lukashenka had arrested for incompetence before running cameras in 1997), in March 1999, the head of the Mahilioŭ regional administration, Aliaksandr Kulichkoŭ, was taken into custody by the president's secret service during a broadcasted "presidential working session." The evening before, an extensive investigation by local KGB forces had brought allegedly incriminating evidence to light. In this case it cannot have been a matter of discussing the causes, but rather of the ritualization of ruthless surveillance from above. Lukashenka did not even let the governor speak before he was led away. What most clearly recalled the Soviet-era machinery of repression was his forced confession, which was published only a few minutes later in the form of a presidential decree. The president indicated in this that the Governor of Mahilioŭ had been released from his office "at his own wish" and would have to reckon with disciplinary measures. In a time of crisis, the president had once again played the role of the "advocate of the little people," who had tipped him off in letters of complaint to the illegal activities of the local administration.[31]

Further, several of "Lukashism's" semiotic peculiarities should be mentioned. After the Belarus Republic had in 1991 initially taken up the white-red-white flag and the state coat of arms "Pahoniia," both of which bore symbols from pre-Soviet Belarusian history and returned the interpretation of history to the realm of the national, change came very quickly under the new president. Since 1995–1996, the official interpretation of the past (comparable to a state of siege), the culture of remembrance surrounding memorials, and the holiday calendar have followed a neo-Soviet and Panslavic scheme.[32] Lukashenka's political speech—exclusively in Russian—is sprinkled with semantic and rhetorical Sovietisms. Again and again, the president sees his country as threatened by "enemy elements" and "factions" that are to be "exposed." The president's supporters among the rural population tend to stress that Lukashenka could have succeeded in doing what was the best for the country if the oppositional camp had not disrupted his policies.

Lukashenka proves to contemporary Belarus that he is a populist even when he publicly discredits the "deal-makers," private (mostly small) entrepreneurs. The dismissal of the kolkhoz leader Vasil Staravoitaŭ in mid-October 1997 and his subsequent imprisonment along with Minister Liavonaŭ in mid-November were received with satisfaction among the rural population not least because Staravoitaŭ's kolkhoz had been a semi-private enterprise able to pay its employees' above-average wages punctually. As a typical sign of the inadequacy of Belarusian social development, successful private economizing finds no valorization there, but instead induces destructive feelings of

---

[31] *Belorusskaia delovaia gazeta* 15 March 1999 [Internet edition: http://bdg. press.net.by/].

[32] Rainer Lindner, "Besieged Past: National and Court Historians in Lukashenko's Belarus," *Nationalities Papers* 27 (1999): 631–48.

envy. One finds oneself as a historian reminded quite unexpectedly of the end of the New Economic Program era in the late 1920s, with its contempt for the *NEP-meny*. The arrests, furthermore, have once and for all confirmed the impression that it can happen to anyone in the meantime, and businesspeople particularly cannot feel themselves secure from attacks on the part of the state. On 16 March 1999, the president clearly indicated his skepticism concerning private enterprises in a decree. The document he signed on that day treats "regulation of state registration and liquidation of economic entities" in Belarus. According to Belarusian television, the decree establishes "strict rules of behavior in the domestic economy," including legal responsibility for businesses that "have done harm to state and public interests." Uladzimir Kariahin, head of an organization representing Belarusian private entrepreneurs, has predicted that the decree will entail a "colossal change in ownership" in Belarus. Many businessmen will find themselves on a "black list" of those prohibited from setting up new businesses for several years because of their failure to comply with the decree.[33]

Last to be mentioned in relation to the populist game are the media, which deserve an analysis of their own. As is the case in other transforming societies, in Belarus, full freedom for the media remains one of the most vulnerable areas of the body politic. At the moment, I would merely like to indicate that Lukashenka has created a topography for the extent of the media's influence that simultaneously permits an adequate surveillance of the population while allowing for a reservoir of alibis before the international community of states. The president controls the media outside the capital, television in particular; however, in Minsk, opposition newspapers are still available. Admittedly, they are no longer printed within Belarusian borders, but rather in Lithuania or Poland, just as the first Belarusian-language newspapers after the Revolution of 1905 were. Information from the Internet also manages to slip through the president's press censorship; however, he is willing to take the stubborn intellectuals in Minsk and a few Internet users in stride while the entire country is exposed to his propaganda TV. Be this as it may, we can perceive

---

[33] RFE/RL Newsline 3(54) Part II, 18 March 1999.

some glimmers of hope. On 29 October 1997, the upper house of the Belarusian parliament rejected 22 amendments to the media law as unconstitutional, including one that would have banned the dissemination of information defaming the president.

With these measures, Lukashenka has kept the Belarusian population under control up to now, but time is working against him. Since mid-March 1999, part of the oppositional spectrum has been consolidating itself. The force of unification in this process comes from the projected election date of 16 May 1999. The institutional framework for this coalition was brought into existence through the creation of a "Rada [Parliament] of democratic forces." The political forces of opposition that Lukashenka sought to force out of office have drawn into position. Of course, one can hardly rely on this, because the opposition operates within a hermetically sealed system of discourse. The great acclaim that Lukashenka enjoys does not result alone from the populist-naive charisma he disseminates, but from the wear and tear suffered by the term "democracy" through the Russian example and the disavowal of the market economy in the swamp of Russian oligarchy—which Lukashenka claims to have hindered in Belarus. Although the decline of the Belarusian economy during the first quarter of 1999 has prejudiced parts of the union against the government's policies, the lack of contours in the opposition's alternative economic policy has damaged its public attractiveness. The vicious circle of the country's incompletely structured elite, which according to its nature encompasses not only the governmental but also the oppositional side, closes here. The country's hope lies with its youth, with the student body of the European Humanities University, and with the engineering schools and the teachers' seminars. It is here that the country, with its excellent educational structures, shows all the signs of being capable of putting the first generation of the post-Soviet elite on the market in five years at the latest. It appears that Belarus is in need of the coming change in generations more urgently than any other European country.

Cracks in the Monolith:
Dynamics within the Presidential Administration

Without his machinery, Lukashenka would be incapable of political action. Since 1994, he has created a state within the state in the form of the presidential office, which is the hub of government and holds the sole authority to set guidelines. He calls his administration the "think tank" (*mozgovyi tsentr*) of his presidential leadership,[34] even after five years of erratic and contradictory politics. The Presidential Council, the Security Council, and several committees, for instance on fighting corruption, on regional tasks, on foreign policy, and on public relations, make up the president's administration. A legal department was added in 1994. The four presidential deputies are simultaneously the chairs of the committees. There also are assistants to the president and the former supply department of the Council of Ministers.

At the beginning of the president's term of office, the administration, including all technical support, was made up of 180 people. After an initial change in cadre, the highest echelon in the administration has hardly altered. Lukashenka has been ruling for the past three years through a solid core of people. In 1999, those belonging to this close circle were: the head of the administration Mikhail Miasnikovich, his first deputy Uladzimir Russakevich, and deputies Ivan Pashkevich and Aliaksandr Abramovich. Piotr Kapitula functions as chief advisor. Ural Latypaŭ, who was the foreign minister until November 2000, has become head of the Security Council without giving up his advisory activities. Viktar Sheiman, who is part of the presidential council and was in charge of security matters for a long time, and Uladzimir Zamiatalin, who is responsible for matters of ideology, but who has in the meantime attained a position in the Cabinet of Ministers, embody the regime's internal authoritarianism. This staff leads the country, as it also does, on occasion, the president.

The state leadership, too, finds itself—or so it appears—at a turning point. The government under newly appointed Premier Uladzimir Iarmoshin is busy with the adversities of a crisis of economics and supply and at the same time sees itself confronted with certain adjustments in its responsibilities. This adjustment in the direction of the presidential administration did not arise by chance. A crisis panel, the president's "Republican Staff," which is to take over

---

[34] Roman Iakovlevskii, "Kadry reshaiut vse! Komanda molodosti ch'ei-to, bez kotoroi nam ne zhit'," *Belorusskaia delovaia gazeta* 27 (18 July 1994) [Internet edition: http://bdg.press.net.by/].

the coordination of stabilization and surveillance measures, joined the presidential administration in the fall of 1998. What is remarkable is that the panel is not filled only with party followers of the president. Lukashenka has more than once criticized the government as the country's situation began to worsen after the long-distance impact of the Russian financial crisis in 1998. "How can it be that we're doing so badly with such high growth rates?" the president was quoted as saying, and even a remark of his about a "trend to economic collapse" that could no longer be ruled out made the rounds at the end of the year. While Lukashenka previously spoke of momentary "bottlenecks," the drastic results of the political class' skepticism about reform and fear of modernization have manifested themselves in the meantime.[35] Leading politicians, such as the former Deputy Minister of Economics Andrei Tur, have been drawing attention to the dramatics of the economic situation since November 1998.

Thus, policies in this time of crisis are no longer being directed "in secret" at the upper level. Information regarding difficulties has been seeping out of the administration. Likewise deserving of mention are the attempts undertaken by the administration and the Ministry of Foreign Policy to normalize relations with the West, such as were formulated from the sidelines of the annual "Minsk Forum" between 1997 and 2000. The composition of the personnel of the president's administration is an expression of the disunity and the frequent incoherence of Lukashenka's policies. Just as the economic crisis and political repression in Belarus both promote and prevent a unification of the states,[36] so is the administration's advisory staff an admixture of advocates and adversaries of such a step. Lukashenka himself, too, vacillates on this issue. When people such as one of the moderate department heads, for example, Aliaksandr Danilaŭ or Ural Latypaŭ, are forced to get along with hardliners such as Viktar Sheiman, it is hard for the outsider to comprehend, but this makes the contradictory

---

[35] Rainer Lindner, "Für Brot und die Einigkeit der Slawen! Alexander Lukaschenko und sein weißrussischer Weg in eine 'Transformationsdiktatur,'" *Frankfurter Rundschau* 8 September 1998: 17.

[36] Ingmar Oldberg, "Sunset over the Swamp: The Independence and Dependence of Belarus," *European Security* 6 (Autumn 1997): 110–30.

and erratic course of presidential policy all the more explicable. Western policymakers must understand that the constitution of the presidential council is designed to involve as many of the president's advisors as possible in a discourse. The "Minsk Forums" and other conferences have been instrumental in taking a number of steps in this direction; at least they helped to identify the cracks in the monolith.

Conclusion

In Belarus, policies to preserve the established order and attempts to liberalize the economy and society very clearly clash with one another. The "Belarusian *Sonderweg*" of a conservative transformation in terms of a dampened or delayed political change and of a dominant executive has to this point prevented one thing: there has been no shooting, neither in the renegade provinces such as there has been in Chechnya, nor—as was recently repeatedly the case in St. Petersburg—in the streets. Nevertheless, we should not judge the mere absence of violence to be the goal of a society in transition.

The country, which Western perception has labeled a *terra incognita* before and since its independence in 1991, has suffered a drastic loss of standing since 1996. Lukashenka has nonetheless still been able to turn the ill feeling in Western Europe and the breaking of contacts to his own advantage. In numerous Russian provinces, he is perceived as a man who does not go begging to the Western-dominated financial institutions, who pays his people's wages promptly, and, beyond that, between 1997 and the first half of 1998, had a sectoral economic consolidation to show for himself. In the face of NATO and EU enlargements at the western border of his country, Lukashenka has threatened to build Belarus up as a stronghold against Westernization and the subordination of Eastern Europe camouflaged as transformation aid and as the arena of a neo-Soviet and Panslavic renewal. The crisis in Russia and its long-distance effects on Belarus have changed the situation. Now, because, in the eyes of the Belarusian president Russia is no longer a 100 percent partner and the "Belarusian economic wonder" faces its own collapse like a house of cards, the leaders of the state find themselves confronted by demands for an adjustment of course. Lukashenka must now reconsider his economic and foreign policy principles if he aspires, through the

"Belarusian model," to remain interesting as a politician in Russia's eyes. Whether he will at the same time take steps to decrease tensions in domestic politics remains questionable at the moment.

This meeting's organizers are correct in assuming that "this strategic geopolitical space is under the firm control of an unpredictable, undemocratic leader whose appeal and influence has spread beyond Belarus' borders." One thing is certain: "while Belarus' importance is growing, our understanding of that country remains woefully inadequate. Belarus indeed is a country the West can no longer ignore."[37] In the face of a Belarusian "anomaly," the Western community's policy of helping to transform and stabilize this country is obviously limited in its ability to bring about change in the political and economic trends there. One reason for this is certainly the inability of, and sometimes the lack of economic interest in, the Western countries to bring to bear the package of instruments that are available for EU accession candidates; however, an extra effort, partly in coordination with other international and national (Belarusian) actors is worthwhile and necessary, given that the success of NATO and EU enlargement and the aim of the creation of an all-European zone of cooperation and prosperity will also depend on the fate of a country as relatively small but strategically important as Belarus. In its consideration of a fuzzy mixture of sanctions and rewards (carrots and sticks), the West should include the following proposals:

The Western and Atlantic institutions should re-institute and force a critical dialogue with the Lukashenka administration, even before the officially proclaimed return to democratic patterns. The EU and the European Council must come to perceive the growing external isolation of Belarus as a potentially dangerous development at the new Eastern NATO and future EU border.[38] The integration of Belarus within the extended European framework presents a better option than does its isolation. Belarus must not be perceived as a buffer zone

---

[37] Rainer Lindner, "Minsk-Forum II als Rundtischgespräch," *Belarus News* 4 (1998): 24–25.

[38] See Rainer Lindner, "Belarus at the Abyss? Dangerous Options at the Further EU Eastern Border," [Briefing Paper for Conflict Prevention Network (CPN) of the European Commission and the European Parliament], Brussels, November 1997.

between an enlarged EU and NATO and a number of post-Soviet republics under the domination of Russia. In times of Belarusian-Russian disturbances, Lukashenka's attitude toward the West has historically tended to be more elastic than in times of euphoric integration. The contradictions in Belarusian political declarations or actions must be perceived as an outward sign of the potential to influence the character of Belarusian politics. While Russia will remain the EU's primary country of reference within the region, it is important for the EU to develop an independent policy for Belarus. In this context, it was a step in the right direction that the European Commission's plans since 1999 also covered continuing humanitarian aid in Belarus and the reconsideration of the World Bank to open a permanent mission in Minsk, since "some progress on a number of issues" has been achieved in negotiations with this country.[39] The Council of Europe, to which Belarus is seeking full membership; the EU; and the OSCE must coordinate their policies on Lukashenka. The Minsk government must realize that the EU, the Council of Europe, and the OSCE subscribe to the same guiding principles and rest their policies on the same conditions. Lukashenka, with the help of new members Ukraine and Russia, must continually be confronted with the human and civil rights guidelines of the Council of Europe.

Before the backdrop of the individual and sociocultural preconditions of Lukashenka's person, the only path that can be taken in the direction of a normalization of mutual perception is that of a discourse offensive. Lukashenka must become familiar with what he—because of an isolation of his own making, but one that was also forced upon him by the West—up to this point has not been able to become familiar with: the advantages from which his country and thereby his claim to leadership could benefit due to cooperation with Russia and the post-Soviet space and with the West. A resolution of the diplomatic crisis and a rapprochement on the part of Western institutions like the World Bank and the EU would present the opportunity for this. Invitations to visit Western states, the opportunity to present the fruits of production at trade shows (as Belarus did in 2000 at the "Expo 2000" in Hanover, Germany), and scientific

---

[39]   RFE/RL Newsline 3(55) Part II, 19 March 1999.

conferences and opportunities to encounter the representatives of all political forces could serve to broaden his horizons.

With respect to the current election campaign and the expected increasing severity of the situation in Belarus, the West would be well advised to support the opposition's initiatives, but at the same time to keep in mind that the prerequisite for the present situation was a plebiscite, the one-sidedness of which, but not its verdict on the line to be taken, may have been manipulated in the president's favor. Despite all criticism of the president's style of leadership and his dissemination of truths, the West should take into account that the majority of the population continues to support his course. The shifting of phases of democratic and market-economy modernization from Western to Eastern Europe is not to be altered through the will of the West alone. This Belarusian transformation requires a change in generation and the West should try, through economic investments, through the seeking of contacts at all level, and through support of forces with a share in the future, to accelerate this process. The ideal scenario would be a long-term, democratically-realized change of the political system from within through an altered system of nationwide values and a reprogramming of Lukashenka's political attitudes, which could lead to a "soft contiguity" of the West and the post-Soviet space on its territory.

The critical dialogue with Belarus must demand the preservation of human rights, but at the same time should regulate possibilities for political and economic action—as has been done with China, Cuba, Iran, and North Korea since 2000. More than ever, the West should regard Belarus as an economic partner. Germany has achieved much and is—after Russia—the country's most important partner in foreign trade. The chances of the West to lead Lukashenka's anti-West system with investment success *ad absurdum* should not be underestimated in the long run. The positive experiences of German-Polish "Euro-Regions" represent a proven model for the encouragement of cooperation across borders, which could also work for cooperation with border areas in Ukraine, Belarus, and Moldova. New methods of dialogue with the participating actors; a meaningful combination of diplomacy and "paradiplomacy";[40] differentiated relations concerning borders, trade, migration, and minorities; and an adjustment of justice are necessary prerequisites for the complete settlement of differences. Next to the decrease of the socioeconomic asymmetries, the synchronization of political and jurisdictional culture exemplifies the key question of the eastern enlargement and of the new neighbor policy—a big challenge for Western foreign policy.

[40] Brian Hocking, *Localizing Foreign Policy: Non-Central Governments and Multilayered Diplomacy,* (New York, 1993); ed. Francisco Aldecoa, *Paradiplomacy in Action: The Foreign Relations of Subnational Governments,* (London, 1999) [=Cass Series in Regional and Federal Studies; Bd. 4]; Rainer Lindner, "Neue Nachbarn: Ukraine, Belarus und Moldowa als Anrainer von Nato und erweiterter EU," in *Stabilität und Kooperation: Aufgaben internationaler Ordnungspolitik,* eds. Jens van Scherpenberg and Peter Schmidt (Baden-Baden, 2000), pp. 310–27.

4

Patricia Brukoff
The Belarusian Economy: Is It Sustainable?

In 1998, cracks began to show in the Belarusian economic "model," as imbalances caused by the macroeconomic policies that had been pursued over the previous three years became more pronounced. At the same time, even before its economic crisis emerged in August 1998, Russia began to withdraw its support and subsidization of the Belarusian economy. This confluence of events drove economic developments in Belarus in 1998–1999 and threatened to result in further deterioration. In 2000, Russia's unexpectedly rapid recovery from the 1998 financial crisis eased economic conditions for Belarus to some extent, but direct Russian support for the Belarusian economy has declined and now frequently comes with strict policy conditions.

This paper will argue that, while Belarusian economic policies could likely translate into the strong economic growth observed in the period 1995–1997, they could generally be expected to result in precisely the negative effects that are now coming to the fore. To develop this argument, this chapter will address two separate, but closely related, questions: First, can current Belarusian economic policies sustain the growth performance and relatively stable living standards recorded over the past few years? Absent other intervening factors, the answer to this question is no. The second question is, will the Belarusian economy be sustained? This question points to the exogenous factors that are primarily responsible for allowing the Belarusian authorities to avoid adverse outcomes until recently. Nor can it be answered definitively at this point, but the discussion below will demonstrate that Russian support for Belarus via high levels of implicit and explicit subsidization underpinned Belarus' economic performance in the mid- 1990s and that, absent such support, the country's current economic policy framework will not result in any subsequent improvements in output or standard of living for the population.

To address these questions, we will first put the Belarusian "model" of continued strong state economic control and minimal tolerance of private sector activity in the context of the broader experience of other transition economies. Second, we will discuss how the policy mix that was pursued could be expected to lead to both the early positive and later negative outcomes observed in the period since 1996. Third, we will outline the implicit and explicit sources of Russia's support for the Belarusian economy and the extent to which these have changed over time. Fourth, we will explore the economic imbalances that are now emerging in Belarus. Fifth, the changes that are taking place in Belarus' relationship with Russia will be considered. Finally, we will examine the trajectory of Belarusian economic policy and performance in the context of post-crisis regional economic recovery.

Belarusian Economic Policies in Context: No "Third Way"

When the performance of the Belarusian economy is viewed in terms of total output, the country appears to have fared far better in the transition process than most of the former Soviet Union[1] (Table 1). Inflation in Belarus slowed sharply in the initial stabilization period, while the exchange rate remained relatively stable. Output declined less dramatically and turned positive much sooner (Figure 1). That this occurred despite the country's slower pace of stabilization and reform makes Belarus something of an outlier relative to the rest of the transition economies, whose macroeconomic performance is

---

[1]   Uzbekistan, like Belarus, has taken a very gradual approach to reform and has also enjoyed better growth performance and relatively more stable macroeconomic conditions than other FSU countries. For more on Uzbekistan, see Stanley Fischer and Ratna Sahay, "The Transition Economies After Ten Years," *IMF Working Paper* 00/30 (Washington, DC: IMF, 2000); and, Jeromin Zettlemeyer, "The Uzbek Growth Puzzle," *IMF Staff Papers*, September/December 1999, Vol.46, No. 3 (Washington, DC: IMF).

summarized quite ably by Fischer and Sahay. These authors draw upon the last ten years of research on transition in support of the view that the most successful transition economies are those that have both stabilized and undertaken comprehensive reforms and that more and faster reform is better than less and slower.

Table 1
Macroeconomic Characteristics of Selected CIS Countries

Country	Starting Date of Stabilization Program	Real Output Ratio 1999/1989	Average Inflation 1989–1999	PPP GDP per Capita 1999
Armenia	1992	0.48	106.5	2,469
Azerbaijan	1992	0.47	233.2	2,404
Belarus	**1992**	**0.81**	**162.4**	**6,485**
Georgia	1992	0.31	17.9	3,950
Kazakhstan	1992	0.61	77.3	4,351
Kyrgyz Republic	1992	0.61	22.3	2,419
Moldova	1992	0.31	16.5	1,847
Russia	1992	0.55	88.0	6,815
Tajikistan	1992	0.29	688.5	1,045
Turkmenistan	1992	0.61	4.9	4,589
Ukraine	1992	0.35	169.4	3,276
Uzbekistan	1992	0.97	304.5	2,157

Source: International Monetary Fund, "World Economic Outlook," October 2000.

Figure 1
Belarus: Real GDP Growth, 1992–2000

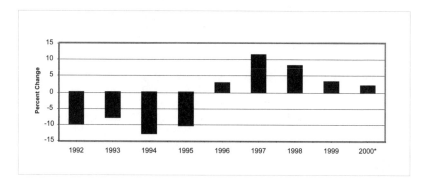

Source: European Bank for Reconstruction and Development, *Transition Report 2000.*
*projection

The strong growth performance and, until 1997, relative price and exchange rate stability achieved by the Belarusian economy are the predictable result of the economic policies pursued by its authorities. Some observers point to the Belarusian authorities' apparently tight fiscal stance as a contributing factor: continued tight state control over the country's enterprises has allowed revenue collection to remain relatively high, financing reported levels of government expenditure without opening up budget deficits such as those observed in Russia and other transition economies. Fiscal policies, however, have not been as tight in reality as the reported small budget deficits would indicate. This is because the official fiscal data do not reflect the authorities' reliance on extrabudgetary funds and substantial quasi-fiscal spending financed by directed credits from the National Bank of Belarus, exchange rate subsidies, and the accumulation of internal and external arrears.[2] If proper account is taken of this spending, the measured budget deficit would be much more substantial (Table 2). This combination of loose fiscal and accommodative monetary policies resulted in an infusion of resources into the economy. This, in turn, allowed the perpetuation of existing economic structures,

[2]   Economist Intelligence Unit, *EIU Country Report: Belarus, Moldova* (August 2000): 17.

enabling firms and farms to continue purchasing inputs, paying wages, and producing outputs as before.

Table 2
Belarus: Official vs. Estimated Actual Fiscal Outcomes, 1997–2000 (in percent of GDP)

	1997	1998	1999	2000 (1st half)
Revenue	45.5	44.5	45.7	38.6
Expenditure	46.2	44.8	47.9	39.7
Balance	-0.7	-0.3	-2.2	-1.1
Adjusted Balance (includes quasi-fiscal operations)	...	-3.3	-5.7	-2.5

Source: International Monetary Fund, "IMF Concludes Article IV Consultation with the Republic of Belarus," Public Information Notice, No. 00/88, October 2000.

The Policy Mix: Early Positive and Later Negative Outcomes

Economic theory and practice would predict a number of less-welcome effects commonly associated with this policy mix. At the macro level, the strategy of money-led growth could be expected to erode the value of the country's currency, sparking inflation and depreciation (Figure 2). At the micro level, the absence of market-driven price signals or meaningful enterprise restructuring would mean that no tight relationship existed between demand for the output of Belarusian enterprises and the amount supplied. This should result in a misallocation of scarce resources and negative value-added production, which, in turn, should have become evident through the accumulation in inventory of unwanted output. Furthermore, these effects would be expected to generate growing external imbalances: importation of inputs relative to production would remain constant, but external demand for the resulting unwanted output would decline. In the absence of continued external financing or an adjustment in the exchange rate, the resultant gap would become unsustainable, prompting a downward movement in the country's consumption of imports (particularly energy) and a sharp decrease in output.

Figure 2
Belarus: Trends in Inflation and Money Supply, 1995–2000

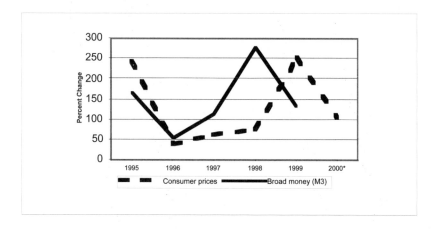

Source: European Bank for Reconstruction and Development, *Transition Report 2000.*
*projection

During the period 1995–1997, Belarus managed to avoid these negative phenomena. Strict administrative controls, rather than market-based outcomes, played a significant role. Inflation was kept in check through the maintenance of price controls, both formal and informal. Exchange rate stability was preserved by means of strict administrative controls over currency convertibility and rationed access to scarce hard currency.[3] But these strategies alone would have provided only transitory stability for the Belarusian economy. Price controls could be expected to result in shortages, queues, and rationing. Reliance on exchange rate controls would increase once hard currency reserves were depleted through intervention in defense of the official exchange rate, with rates offered by the informal sector increasingly diverging from the official rate.

[3] Economist Intelligence Unit, *EIU Country Report: Belarus, Moldova* (August 2000): 16; European Bank for Reconstruction and Development, *Transition Report* (1999): 194.

Russia's Vital Role in the Belarusian Economy

These predicted outcomes are now becoming apparent in Belarus, but they took longer to emerge than in other countries where a similar policy mix has been pursued. This is due in large part to official and quasi-official Russian support of the Belarusian economy, which provided an outlet for the pressures accumulating within the economy and allowed the authorities to avert these negative phenomena for a considerable period. This support took two forms.

First, preferential trade arrangements that exist between the two countries have provided an important outlet for exports of Belarusian output to Russia. Exports to Russia have grown dramatically since 1996; they rose 50 percent in 1997 alone and represented 55 percent of Belarusian exports at end-1999.[4] To the extent that Belarus exports to Russia on a cash basis, the country enjoys a considerable advantage over competitors resulting from preferential tariff treatment flowing from the country's union treaty with Russia. In addition, barter trade continues to be a feature of Belarusian trade with Russia; in 1999, the share of barter operations was 42.1 percent of Belarusian exports to Russia and 36.3 percent of Belarusian imports from Russia.[5] The continued substantial role of barter trade reflects the growing difficulty on the part of exporters in making cash payments to suppliers, as well as increasing efforts to evade the Belarusian authorities' hard currency surrender requirement.

The second and still more important form of Russian support for the Belarusian economy is the provision of energy supplies on terms that involve substantial explicit and implicit subsidization. In the first instance, Russia has consistently charged Belarus a lower price for natural gas than that paid either by other CIS countries or by non-CIS importers (Table 3). As of October 2000, the price was $31/TCM (thousand cubic meters), compared to the non-CIS price of $96/TCM.[6] Two additional forms of subsidization, however,

---

[4]   International Monetary Fund, "Republic of Belarus: Recent Economic Developments and Selected Issues." *IMF Staff Country Report,* No. 00/153, p. 20.

[5]   Arkady Moshes, "Russia's Belarus Problem," Memo No. 182, Program on New Approaches to Russian Security Policy: Policy Memo Series (January 2001): 1.

[6]   Arkadii Moshes: Gosudarstvennyi Komitet Rossiiskoi Federatsii po statistiki, *Sotsial'no-ekonomicheskoe polozhenie Rossii,* (November 2000): 2.

complicate the calculation of a specific price equivalent charged by Russia per unit of gas shipped to Belarus: these are, first, Russia's tolerance of non-payment for energy exports and, second, the prevalence of non-monetary forms of remuneration that comprise a large share of payments made by Belarus. Energy imports are paid for almost exclusively on barter terms, and offset arrangements involving industrial goods are used to settle arrears.[7] In-kind payments include the provision of: transit services to Gazprom for shipments carried to Western Europe by the Belarusian pipeline network; labor and material inputs for construction of the new Yamal pipeline; and agricultural and manufactured goods to Gazprom.

Table 3
Average Prices for Russian Natural Gas Exports, 1997–2000 (in dollars per 1,000 cubic meters)

	1997	1998	1999	2000
To Belarus	49.1	49.9	30.4	31.0
To Other CIS Countries	71.4	57.2	n.a.	55.8
To Rest of the World	88.6	72.2	n.a.	102.5

Sources: International Monetary Fund (2000), "Republic of Belarus: Recent Economic Developments and Selected Issues," *IMF Staff Country Report* No. 00/153; *Russia in Figures '99*, State Committee of the Russian Federation on Statistics; Interfax News Service, "Russia Exported 6% Less Gas in 2000 than in 1999," Interfax News Service, 8 February 2001.

In spite of the low prices and relatively easy repayment terms that these mechanisms create, Belarus continued to fall behind in its payment for gas imports from Russia. Although the Belarusian authorities reduced these arrears in 1997, they have been unable to prevent an accumulation of new debts since the beginning of 1998. As of end-1999, Belarus' gas payment arrears, owed mostly to Russia, amounted to approximately $243 million, and those on payments for

---

[7]   International Monetary Fund, "Republic of Belarus: Recent Economic Developments and Selected Issues," *IMF Staff Country Report,* No. 00/153, p. 23.

electricity, owed mostly to Russia and Lithuania, were $96 million.[8] Taken together, these debts are equal to 3 percent of the end-1999 GDP.[9]

Economic Imbalances Now Coming to the Fore

Belarus' ability to contain the negative effects of its economic policies is now diminishing, and the imbalances generated by these policies are overwhelming the nation's capacity to compensate. This was first demonstrated by the currency crisis that hit Belarus in March 1998. After a month of heightened pressure on the exchange rate brought on by the credit emissions described above, the crisis broke out on 13 March, with the official exchange rate dropping 43 percent on the Moscow Interbank Currency Exchange (MICEX). The decline was precipitated by the failure of a Belarusian delegation to reach agreement with Russia on a financial aid package in support of the Belarusian currency. The authorities ordered the rollback of both the exchange rate and price increases triggered by the devaluation, tightened controls on ruble transactions with non-residents, and persuaded Russian authorities to suspend ruble trading on the MICEX.

In the aftermath of the Russian financial crisis, Belarus' extreme dependence on the Russian economy led to a sharp slowdown in economic activity. Output growth declined from 8.5 percent in 1998 to 3.5 percent in 1999. During the same period, the current account deficit dropped from 6.1 percent/GDP to 2.2 percent/GDP as slower domestic and external demand resulted in a sharp contraction in both imports and exports. In response, the Belarusian authorities again resorted to expansionary monetary policy to spur economic activity. To contain the pressures this placed on prices and the exchange rate, the authorities increased the extent of price controls and strengthened their grip on access to hard currency. This resulted in the emergence of approximately five different official exchange rates. Even with these controls in place, inflation spiraled, the exchange rate continued

---

[8]   International Monetary Fund, "Republic of Belarus: Recent Economic Developments and Selected Issues," *IMF Staff Country Report,* No. 00/153, p. 23.

[9]   Economist Intelligence Unit, *EIU Country Report: Belarus, Moldova* (August 2000): 6. Belarus' 1999 GDP in dollar terms calculated at an estimated market exchange rate was equal to $11.5 billion.

to depreciate in the parallel market, and official foreign exchange reserves, which were at the equivalent of less than one month of imports, remained extremely low.[10]

In addition to the collapse of the exchange rate and sharp depletion of official reserves, other signs point to the authorities' attenuated ability to keep economic imbalances in check. As prices for "socially important goods" remained nominally fixed, indications of repressed inflation started growing in the last quarter of 1998. Shortages were increasing, queues were appearing, and rationing of staple goods had reemerged. In spite of the presence of increasingly pervasive price controls, measured inflation jumped, reaching about 180 percent in 1998 and 250 percent in 1999. It should be noted that this undoing of Belarus' earlier successful stabilization is consistent with another finding by Fischer and Sahay: their review of country-level data showed that the stabilization process was not sustained in countries that had persistent fiscal deficits and slow structural reforms.

Perhaps most telling is the decline in living standards and increase in poverty that has taken place in Belarus over the past three years in spite of the country's strong overall growth performance. Even with several years of emphasis by the Belarusian authorities on employment, benefits, subsidies, and economic growth, almost 47 percent of the population lived below the minimum subsistence level (equivalent to $50 per month) as of the first quarter of 2000, compared to less than 44 percent at end-1998 and 32 percent in 1997. Government wage arrears, which were virtually eliminated in 1994, rose to approximately $36 million as of June 2000, and per capita consumption of meat, potatoes, sugar, and other dietary staples has fallen by more than one-third over the past ten years.[11]

[10]   International Monetary Fund, "Republic of Belarus: Recent Economic Developments and Selected Issues," *IMF Staff Country Report,* No. 00/153, p. 6; "IMF Concludes Article IV Consultation with the Republic of Belarus." *Public Information Notice*, No. 00/88 (October 2000).

[11]   European Bank for Reconstruction and Development, Economist Intelligence Unit, *Transition Report* 2000: 22.

A Changing Relationship with Russia

Signs that Russia was becoming less willing to help Belarus became apparent prior to the Russian financial crisis, as illustrated by the March 1998 collapse of negotiations for additional support for the Belarusian economy. Following the onset of the financial crisis in August of the same year, the unwillingness of the Chernomyrdin and Kiriyenko governments to assist Belarus was replaced, at least temporarily, by the inability of the Primakov government to spare the necessary resources. The worsening situation, combined with the loss of Russian support, appears to have motivated the Belarusian authorities to search elsewhere for help. In particular, Belarus' straitened economic circumstances spurred an attempt to reengage with international financial institutions, in particular with the International Monetary Fund (IMF), which had no lending programs in the country at that time. In the fall of 1998, after two years of very public rejection of IMF policy recommendations, Belarus changed course requesting financing from the IMF to compensate for the sharp downturn in exports to Russia and a poor harvest. Discussions toward this end, however, yielded no results.[12]

Although Russia resisted Belarusian requests for direct financial assistance in 1998, the degree of subsidization appears to have increased substantially starting in 1999, as demonstrated by a sharp reduction in the already below-market prices charged for natural gas deliveries (Table 3). These lower prices have remained in effect, even as international energy prices surged starting in late 1999. While this form of assistance has intensified, Russian expectations regarding adjustments in Belarusian economic policies also appear to have risen. The prospect of direct Russian financial assistance for Belarus conditioned on the implementation of particular economic reforms represents this latest twist in Belarusian-Russian economic relations. In November 2000, Russian Prime Minister Mikhail Kasyanov announced that Russia would lend Belarus $150 million to create a national currency stabilization fund. This approach appears to be modeled on Russia's interaction with the IMF, in that disbursement

---

[12] *Statement by the Hon. Gennady Novitsky, Governor of the World Bank for the Republic of Belarus, at the Joint Annual Discussion,* Board of Governors of the World Bank and International Monetary Fund, Press Release No. 13, 28–30 September 1999.

would depend on fulfillment by the Belarusian authorities of economic reforms identified by Russia as critical for advancing the convergence of the two countries' economies ahead of the eventual economic and monetary union now planned for 2005.[13] It remains to be seen whether the Belarusian authorities will implement the policies required to unlock this support, although recent efforts to liberalize the foreign exchange market, which culminated in September 2000 in a unified exchange rate for the Belarusian ruble, appear to be a move in that direction.[14]

Future Sustainability

The negative consequences of the policy mix chosen by the Belarusian authorities, such as high inflation in the presence of strict price controls, continued accumulation of arrears on energy imports, and worsening living standards, have become increasingly visible even as the regional economy has strengthened substantially starting in the second half of 1999. These factors point to the conclusion that the growth performance and relatively stable living standards recorded by the Belarusian economy over the past few years cannot be sustained by a continuation of current economic policies. Furthermore, the above discussion has shown that the extent of continued Russian goodwill and Russian economic developments will determine whether the Belarusian economy can continue to perform at current levels in the absence of any change in current macroeconomic policies. Belarus' increased dependence on Russia resulted in a substantial worsening in its economic situation in connection with Russia's financial crisis. And, while there has been some easing of economic difficulties for Belarus stemming from the faster-than-expected post-crisis recovery in Russia, it remains to be seen whether the various forms of Russian subsidization will continue, especially given signs of changing Russian attitudes toward Belarus.[15]

---

[13]   Interfax News Service, 14 November 2000; "Kremlin Plays Role of IMF in Belarus," *The Moscow Times.com*, 15 November 2000.

[14]   "IMF Concludes Article IV Consultation with the Republic of Belarus," *Public Information Notice,* No. 00/88 (October 2000).

[15]   Further sources referenced for this study include:

Economist Intelligence Unit, *Country Report: Belarus, Moldova* (London: The Economist Intelligence Unit Ltd., 2000).

European Bank for Reconstruction and Development, *Transition Report 1999* (London: European Bank for Reconstruction and Development, 1999).

European Bank for Reconstruction and Development, *Transition Report 2000* (London: European Bank for Reconstruction and Development, 2000).

International Monetary Fund, "IMF Concludes Article IV Consultation with the Republic of Belarus," *Public Information Notice*, No. 00/88 (Washington, DC: International Monetary Fund, 2000).

International Monetary Fund, "Republic of Belarus: Recent Economic Developments and Selected Issues," *IMF Staff Country Report* No. 00/153 (Washington, DC: International Monetary Fund, 2000).

International Monetary Fund, "World Economic Outlook," *World Economic and Financial Surveys*, October 2000, Washington: International Monetary Fund.

Moshes, Arkady, "Russia's Belarus Problem," *Program on New Approaches to Russian Security, Policy Memo Series*, No. 182 (Cambridge: Harvard University, 2001).

5

Leonid Zlotnikov
Possibilities for the Development of a Private Economic Sector and a Middle Class as a Source of Political Change in Belarus

Nobel Prize winner Ronald H. Coase (and, still earlier, Marx) defined private property as "a bundle of rights" used in making economic decisions. The essential distinction between a market and a command economy lies in the field of decision-making. Properly speaking, "private property" and "market economy" can be viewed as convertible notions. This is why evaluating the possibilities for private sector development in Belarus is the same as evaluating the possibilities for the formation of a liberal market economy as a whole. This is significant because an analysis of private sector development in Belarus has to begin with an analysis of the "bundle of property rights" that private property involves.[1]

Belarus' present economic model is determined by at least six factors. These are: the interaction of the material interests of different groups of the population; cultural values and ideas on how to achieve them; the necessity of solving the main tasks of economic development; the influence of events in Russia; international financial organizations; and, the success of market reforms in neighboring countries. The present evaluation of the possibilities for private sector development in Belarus is based on an analysis of the interaction

[1]   I would like to thank an anonymous reviewer for bringing this point to my attention.

among these factors and on the experience of reforms during the first decade of independence, as well as on ideas about the direction of Belarusian society as a whole.

Of all the Central and East European states, it has been Belarus that has moved least in the direction of market reforms. The transformation process was practically stopped after Aliaksandr Lukashenka's election as president in 1994. In the first part of this chapter, I will seek to explain why the transformation process has lagged behind in Belarus. In the second part, I will analyze the attitude of the population and other subjects of politics and economy to private sector development. In the third part, I will examine the influence of various external factors (Russian political and business circles, international financial organizations, and Western investments) on private sector development. The fourth part of this chapter shows that in the years between 1996 and 2000 Lukashenka managed to create an economic model similar to what existed in Nazi Germany. To conclude, I will examine some possible scenarios of economic development in Belarus.

The Conservative Revolution

In 1994, after Lukashenka's election as president, market reforms were at first stopped and then turned backwards. The former elite was discouraged from making strategic decisions on the development of the society. Power, in the person of Lukashenka and his closest associates, passed into the hands of "ordinary" people. The liberal-democratic approach to development was rejected. Similar events had taken place in the twentieth century (in Russia, for example, in 1917, and in Germany in 1933). In all three cases, what Friedrich Hayek calls "harmful conceit," authoritarianism, and a traditional system of values prevailed. All this can be generalized in the notion of "conservative revolution." In the present author's opinion, the roots of the deeper conservatism of Belarusian society should be sought in the peculiarities of Belarus' development.

Two important historical facts should be pointed out: (1) the lower level of industrial development of Belarus before the revolution; and (2) the higher rates of economic growth after it, especially in the post-1945 period. Before 1917, in spite of the fact that Belarus was located near industrial centers, it was no more than one of Russia's backward borderlands. Industry consisted mainly of small peat mines, logging enterprises, and paper and cement factories. In 1940, towns contained only 21.3 percent of the population (versus 34.4 percent in Russia). Capitalist relations in Belarus were developed to a much lesser extent than in Russia or Ukraine.

The growth rate of industrial production in Belarus for the period between 1960 and 1985 was higher on average than in the USSR; these were 9 and 4.9 times, respectively. This led to a significant growth of the urban population. In the period between 1959 and 1987, the urban population of Belarus increased by 262 percent (Minsk's population tripled). By way of comparison, the figure for Russia during the same period was 173 percent. In that period, in terms of population growth rates among the world's cities, Minsk was outpaced only by Mexico City.

Thus, the peculiarities of Belarus' recent history have caused two developments that are of an economic nature and that influenced, in my opinion, the relative unwillingness of the population to undertake market reforms. First, in comparison with other former Soviet republics, a larger share of the urban population and elite of the society happened to be first-generation immigrants from the villages. This stratum of the population, in a larger degree, preserved feudal-patriarchal values, that is, a negative attitude toward incomes derived from trade and exchange, a weak perception of human rights values and legality, and a tendency to valorize authoritarianism. Second, during the Soviet period, the living standards in Belarus were growing faster than in the other republics of the USSR. (Belarus had a low initial income and the highest rates of national income growth.) This led to a higher degree of satisfaction with the existing system and the absence of a reform wing in the leadership of the Communist Party prior to the beginning of reforms.

During the Soviet period, the Party and state bureaucracy, as collective owners of most of the economy, received certain "dividends" or benefits. Naturally, these privileged groups tried to delay the process of property redistribution on the basis of other principles. At the same time, it was frightened by the failure of socialism in the countries of Central Europe and could not but see that, in 1990–1991, the idea of a market economy had become a myth that seized the imagination of the masses. This is why the bureaucracy had to maneuver. At the 31st and last congress of the Communist Party of Belarus (November 1990), its newly elected leader, Anatolii Malafeiaŭ [Malofeev], declared: "We have to think once more about how to blend our political platform with market relations, how to fill them with contents that will help to preserve socialist choice."[2]

To the present, orthodox Communists who have set themselves the task of preserving socialist structures in market forms hold leading posts in the state: for example, Siarhei Linh [Sergei Ling] (former Secretary of the Central Committee of the Communist Party of Belarus) was at the head of the government until February 2000; Malafeiaǔ (former First Secretary of the Central Committee of the Communist Party of Belarus) is at the head of the legislative branch of power; Mikhail Miasnikovich (former head of the department of the Central Committee of the Communist Party of Belarus) is the head of the Presidential Administration.

During the first years of independence, the country's party and bureaucratic elite did everything possible to preserve the system of the command economy. Under the conditions of economic decline and the development of market relations, however, it had to give its enterprises the right to manage those products destined to be exchanged for necessary raw materials and a partial freedom to set prices.

The liberalization of the economic activity of state enterprises, shortages of goods and artificially low prices, the development of black markets in neighboring countries—all this created favorable conditions for corruption. In Minsk, for instance, the price of a "MAZ" truck in 1991 was $30,000–$35,000, which was approximately half of what it was in the other republics of the USSR. Bribes for the right to buy one truck at the state price reached $15,000–20,000. The plant was surrounded by middlemen. According to our estimates, middlemen pumped about $1.5 billion out of the state sector from "MAZ" alone. During periods of goods shortages, the story was repeated at other plants as well.

Around the time of the election of the first president of Belarus in July 1994, the country's economic situation continued to worsen. The government's populist policies caused rapid inflation. In 1993–1994, prices increased 432 times, while the GDP volume declined by 20 percent. Corruption flourished. Property and power were concentrated in the hands the state bureaucracy, and an economic model of oligarchic capitalism similar to that prevalent in Russia was formed.

---

2   *Sovetskaia Belorussiia* 29 November 1990.

Between 1990 and 1994, the standard of living was cut by at least half (by two-thirds in some cases) and social stratification was noticeably exacerbated. The income differential between the top 10 percent of the population and the poorest 10 percent increased to 1,300 percent (versus 1,500 percent in Russia in 1995, up from 450 percent in 1991). This difference surpassed the threshold at which authoritarian regimes instead of democracies tend to be established. Communist and populist propaganda of various sorts skillfully channeled people's dissatisfaction with their position and the unfair (in their opinion) enriching of entrepreneurs into a rejection of market reforms and democracy.[3]

It should be noted that it was the Left that achieved the mass rejection of market reforms. If, in December 1994, there had been a referendum, according to the results of a national sociological poll conducted by the Independent Institute of Socioeconomic and Political Studies (IISEPS), 30.3 percent of those polled would have voted for a "market economy" (against 62.6 percent at the end of 1990). Thus, the readiness of the population to accept market reforms, unknown to it at the end of 1990, had dissipated by the time of the presidential elections. The "window of opportunity" for the establishment of a private sector in Belarus was closed.

Lukashenka's election as president cannot be explained only by his populist economic slogans. It became the expression of protest by the masses who did not get anything in the course of property transformation. Lukashenka's ascent to power can be explained using the conceptual scheme of the "revolution of the masses" formulated by the Spanish philosopher José Ortega y Gasset. People who did not belong to either the political, economic, or cultural elite of the society and who did not have the necessary education or experience to govern the state entered the top tiers of power. Now these people govern the Belarusian economy, acting according to the notions of "ordinary" people by favoring simple and quick solutions to complex social problems. The "fatal conceit" of "ordinary" people's intellect does not leave any place for the market as a mechanism of self-regulation of the economy, replacing it instead with a command system. A similar process took place in the Germany of the 1930s and in Bolshevik Russia. At the same time, however, the new leaders, unlike the Bolsheviks, rely in their activities upon a system of traditional, pre-

---

3   *Belorusskaia niva* 9 September 1992

bourgeois values that appear to be preserved in Belarusian society to a greater extent than in neighboring countries. From this springs President Lukashenka's negative attitude towards intermediaries and financiers and his ideas of a "natural" hierarchical system of individual power and the organic unity of the society.

In general terms, a conservative revolution (a regular "revolution of the masses") has taken place in Belarus. By this I mean the conservatism that sprang up in reaction to the French revolution and the Enlightenment and that is organically incompatible with a well-developed system of market relations.

Various Political Actors' Attitudes to the Private Sector

The Electorate

The readiness of the population to accept a market economy can be estimated by gauging its attitude toward the values of capitalist society. In a national poll (IISEPS, June 1997),[4] those polled were asked questions designed to reveal their attitudes toward separate elements of market relations. If, as a whole, 30.4 percent of the respondents spoke for "market economy with insignificant state regulation" (the same number spoke in favor of a "planned economy" as well), the answers to more precise questions testify to the fact that people who really support the values of a market economy constitute less than 30 percent.

Later opinion polls showed that the number of those who prefer a market economy is increasing gradually. This can be seen from a number of national polls carried out by IISEPS (1999, see Table 2.1).[5]

---

[4]   Aleksandr Feduta, "Bol'shaia zhratva," *Belorusskaia delovaia gazeta* 2 August 1999.

[5]   "Molodezh i grazhdanskoe obshchestvo. Belorusskii variant," ed. Oleg Manaev, IISEPS, Minsk, 1999. In the nation-wide polls conducted by IISEPS from which the results are used in this chapter, 1490–1500 people over the age of 16 were polled. The margin of error is less than 3 percent.

Table 1
Distribution of respondents' preferences in relation to the type of economy (percent)

Issue	Nov. 1994	June 1995	Nov. 1997	Sept. 1998	June 1999
Market economy	51.0	52.1	69.0	74.6	72.1
With slight state regulation	—	—	32.8	35.2	36.8
With considerable state regulation	—	—	36.2	39.4	35.3
Planned economy	46.3	45.1	25.7	22.8	24.7

The question "How, in your view, should the price of a product be determined?" reveals more precisely the attitude to the market. Only 23.1 percent of those polled in November 1997 answered that it should be determined by supply and demand. The number of those who felt disposed to socialism was much larger, with 31.6 percent answering that it should be determined "by production costs" or "by the state proceeding from the interests of the population" (27.2 percent). Only 9.6 percent responded positively to the direct question "Must the prices be free?" (the state must regulate the prices of all goods and services–43.8 percent; of some of them–37.1 percent).

The population's views on the role of the state in price-formation have remained stable over time. A nationwide poll conducted in March 2000 produced approximately the same results as the 1997 poll, with 45.5 percent agreeing that the state must control the prices of all goods and services and 37.2 percent "some goods and services."[4]

The values revealed for the population reflect a low tolerance for risk and to taking personal responsibility for one's own destiny, and a relatively high acceptance of social inequality. A considerable portion of those polled thought that the director of an enterprise must have a salary not more than two times larger than the average (56.7 percent). Two-thirds considered the resale of goods as "dishonest" or "rather dishonest." Not more than 28.3 percent considered incomes from the lease of apartments, resale of goods, shares, or entrepreneurial activity to come from honest sources.

---

[4] "Belarus i mir. Resul'taty sotsiologicheskogo oprosa," 2–10 March 2000, "Novak" Laboratory, Report.

According to Belarusian poll data, the same social phenomenon that researchers have already noted in Russia is also seen in Belarus. This is what could be called a "transition state of economic mentality." Both "the spirit of socialism" and "the spirit of capitalism" are present simultaneously in people's needs and orientational behavioral motives.

The mass mentality retains the ideology of equality and justice, accepts the necessity of considerable state regulation of the economy, and underestimates the significance of ideas and the art of governing in the creation of a country's wealth. As a result, only 3.7 percent of the polled think that the leaders create the wealth of the country (workers, peasants–55.5 percent). Income accrued from trade and financial lending-based activity (usury) is still looked upon negatively, and the tendency to take risks is slight (65 percent of those polled are ready to receive a salary that is not necessarily high, but that is guaranteed).

Yet this is a paradoxical situation: at the same time, the population is "for" having a wide choice of high-quality goods at free prices (77.9 percent), thinks that private enterprises work more effectively (48.3 percent) than state ones (44 percent), and is in favor of allowing the purchase and sale of land (with limitations). Twenty-eight percent of those polled are ready to work at private enterprises, 14 percent have dealt with the resale of goods, and 12.8 percent were engaged in individual labor activities.

Thus, the population is ready to support the market, but without capitalism and without businessmen. According to a poll conducted in 1996 in Russia, 69 percent wanted the nation to return to pre-1985 conditions; only 25 percent favored the development of Russia along a capitalist path. It can be supposed that similar answers would have been given in Belarus as well.

The ratio of those who support market values changes considerably depending on the place of residence and level of education. This can be seen in Tables S2 and S3 (supplementary tables follow the end of the chapter). The more educated the people and the closer they live to the capital, the more they accept the capitalist model.

The results of a 1997 national poll conducted by IISEPS[6] also show that Lukashenka's electorate is composed of those people who reject market values (see Table 1 and Table S4).

---

[6]   Oleg Manaev, "Po tonkomu l'du. Sotsiologicheskii portret elektorata Aleksandra

Table 2
Social and demographic portrait of Lukashenka's supporters

Social and demographic characteristics	Would vote for Lukashenka tomorrow	
	Yes	*No*
Gender		
Female	50.2	49.8
Male	39.8	60.2
Age		
16–19 years old	31.7	68.3
20–24	30.8	69.2
25–30	19.7	80.3
30–39	29.3	70.7
40–49	40.1	59.9
50–59	48.6	51.4
60 and older	81.7	18.3
Education		
Up to 4 years	88.2	11.8
Up to 8 years	54.3	45.7
Secondary school, specialized school	35.6	64.4
Secondary specialized	34.3	65.7
Unfinished higher and higher	24.6	75.4
Social Status		
Leader	21.6	78.4
Specialist	29.4	70.6
Employee	31.4	68.6
Skilled worker	32.6	67.4
Unskilled worker	46.7	53.3
Retired	77.9	22.1
Housewife	46.1	53.9
Pupil	32.9	67.1
Unemployed	30.3	69.7
Place of Residence		
Minsk	17.5	82.5
Regional centers	35.8	64.2
Large cities	38.0	62.0
Small towns	40.2	59.8
Village	69.9	30.1
Minsk region	50.0	50.0
Brest region	46.5	53.5

Lukashenko," *Belorusskaia delovaia gazeta* 1 September 1997: 4–5.

Table 2 (con't)

Social and demographic characteristics	Would vote for Lukashenka tomorrow	
	Yes	*No*
Hrodna region	36.1	63.9
Vitebsk region	52.8	47.2
Mahilioŭ region	64.1	35.9
Homel region	54.0	46.0

The social and demographic portrait of the president's supporters is very characteristic. These are, first of all, relatively uneducated and elderly rural dwellers, mainly retirees, among whom there are more women than men, and inhabitants of the eastern regions of Belarus. Also characteristic is the economic status of the president's supporters, which fully coincides with their social and demographic status—mostly the poor part of the population that has difficulty making ends meet.

Lukashenka's adherents reject economic reforms in principle, because such reforms benefit only "swindlers and rascals" and draw the country still farther away from what it was like in the USSR. In short, the majority of the electorate represents the personification of classical anti-market stereotypes colored by nostalgia for the past.

But it would be wrong to limit the present analysis to such characteristics, which describe the dominant social type of presidential supporters. From the data produced by the above-mentioned poll, it follows that there is still another type of presidential supporter characterized by social dynamism and by having a quite market-oriented, democratic, and tolerant mentality. One-fifth of such individuals sympathize with the opposition; one-fourth prefer a U.S.-type economy; one-fourth have higher or incomplete higher education; one-third have a good economic position; almost one-third are young men; almost half are proponents of Belarusian sovereignty, etc. This second type of Lukashenka supporter will be called the "socially dynamic type." The first type outnumbers the second approximately 2:1. Obviously, these groups are antagonists having different life prospects and, therefore, it is impossible to develop a state policy based on their combined support. Probably, the "socially dynamic" type continues to support the president only because they have not found a leader capable of realizing their actual social interests.

The President

Today, Aliaksandr Lukashenka is the country's most influential political actor. His decisions are determined by many factors, most importantly by his convictions and world-view, his desire to preserve power, and by the necessity to find a solution to the current problems faced by Belarusian society.

Lukashenka's views, as can be surmised from numerous interviews, are deeply conservative. Here is a short summary of his opinions regarding private sector development: All the processes in the society must be under the control of one leader. The division of powers in Western democracies, in his opinion, is more an illusion than a reality. In fact, even in the United States as well as in Belarus, only one man controls everything. The Belarusian president must have the right to make any and all decisions concerning the governing of the society, for example, to dismiss not only the chairman of the Constitutional Court or the chairman of the National Bank, but the director of any enterprise or school in the most remote district of the country as well.

The main motive for an entrepreneur, according to the president, should not be the desire for profit, but the desire to benefit society. "The spirit of gain" is incompatible, in his opinion, with the spiritual values of the Slavic-Orthodox peoples. Lukashenka has an especially negative view of financial and trade enterprises. He has said repeatedly that society must rid itself of such enterprises as it would rid itself of "louse-infested fleas." At a conference on the new system of registration for enterprises held on 12 March 1999, he decreed that enterprises that dealt with the purchase and sale of goods would not be allowed to register. Further, if regional leaders believe there is a need for trade firms, then they must register them on their own responsibility. As a result, in the year starting in the autumn of 1998, only several dozen such enterprises were registered.[7] In the city of Minsk as of 1 April 2000, not more than 2 percent of enterprises and private entrepreneurs were re-registered.

The president prizes the values of justice and equal distribution. He has repeatedly declared that Belarus looks for its own model of economic development different from both capitalism and socialism.

---

[7]   S. Balykin, "Problemy predprinimatelei nachinaiutsia s registratsii," *Narodnaia volia* 20 August 1999.

The main characteristic of this new society must become, in his opinion, justice that results, first of all, in distribution according to labor. This is why the market principle of price-formation based on supply and demand in Belarus is being replaced mainly by that of price-making.

Beginning in 1997, the president, through his decrees, has determined the monthly limits for price growth. In 1998, for example, the monthly increase of prices for every product was not to exceed 2 percent (4–5 percent per month in 1999 and 2000, which is much lower than the inflation rates). In order to increase a price over the determined percent, an enterprise has to appeal to local executive committees and substantiate the necessity for such a change. The punishment of enterprise directors for violating price-formation decrees has become a mass phenomenon. Lukashenka has repeatedly affirmed that the former socialist economic system justified itself and that Belarus' economic crisis was caused 50 percent by the disintegration of the USSR and 50 percent by the decline of executive discipline.[8] This is why it is necessary not to reform, but to perfect, the former system. In his opinion, with a good director, a state enterprise can work as effectively as a private one.

Yet Lukashenka has severely limited the freedom of maneuver of state enterprise directors. Every year, by decree, he affirms the "forecast" of the growth of production volumes in the national economy for enterprises of all ownership forms. At the end of 1998, for example, eight directors of private enterprises were called to the executive power bodies and asked to explain why they had not increased production volume.

In the name of power preservation, the president must act in accordance with the expectations of his electorate ("ordinary people") by suppressing private trade, intermediaries, financiers, and bankers; establishing "just prices"; etc. And he does it. A durable system has taken shape: the president analyzes the people's moods and reflects them in his words and actions. This, in turn, reinforces even more marginal moods among "ordinary people."

It is now difficult for the president to change his negative attitude toward the private sector, not only because it contradicts his convictions, but also because it could lead to a loss of electorate.

---

8   *Gomel'skie novosti* 1 December 1994.

Having become president, Lukashenka revealed his archaic notions about his role in the state and on the ways of governing the country. A presidential fund, equal in size to the state budget was created.[9] No one has the right to control Lukashenka's expenditures. (This right of uncontrolled expenditure was approved by the people in the November 1996 referendum in which they also approved a new constitution that authorized the introduction of an authoritarian regime.) A number of profitable enterprises were put under the authority of the management of affairs of the Presidential Administration *(Upravlenie Delami Administratsii Prezidenta)*. Incomes from the lease of different kinds of state property also flow there.

The largest source of income to the presidential fund flows from different privileges that were given by the president, mainly to Russian private enterprises, for the import of goods into the Customs Union area shared with Russia.[10] In this way, large sums of un-accounted money came into this fund.[11] It is common knowledge that Lukashenka paid additional salaries to high-ranking officials in cash dollars or paid expenses for holding large events from this fund. At the legal proceedings involving former Agriculture Minister Vasil Liavonaŭ [Leonov], for example, Liavonaŭ revealed that the dollars that had been found in his office by preliminary investigators had been given to him personally by Lukashenka.[12]

Managing this virtual second budget of the country by himself and without oversight, Lukashenka satisfies his personal "needs" at the expense of this fund. Among other things, he built a new house for his mother, repaired his wife's house, buys many expensive suits for himself, and gives presents.[13]

For Lukashenka, all other principles are subordinate to the principle of the preservation of power. This is why he is not tolerant of

[9]   According to an assertion of ex-premier Mikhail Chyhir [Chigir], made by him in the letter to Lukashenka from prison. See *Narodnaia volia* 12 August 1999.

[10]   On this topic, see also Chapter 7 of this volume, "Lukashenka's Role in Russian Politics," by Arkady Moshes.

[11]   Aleksandr Feduta, "Zavkhoz respubliki," *Belorusskaia delovaia gazeta* 12 August 1999.

[12]   *Belorusskaia delovaia gazeta* 28 August 1999.

[13]   See interview with Iu. Chyhir, wife of the arrested ex-premier Mykhail Chyhir, *Belorusskaia delovaia gazeta* 2 April 1999.

people in his circle who appear to have the potential to become rivals. In a letter from prison, for example, ex-premier Mikhail Chyhir [Chigir] recalls that, at the time of his appointment to the post of prime minister, Lukashenka asked him not to appear on TV without a pressing reason. In order to discredit Chyhir, his children were repeatedly arrested and beaten by the militia. In addition, different "witnesses" were made to give false evidence that Chyhir's children had committed economic crimes.[14]

The rough and tumble style of communication that the president has with his subordinates, which can be seen at every press conference broadcast on radio or TV, should also be noted. The head of administration of Mahilioŭ [Mogilev] region, A. Kulichkoŭ [Kulichkov], for example, was dismissed from his post right in front of the TV cameras during a press conference broadcast by Belarusian TV. He was immediately removed by guards from the conference hall. The decree announcing his dismissal appeared only afterwards.

The realization of the president's economic worldview in his actions does not contribute to the development of a private sector. A. Patupa, vice-chairman of the Belarusian Union of Entrepreneurs, speaking at the Congress of the Union in February 1998, summarized the situation very well: "We have returned to a command-administrative system. Market structures existing at the present moment are, in fact, decorative and can be destroyed at any time."[15]

The Presidential Administration and "Nomenklatura Entrepreneurs"

The Presidential Administration is composed of Lukashenka's closest and most trusted advisors. All main decisions are made here. Other power bodies (the Council of Ministers, the National Chamber) are only passive players. But even in the Administration, there are few people who really influence the president's decisions. It is known, for example, that the economic department of the Presidential Administration suggested that the dollar exchange rate be established on the basis of supply and demand. But these suggestions were constantly rejected.

The small circle of people who, in fact, govern the country and who were shown in the series of articles in the *Belorusskaia delovaia*

---

[14]   M. Chigir, "Otkrytoe pis'mo gr. Lukashenko," *Narodnaia volia* 12 August 1999.

[15]   *Belorusskaia delovaia gazeta* 23 February 1998.

gazeta (*Belarusian Business Newspaper*),[16] comprise only half a dozen or so men. Almost all of them come from the middle ranks of the Army, the Ministry of Internal Affairs, and the KGB (with the exception of Mikhail Miasnikovich, head of the administration) and have had no prior experience in governing a country. The representatives of the intellectuals who helped Lukashenka come to power either left the administration on their own or were dismissed. Orthodox Communists who once headed the government and held legislative power are not in this influential circle.

Within the Presidential Administration, two groups of people who make money for the president's fund have taken shape. One of them deals with the arms trade (Secretary of the Security Council V. Sheiman) and the second with other kinds of commercial activity (manager of the affairs of the Presidential Administration Ivan Tsitsiankoŭ [Titenkov]). Under the umbrella of the administration, several groups of commercial enterprises that captured the most profitable business spheres have been created.[17]

People doing business under the protection of the Presidential Administration do not forget about their own interests. An interesting example was given by a Belarusian newspaper. Entrepreneurs working under the protection of the administration were buying up cars that had been confiscated from other entrepreneurs at prices ranging from one hundred to one thousand times lower than the normal ones.[18] The heads of state organizations who created obstacles to the actions of "nomenklatura" entrepreneurs were dismissed. Thus, Tamara Vinikava [Vinnikova], former head of the National Bank, asserts that the reason for her arrest was the actions of those people close to the president whom she prevented from earning millions of dollars through dubious deals.[19]

Enterprises founded by the Presidential Administration ("Beltorgvneshinvest," for example) are formally state enterprises. From the political and economic point of view, however, they are the private property of small group of individuals who have real power in

---

[16] *Belorusskaia delovaia gazeta.* Series of articles "Bol'shaia zhratva," spring–summer 1999.

[17] Aleksandr Feduta, "Bol'shaia zhratva," 2 August 1999.

[18] "Baza deshevoi rasprodazhi," *Belorusskaia delovaia gazeta* 27 August 1999.

[19] Interview of Tamara Vinikava, *Belorusskaia delovaia gazeta* 2 April 1999.

the country, as the profits of these enterprises remain at their disposal. These people are interested in some kind of freedom for entrepreneurship because the return to a strict Soviet-style planned economy would mean the expansion of the circle of owners of these enterprises at the expense of other groups of state bureaucracy.

The Bureaucracy

After gaining independence and after the dissolution of the Communist party (and especially during the Kebich government of 1991–1994), the state bureaucracy became the country's absolute master. The attempts made by the country's higher leadership to maintain the course of Belarus' development in accordance with socialist principles only created conditions for corruption and appropriation of state property. Ideological directives were quickly dissolved. The bureaucracy itself began privatization according to the decision and rules drawn up by the Council of Ministers (1991) two years before the adoption of the "Law on Privatization" by the Supreme Soviet.

In Belarus as well as in Russia, bribery, as the primitive form of "participation" of the bureaucracy in the appropriation of incomes of the private sector, grew into cooperation with private business groups that needed its support. During Kebich's tenure as prime minister, directors of large enterprises founded the Economic Council. Belarusian scientific and industrial associations and leaders of unions of entrepreneurs had direct telephone access to the Prime Minister and accompanied him on foreign trips. After Lukashenka came to power, these communication lines were cut.

The model of oligarchic capitalism and corporative-bureaucratic organization began to form in Belarus between 1991 and 1994. This was slower than in Russia, because of cultural and historical differences. The agrarian lobby headed by Minister Liavonaŭ, for example, suggested a mechanism for the privatization of the agrarian-industrial complex that would transfer the enterprises of the complex (production, processing and sale of agricultural products, financing, and insurance) into the private property of a small financial group.[19] Liavonaŭ later was arrested.

---

[19] L. Zlotnikov, "Korporatsiia 'Agrokredit'—sovokupnyi zemlevladelets," *Belorusskii rynok* 19 (1994).

Lukashenka's ascent to power temporarily interrupted the development of private sector and market relations in the direction of a Russian-model form of oligarchic capitalism. All previously created bureaucratic clan groups lost their influence over decisions made by the president. At the same time, having no other candidates, he had to form his executive "vertical line" from the same immortal bureaucracy. Only Lukashenka's closest advisors, concentrated in the Presidential Administration, accommodated new people. The main economic policy decisions are made by this group. These decisions reflect the preference of "ordinary" people for simple and quick solutions to complex economic problems.

Immediately after Lukashenka came to power, an original project to introduce subsidiary (full) responsibility of the founders of economic entities took shape in his administration. In accordance with this project, for instance, the shareholders would have to be able to respond with their private property for debts incurred by their joint-stock companies. This project, however, does not correspond to the interests of other groups of the bureaucracy. The project of subsidiary responsibility met strong resistance from the bureaucracy and was rejected.

The idea of expansion of responsibility of individuals for the liabilities of enterprises, however, found its reflection in some recent presidential decrees. The official who registers a new enterprise, for example, will have to pay a fine if, in the future, this enterprise does not pay taxes or debts to other creditors. Similarly, if an enterprise engaged in exports does not receive payment for the goods exported within two months, the employee of the enterprise who made the decision on the export must pay a large fine. Some decrees are directed simply at the appropriation of the means of enterprises. The decree of 16 February 1999, for example, took money from those legal entities that had currency in their accounts in the form of a peculiar tax on the growth of the currency rate.

The incompetence reflected by decisions made in the Presidential Administration can be seen in the new Civil Code and other documents.[20] These decisions are made, as Lukashenka has declared repeatedly, in the interests of "ordinary people." They do not correspond to the bureaucracy's own interests, nor to its ideas on ways

---

[20]   V. Demidov, "Osinovyi kol v grazhdanskii kodeks," *Belorusskaia delovaia gazeta* 2 November 1998.

out of the crisis. Many specialists in state control bodies during the period between 1992 and 1994 had received training either abroad or in Belarus with the participation of foreign experts. This is why the president's populist decisions do not resonate with them. Adherents of market reform either left the government on their own or were dismissed from their posts. The new people who have entered the government are less competent. The posts of vice-premier for economic issues and then the chairman of the national bank, for example, were occupied by individuals with no training in economics.

Tension is increasing between the top (Presidential Administration) and lower levels of the power structure. This is conditioned by the fact that the negative consequences of incompetent economic decisions at the highest level are blamed by Lukashenka and the mass media on ministers, local authorities, and enterprise directors. In the course of Lukashenka's regime, the bureaucracy, except for the president's closest advisors, has lost confidence in its future.

In summary, above the state bureaucracy a new power center has appeared that is trying to turn the bureaucracy, which has already tasted power, again into an instrument to satisfy the interests of the president's electorate, that is Lukashenka's "ordinary people."

The Entrepreneurs

The majority of those employed in the non-state sector (650 mainly medium-sized enterprises) work in so-called "collective" enterprises formed when their labor staff bought out the company. At these enterprises, the workers do not feel that they are either owners or entrepreneurs. Employees of state enterprises that became joint-stock companies also do not feel that they are either owners or entrepreneurs. Neither do the shareowners who received shares in exchange for privatization vouchers see themselves as entrepreneurs. As of the end of 1998, 70 percent of the population had received their privatization vouchers. Only 12 percent of them exchanged them for shares. And, of those who did so, practically none received any dividends. The vouchers depreciated quickly to the point where a citizen could sell all of them for only $3 to $5.

A considerable portion of the population is involved in the shadow economy ("shuttle trading" of goods brought from Poland and Russia, repair and building of private houses, country cottages, etc.).

Employment statistics testify to this fact: from 1991 through 1998, the number of people employed in the national economy was reduced by 760,000, yet the number of officially unemployed at the end of 1998 totaled only 105,000.[21]

Small and medium-sized enterprises (SME) in Belarus function under hard conditions. A poll of leaders of such businesses carried out by IISEPS in May 1997 showed that the state organs treat SME "negatively rather than positively" (63.2 percent) or "negatively" (23.2 percent). Nearly three-quarters (73.7 percent) of those polled claimed that corruption prevents their activity; 82.1 percent blamed high taxes, and 86.3 percent unstable legislation.

The leaders of small and medium-sized businesses are the most influential force behind democracy and the development of the private sector of the economy. More than half of them (56.8 percent) support development of a free market economy, while only 1.1 percent favor a planned economy.

The results of other polls show that people who participate in the non-state sector of the economy are approximately twice as likely to support market economy values (they have a higher tolerance for risk, a higher opinion of the efficiency of private enterprises, freedom of prices, etc.). They are also more likely to have a favorable attitude toward democratic values.[22]

The hard conditions of economic survival encourage small businesses to unite. A trade union of small entrepreneurs and "shuttle traders" now numbers 70,000 members and has already organized several strikes calling for the protection of the rights of small traders. At their congress, the two main unions of Belarusian entrepreneurs were sharply critical of the state's economic policy and demanded more freedom for entrepreneurship.[23]

In agriculture, small and medium-sized private businesses are only marginally developed at the moment. As of 1 January 1999, there were 2,640 private farms (versus 3,034 in 1996) in Belarus. Less than one percent of the nation's agricultural land is in the hands of private farmers. It was mainly the head specialists of collective and state

---

[21] *Statistical Yearbook of the Republic of Belarus, 1998.*

[22] Pelipas, "Uspekh v biznese izmeniaet mirovozzrenie," *Belorusskii rynok* 46 (1997).

[23] See, for example, A. Makhovskii, "Druz'ia, pechalen vash soiuz," *Belorusskaia delovaia gazeta* 23 February 1998.

farms who became farmers. State support of farmers is practically nonexistent. Farmers receive lifetime use of land with the right to transfer it through inheritance, but not to sell it. When the farmer ceases working his land, it is returned to the state.

Belarusian statistics classify all joint-stock companies as belonging to the non-state sector, even if 100 percent of the shares belong to the state. There are no statistics on the number of truly private enterprises formed as a result of privatization. During the entire period of reforms (1991–1998), 3,112 enterprises (16 percent of the total), including 1,496 involved in trade and services moved into the non-state sector. These enterprises employ 656,000 people. In 1999, the growth of the non-state sector practically stopped.

During the years of reforms, 57,000 new small enterprises appeared, and 160,000 private entrepreneurs were registered without the formation of a legal entity. The non-state sector accounts for 15 percent of all employees in Belarus.[24]

It can be roughly estimated that those involved in entrepreneurial activities or owning private property make up no more than 5 percent of the employed in the national economy, or no more than 2.5 percent of the population of Belarus. It is widely agreed that these people comprise the nation's "middle class." Thus, Belarus' middle class is too small to influence the development of the society. Moreover, the economic system that has taken shape in Belarus does not assist the development of the private sector or the growth of the middle class' influence.

State Enterprise Directors: The Directorate

Directors of large enterprises that are still state-owned lost their privileged position in society after Lukashenka came to power. Their monthly salary ($70–100) is only double or triple the average worker's and is one-tenth to one-twentieth that of Russian directors. They are ordered by the state, in a summary manner, to improve their companies' indicators. Laws and regulations are constantly changing and are often contradictory. Enterprises are submitted to continuous inspections. One poll of directors of such companies showed that, on average, each enterprise is subjected to twelve inspections per year.[25]

---

[24] *Statistical Yearbook of the Republic of Belarus, 1998.*

[25] *Belorusskaia delovaia gazeta* no. 20 (1998). [Note that *Belorusskaia delovaia*

Punishment of directors is commonplace. In 1997, for example, fifteen heads of enterprises were dismissed and thirty-one were under investigation (about 15 percent of the total number).[26] Political activity by directors has declined in recent years. Their political party (the Belarusian Scientific and Industrial Congress) ceased to exist in 1999. Their attitude toward the regime was put into sharp relief by Vasil Shlyndzikaŭ, one of the former leaders of a large machine-building concern and now an opposition leader, who said: "Society must be protected from tramps and demagogues coming to power."[27]

The decline in the social status of directors of large enterprises after 1994 does not yet mean that they will assist in the transformation of the Belarusian economy into a liberal market economy. In the mentality of this kind of elite, as noted by Russian political scientist G. Diligensky, the idea of a command-administrative political power as higher value has taken root.[28] Hence, the elite's tendency towards nostalgia for a planned economy. In market relations, they strive to enter the system of power and use it as an instrument of private appropriation. It was through their assistance that the "oligarchic" model of the economy took shape in Russia in 1991–1994. A similar model was formed in Belarus as well.

Until recently, the social and psychological profiles of upper-level managers in Russia and Belarus were practically the same. This is why Diligensky's conclusion regarding the tendency of the directorate of large enterprises towards the formation of an oligarchic model of capitalism holds true for Belarus as well. The history of the development of goods stock exchanges in Belarus before Lukashenka's ascent to power confirms this conclusion. In 1992–1993, goods stock exchanges became rivals to state enterprises. This is why the latter lobbied for raising the requirements for allowing stock exchanges to operate. As a result, from almost forty goods stock

---

gazeta changed its numeration system in 1998, thus the different forms of citation for that year.]

[26] *Belorusskaia delovaia gazeta* 9 March 1998.

[27] V. Shlyndikov, "Direktorat ustal, vlasti bezialostnyi v bor'be s nim," *Belorusskaia delovaia gazeta* no. 59 (1997).

[28] G. Diligenskii, "Politicheskaia institutsionalizatsiia v Rossii: Sotsial'nyi, kul'turnyi i psikhologicheskii aspekty," *Mirovaia ėkonomika i mezhdunarodnye otnosheniia* 8 (1997).

exchanges, by 1995, only eleven remained and only one of them was fully functional.

Influence of External Factors on the Development of
Market Reforms in Belarus

Influence of Russian Political and Business Circles

The geopolitical strategy of almost all Russian political forces assigns a key role to Russian-Belarusian integration. This leads to the economic support of Belarus by Russian politicians. Gas, for example, is supplied to Belarus at prices some 30–40 percent lower than to neighboring Ukraine and Lithuania. Furthermore, Belarus has never paid for part of the gas supplied, and, in 1996, a debt in the amount of $1.4 billion was written off. In the opinion of Russian experts, the Belarusian side is intentionally dragging out the adoption of unified customs and tax legislation. Such customs policy caused damage to Russia in the amount of about $1.5 billion.[29]

Russian business circles did not have a great influence on the development of Belarus' private sector. This is, first of all, because the investment climate in Belarus turned unfavorable for entrepreneurs. Even in those rare cases in which Russian entrepreneurs bought up control packages of shares of Belarusian enterprises, they soon became convinced that it would be better to sell them.[30]

It should be taken into consideration that, as a whole, direct foreign investments in the Belarusian economy are very small: $270 million for the entire 1992–1998 period or $27 per capita. By way of comparison, the corresponding figure in Poland was $532 per capita; in Estonia, it was $527. Direct investments, together with credits for the above-mentioned period totaled $2.2 billion. As a result, the collective investment fund of all foreign enterprises and joint ventures (including Russian) in 1993 totaled $100.4 million; in 1996, this was reduced to $50 million. Russian gas (Gazprom) and oil companies have repeatedly tried to obtain shares of property in pipelines, in oil-processing plants, in production of mineral fertilizers ("Azot," Hrodna) and some other enterprises. In spite of prolonged negotiations

---

[29] "Politicheskoe i èkonomicheskoe razvitie respubliki Belarus. Perspektivy rossiisko-belorusskoi integratsii." Institute of CIS (Moscow, February 1997).

[30] T. Manenok, "Kooperatsiia ne poluchilas'," *Belorusskii rynok* 41 (1997).

with Gazprom and promises by the Belarusian government to make Beltransgas (Belarus' gas transportation monopoly) a joint-stock company with the aim of transferring a part of the shares in exchange for the gas debts, these efforts have not borne fruit.[31]

Russian oil companies are interested in acquiring the property of Belarusian oil-processing plants, oil pipelines, and oil product sales systems. In 1993, before Lukashenka came to power, the oil-processing plant in Mazyr [Mozryr] was converted into a joint-stock company. Now, 43 percent of the shares of this plant belong to the Russian-Belarusian joint venture Slavneft. As for another oil-processing plant (Navapolatsk [Novopolostk]), in spite of its being in dire need of reconstruction (the state does not have the necessary funds for this purpose), it has not been privatized.[32]

The only Russian company that has managed to acquire and create its own objects on Belarusian territory is the oil company LukOIL. This company has invested about $30 million, mainly into the Mazyr oil-processing plant and refueling stations (most notably into the creation of its own network of service stations).

The presence of private enterprises, including Belarusian ones, in the oil product distribution network has favorably influenced the oil product market. In winter of 1998–1999, with shortages of gasoline and diesel fuel and long lines at state refueling stations, these products could be bought at private stations at higher prices.

In short, it can be said that with Lukashenka's rise to power the influence of Russian capital on the formation of a private sector in Belarus has become minimal. The influence of those Russian political circles who reject the values of a market economy and democracy is much stronger. The strengthening of Belarus' trade relations with Moscow can be mentioned as an example. In 1998, Moscow's share in the total volume of Belarusian exports to Russia totaled 29 percent; by 1999, this had risen to 34 percent. Moscow buys a great deal of equipment for communal services (trolleys, buses, elevators, etc.) from Belarus. It is reasonable to suppose that this process has been assisted by Moscow's mayor Yuri Luzhkov, whom Lukashenka considers to be a friend. The Moscow press charges that Luzhkov has equipped the city's communal services to the detriment of its budget

---

[31] V. Mahovsky, "'Beltransgas' trebuet den'gi," *Belorusskaia delovaia gazeta* 7 September 1998.

[32] This topic is discussed in length in Chapter 7 of this volume.

(Belarusian equipment is more expensive than Western products of similar quality). From this point of view as well, Lukashenka encourages the suppression of the private sector in Russia itself, because he reinforces the influence of Leftist political forces there.

Influence of the West

The influence of the West on the formation of a market economy in Belarus has been felt mainly via three channels. First, via the inflow of direct investments and credits to the private sector; second, via the influence of international financial organizations; and, third, via the training and retraining of personnel.

The role of foreign direct investments in the development of small and medium-sized private enterprises in Belarus has been limited. In 1996, for example, per capita direct investment in Belarus was only $2 (vs. $68 in Latvia, $60 in Poland, and $117 in the Czech Republic). The climate for foreign investments as a whole is unfavorable. According to the investment ratings published by the journal *Institutional Investor* in 1997, Belarus was in 118th place among the 135 countries under consideration. Researchers also note the capital flight from Belarus and the outflow of foreign capital.[33] The number of joint ventures in Belarus, for example, declined from 455 in 1994 to 147 in 1996, while the number of foreign enterprises more than halved from 262 to 126.

Due to the unfavorable investment climate, of all the credit lines intended to foster the development of the private sector, only one has remained open for Belarus—that of the European Bank for Reconstruction and Development (EBRD). Its attempts to encourage the development of small private enterprises by way of giving small hard currency credits have yielded practically nothing. In 1994, a sum of only $30 million was allocated for these purposes. But by the end of 1998, this money had not been expended. First of all, under the government's populist currency policies, exports are unprofitable and there are practically no hard currency-repaying projects. Besides, about 60 percent of the enterprises involved cannot fulfill requirements to fulfill the pledges they make.

---

[33]   "Development of the non-state sector of economy and investment climate of the Republic of Belarus," UN Development Program. Project RER/95/03c. Informational analytical report (Minsk, 1997).

Within the framework of the UN development program, there is at present a project for the creation of business incubators for small enterprises. This undertaking is small, however, and cannot be expected to have a noticeable influence on the development of the private sector in the foreseeable future.

After Lukashenka's ascent to power, international financial organizations lost their influence on Belarus' economic development. Neither the IMF nor the World Bank has allocated any credits since 1996. The IMF mission and the World Bank's representative have left Belarus.

Now that the period of the growth of the Belarusian economy (1996–1998) at the expense of short-term resources is over, the government is in dire need of foreign credits. Under these conditions, the government can agree to partial fulfillment of foreign requirements in order to obtain these credits (liberalization of currency rate and prices, privatization of individual objects).

One of the few positive results of the influence of international organizations has been the improvement of the education of managers who have undergone training or participated in internships abroad. These specialists are now adherents of market reforms. It is desirable to continue the training of the government staff. This is the future elite of the country.

The credits provided by the IMF, the World Bank, and other organizations have had few positive results in terms of the development of the private sector. These monies were used for solving current problems in the state sector. For example, from $100 million in System Transformation Funds (STF) credits, $20 million was used to cover the losses of only one facility–the Minsk Tractor Factory.

In many experts' opinions, the most desirable form of support for private enterprises, instead of credits to the government, would be the creation of a private fund for the support of entrepreneurship, with the participation of Western partners interested in private sector development in Belarus. In addition, it should be taken into account that there are few private enterprises in Belarus and that those that have been newly created cannot provide the required level of pledge liabilities. The reduction of pledge liabilities is one of the main conditions of private sector development.

Formation of the "German" Model of Socialism

Once in power, Lukashenka could not immediately change the flow of economic processes according to the demands of "ordinary" people. This was because he had to rely on the former state bureaucracy and had to take into account their understanding of market reforms. When he invited Chyhir to become his Prime Minister, for example, Lukashenka promised him the freedom to make economic decisions on his own.[34] The program to extricate the nation from the crisis that arose from Lukashenka's instructions in 1996 reflected the lobbying interests of different groups of the nomenklatura (industrialists, agrarians, bureaucracy). At the same time, it contained a number of measures on economic liberalization and financial stabilization. In 1994–1995, the National Bank managed to stabilize the Belarusian ruble exchange rate and even to accumulate hard currency resources. This helped to draw in foreign investments.

In 1996, however, the situation changed. Three lobbying groups formed around the Presidential Administration: the construction lobby (represented by Piotr Prakapovich, now chairman of the National Bank); the industrial (represented by Mikhail Miasnikovich, head of the Administration); and the agrarian lobby (represented by the president himself). These lobbies reflect the interests of large state enterprise directors and chairmen of collective farms and oppose market reforms as possibly leading to a redistribution of power and property. Under their influence, a "Program of Socio-Economic Development for Belarus up to the Year 2000" was adopted, the main priorities of which became the interests of the main lobbying groups (food, residential construction, export-oriented industry).

In 1995–1996, a considerable number of heads of state institutions, including the army, the KGB, and the Ministry of Internal Affairs, were changed. Having strengthened his position, Lukashenka began to limit the freedom of entrepreneurship more decisively. As early as 1996, privatization had practically been stopped (except for a small number of objects of trade and services). By one of his decrees, for example, the president united a joint-stock company with a state bank (Presidential Decree No. 340 of 30 August 1995). Another presidential decree reduced the share of private shareholders in the authorization fund of commercial banks (Presidential Decree No. 209

---

[34] M. Chyhir. "Otkrytoe pis'mo gr. Lukashenko," *Narodnaia volia* 28 August 1999.

of 24 June 1996) by several times. Beginning in 1997, the president has determined the "forecast" indices of economic development that are interpreted by the executive power as directive tasks. Since 1998, these decrees have determined the limits of monthly growth of prices as well. Both state and non-state enterprises are obliged to follow these indices.

Lukashenka has gradually created unfavorable conditions for entrepreneurship. Regulations constantly change. In addition, changes are often introduced with retroactive force or enter into force the very day of their (often unexpected) announcement, creating chaos that leads to the bankruptcy of many firms. One of the recent hard blows to the private sector was the president's telegram to regional executive committees directing them not to register private enterprises if, in their charters, there is no subsidiary responsibility for the founders, that is, if the charters do not spell out the founders' legal responsibility to cover the debts of the enterprise with their own personal capital.

Those leaders of private enterprises who tend to be obstinate are thoroughly inspected by the tax authorities; sometimes they are arrested and held in prison without formal charge for prolonged periods. Under these conditions, directors of private enterprises are likely to obey all government orders, without particular regard to their legality. In the autumn of 1998, for example, when the rates of growth of industrial production volumes became lower than those that had been established by the presidential decree at the beginning of the year, directors of private enterprises along with the leaders of state enterprises were called to the local executive bodies to explain the reasons for the reduction.

Besides the payment of taxes, private enterprises are continuously subjected to extortion: for the building of sports facilities, for food purchases, for the spring sewing campaign,[35] etc. Directors of private enterprises cannot refuse to make such "donations" without the risk of getting into difficulty. In January–March 1999, commercial banks found themselves in such a situation when they were obliged to allocate large credits to collective farms, at negative interest rates. It was known beforehand that most of these credits would never be returned.

---

[35] This is the period during the spring when Belarusian farmers undertake their sewing chores. This work requires fuel for tractors and, thus, large sums of money.

As a rule, entrepreneurs cannot find protection in the courts since, according to the Constitution of 1996, the president appoints all judges in the country. Thus, since 1996, Lukashenka has created what could practically be called an "ochlocratic" economic model, similar to that existing in Nazi Germany in the 1930s. The economist Ludwig von Mises called it the "German type" model of socialism. In this model, the notions of "ordinary" people on the functioning of the economy are realized.

The Private Sector in Belarus:
Possible Scenarios of Economic Development

The possibilities of private sector development depend, to a decisive degree, upon the choice of the economic model of development.

An analysis of systems of values and material interests of different groups of Belarusian society, of Belarus' experience in the years since independence, and of the experience of economic reforms in Russia shows that development of the Belarusian economy could take place according to three possible scenarios or models (according to Tatiana Zaslavskaia's classification).[36]

1) The "ochlocratic" model, that is, a model that corresponds to the ideas of "ordinary" people on the functioning of the economy. ("Ochlocracy" literally means "mob rule.") If the control of the economy falls into the hands of such "ordinary" people who are not cognizant of the great complexity of the economy and who try to govern with the help of "ordinary" methods (which is what happened in Belarus), then the "ochlocratic" economic model is formed. Cuba or North Korea are examples of this.

In Belarus, Lukashenka, his electorate, and the key figures of his team making strategic decisions in the name of the interests of "ordinary" people are the force that is dragging Belarusian society to an "ochlocratic" model of development. With this model, there can be no real development of the private sector.

---

[36] Tat'iana Zaslavskaia, "Real'na li democraticheskaia pereorientatsiia nashei ėkonomiki?" *EKO (Ėkonomika i organizatsiia promyshlennogo proizvodstva)* 1997 (11): 25.

2) The "oligarchic" model. Belarus (as well as Russia) developed according to this model before Lukashenka's election in 1994. Development according to this model corresponds to the interests of the bureaucracy, directorate, and nomenklatura entrepreneurs. In this model, the private sector is developed, but competition is suppressed, the economy is inefficient, the polarization of incomes is large, and the political system is unstable.

3) The "democratic" model. Similar models function in developed capitalist countries. The adherents of this model are representatives of small and medium-sized business, skilled workers, and the most educated strata of society. From the point of view of the efficiency of the economy and of raising the level of social development, this is the most attractive model.

If economic decisions were made only by "ordinary" people, the Belarusian economy would develop according to the Cuban model. As things stand today, however, Lukashenka cannot restore a command economy. He has to rely, although only partially, upon the bureaucracy that was formed before he came to power. This group of people is interested in the preservation of the private sector that was formed earlier as the source of its illegal income. Nomenklatura entrepreneurs are interested in the preservation of market economic forms as well. This is why the president has to tolerate the existence of a private sector. In Belarus, as a result, an economic model similar to the "German model" of the 1930s has taken shape. In this model, private property exists formally, but in its functioning it is, in reality, subject to commands from the political center. The fact that Belarus is a country with a small, open economy and is surrounded by countries with market economies also is important. This is why it is simply impossible to restore the command-administrative system in its previous form in Belarus.

The model existing in Belarus is unstable. If Lukashenka were to remain in power for a rather long time and if the Left were to come to power in Russia, the private sector would be suppressed as, for example, Stalin suppressed the private sector in the USSR at the end of the 1920s. Another possibility would be that the bureaucracy, which is currently suppressed, will find a way to replace a president who does not please it.

Will economic necessity force the president to liberalize the economy, as occurred during the Kebich government in 1992–1994? Most likely, no. This is because the values of Lukashenka himself, as well as those of his closest associates, are deeply conservative and are based on emotions more than on analysis. These values are more stable than those of communism. It is possible that, with the aim of getting credits, the government will implement some of the IMF's recommendations for at least a while. But it is unlikely that Luka-shenka will reject his populist economic policy together with his convictions and his electorate.

Will the impoverished population get out into the streets to demand market reforms? Most likely, no. This is because the preferences of the population are rather anti-market. Besides, Lukashenka's policies have achieved equality—in poverty. As is well known, any reduction of income differentials diminishes the probability of revolution.[37]

In Belarus, however, there is still the high probability of a transition to a market economy through democratic means. An analysis of the Belarusian electorate carried out by Professor Oleg Manaev, director of the Independent Institute of Social, Economic and Political Studies (IISEPS) on the basis of 1994–1999 national polls gives reason for such hopes.[38] Sociological polls show that since 1994 the number of supporters of market reforms has been growing gradually. In June 1994, for example, those who were for a "market economy with slight state regulation" made up 30.4 percent of those polled; by November 1999, this had risen to 40.5 percent. Faithful Lukashenka disciples, that is, those who share his system of values and views, made up 20 to 25 percent of the electorate in 1999. The rest of Lukashenka's electorate are either people with a mixed system of values or the "socially dynamic type" who have yet to find their leader (about 20 percent). The number of people of this type is declining in Lukashenka's electorate and is being replaced by adherents with an anti-market and egalitarian mentality who for some reason did not vote for Lukashenka earlier.

---

[37]   Cf. the ideas expressed in Pitirim Sorokin "Hunger and Ideology of the Society" (in Russian: "Golod i ideologiia obshchestva," in his *Obshchedostupnyi uchebnik sotsiologii. Stat'i raznykh let* [Moscow, 1994]).

[38]   Oleg Manaev, "Po tonkomu l'du," p. 5; idem, "Belorusskii ėlektorat: Za i protiv prezidenta," *IISEPS NEWS* 1998 (1). See also *IISEPS NEWS* December 1999 (4).

Lukashenka can become, as Manaev notes, "a hostage of his black and white electorate and can preserve his influence only by satisfying more and more primitive and aggressive expectations." Along with such a development, social polarization will increase.

Hard-core adherents of a liberal market economy (the "democratic" model) make up about 20 percent of today's electorate. This is the most active and educated part of the society.

The mentality of approximately 50 percent of the electorate represents a conflicting system of views and expectations. Their behavior is unpredictable. This part of the electorate is not interested in a renaissance of Belarusian culture, nor do they express any aspirations for a return to the socialist past. This part of the society is mostly interested in future stability, and this is why economic education and the propagandizing of market values can influence its position. Support of market reforms by this hesitant part of the electorate can also be reinforced by propaganda pointing to the positive changes in the life of the residents of countries that neighbor Belarus and that are going along the path of reforms (the Baltic countries and Poland, for instance). This part of the electorate can become a resource for redirecting society, through democratic means, toward private property, a market economy, and democracy.

Moving in the direction of the "ochlocratic" economic model, Lukashenka is acting not only against the interests of adherents to the "democratic" model. He also has impinged upon the interests of adherents to the "oligarchic" model and even against the interests of the "nomenklatura" entrepreneurs. The June 1999 arrests of the well-known director of a metallurgical plant and a leading "nomenklatura" entrepreneur showed once again that, in Belarus, nobody is protected against the tyranny of the dictator.

A widening rupture is emerging in Lukashenka's relationship with the leaders of agricultural enterprises who supported him earlier. The arrest of well-known agrarian reformers meant the end of those agricultural leaders' hope for beneficial (for them) change in that sector. As a result of the deepening economic crisis, state allocations to agriculture have been reduced. More than 50 percent of the nation's agricultural enterprises are unprofitable and are continuing to fall into even more dire straits. At the same time, they have to comply with unrealistic and increasingly rough commands from the president, and this, of course, only exacerbates their situation. This is why farms ignore commands from above. At a September 1999 meeting of the

Ministry of Agriculture and Food, for instance, it was noted that "governmental directives and even Presidential Decrees in some places are simply being ignored."[39]

There are growing contradictions between business and state elites, on the one hand, and the narrow circle of people around Lukashenka who govern the country, on the other. As an example, the conclusion that was reached at a meeting of the Council of Ministers at the end of August 1999 should be noted. At this meeting, it was claimed that the policy of currency regulation carried out by the National Bank lies at the root of the economic crisis. In addition, it is widely acknowledged that the present incompetent currency policy is personally dictated by the president and that the chairman of the National Bank, Prakapovych (by the way, a construction engineer by education and work experience), is not at fault. But the very fact that this "protest" took place, and its form, is very telling of the growing contradiction between business and state elites.[40]

Even Lukashenka's cultural differences with the elite of the society and his closest advisors (inability to speak, roughness and boorishness in addressing subordinates, etc.), while strengthening the president's unity with "the people," nonetheless create tension in relations between him and the elites and subordinates around him.

Generalizing, it could be said that it is highly probable that the current authoritarian regime in Belarus will change. The decline in the standard of living will reduce Lukashenka's electorate. Because tensions already exist between the president and business interests, the political and cultural elite can influence matters so that, once an election is held, the election commission may decide against manipulating the results in Lukashenka's favor.

There will be real prospects for the development of the private sector only if there is a change of the established regime. The most likely possibility is that, after such a change, Belarus will go along the path of "oligarchic" capitalism and a movement for the formation of a "democratic" model will grow within the society.

---

[39] "Resoliutsii pravitel'stva ne osuzhdaiut'sia, a vypolniaiut'sia," *Belorusskaia niva* 7 September 1999.

[40] "Strasti vokrug koshel'ka," *Sovetskaia Belorussiia* 28 August 1999.

Leonid Zlotnikov

Supplementary Tables[41]

Table S1. Differences in views of respondents depending on place of residence (in percent)

	Hrodna region	Mahilioŭ region	Belarus
For market economy with small state regulation:	40.5	19.3	30.4
For planned economy:	17.9	43.8	30.3
Hopes for emerging from the crisis are connected:			
With the president of the republic	40.2	61.8	50.7
With Belarusian entrepreneurs	14.2	7.7	15.8
With heads of state enterprises			
With state farms, collective farms	11.2	27.6	19.6
With the help of the West	28.2	10.4	16.6
Must not be in private property:			
Large enterprises	17.6	44.5	32.1
Banks	19.9	49.1	30.4
Agricultural lands	16.4	39.6	32.5
Transport, communication, power engineering	29.5	49.6	35.3
Medical establishments	31.2	54.4	41.1
Schools	37.8	52.2	39.4
Economically more effective property:			
State	39.7	60.5	44.0
Private	53.8	33.1	48.3
Responsibility for worsening of the economic situation lies with:			
President of the republic	70.0	34.5	49.3
Local authorities	23.5	13.3	25.2
Mafia	16.0	51.0	35.6

[41] All data from IISEPS. In the nation-wide polls conducted by IISEPS from which the results are used in this chapter, 1490–1500 people over the age of 16 were polled. See Oleg Manaev, "Po tonkomu ľdu."

	Hrodna region	Mahilioŭ region	Belarus
Inhabitants of Belarus live worse than the people in the West because they are less industrious:	2.2	11.2	6.2
The following type of economy is preferable:			
As in the former USSR	15.8	27.6	27.5
As in Poland or the Baltic countries	19.2	2.2	6.9
As in today's Russia	0.0	0.9	0.9
As in today's Belarus	4.1	5.8	4.2
As in Sweden, Denmark	13.9	18.1	19.5
As in the United States	10.2	10.6	10.3
Integration with Russia can improve economic situation in Belarus:			
Yes	40.2	59.3	53.6
No	19.8	3.4	11.6
Choice of social services (education, health care, etc.):			
Free of charge, without choice, with low level of service	53.9	62.6	51.4
For money and choice according to the quality	44.5	28.9	46.5

Differences in moral values

	Hrodna region	Mahilioŭ region	Belarus
What do you feel is needed for a happy life:			
Family	66.6	50.0	60.3
Conscience	48.5	34.5	42.6
Human rights	31.0	37.7	43.2
Money	39.9	47.1	47.7
Spirituality	31.5	17.5	27.9
Property	13.3	20.8	21.2
Collectivism	0.9	17.8	10.1
Freedom	0.1	6.2	3.9
Individualism	8.4	2.3	4.8

Leonid Zlotnikov

	Hrodna region	Mahilioŭ region	Belarus
Usury is:			
Normal useful activity	35.4	19.6	32.6
Dishonest, parasitic kind of earning	35.4	47.4	38.6
Honest sources of income are:			
Salary	68.8	79.5	74.0
Unemployment allowance	17.0	26.3	20.1
Interest on money kept in the bank	24.3	43.4	29.4
Income on shares			17.7
Money received from the lease of flat	16.1	19.3	15.8
Entrepreneurial profit	14.7	14.8	16.4
All above-mentioned incomes are honest	35.0	19.5	28.3
The following characteristics in people are valued the most:			
Ability to take into account views and convictions of others	40.6	20.9	39.0
Faith in God	61.6	18.5	30.6
Tolerance	34.3	17.8	27.2
Charity	11.4	7.2	12.1
Ability to fight difficulties	39.2	29.2	35.9
State must help:			
Young people	30.9	19.9	30.8
Families with many children	67.2	30.3	46.1
All who have low income	46.5	28.6	42.1
(invalids, the elderly)			75.1
In social life what is valued the most:			
Guarantees of human social rights (access to Education, health care, etc.)	53.1	69.2	64.9
Equality of all citizens under the law	51.1	63.9	61.3
Freedom of choice of convictions and behavior	30.1	21.3	27.1

	Hrodna region	Mahilioŭ region	Belarus
In social life what is valued the most (con't):			
Non-interference of the state with the private life of citizens	12.8	21.2	23.0
Legality of power	38.5	51.0	38.0
Righteousness of power	30.1	19.9	19.0
Wealth	13.9	14.3	16.9
Attitude to political life			
If elections were held tomorrow, Luka-shenka would be elected president.	36.3	64.1	45.4
Expansion of NATO to the East represents a threat:			
Yes	15.7	33.7	31.2
No	21.4	9.6	20.1
Belarus and Russia must unite into one state.	12.5	22.7	16.3
In reality, integration of Russia and Belarus must include:			
Absence of border between countries	65.7	65.7	65.5
A common outer border guarded together	28.5	56.3	36.7
A common president	8.6	26.1	12.6
A common currency	30.2	51.0	41.9
Common laws	14.9	36.9	29.3
Would like to live:			
In Belarus	62.5	59.0	
In Poland	11.6	0.0	
In the former USSR	2.2	6.7	
Belarus must be a sovereign state.	88.5	82.0	85.4

Table S2. Differences in respondents' views depending on their education (percent)

	Up to 4 years	Up to 8 years	Secondary school	Secondary specialized school	Higher educational establishment
How much, in your opinion, should the head of an enterprise get in comparison with other employees:					
At the level of average salary of employees	25.5	24.9	15.4	13.5	6.2
2 times higher than on average	34.7	41.8	41.3	42.3	34.1
3–5 times higher than on average	14.3	13.4	19.3	18.5	29.4
6–10 times higher than on average	4.6	5.1	4.9	4.0	9.1
What must, in your opinion, the price of a product be determined by:					
Expenditures on its production	25.2	24.2	34.0	33.8	38.0
Supply and demand	4.6	16.6	25.8	30.0	36.9
Established by the state proceeding from the interests of the population	26.6	39.0	27.1	26.1	16.1

	Up to 4 years	Up to 8 years	Secondary school	Secondary specialized school	Higher educational establishment
What is your attitude to usury—lending money at interest:					
It is a normal useful activity	17.4	25.9	35.7	36.6	45.0
It is a dishonest, parasitic way of earning money	44.0	49.4	35.6	35.8	28.3
How do you explain the growth of prices:					
The state does not exert control	39.4	45.3	40.1	36.2	33.2
Enterprises increase prices	36.3	24.6	18.3	20.5	19.5
The state prints excessive money	10.4	12.7	26.2	22.6	35.0
Enterprises' expenditures increase	—	17.8	24.5	22.3	28.6
High taxes	17.4	37.3	36.9	46.3	53.3

Table S3. Differences in respondents' views depending on the type of populated area (percent)

	Minsk	Regional cities	Large cities	Small towns	Villages
How much, in your opinion, should the head of an enterprise earn in comparison with other employees:					
At the level of average salary of employees	13.4	10.6	9.2	17.9	23.5
2 times higher than on average	31.8	34.8	45.9	39.7	43.5
3–5 times higher than on average	25.9	29.6	18.0	14.7	13.0
6–10 times higher than on average	5.4	7.8	5.8	3.7	4.8
What must, in your opinion, the price of a product be determined by:					
Expenditures on its production	29.7	31.6	30.7	28.1	35.2
Supply and demand	32.3	35.0	29.7	20.6	12.5
Established by the state proceeding from the interests of the population	20.0	19.6	19.1	34.7	31.9
What is your attitude to usury—lending money at interest:					
It is a normal useful activity	41.9	30.2	39.0	36.1	24.5
It is a dishonest, parasitic way of earning money	33.6	37.0	39	29.5	47.7
How do you explain the growth of prices:					
The state does not exert control	31.7	34.7	32.5	42.1	44.9
Enterprises increase prices	18.4	22.9	21.9	17.8	28.7
The state prints excessive money	32.5	27.6	40.6	12.5	10.0
Enterprises' expenditures grow	25.4	29.3	16.9	15.7	15.5
High taxes	59.8	39.3	34.0	34.6	29.6

Table S4. Electoral Support for Lukashenka

Socio-Economic Status	Would vote for Lukashenka tomorrow	
	Yes	No
Level of Income:		
Poverty	52.2	47.8
Below average	44.0	56.0
Average	43.2	56.8
Above average and high level	34.5	65.6
Do present-day incomes allow you to eat normally:		
Do not allow	50.5	49.5
Hardly allow	48.6	51.4
Quite allow	34.5	65.5
Do present-day incomes allow you to purchase necessary clothes and footwear:		
Do not allow	54.4	45.6
Hardly allow	42.7	57.3
Quite allow	27.4	72.6
Do You Have Property (Land Area, Sales Equipment, Car, Tractor, Etc.) used for Earning Money:		
No	48.3	51.7
Yes	38.0	62.0
Change in Material Circumstances:		
Worsened	46.9	53.1
Improved	58.9	41.1
Change Of Economic Situation in the Country During the Past Year:		
Worsened	37.8	62.2
Did not change	43.9	56.1
Improved	58.3	41.7

6

Margarita M. Balmaceda
Belarus as a Transit Route: Domestic and Foreign Policy Implications

Introduction: Transit as a Belarusian Metaphor

The issue of transit lies at the intersection of several broader theoretical questions. Through understanding transit of goods across borders, we can understand the larger questions in post-Soviet societies concerning (1) the relationship between domestic and foreign policies; (2) the interaction of domestic and foreign interest groups; and, (3) the effect of economic factors on international relationships. An examination of transit issues in Belarus, in particular, offers interesting insights from each of these perspectives and highlights a number of key features useful for understanding the current regime.

Already half a century ago Albert Hirschman paid attention to the role of transit as a means of building economic power by the transit country itself.[1] Yet, in my view, this is not an unqualified advantage: dependence on the revenue created by transit services may similarly leave a country in a vulnerable position. Belarus' transit situation exemplifies the best and the worst possibilities offered by being a transit country in conditions of an authoritarian regime and a tense regional security situation.

---

[1]   See Albert Hirschman, *State Power and the Structure of Foreign Trade* (Berkeley, 1945), pp. 33–34. For a discussion of the ambiguous role of transit trade in another complex relationship in Belarus' neighborhood, that between Russia and Ukraine, see Paul J. D'Anieri, *Economic Interdependence in Ukrainian-Russian Relations* (Albany, New York, 1999), especially chapters 3 and 5.

Transit is one of the keys to Belarus' future, but also to some of the problems it faces. Transit sheds light, as well, on the hold on power of Aliaksandr Lukashenka, the Belarusian president since 1994. A country twice devastated in this century by wars waged on its territory, Belarus knows from experience the pros and cons of its geographical situation. In this chapter, I shall look at several aspects of Belarus' role in transit, including (1) its effects on Belarus' international relationships with both the East and the West, and (2) its role in either cementing or eventually weakening Lukashenka's hold on power.

Belarus' geographical position is an important element in the geopolitics of the Central-East European area. It has been observed that the much-discussed (but more modestly implemented) Belarus-Russia Union[2] has important implications for regional politics because Belarus' "defection" from a possible "Baltic-Black Sea axis"[3] has damaged chances for regional cooperation. The removal of Russian-dominated Belarus from the picture has had the effect of "cutting off" Ukraine from the Baltic republics.[4] The issue of transit is closely linked to this assessment; as we shall see below, the close strategic relationship between Belarus and Russia also limits the potential for both economic and transit cooperation in the region.

Belarus' geographical location not only has created new possibilities for the country, but it also has allowed the Belarusian economy (and, more specifically, the presidential administration and Lukashenka himself) to access income that has been used, in part, to solidify his personal power. In addition, the transit phenomenon has allowed Lukashenka to increase his power vis-à-vis Russia and some important Russian actors, while simultaneously reflecting certain broader contradictions in the Russian-Belarusian relationship.

Indeed, transit has become a complex and controversial area in the Russian-Belarusian relationship. The transit link with Russia involves

---

[2] On this topic, see Margarita M. Balmaceda, "Myth and Reality in the Belarusian-Russian Relationship: What the West Must Know," *Problems of Post-Communism* May–June 1999: 3–14.

[3] That is, the Zone of Security and Cooperation in Central-East Europe, proposed by Ukrainian President Leonid Kravchuk in 1994.

[4] Taras Kuzio, *Ukraine's Security Policy* (Washington, DC, 1995), p. 80

the transport through Belarusian territory to Russia of at least two commodities: energy, and consumer goods. An investigation of these two issues, using case studies on energy, consumer goods, and transit services, can tell us a lot about the real state of the relationship between Russia and Belarus.

Energy and Politics in the Belarusian-Russian Relationship

Energy resources play an important role in Belarus' transit regime. In turn, energy transit is part of a larger energy picture in which infrastructure, subsidies, and pricing arrangements are important. For this reason, this section starts with a brief description of the larger energy situation.

With few energy resources of its own, Belarus is one of the countries of the Commonwealth of Independent States (CIS) most dependent on Russia for energy supplies. It is even more dependent than Ukraine, relying on Russia for about 90 percent of its energy overall.[5] So far, and despite increasingly frequent threats from Russian energy companies, the country has managed to receive relatively stable oil and gas supplies from Russia at subsidized prices.[6] This subsidy arrangement, to this point, has allowed Belarus to pay for energy mainly through barter.

Energy subsidies from Russia have had a tremendous domestic and political impact inside Belarus. First, low energy prices and easy credit have meant a direct subsidy to the Belarusian economy. According to some estimates, lower prices for energy resources in 1997 earned Belarus $400 to $500 million dollars per year in indirect Russian subsidies.[7]

---

[5]   Ustina Markus, "Belarus, Ukraine Take Opposite Views," *Transition* 15 November 1996: 20–22.

[6]   Estimates vary as to the size of the subsidy. See, for example, Kathleen J. Mihalisko, "Belarus: Retreat to Authoritarianism," in Karen Dawisha and Bruce Parrott, eds., *Democratic Changes and Authoritarian Reactions in Russia, Ukraine, Belarus and Moldova* (Cambridge, 1997), p. 273. What is crucial is not the subsidized price *per se*, but the ability to pay by means of barter.

[7]   Liavon Zlotnikaŭ [Leonid Zlotnikov], quoted in Jan de Weydental, "Belarus: Government Lauds Economic Growth, But Future Uncertain," RFE/RL 18 April 1998. For example, in 1997, for each ton of oil that Russia exported to Belarus through official channels, Russian producers lost $40–$50. (This was because of very

Second, fuel loans, which account for a large part (90 percent) of the reserves of the Belarusian economy,[8] have given the economy much-needed "breathing space." Moreover, thanks to two agreements signed on 2 April 1996 and 2 April 1997, Belarusian debts to Russia, which had stood at about $1 billion, were forgiven "in honor of the establishment of the Commonwealth" of Russia and Belarus.[9] The effect was felt not only by the economy as a whole but by specific factories as well, especially those paying for Russian energy with their own production.[10]

Third, what might be most important in these arrangements is not the low prices themselves, but the potential for conducting trade by barter. Barter accounts for about 50 percent of the total commodity turnover between the two countries[11] and 74 percent of Belarus' energy imports from Russia.[12] Barter is important not only as a means of financing imports from Russia, but also as the key to the perverse functioning of the "Belarusian economic miracle."[13] According to governmental statistics, Belarusian industries pushed gross domestic product (GDP) growth by 10 percent in 1997; even more spectacular results were promised—but not delivered—for 1998.[14] The only

---

low prices charged for the oil supplied to Belarus as part of bilateral intergovernmental agreements with Russia.)

[8]   Tatiana Manenok, "Belarus: Last to Reform," *Minsk Economic News* July 1997.

[9]   Vadim Dubnov, "The New Abroad: Russia-Belarus," *Novoe vremia* 9 March 1997: 23 [in FBIS-SOV-97-061]. Many have seen this debt-forgiveness as Moscow's "thanks" to Minsk for agreeing to the construction to the Yamal pipeline through its territory. See Hryhorii Musiienko, "Why Has Yeltsyn Recalled Kuchma After Falling Out With Lukashenka?" *Vechirnyi Kyïv* 19 September 1997: 1, 4 [in FBIS-SOV-97-266].

[10]   Irina Selivanova, "Ékonomicheskaia integratsiia Rossii i Belorussii i ee vliianie na razvitie narodnogo khoziaistva Belorussii," in D. E. Furman, *Belorussiia i Rossiia: Obshchestva i gosudarstva* (Moscow, 1998), p. 323.

[11]   "'Belorusskoe chudo' svoeobraznoe i opasnoe," *Belorusskaia delovaia gazeta* 23 February 1998: 3, in FBIS-SOV-98-058.

[12]   N. Galko, "Bank 'Imperial' vezhlivo pred"iavil Minsku schet," *Nezavisimaia gazeta* 11 April 1998, quoted in Selivanova, op. cit., p. 324.

[13]   On the Belarusian "economic miracle," see also David R. Marples, "Belarus: Exploring the 'Economic Miracle,'" *Analysis of Current Events* 10(6) June 1998: 4.

[14]   See Robert Lyle, "Belarus: 'Lukanomics' Impacts Economic Decline," *RFE/RL*

problem is that much of this production, financed by cheap government credits and imposed by decree on enterprise managers,[15] consists of outdated, uncompetitive goods for which there is limited demand and which can only be disposed of through barter with Russia.[16] Lukashenka knows full well the advantages of such deals: where else would he be able to sell the thousands of tractors produced by the Minsk Tractor Factory and thanks to which Belarus became—at least on paper—the fastest-growing economy in Europe in 1997? Although in 1997 and early 1998 the Russian side tried to limit the role of barter in this trade, following the August 1998 Russian financial crisis there was more pressure to continue the system.

Yet some barter arrangements have backfired on Belarus. In the wake of the August 1998 crisis, Russia, unable to continue paying for massive food imports from the West, approached Belarus to include items such as eggs, poultry, and dairy products in the barter agreements. As a result, these products, which are subsidized inside Belarus and thus are some of the few accessible to the impoverished population, have periodically disappeared from stores.[17]

Moreover, there have been many disagreements between Belarus and Gazprom (the Russian gas production and export giant) that reflect the larger problems and conflicts in the Russian-Belarusian relationship.[18] Lukashenka prefers to maintain a "unified energy

Newsline (23 March 1998).

[15]   For example, the president's orders in late 1997 to "dramatically increase production towards the end of the year" (Lyle, "Belarus: 'Lukanomics' Impacts Economic Decline").

[16]   The way in which these barter arrangements really takes place defies even the most sophisticated imagination: Belarus owes Gazprom for gas and pays in goods; Gazprom owes the central Russian government for overdue taxes and pays in Belarusian goods; the central Russian government owes the regions for wage and pension arrears and also pays with these same Belarusian goods. See Andrei Makhovskii, "Bol'shoi pokhod na Moskvu ob"iavilo belorusskoe pravitel'stvo," *Belorusskaia delovaia gazeta* 11 December 1997: 6.

[17]   See Andrei Makhovskii, "Gas-for-food deal bodes ill for Belarus, as shortages aggravate," *Minsk News* 17–23 November 1998: 2 [reprinted from *Belorusskaia delovaia gazeta*].

[18]   For more on this topic, see Chapter 11 herein, "Power and the Yamal Pipeline," by Astrid Sahm and Kirsten Westphal.

balance" between Belarus and Russia and, correspondingly, for Belarus to pay domestic Russian prices; however, Gazprom insists on a different price structure for Belarus.

Gas Transit: The Yamal Pipeline and Its Implications for Belarus and Lukashenka's Domestic Power

The most significant factor in gas transit for Belarus is the Yamal pipeline. Of the various new options open to Russia for gas transport, the pipeline merits the greatest attention. This gigantic project was conceived to develop gas fields in Siberia and to transport gas to Western Europe by way of a 6,670 kilometer pipeline passing through Belarus, Poland, and Germany. The total price tag for the project was an estimated $36 billion.

The Yamal pipeline plays an important role in Gazprom's medium-term plans. Once finished, the pipeline will handle an estimated 68 billion cubic meters (bcm) of gas annually. This would allow Russia to double its gas transit to Europe, fitting in well with Gazprom's plans for strategic expansion in Europe.[19]

For Gazprom, the Yamal pipeline offers two advantages: (1) a route to Western Europe shorter than the current one, and (2) 30 percent lower costs than the current route.[20] Therefore, it should not surprise us that Gazprom, concerned about building the Yamal pipeline through Belarus and the stability of subsequent gas deliveries through it, is one of the major lobbyists for a Russian-Belarusian union.[21] Indeed, the union of Russia and Belarus could be a further guarantor of stability in this section of the pipeline. From a Russian perspective, the stability of gas transport through a Belarus linked to Russia by a union treaty is especially appealing in comparison to the definite risks (from a Russian perspective) associated with gas transit

[19]   This topic will be discussed in more detail in Westphal's and Sahm's paper, therefore I will limit myself to discussing Yamal's implications for the Russian-Belarusian relationship and for Lukashenka's power.

[20]   Interview with Aman Tuleev, Russia's Minister for CIS Affairs, on Russian TV, 23 April 1997 [in FBIS-SOV-97-085].

[21]   Valerii Solovei, "Nadezhdy i strakhi rossiiskikh politikov (diskussiia o rossiisko-beloruskom soiuze), in D. E. Furman, *Belorussiia i Rossiia: Obshchestva i gosudarstva* (Moscow, 1998), p. 427.

through Ukraine.[22] In addition to its strategic significance, the Yamal project is also important domestically, not simply for Belarus as a whole, but also for Lukashenka's own power, image, and discourse. There are four main elements of Yamal's significance for Lukashenka:

1. In economic terms, the project means not only an investment of $2.5 billion—quite a significant sum for an economy of Belarus' size,[23] but also employment for over 2,000 Belarusian technicians and specialists. It is worth noting that, in contrast to the pipeline segment being built through Poland, which is a joint investment, the costs of building the pipeline segment through Belarus are being covered fully by Gazprom. (This also means that technically, the pipeline will be the property of Gazprom.)[24]

2. In foreign policy terms, the Yamal pipeline represents support for and a certain embodiment of Lukashenka's view of integration in the post-Soviet space. Lukashenka's warm reception of the Yamal pipeline idea reflected, first, that the project vindicated his official positions in favor of a strengthened CIS, rewarding the advocates of a closer economic union and punishing those countries opposing it. Indeed, Lukashenka felt Yamal was both a good answer and a lesson in response to the uncooperative approach of Ukraine to CIS integration. (Ukraine has refused to join either closer military or customs union agreements within the CIS and has remained lukewarm towards any attempts at closer CIS integration.) Lukashenka's position echoed the views of many Moscow analysts and politicians, who would favor the process of Russian-Belarusian integration because it puts pressure on Ukraine to "adopt a less ideological and more pragmatic foreign policy stance."[25] One must remember that the

[22]   See Margarita Mercedes Balmaceda, "Gas, Oil and the Linkages between Domestic and Foreign Policies: The Case of Ukraine," *Europe-Asia Studies* 50(2) 1998: 257–86.

[23]   "Bankiry uchatsia vyzhivat'," *Belorusskaia delovaia gazeta* 29 December 1997.

[24]   See Vadim Sekhovich, "Zalozhniki truby," *Belorusskaia delovaia gazeta* 29 March 1999: 19.

[25]   Author's interviews, Moscow, 20 March 1997.

Yamal pipeline represents a considerable threat to Ukraine because its presence would reduce Ukraine's role in the profitable system of gas transit from Russia to Western Europe.[26]

3. In terms of the Russian-Belarusian relationship, the Yamal pipeline can be seen as its backbone. As Lukashenka himself stated: "The Yamal-Europe system gives specific substance to the treaty on the creation of the Community of Belarus and Russia and renders the fuel and energy complexes fundamental components of our states' economies."[27] There might be much truth in these words, considering that the Yamal project puts a concrete economic actor— Gazprom—behind the political project and adds a powerful lobbyist to it.

4. Concretely, vis-à-vis Gazprom, some additional factors improve Belarus' position in negotiations with the company: (a) Gazprom apparently still hopes that the Beltransgas company, now owned by the Belarusian government, will be transformed into a share-holding company (allowing Gazprom to buy a stake in it). This would increase Belarus' bargaining power, because Gazprom would have reason to be more accommodating to Belarus. Thus, Belarus would seem to have more leeway on the payments question.[28] (b) A second factor improving Belarus' bargaining position is the very fact of the Yamal gas pipeline being under construction. Indeed, in the fall of 1998, when Belarus did not pay for gas, "Gazprom, keeping this secret from the Moscow 'public,' accepted a request by the Belarusian government and doubled its gas deliveries to Belarus."[29] (c) Belarus is a relatively large consumer of Gazprom's gas (about 17 bcm per year).[30] (d) Finally, given that Gazprom is so closely related to

---

[26]   See Balmaceda, "Gas, Oil, and the Linkages."

[27]   Aliaksandr Lukashenka, remarks on the occasion of the start of work on the Yamal pipeline, in the city of Slonim, Belarus; quoted in *Trud* (Moscow) 30 October 1996: 1–2.

[28]   Andrei Makhovskii, "Zakonchilsia ocherednoi raund peregovorov s 'Gazpromom,'" *Belorusskaia delovaia gazeta* 15 January 1999: 1

[29]   Ibid.

[30]   Semen Novoprudskii, "Tovarishch ne ponimaet," *Izvestiia* 18 March 1999: 6.

Russian governmental policy, to a certain extent, it is simply "compelled to serve the integration ambitions of the two Slavic states."[31] Keeping in mind Lukashenka's contradictory attitudes towards Russia (for example, while loudly proclaiming his desire to create a real and deeper union between the two countries, he is actually deeply suspicious of the Russian leadership, which he often accuses of various acts of "treachery"), the symbolic importance of such elements of power should not be underestimated.

For these reasons, the Yamal project has helped to increase Lukashenka's popularity inside Belarus. Indeed, Lukashenka himself admitted in November 1996 that the pipeline's construction has added some points to his popularity rating.[32]

At the same time, Lukashenka's belief (similar to that held by the Ukrainians some time ago) that "having control over the pipeline" or "sitting on the pipe" would give him some real leverage over Russia may be overstated. The project has repeatedly been delayed, and it is unclear whether Lukashenka will be able to extract as many advantages from it as he originally expected. Moreover, as has been shown in the cases of Slovakia and Ukraine, Russian energy companies (and Gazprom, especially) are very adept at changing and making their transport options flexible enough so as not to be dependent on a single option.[33]

Oil Refining and Oil Transit

Although better known in the West for its role in gas transit, Belarus also plays an important role in oil transit. Today, about half of Russia's oil exports go through Belarus.[34] Here, the Soviet legacy is very important: not only is Belarus the former USSR's westernmost republic, but also some of the USSR's most modern refining facilities are located in Belarusian territory.

---

[31] Ibid.

[32] *Rossiiskaia gazeta* (Moscow) 15 November 1996 [FBIS-SOV-96-222].

[33] On the Slovak case, see Alexander Duleba, *The Blind Pragmatism of Slovak Eastern Policy: the Actual Agenda of Slovak-Russian Relations* (Bratislava, 1996).

[34] Author's interview with Yuri Shevtsov, European Humanitarian Fund, Minsk, 19 December 1997.

Belarus' location is also important in terms of energy alternatives for the region. Had Belarus not "defected" from the embryonic grouping of Baltic-Black Sea countries, the potential for the creation a Baltic-Black Sea corridor would be much more realistic. In perspective, such a grouping, if developed into an economic as well as political partnership, might have created its own energy transport infrastructure and new oil transport possibilities. New corridors through Latvia and Lithuania to the Baltic Sea and through Ukraine to the Black Sea might have created new energy transport alternatives for these countries. This could have had very important implications, because it could mean not only that these countries would break their energy dependence on Russia, but also would become a real source of competition for Moscow in terms of the re-export of Caspian oil to Europe.[35] However, after the building of the Yamal pipeline, "the Baltic-Black Sea corridor becomes divided into two separate directions: Southern and Northern,"[36] limiting these countries' energy options and giving Russia increased possibilities to play one country against another (that is, Belarus vs. Ukraine) in its search for cheaper energy transit possibilities.

One of the pipelines transporting Russian oil to Europe passes through Belarus. Although the amount currently carried by the pipeline is smaller than that carried by the Druzhba pipeline through Ukraine, Ukraine is demanding very high transit tariffs from Russia. Therefore, in oil, as in gas transport, Russia is reorienting itself towards Belarus.[37]

The Oil Refining Sector in Belarus

Belarus' attractiveness in terms of oil transit is compounded by its oil refining capabilities. Belarus had some of the largest and most modern oil refining facilities in the USSR. Its oil refining capacity is comparable to Ukraine's: 11 million tons per year compared to Ukraine's 12 to 12.5 million tons per year.[38]

---

[35]   Selivanova, "Ėkonomicheskaia integratsiia Rossii i Belorussii," p. 317.

[36]   Ibid.

[37]   Ol'ga Romanova, "Farewell of the Slav Woman," *Moskovskie novosti* 19–26 October 1997 [in FBIS-SOV097-303].

[38]   Natal'ia Grib, "Alians 'Lukoila' i 'Slavnefti.' No Comment!" *Belorusskaia*

Yet, even in the overall context of Belarus' "phenomenally growing" economy, oil refining did not look very good in 1997. The president himself reported growth in all regions and branches of the economy, except for the fuel branch, which had problems financing purchases of oil and gas condensate. Production in the Mazyr (Mozry) refinery, for example, went down by 12.5 percent.[39] These problems were primarily caused by the lack of stable oil supplies from Russia. The desire to solve this problem and assure stable oil supplies to keep these refineries in operation is the major reason the Belarusian government has been somewhat flexible in its dealings with several Russian oil companies.

Indeed, this situation has led the Belarusian government to seek new solutions. One solution uses the *davatel'skoe syr'e* system (import–refine–re-export raw materials), which means that raw material is imported to be processed, but is later returned in part or in full to the country of origin. With this new system, after October 1998, the supply of oil to Belarus increased significantly—but this has not meant that more fuel is available for sale.[40]

The crisis in the oil refineries has raised the question of the need to involve Russian oil companies more directly in their work. We shall discuss this issue next.

The Ownership of Refining Companies

Since Belarus' independence, Russian oil companies have been interested in Belarusian oil refining capacities, and here the issue of transit is essential. Cooperation between Belarusian refineries and Russian oil companies could be beneficial for both sides (at least in Lukashenka's assessment). Lukashenka's hopes were based on the following division-of-labor scenario: Russian companies would supply the raw materials, Belarusian companies would refine the materials, and the (expectedly large) sales market would be shared by both. From the perspective of the Russian companies, this arrange-

---

gazeta 18 January 1999: 13.

[39] Lukashenka's speech to the Council of Ministers, 26 January 1998, in *Respublika* (Minsk) 28 January 1998.

[40] Natal'ia Grib, "Deshevyi benzin ne poiavit'sia," *Belorusskaia gazeta* 11 January 1999: 16.

ment could mean good news as they could complete their own technological cycle: "extract oil in West Siberia, deliver some of it to Belarus, and with their local partners, refine it and sell it either on the spot or send it for export, including to Russian regions."[41]

The potential sales market discussed above is very much related to the geographical location of Belarus and the refineries, so here the transit issue is essential. In particular, from the perspective of the Russian oil companies themselves, it is more advantageous to supply the nearby Russian regions with oil refined in Belarus than in Siberia or the Volga region, where many of the Russian refineries are located. Moreover, oil refined in Belarus is easier to export to the West.[42] Access to the European *refined* oil products market is especially important for these companies because this market is seen as more promising than the market for crude oil.[43]

Because of geographical convenience and the potential to "complete the production cycle," Russian oil companies have been keen to acquire full or partial ownership in Belarus' two refining complexes, in Mazyr [Mozyr] and Navapolatsk [Novopolotsk].

Mazyr Refinery

The Mazyr Oil Refinery, located in southeast Belarus in Mazyr, is approximately 200 km from the Polish border and 50 km from the Ukrainian border. The refinery is geographically attractive because it is the westernmost enterprise from which Russian oil products can be exported to Europe.

The Mazyr Refinery was made into a share-holding company in 1993 by the Kebich government, and Russian oil companies have important interests there. In 1994 the Slavneft Joint Company was established as a Russian-Belarusian joint venture. The major stakes are held by the Slavneft Oil Company (based in the Russian Federation), with 42 percent ownership; the Belarusian government, with 42 percent; workers and managers, with 8 percent; and private

---

[41]   "Lukashenka, Serov Discuss Joint Oil Scheme," FBIS-SOV-96-202 [originally in *Rossiiskaia gazeta* 12 October 1996: 5–6].

[42]   Ibid.

[43]   See interview with Belarus Foreign Trade Minister Mikhail Marynich, in *Vo slavu Rodiny* (Minsk) 28 June 1997: 1 [in FBIS-SOV-97-185].

investors holding the final 8 percent. Mazyr represents 15 percent of the total value of the Slavneft Joint Company, and so is an important constituent of Slavneft Joint Company—and, presumably, important to the Belarusian government. Nonetheless, relations between the Belarusian government and the Mazyr leadership have not been smooth. Lukashenka made accusations that although Mazyr belonged to the Slavneft Joint Company, the Russian government sold a large block of stock in the company without consulting Belarus.[44]

Indeed, in part because of its interests in Mazyr, Slavneft Joint Company is considered "one of the tastiest morsels in the upcoming struggle for oil." Yet, at first, its shares were not priced very high, in part because its partial ownership by Belarus was seen as an added risk factor.

The Slavneft Joint Company's potential overwhelms these "minuses," however, and the company is expected to be sold and privatized (that is, a Western or other investor will be found to help with the reconstruction of the factory) very soon. Some of the company's merits are its wide geographical reach (it extracts oil in Russian Siberia and owns an enterprise in Belarusian territory), and its abovementioned important interests in the well-located and attractive Mazyr Refinery.

Naftan Refinery in Navapolatsk

The Naftan Refinery in Navapolatsk (north-central Belarus), one of the objects of discussion between the Belarusian government and the oil companies Yukos and LUKoil, is also important for geographic and transit reasons: (1) its location is closer to Western markets than Russian refineries; (2) two oil pipelines, the Surgut-Polatsk and the Samara-Ventspils, meet there; and (3) the Samara-Polatsk oil products pipeline also passes there. Naftan also became very important for Russia during the 1997 Chechen War, for its output helped to

---

[44]   Interview with Aliaksandr Lukashenka in *Delovoi mir* (Moscow) 18 December 1997: 1, 3. Note that this is another example of the paradoxical way in which Lukashenka deals with Russia. He proclaims a desire to create a meaningful partnership between the two countries, yet he repeatedly accuses the Russian government of various acts of unilateralism and of not working toward a more significant union.

compensate for the loss of the Grozny oil refinery in Chechnya.[45]

In contrast to the Mazyr Refinery, the Naftan Refinery is strictly government property. Indeed, in informal discussions, both members of the Belarusian Supreme Soviet and Lukashenka have expressed the opinion, "We 'gave' [Russian investors] one of the country's most important economic objects [the Mazyr Refinery] and we won't give them another."[46] The Belarusian government has never fully allowed the auctioning of the Mazyr Refinery. The government has repeatedly given the green light, but later retreated. Yet, Russian oil companies expect privatization to happen eventually, and a struggle between LUKoil and Yukos for the refinery "is already beginning."[47] Indeed, the case of Mazyr is one of the clearest examples of Lukashenka's contradictory policies towards Russian capital and investors. In a very frank interview with a Belarusian newspaper published under the title "Russia Is Building People's Capitalism in Union with Us, but without Us," then-Russian Deputy Prime Minister Boris Nemtsov deftly described the position of the Belarusian leadership about a

---

[45] Russian government official, quoted by Moscow Interfax, 3 April 1997 [in FBIS-SOV-97-093]. Belarus and the Navapolatsk Refinery also have strategic and transit importance for the Baltic states. For example, in April 1998, Latvian officials announced they had decided on two options for a crude oil pipeline to the Baltic port of Ventspils, called the "Western Pipeline System" (WPS). In addition to an option to begin the system in Nevel, Russia, the Latvian side was seriously considering the idea of starting the pipeline system from Polatsk, Belarus. The Polatsk option has several advantages, including (1) its construction would be shorter in time and cheaper ($435 million vs. $510 million); (2) it would follow an existing crude oil line; (3) it offers a better rate of return; (4) it would provide a better connection to Samara, a collection point for "eastern and southern oil flows"—WPS President Janis Blazevis, quoted in Spencer Star, "Latvia Narrows Choice on Oil Route," *Platts Oilgram News* 22 April 1998 [through Lexus-Nexus]. Yet, which route will be selected will depend largely on the "degree of interest from Russian oil exporters and the political influence of the countries through which the pipeline will cross"—Ojars Kheris, deputy chairman of Ventspils Nafta, quoted in Star, "Latvia Narrows Choice."

[46] Lukashenka said, "Why should we sell two oil processing plants? After all, property equals power. I won't give it to them, because I need to exercise power," *Belaruskii monitoring* 31 August 1995, quoted in Yuri Drakokhrust and Dimitriy Furman, "Perepetii Integratsii," in D. E. Furman, *Belorussiia i Rossiia: Obshchestva i gosudarstva*, p. 365n62.

[47] Vadim Dubnov, "Fried Bulbs. Dinner is Served," *Novoe vremia* 26 January 1997: 16–19.

union with Russia as a political game: "On the one hand, there is constant talk about economic integration; and, on the other, all possible juridical, administrative and economic obstacles are created to prevent this integration from really happening."[48]

Another issue that has created problems is Belarus' frequent participation in the illegal re-export of Russian oil initially supplied to Belarus at lower-than-world prices. This creates losses for Russian oil exporters, which lose part of their profitable exports to other countries. In 1994, a Russian journal estimated that up to 20 percent of the oil flowing through Belarus' pipelines was illegally repumped (*perekachalsia*) abroad.[49]

Other Energy-related Investments from Russia

In addition to direct investments in the pipeline and refining sectors, Russian energy companies—following their practice in Central and Eastern Europe—have started to invest in various areas of the Belarusian economy, despite a generally negative investment climate and the lack of adequate legislation. This investment is likely related to their desire to acquire long-term positions in Belarus. It would seem as if Russian companies are working to strengthen their positions in those sectors of Belarusian industry that are still strong and useful (e.g., those related to energy and transit), while trying to keep a distance from more unsalvageable aspects of the Belarusian economy (e.g., by avoiding a monetary union).[50]

Gazprom, for example, already owns 30 percent of the stock of the Navahrudski Gas Equipment Plant and is already sizing up Hrodna Azot, a major producer of nitrogen fertilizer—one of Belarus' principal exports. Moreover, Gazprom not only will be the de jure or de facto owner of the Yamal pipeline, but its interest in acquiring control of other parts of the Belarusian pipeline system may lead it to increase its stake in those parts as well.[51]

---

[48] Interview with Boris Nemtsov ("Rossiia stroit narodnyi kapitalizm v soiuze s nami, no bez nas," *Belorusskaia delovaia gazeta* 25 September 1997: 7.

[49] Selivanova, "Ékonomicheskaia integratsiia Rossii i Belorussii," p. 326.

[50] See also Vadim Dubnov, "The New Abroad: Russia-Belarus," *Novoe vremia* 9 March 1997: 23 [in FBIS-SOV-97-061].

[51] Vadim Dubnov, "Fried Bulbs. Dinner is Served."

Another important element of Russia's investments in Belarus has to do with Russian banks, some of which have been allowed to establish branches in Belarus. Here, we are talking about not only Belgazprombank (owned largely by Gazprom) but also other banks, such as Imperial, which have close ties with Gazprom and are part of the system of debt repayment from Belarus to Gazprom. Imperial, for example, has plans to start investing in a broad set of areas, such as wood processing, paper, and fisheries.[52] Yet, at the same time, Lukashenka, in practice, has shut the door on Russian investments in the Belarusian privatization process.

Belarus and Electricity Transit

Belarus' power grid is connected to grids in Lithuania, Russia, Ukraine, and Poland, and imports a significant amount of the electricity it uses. In 1998, Belarus produced 23 billion kilowatt-hours [bKw hrs] of electricity and imported 10 bKw hrs, seven of which were imported from Lithuania and the remainder from Russia.[53] At the same time, for locally produced electricity, Belarus is almost completely dependent on Russian oil, coal, and natural gas to fuel its electric power generation plants.

A very large part of the gas imported from Russia (61 percent) is used to supply Belarusian electric power stations. Belarus seems to have made a political decision to try to limit its electricity imports from Lithuania, even when producing the same amount of electricity at home with imported Russian raw materials is more expensive. Indeed, it costs approximately 45 percent more to produce electricity in Belarus from imported Russian gas than to import it.[54] Therefore, the state could save around $200 million per year by importing electricity directly.[55] While such a policy may not make sense from an

---

[52] Selivanova, "Ėkonomicheskaia integratsiia Rossii i Belorussii," p. 330.

[53] Author's interview with Leonid Zlotnikov, 2 April 1999.

[54] It costs $0.0229 to import 1 Kwhr of electricity from Lithuania, and $0.031 to produce it in Belarus with imported gas. Data from *Belorusskaia delovaia gazeta* 27 October 1999: 6; and author's interview with Leonid Zlotnikov, 2 April 1999.

[55] Andrei Makhovskii, "Tsena ėnergeticheskoi bezopasnosti," *Belorusskaia delovaia gazeta* 27 October 1997: 6.

economic point of view, an explanation can be found in either (1) the government's desire to keep the giant energy-producing stations open at any cost because of national pride and the benefit of retaining this large source of employment, or (2) the Belarusian administration's complex political game with Gazprom. In this game, Gazprom does not want Belarus to diversify its energy sources, while the Belarusian government knows that the more it imports from Gazprom, the more Gazprom will be dependent on Belarus.[56]

At the same time, there have been many problems with Belarus' purchase of Lithuanian energy. Given its lack of hard currency, Belarus must arrange complicated deals: Belarus sells its products to Moscow, Moscow pays Belarus, Belarus pays the intermediary company, and the intermediary pays Letuvos Energii, Lithuania's electricity company. Payments in arrears and huge (and perhaps illegal) profits for the intermediaries are but a few of many complications that have arisen.[57]

Because of these factors, in mid-February 1999, the Lithuanian Seim (Parliament) discussed the question of discontinuing energy deliveries to Belarus. However, it is unclear how this could be realized in practice. Lithuania still has not made its way into Western energy markets, and after Russia refused to buy energy from Lithuania (foremost for political motives), Belarus has remained its only foreign buyer of energy.[58]

Therefore, although Belarus cannot produce electricity for export and actually has to import much of it, its location and infrastructure (Belarus participates in several international projects, such as the Russia–Belarus–Poland–Germany Energy Bridge and the Baltic Energy Bridge) give the country important possibilities in terms of energy transit.

One of these possibilities became known in 1999, when Russia's United Energy Systems (EES) unveiled an ambitious program for the sale of Russian electricity to Western Europe through Belarus and Ukraine. According to EES experts, two factors make this a very real

---

[56]   Ibid.

[57]   Yurii Voloshin, "12 millionov dollarov—kak korova iazykom," *Belorusskaia delovaia gazeta* 22 February 1999: 16.

[58]   Ibid.

possibility right now. First, the liberalization of the European electricity market means that large companies can now buy electricity from foreign countries; by 2005, about 40 percent of electricity consumers in Western Europe will be able to buy electricity from abroad. Second, the arrival of the Green Party in the government coalition in Germany implies that Germany will gradually move away from the use of nuclear power stations.[59]

Belarus could become a necessary intermediary country in the project because West European and Russian electricity use different standards, and it needs conversion. To do this, Russia can either build new converters on the border between the CIS and Central Europe, rehabilitate old converters located on the borders between Hungary and Austria, and Poland and Germany (earlier the COMECON countries used the same standard as Russia, but now they use the West European standard), or move the converters to the western borders of Ukraine or Belarus. The latter would seem be the best and cheapest option, and one that could include Belarus directly. The project could be put in place between 2005 and 2010, with the necessary infrastructure costing around $2 billion. The project might be useful to Belarus because it would funnel in significant investment and offer a way to repay the money it owes to EES for electricity.[60]

Consumer Goods Transit

Transit, Trade, and Customs Agreements in the Russian-Belarusian Economic Relationship

For all the talk about Belarus and Russia being at the vanguard of economic pro-integration tendencies in the CIS, their actual behavior shows quite a different reality. The economic aspects of the Ustav (statute), the basic document of the union of Russia and Belarus, signed on 23 May 1997, have remained mainly on paper. Yet, Belarus still conducts more than 50 percent of its foreign trade with Russia.[61]

---

[59] See Vladislav Kuz'michev, "Chubais vosstanavlivaet ėnergeticheskie sviazi byvshego SSSR," *Nezavisimaia gazeta* 5 February 1999: 4.

[60] "Cherez Belarus proliazhet energomost iz Rossii na Zapad," *Belorusskaia delovaia gazeta* 15 February 1999: 18.

[61] Andrei Makhovskii, "Bol'shoi pokhod na Moskvu."

(See Table 1 for overall trade figures for Belarus.) Statistics about trade with CIS countries are even more dramatic. The proportion of Belarus' trade with the CIS, compared to its trade with the rest of the world, is growing, and now stands at a ratio of 4 to 1.[62]

Table 1
Basic Trade Statistics for Belarus (1996–1997 in US$)[63]

	Total Foreign Trade
1996	$12.0 billion
1997	$12.0 billion

	Negative Balance
1996	$1.2 billion
1997	$1.4 billion

	1997 Trade with Russia
Exports to Russia	$2.5 billion
Imports from Russia	$3.5 billion

Source: Andrei Makhovskii, "Bol'shoi pokhod na Moskvu ob"iavilo belorusskoe pravitel'stvo," *Belorusskaia delovaia gazeta* 11 December 1997: 6. Figures for 1997 are estimates.

After its entry into the Customs Union in 1996, Belarus raised import tariffs to the level of Russia, with the result that imports from "far abroad" were reduced and the production of certain goods (such as tires, TVs, etc.) inside Belarus sharply increased, along with their export to Russia. (For example, from 1995 to 1997, the production of color TVs increased by 60 percent and their export to Russia increased by 27.3 percent.)[64]

Yet, little economic integration has taken place in practice, in great part because of lack of cooperation of the Belarusian government. Agreements on monetary union remain far from

[62]   That proportion has growth from 3.4 to 1 in 1996 to 4.1 to 1 in 1997; E. Konstantin "Belorusskaia igra na rossiiskikh vesakh," *Svoboda* 1 October 1997: 4.

[63]   Andrei Makhovskii, "Bol'shoi pokhod na Moskvu." Figures for 1997 are estimates.

[64]   Leonid Zlotnikov, "Vyzhivanie ili integratsiia?" *Pro et Contra* Spring 1998: 84.

implementation. The first reason for this has been the reticence of the Russian Central Bank to tie the Russian economy to the economy of a country that has followed policies opposite to Russia's, remains largely unreformed, and thus faces very different problems from those faced by Russia. The contradiction here is that, rather than using its relationship with Russia as a stimulus to inch closer to the reform policies pursued by that country, "Belarus is using partnership with Russia as an escape route to avoid any radical changes in the economy."[65]

Despite the lofty words used by Lukashenka to describe the union with Russia, there are some very real problems and unfinished business in the Russian-Belarusian Customs Union, problems that cannot but affect the issue of transit. First, there is no common customs policy for the two countries, as the various customs tariffs have yet to be harmonized. Second, while Belarusian goods pay no duties in Russia, Russian goods transiting through Belarus on their way to the West must pay duties in Belarus.[66] Moreover, Belarus has been able to collect the lion's share of import duties on all goods moving from the West that must cross Belarusian territory before reaching Russia.[67] This occurs even though proceeds are supposed to be transferred to the country where the goods will ultimately be used[68] or divided between the two countries according to a formula that takes into account the type of goods involved and the size and trade turnover of each country. Indeed, Russian authorities claimed that the Russian central budget loses "hundreds of millions of dollars in customs tariffs paid in Belarus for goods . . . ostensibly for use in Belarus, but in fact consumed in Russia."[69]

A third problem in the Russian-Belarusian Customs Union is the lack of coordination of customs policies towards third countries, a situation which might lead to a virtual "customs war." In 1997, for

---

[65] David R. Marples, "Belarus: Exploring the 'Economic Miracle,'" p. 4.

[66] Selivanova, "Ėkonomicheskaia integratsiia Rossii i Belorussii," pp. 325–26.

[67] Marples, "Belarus: Exploring the 'Economic Miracle,'" p. 3.

[68] "FM U.S. Embassy Minsk to Washington," 21 October 1998 [from Business Information Service for the Newly Independent States (BISNIS), at <http://www.itaiep.doc.gov/bisnis/country/981021br.htm>].

[69] Ibid.

example, Belarus brought its customs duties into parity with Russia's and imposed a value-added tax on Ukrainian products. However, without informing Russia, it signed a bilateral agreement with Ukraine, overturning any limits on trade between the two countries. This allowed the unlimited entry of Ukrainian products into the Russian market, unhindered by customs barriers.[70]

Finally and most importantly, the openness of the Russian-Belarusian border and the ineffectual work of the Belarusian customs units have created problems to the point that the phrase "Belarusian corridor" has been coined as a synonym for the passage of smuggled goods through Belarusian territory.

The Issue of Used Car Imports

The issue of used car imports into Belarus provides a good example of some of the ways in which Belarus' (i.e., Lukashenka's) and Russia's interests collide, putting further strains on their customs relationship. After Belarus and Russia established the Customs Union in 1995, Russia insisted on protection for its car manufacturers from the large number of second-hand cars brought into Russia from Western Europe, in particular through Belarus. In response, in April 1997, Belarus imposed restrictive measures, for example, limiting a Belarusian citizen to the sale of only one car every two years. Following this decree, trade in used cars brought from Western Europe sharply decreased, but so did Belarusian government revenues. As a result, in September 1998, the Belarusian government significantly liberalized its laws on the import and sale of used cars. Given the shortage of hard currency and the government's lack of success in getting people to deposit their money in the official banking system, government officials reasoned that allowing people to import cars more freely would increase hard-currency government revenue through vehicle registration fees and customs payments.[71]

With the new regulations, the government of Belarus seems to be more clearly delineating its own economic interests vis-à-vis Russia's. At the same time, this new element makes even more apparent the tremendous threat to Russia represented by the unregulated border

---

[70]   Selivanova, "Ėkonomicheskaia integratsiia Rossii i Belorussii," p. 326.

[71]   "FM U.S. Embassy Minsk to Washington."

with Belarus—the border with a "hole." The new measures (and their potential consequences) also show some of the latent conflicts of interest between Belarus and Russia on this matter.

Official Transit Links and Their Significance

In addition to gas and oil transit, the transit of consumer goods has been very important for Belarus. After 1991, because of unstable relationships with the Baltics and Ukraine, Russia began to reorient its exports transit to move through Belarus. Indeed, the amount of goods transported through Belarus has increased significantly since the beginning of Gorbachev's reforms in the late 1980s. In the last 12 years, truck cargo transit has increased almost 11 times and light vehicle transit by 90 times.[72] This, in turn, has allowed the Belarusian government in Minsk to increase the country's revenues. Keeping in mind that 42 percent of Russia's import-export activity goes through Russia's western border and that 70 to 80 percent of that is linked to transit through Belarus, the importance of this transit for Belarus is readily apparent.[73] According to Belarus' official budget, about one percent of the country's revenues come from transit services.[74] This includes neither indirect transit-related activities, nor illegal transit activities, both highly profitable. Therefore, while the significance of *official* transit links to the official budget is not so significant, the significance of unofficial transit payments, and of these payment to structures close to the president, can be quite considerable.

Effect of the Russian Crises on Transit Links

The August 1998 economic crisis in Russia had important effects on Belarus' transit business, and indirectly, on other parts of its economy as well. First, after the crash, Russia sharply reduced its imports from the West, which led Belarus to lose a large amount of cargo transit revenue. This has had broader implications because "new sources of budget financing need to be sought,"[75] including the sale and barter of

[72] Sergei Vasil'tsov, "Respublika Belarus' namerena poborot'sia za transitnye koridory," *Belarusskaia gazeta* 15 March 1999: 21

[73] Selivanova, "Ėkonomicheskaia integratsiia Rossii i Belorussii," p. 326.

[74] See *Statisticheskii sbornik 1997* (Minsk, 1998).

[75] Viktor Demidov, "All Change in the Economic Front," *Minsk News* 17–23 November 1998: 1 [reprinted from *Belorusskaia delovaia gazeta*].

food products to Russia. The deepening domestic crisis in Belarus is creating new challenges. Cheap, price-controlled food products are becoming harder to find in Belarus as the country repays Russia for gas and oil with Belarusian food products. (Russia itself unable to continue large-scale food imports from the West.) At the same time, prices in Belarus remain lower than in Russia, and many traders make a good profit reselling Belarusian products in Russia.[76] As a result, the customs police have strengthened their control of the border with Russia.

The Russian crisis has had other effects on transit-related aspects of the Belarusian economy. The reductions in imports and cargo from the West to Russia has worsened the situation of Russian truck cargo services and heightened tensions with Belarusian cargo companies. At the end of 1998 and early 1999, there was a virtual war between Russia's Ministry of Transport and Belarusian trucking companies carrying cargo from Western Europe to Russia. This confrontation took place within a broader situation, where "a very hard 'battle' is going on for the control of transit, especially truck transit routes in the east-west and Baltic Sea-Black Sea" directions.[77]

On January 1999, the Russian Ministry of Transport unilaterally decided to require permission for trucks to enter Russia, causing, at one point, 500 Belarusian trucks to be left waiting at the border.[78] (Altogether, about 2,000 Belarusian trucks are involved in international cargo, including shipments between Western Europe and Russia.)

According to some, the reason for these measures was Russia's "jealousy" that the Russian trucking sector has been in crisis since 1996–1997, while the respective Belarusian sector is doing much better.[79] Indeed, Belarusian companies, offering lower prices, have occupied nearly 25 percent of the Russian market in this area.[80] Russia hoped that by creating obstacles for Belarusian companies,

---

[76]   Ibid.

[77]   Vasil'tsov, "Respublika Belarus' namerena poborot'sia," p. 21

[78]   *Minsk News* 26 January–1 February 1999: 1

[79]   Viacheslav Dovnar, president of Belintertrans, a truck shipments company, in *Minsk News* 26 January–1 February 1999: 1.

[80]   *Minsk News* 26 January–1 February 1999: 1

they could get more business themselves. In fact, Russia's measures are creating problems for Belarus. Some West Europeans, fearing Russia will refuse entry to trucks, do not want to give cargo destined for Russia to Belarusian companies. Finally, in late January, the conflict was resolved when Russia's transport ministry was forced to exempt Belarusian trucks from the licensing process.

This is another example of how the so-called "Union of Russia and Belarus" is not really working in the areas where it should. Indeed, this latest crisis is related to broader issues in the Russian-Belarusian trade and customs relationship. In late 1998, the Belarusian side erected police checkpoints on the border with Russia to protect the Belarus domestic consumer market from "unsanctioned food exports to Russia, and Russian customs could not be expected but to react in kind."[81]

Illegal Transit Links and Their Significance

The Use and Abuse of Open Borders

Such is Minsk's relationship with Russia that whatever incipient borders started to take shape between the two countries in the first years after independence were basically abolished by Lukashenka and Russian president Boris Yeltsin in a solemn ceremony in May 1995. Thus, not only can we associate Belarus with the image of a "black hole in Europe," but a hole in a much more literal sense as well: the "hole"—albeit official and sanctified—in the border between Belarus and Russia.

In theory, Russia and Belarus belong to the so-called "Union of Five" Customs Union (Russia, Belarus, Kazakhstan, Kyrgystan, and Tadzhikistan) committed to open and transparent trade borders between member countries. Yet, the existing agreements work to the clear disadvantage of Russia, which loses in trade with an unliberalized Belarusian economy.

The open border was intended to facilitate trade between the two countries, but it has turned into something different, and smuggling is common. One of the ways this happens is that particular "foundations" gain a series of special privileges—legally, through the

---

[81] Ibid.

granting of special customs exceptions, or illegally, by special "under the table" deals—to import profitable consumer goods (vodka and cigarettes, among others) free of duty. The tax exemptions supposedly were intended to cover only the Belarusian market. However, these exemptions can create substantial profits in the following way: the various "foundations" or entrepreneurs import goods duty free. Instead of selling them in Belarus, they export them back through the "abolished" border to Russia. The situation became so critical that, in the summer of 1997, Lukashenka had to create a special interdepartmental commission to strengthen customs controls at Belarus' borders. Yet, when the Russian side decided to contribute to this process by creating special mobile units to work on the Russian-Belarusian border (de facto recreating the border that had been so solemnly abolished a couple of years earlier), "the Belarusian leadership was greatly displeased."[82]

The smuggling of alcohol created some of the most serious problems in the Russian-Belarusian relationship, especially around 1995 and 1996, when Russia was drowning in cheap and low-quality (and thus possibly dangerous) vodka that was smuggled from Belarus, under the name of *Chernaia Smert'* (Black Death).[83] Such large-scale alcohol smuggling was also significant because it signified one of the ways in which Belarus was able to siphon off resources from Russia. Data compiled by Leonid Zlotnikov gives an idea of the size of this operation. From 1995 to 1996, for example, the import of alcoholic beverages to Belarus grew 36 times overall. Imports from the "far abroad" grew 87.8 times.[84] From all this, the amount actually sold in Belarus decreased (the 1996 level was 76 percent of the 1995 level), while the officially accounted-for exports to the rest of the CIS grew only 4.3 times.[85] From this, we can speculate that the missing millions of bottles of vodka went back to Russia.

---

[82]   Selivanova, "Ékonomicheskaia integratsiia Rossii i Belorussii," p. 325

[83]   "Sakharnaia kontrabanda s blagosloveniia ékzarkhata," *Belorusskaia delovaia gazeta* 24 February 1999: 2.

[84]   Leonid Zlotnikov, "Uverennym kursom k 'ziiaiushchim vysotam,'" *Belorusskii rynok* 1 (1997): 13.

[85]   Ibid.

One of the central actors in this scandal was the Torgexpo enterprise, which, in February 1996 alone, imported about $100 million worth of liquor—the equivalent of 10 liters of vodka for every Belarus inhabitant. Torgexpo had a very special deal with the state. All firms, with the exception of Torgexpo, had to pay $4 per dollar in the contract to cover taxes, excise duties, and so forth.[86] Created in August 1995, by November 1995 Torgexpo had been granted heavy tax concessions, most notably the right to bring into Belarus alcoholic beverages valued at $500 million, with the intention of supplying the population's "New Year's Eve needs."[87] According to opposition leader Anatol Liabedzka [Lebedko], however, about 95 percent of the vodka went to Russia. Under a single contract, Torgexpo imported goods (mainly, vodka) valued at $500 million, and as a result, the Belarusian and Russian treasuries lost $2 billion.[88] According to a report by the *Belorusskaia delovaia gazeta*, while visiting Minsk, Russian Vice Premier Valerii Serov told Lukashenka that Belarus has damaged the single customs area to the tune of $4 billion and demanded that the Belarusian border be controlled by Russian customs. The Belarusian president strongly objected to this demand, arguing that satisfying it would undermine Belarus' sovereignty. As a result, in spring 1997, a small customs war erupted between Russia and Belarus. By July 1997, mobile detachments of Russian customs officers were set up on the Russian-Belarusian border.

The smuggling of sugar into Russia has also become one of the most profitable enterprises available in Belarus, and here favors from Lukashenka have also played a role. As part of his well-known policy of establishing a political and ideological relationship with the Orthodox Church, Lukashenka gave the Department of Foreign Relations of the Minsk Exarchate a license to export sugar. In mid-February 1999, the Vitsebsk police intercepted a 60-ton shipment of sugar destined to be smuggled into Russia, which was being shipped

---

[86]   *Komsomol'skaia pravda* 12 October 1996 [in FBIS-SOV-96-201].

[87]   *Ėkspert* 41 (27 October 1997): 27 [quoted in Selivanova, "Ėkonomicheskaia integratsiia Rossii i Belorussii," p. 325]. See also *Izvestiia* 22 February 1996 and 26 July 1996.

[88]   Interview with Anatoli Liabedzka, *Belorusskaia delovaia gazeta* 11 January 1999: 7.

by Kontogrupp, a company using a license "lent" to it by the
Orthodox Church.[89] This is all the more significant considering that
sugar was very hard to find in Belarusian supermarkets at the time.[90]
Moreover, special licenses and privileges such as those granted by
Lukashenka to the Orthodox Church may be the price he pays for the
Church's political support.

The "Hole" and Russian Subsidies to Belarus

The "hole" in the Russian-Belarusian border and how revenue derived
from it is used by Lukashenka to finance and maintain his rule over
the country is part of the broader issue of the subsidies that Belarus
receives from Russia. According to the Institut Ėkonomicheskogo
Analiza, the estimated Russian subsidy of the Belarusian economy is
$1.5–2 billion per year, while Zlotnikov believes the subsidy to be
closer to $1–1.3 billion per year.[91]

According to data from the Institut Problem Perekhodnogo
Perioda in Moscow, the lack of a fully coordinated customs policy
between the members of the Customs Union caused the Russian
treasury to lose $400 million in 1996, an amount deposited instead in
the treasury of Belarus.[92] Moreover, gas debts to Russia continue to
increase at the rate of $300 to $350 million per year.[93]

Another important, but less obvious, Russian "subsidy" to the
Belarusian economy comes in the form of subsidized oil and gas
prices (see above). Belarus received Russian oil and gas at lower-than-
world prices. At the same time, goods exported from Belarus to
Russia (half of them through barter) are more expensive than similar
imports from "far abroad." In 1997, for example, Russia bought sugar
from Belarus at $513 per ton, while the price paid for sugar imports
from other countries was from $307 to $324 per ton. According to
Leonid Zlotnikov's estimates, Russia, by refusing to buy these

---

[89]   "Sakharnaia kontrabanda s blagosloveniia ėkzarkhata," *Belorusskaia delovaia
gazeta* 24 February 1999: 2.

[90]   Ibid.

[91]   Zlotnikov, "Vyzhivanie ili integratsiia?" pp. 84–85.

[92]   Ibid., p. 84. See also Selivanova, "Ėkonomicheskaia integratsiia Rossii i
Belorussii," p. 325.

[93]   Zlotnikov, "Vyzhivanie ili integratsiia?" p. 84.

products cheaper from elsewhere, is in fact subsidizing the Belarusian economy by $200 to $300 million per year.[94]

At the same time, simply talking about a certain Russian subsidy to the economy of Belarus does not capture the essence of the situation. Rather, one should talk about a very particular relationship, where the immediate players (certain interest groups or political actors, such as Lukashenka) benefit, while the way the relationship works creates growing problems for each of the countries involved. It is not Russia alone that is paying higher-than-world prices for its imports from Belarus. Belarus also imports some items from Russia at higher-than-world prices—for example, metal at 1.5 to 1.8 times higher than world prices.[95] What this protectionism has really created are higher prices for the domestic populations and fewer incentives for technological advancement.

Role of Presidential Structures

How much of these subsidies go to finance the Belarus president's own political apparatus? According to Russian experts, much of the Russian revenue loss results from Lukashenka's own appropriation of duty-free Russian-Belarusian transit deals and from the various advantages given by edict to various firms close to him. According to Lukashenka himself, he has signed over 200 such edicts.[96]

In the tax exemption scheme discussed above, every player seems to benefit: Lukashenka's associates make big profits selling the goods in Russia, and the "privatizer," Lukashenka, gets a big cut. Even Russian economist Yegor Gaidar agreed to be quoted on this situation: "Clearly, [sanctions] would punish Lukashenka. Keeping in mind that the 'hole' in the Belarusian-Russian border is one of the most important, if not the most important, source of income for a significant part of Lukashenka's entourage."[97] The only losers are the official Belarusian treasury and Russia. Anatol Liabedzka has calculated that

---

[94] Ibid.

[95] Ibid., p. 93n11.

[96] See Selivanova, "Ėkonomicheskaia integratsiia Rossii i Belorussii," p. 325.

[97] Interview with Yegor Gaidar, in *Svoboda* 11 November 1997: 5.

so far, Russia has lost $3 to $4 billion in unreceived customs revenues thanks to these "fraternal" arrangements.[98]

Moreover, income from the preferential (*l'gotnyi*) transit of goods to Russia is concentrated largely in the hands of Lukashenka and his closest entourage.[99] Lukashenka uses many of these funds for emergency management, thus helping to reduce socio-economic tensions and to support the needs of the most important industries.[100]

Lukashenka's appropriation of murky business deals on the Russian-Belarusian border fits in well with his broader strategy of "privatizing" semi-underworld operations in Belarus for his own benefit and that of his sprawling administration, whose activities are kept off official books. Lukashenka has not only sought to annihilate any potential sources of independent economic power but has also virtually privatized mafia activities in Belarus, either by his own actions or through the actions of his Presidential Administration.[101] Through this activity and the appropriation of power from other parts of the government, the Presidential Administration thus seems to have become an "official shadow government" in and of itself.[102] The

[98]   Author's interview with Anatoli Liabedzka, 22 December 1997. Liabedzka discussed this issue in a series of articles published in the opposition newspaper, *Narodnaia volia*.

[99]   Selivanova, "Ėkonomicheskaia integratsiia Rossii i Belorussii," p. 326.

[100] Ibid.

[101] Indeed, the situation around the Komarovskii market, the largest in Minsk, represents the way Lukashenka's regime has been able to bring various economic groups—inside or outside the law—under his control. In fall 1996, a scandal erupted around the Komarovskii market after it became clear that access to selling stands was controlled by organized criminal groups. In his characteristic style, the president took the matter into his own hands and decided to turn the market into a state company. Yet, as was made clear by a publication in the pro-government newspaper *Sovetskaia Belorussiia*, a year after the clean-up operation, it continues to be almost impossible for ordinary farmers to sell their products there without bribing someone. What has happened? The words used by Pavel Sheremetev to describe the changes in the Komarovskii market following the fall 1996 "cleanup" seem to characterize many other areas of the economy, in particular, transit activities: "There now we have the same re-sellers, the same Mafia, with the only difference that now it has been put there by the government itself." See Igor Klenov, "Strasti vokrug Komarovskogo rynka," *Belorussiia* 16–18 December 1997: 1; and "Moi prigavor uzhe podpisan," [interview with Pavel Sheremetev] in *Belorussiia* 16–18 December 1997: 1.

[102] Vladimir Dorokhov, "Staryi novyi kandidat," *Belorusskaia delovaia gazeta* 5

Belarusian opposition asserts that the size of the Presidential Administration is "commensurate with the country's yearly budget," equivalent to $11.5 billion in 1998. According to Western observers, the amount of money directly available to Lukashenka is closer to $3 billion.[103]

Yet, the Belarusian government has officially recognized the smuggling problem, and smuggling accusations have been behind—or, most likely, been used as justification for—Lukashenka's latest purges in the provinces.[104] It is also well known that the local mafia very much favors maintaining what are essentially open borders between Belarus and Russia (as well as within the customs union, in general), as this facilitates its various smuggling operations.[105]

Transit, Borders, and the Underlying Contradictions in the Russian-Belarusian Relationship

It is worth noting that these phenomenal losses in revenue also mean that Moscow is likely to try to put an end to this situation, with important consequences. First, such a response could affect the openness of the Russian-Belarusian border in general. Russia is already starting to take some measures to "close the hole," establishing control posts on the supposedly nonexistent border with Belarus. The likely effect will be that other, more legitimate aspects of Russian-Belarusian trade and the openness of the border will be affected as well, changing the very flavor of the relationship. Second, a Russian response could have very important effects on Lukashenka's sources of economic support.

Given these dynamics, the transit question uncovers several paradoxes in the larger Russian-Belarusian relationship. One paradox is the way Lukashenka manipulates the relationship with Russia to his

---

February 1998: 4.

[103] Author's interviews, Minsk, November–December 1997.

[104] For example, the March 1999 demise and arrest of the head of the Mahilioŭ [Mogilev] *Oblispolkom* (Regional Executive Council), Aliaksandr Kulichkoŭ [Aleksandr Kulichkov]. See Iva Kashkan, "'Vertikal'shchiki' voruiut i vooru-zhaiutsia," *Belorusskaia delovaia gazeta* 15 March 1999: 1.

[105] See Viktor Ianin, "Tamozhenyi soiuz—'klondaik' dlia mafii," *Belorusskaia delovaia gazeta* 26 February 1999: 3

own advantage. Specifically, he applies a double standard, emphasizing the union when it is convenient for him, and Belarus' sovereignty when that idea is more useful. Semen Novoprudskii describes the dynamic in the economic sphere: "When it is convenient for her, she [Belarus] considers herself a part of Russia (as in the case of gas supplies or the recent 'war' for the Russian truck cargo market). When this is not advantageous, [she] acts as an independent state (for example, unilaterally broadens the use of the US dollar as a payment method in Belarus, or imposes taxes on Russian shuttle traders)."[106] This dynamic works in the political sphere as well.

A second paradox is that while loudly proclaiming his desire to create a real and deeper union between the two countries, Lukashenka repeatedly accuses the Russian government of various acts of treachery and non-partnership, and of not really working towards a deepened union. This is especially clear in Lukashenka's relationship with several Russian energy companies working in Belarus.

A third paradox is that, despite endless declarations about the deepening of the Russian-Belarusian union and the building of a common state, suspicion between the partners is actually increasing and the border is actually closing up, not opening. One point of tension is the question of who will pay for border services currently provided by Belarus that also benefit Russia. For example, although in principle both countries agree that costs should be covered jointly, and Belarus calculated that Russia should have allocated $65 million in 1996 for this expense, only an insignificant amount was received. Belarus covered these expenses largely on its own.[107]

A fourth paradox is the broader question of Russian subsidies to the Belarusian economy and Russia's role in maintaining the differences and even incompatibility between both systems. Paradoxically, the very survival of Belarus' current economic system, so different from Russia's, is made possible by its close economic link with Russia.[108] In all these areas, the issue of transit reflects the

---

[106] Semen Novoprudskii, "Tovarishch ne ponimaet," *Izvestiia* 18 March 1999: 6

[107] Interview with Vasil Shaladonaŭ, Belarusian deputy minister for CIS Affairs, *Zviazda* (Minsk) 25 September 1997: 2 [in FBIS-SOV-97-272].

[108] Selivanova, "Ėkonomicheskaia integratsiia Rossii i Belorussii," p. 327

tensions and contradictions of the Russian-Belarusian relationship as a whole.

Conclusion: Belarus and European Transit Routes

I conclude with some alternative transit possibilities that offer more positive outcomes for Belarus and the region as a whole. In reviewing some of these opportunities, the focus is on why Lukashenka does not support some of these options and how this is related to both his economic policy and his larger world-view.

Belarus' geographic location and its porous border with Russia make the country a prime target for the illegal transit of immigrants and drug smuggling. At the same time, this same geographical location opens a series of more positive transit possibilities. The current political situation, however, prevents Belarus from taking full advantage of these opportunities.

Profitable European Transit Possibilities and Why Lukashenka Fears Them: Transit and Transport Corridors

Despite the difficult state of its economy after the Russian crash, Belarus does possess some characteristics that have the potential to lead to dynamic growth, and many of these features have to do with transit. Although Belarus has no direct access to the sea, its strategic location makes it a "natural transport route between Russia and elsewhere in Europe"[109] In January 1995, the transport ministers of Belarus, Germany, Poland, and Russia met in Berlin to sign an initial agreement on the construction or upgrading of the international route Berlin-Warsaw-Minsk-Moscow, including rail and highway lines. This work would be subsidized by the European Union.

Despite Belarus' advantageous geographical situation, its leadership has chosen not to use the country's transit possibilities vis-à-vis the West and has limited transit links to those involving Russia,[110] thus making the country even more dependent and

---

[109] "Economic and Trade Overview of Belarus," (updated June 1997) [provided by the Business Information Service for the Newly Independent States (BISNIS), at <http://www.itaiep.doc.gov/bisnis/country/belcon.htm>. For "BISNIS Information Service" a new site has been established. See <http://www.bisnis.doc.gov/bisnis/fact.htm>.]

[110] See comments by Prof. M. Dąbrowski [Dombrovskii], Center for Social and

vulnerable to economic fluctuations in Russia. This became evident in the aftermath of the Russian economic meltdown in 1998. As Russia became increasingly unable to afford food and other imports from the West, Belarus lost a large part of its transit business and revenue.

Lukashenka likely would not mind playing the role of "bridge," benefiting from his country's situation as a "transit point" or bridge between East and West, getting investments from the West to modernize production and exporting the resulting products to the Russian market.[111] But this is not likely to work very well, considering that Belarus is the smallest per-capita receiver of Western investment in Central and Eastern Europe and the former USSR, and most of this investment is concentrated in loans and aid programs.

Euroregions and Trans-border Cooperation

Euroregions—trans-border cultural and economic cooperation units established with the support of the European Union—are still in a very early stage of development. However, they still provide some unique opportunities to help Belarus integrate its economy into larger European-wide processes. In the case of Belarus, the issue of Euroregions has been closely linked to the issue of "free economic zones," because both allow for a certain amount of free economic integration with neighboring states. In April 1996, Lukashenka issued a decree on free economic zones, with the first one established in Bierastie. In 1998, two others were established, in parts of Minsk and Homel.

The Neman [Niemen] Euroregion was announced in April 1996 by the Polish and Lithuanian prime ministers, who invited Belarus and Kaliningrad to participate as well. It includes areas around the Neman River basin in Hrodna [Grodno] Oblast (Belarus), parts of Lithuania, Kaliningrad oblast, and northern Poland. The Bug Euroregion is composed of Ukraine's Volyn Oblast and Poland's border counties. In 1995 (or, possibly, even earlier), Ukraine proposed also including Belarus' border oblasts in the Bug Euroregion.

Economic Research (CASE), Warsaw, interview in "Vremia zaderzhalos' v Belarusi," *Belorusskaia gazeta* 27 October 1997: 15.

[111]   Selivanova, "Ėkonomicheskaia integratsiia Rossii i Belorussii," p. 333.

Why Lukashenka Fears These Possibilities

Lukashenka does not want to support or encourage these transit links with Belarus' Western neighbors for two reasons. First, transit links would probably require changes that make economic policy more investor friendly. Lukashenka dreads this possibility, because an open investment policy would foil his overall plans to control and limit the private sector.[112] Second, Lukashenka knows full well that a real opening of the borders would give Belarusian citizens the opportunity to compare their country's conditions to others', and thus the bubble of official propaganda describing Belarus as an oasis of modest well-being and stability would burst.

At the same time, a series of objective political factors make the development of these transit links especially difficult now. The lack of stable political relations with Belarus' Western neighbors, Poland and Lithuania, also complicates the country's transit situation. For example, Belarus could make very good use of access to the sea through Poland for its cargo, yet its tenuous political relations with Poland make this difficult.[113] (Lukashenka has accused Poland of supporting the Belarusian opposition.) Moreover, Poland has established a visa system with Belarus, in great part because Belarus refused to accept a readmission clause calling for Belarus to turn back illegal immigrants to Poland.

Belarus is unable to take full advantage of the possibilities offered by the transit situation because policy is made according to its possible effects on the president's own policy and not according to its possible benefits for the country as a whole. An opening-up towards the West may destroy the illusion on which Lukashenka's power and popularity are largely based.

Keeping Belarus as closed as possible to foreign influences allows Lukashenka to trumpet his view that the country is doing fine compared with those neighboring states that underwent economic

---

[112] On this topic, see Chapter 5 herein, Leonid Zlotnikov, "Possibilities for the Development of a Private Economic Sector and a Middle Class as a Source of Political Change in Belarus."

[113] Interview with Zbigniew Szymanski [Shimanskii], deputy of the Polish Seim and chairman of the group Poland-Belarus ("Ne starykh raket, a ispol'zovaniia sredstv vo blago naroda," *Belarusskaia gazeta* 1 February 1999: 3).

"shock therapy." Indeed, in today's Belarus, everything may seem perfectly fine only if one does not realize that people can live differently and aspire to different standards.[114] However, only by using such points of comparison can Belarus fare well. It is Belarus' isolation, this lack of points of comparison, that explains both Lukashenka's popularity at home and the inability of the West, in particular the European community, to play a significant role in democratic reform in the country.

Belarus, in fact, has grown so insular and so isolated from the West and Western institutions that the West has lost mechanisms for influencing the situation there. As Vladimir Dorokhov said, it turns out that Belarus' current authorities "do not want the European 'carrot' and are not afraid of the 'stick' either."[115] The points of contact are so few that both carrots and sticks have limited effectiveness. This explains why the sanctions, imposed by the European Union after three months of discussions and consultations with Belarus on human rights in 1997, seemed to have little impact. This also might explain why current European Union sanctions may have only limited impact.

The official Belarusian response towards this question is, after all, also related to Belarus' geographical location and its transit potential. This attitude was summarized in the words of then-Foreign Minister Ivan Antanovich: "Some observers have hurried to say that Belarus is being 'thrown out of Europe.' No, we are not being thrown out anywhere. We, ladies and gentlemen, *are* the center of Europe."[116]

---

[114] The declarations of the leader of a delegation of Russian writers that visited Belarus last December, who was very favorably impressed, say it all: "The trolleys run, people hurry off to work" (author's translation from Radio Maiak, Moscow [21 December 1997]).

[115] Vladimir Dorokhov, "Evropa nam ne pomozhet," *Belorusskaia delovaia gazeta* 2 March 1998: 4 [in FBIS-SOV 98-070].

[116] Ivan Antanovich [Antonovich], January 1997, quoted in *Belorusskaia gazeta* 22 December 1997: 3 [emphasis added].

7

Arkady Moshes
Lukashenka's Role in Russian Politics

The results of the Russian presidential election of March 2000 put an end to speculation about the likelihood of Aliaksandr Lukashenka one day becoming head of the Russian state. Nevertheless, an analysis of the role of the president of Belarus in Russian politics remains of interest, since this role has been, and will most likely continue to be, an important component of Russian-Belarusian relations.

The influence of the Lukashenka factor in Russian politics is very difficult to assess. First, Lukashenka has always had, to a very large extent, a "would be" role in Russian politics. To date he has never had a real opportunity to fully participate in the Russian political game. Therefore, there is the risk of reducing any analysis to speculative description.

Second, Lukashenka's role vis-à-vis Russia is openly dualistic and contradictory. On the one hand, he consistently creates the image of being the leading integrator of the post-Soviet space. On the other hand, he no less consistently emphasizes the imperative of preserving Belarus' sovereignty. He attempts to appear as Moscow's best possible partner, while at the same time, he pretends to be a leader of the Russian opposition. These inherent contradictions of Lukashenka's line of action create a confusing picture of how he is seen in Russia.

Third, it is not always easy to distinguish between the openly positive attitudes in Russia toward the process of an interstate rapprochement and integration as such, and those toward the political representative of Belarus himself in this process. The latter is certainly influenced by the former, although one can assume that a less charismatic and less energetic Belarusian leader would not benefit politically to the degree that Lukashenka has.

Fourth, Lukashenka's role in Russia is mosaic-like. It does not appear whole. This reflects and possibly results from his multifaceted strategy toward Russia.

This chapter intends to add new insights to the discussion of Russia's policy toward the present Belarusian leadership. This policy will be analyzed in connection with the relationships that have been established between Aliaksandr Lukashenka on the one hand, and Russian ruling circles, the Leftist and nationalist opposition, regional elites, and the general public, on the other. Belarusian policy and Russia's reaction to it cannot be dealt with separately, since they form a political construction of challenge and response.

Although Lukashenka has been a noticeable factor in Russian politics within the whole integration context from 1995 through 1999, while at the same time successfully exploiting Russian connections for domestic purposes, his influence should not be exaggerated. As a Russian politician, Lukashenka has no future. His attempts to become one would be immediately neutralized. His advent into Russian politics would have contradicted Yeltsin's plans to use the issue of integration for Yeltsin's own purposes, undermined the political base of the Communists, and threatened the status of many regional leaders, especially the ethnocrats. All these forces would strongly resist the prospect of facing another competitor in Lukashenka.

Even if a legal opportunity for Lukashenka to run for the presidency could have been created, Lukashenka's weaknesses would have become evident. The mass media, predominantly unfriendly toward—but at the same time often ignorant about—Lukashenka, would have opened a mud-slinging campaign that would have quickly destroyed his image as an effective practitioner. In Russia, political structures are a prerequisite for running any successful campaign, as opposed to Belarus, where the absence of those structures can be partly compensated for by the leader's personal energy. The uncertain prospect of forming a single state, the lack of tangible results of political integration, and the prevalence of rhetoric over deeds would further weaken the chances of the Belarusian president in the Russian context.

Having failed to become a factor in the Russian presidential election of 2000, Lukashenka will now have to put increasing effort into staying in power in Belarus.

Goals and Tactics of Lukashenka's Policy toward Russia

Rationale

The essence of Lukashenka's Russia policy can be interpreted in different ways. While one cannot claim to know all of Lukashenka's goals in his pursuit of relations with Russia, at least three goals have been evident throughout his term in office, as is their order of priority: (1) to find additional instruments to help himself stay in power in Belarus; (2) to preserve the present Belarusian economic model, based on post-Soviet economic inertia and control; and (3) to be a factor in Russian politics. These goals will be addressed below in more detail.

For Lukashenka, power in Belarus is the most valuable commodity. Keeping this power is the primary imperative, to which all other goals are subordinate. With Belarus as his only reliable stronghold, Lukashenka can still conduct an effective policy in Russia. Correspondingly, he is extremely sensitive to any process that could weaken his position as the leader of Belarus. The predominance of this priority was reflected in his strongly negative reaction in January 1997 to plans, officially denied by Moscow, of political unification. According to those plans, Belarus, with its six administrative units, would enter Russia as six subjects of federation (or regions), while Lukashenka would be named vice-president or, in his own words, a mere governor-general.[1]

Focusing on integration with Russia as a central political goal, however, does serve to strengthen Lukashenka's domestic popularity, since integration is a popular idea in Belarus. Unlike the Baltic states, and to a lesser extent Ukraine, Belarus, its elite, and its population did not struggle for independence in the late 1980s and were totally unprepared to cope with the situation when the Soviet Union collapsed. Psychologically, a large part of the population, although

---

[1]   "Moskva ne predlagala Aleksandru Lukashenko post vitse-prezidenta," *Segodnia* 21 February 1997: 1; "President Lukashenko nedovolen Moskvoi," *Nezavisimaia gazeta* 22 February 1997: 3.

exact figures vary, still would like to live "together" with Russia. A poll, conducted by the Center for Sociological Studies of the Foundation for National and International Security of Russia in Minsk, Vitsebsk [Vitebsk], and Hrodna [Grodno] (and in 12 Russian cities) in early 1999 showed that 59.6 percent of Belarusians would agree to live in a union state (26 percent were against). Of those, 46.5 percent would prefer a federation, and 12.6 percent a confederation.[2] In spring 1997, when a discussion of the Treaty on the Union of Belarus and Russia was held in both countries, an even higher level of support was cited. Joint bilateral commission member Viacheslav Nikonov pointed out that in Belarus, support for integration reached 78 percent.[3] In the May 1995 referendum, 82.4 percent of participating voters answered affirmatively when asked about the need to develop economic integration with Russia.

These attitudes have undoubtedly helped Lukashenka domestically. For example, according to data from the Sociological Laboratory "NOVAK" in Minsk, after the Treaty on the Commonwealth of the Sovereign States of Belarus and Russia was signed on 2 April 1996, Lukashenka's positive rating rose to 57.8 percent, the highest since his election as president.[4] In Belarus he is considered to be the best candidate to head the union state, which also signals the popularity of his integration course. An Independent Institute for Socioeconomic and Political Studies (IISEPS) poll showed that in fall 1998, despite growing skepticism concerning integration in the aftermath of the Russian economic crisis, 44.7 percent of respondents wanted to see Lukashenka president of the union state.[5]

At the same time, the Belarusian electorate's understanding of integration is somewhat confused and is mixed with a desire to continue to live in a sovereign state. According to the same poll cited above, 60.8 percent of respondents would like to see Belarus independent and neutral. This contradiction in the Belarusian

---

[2] *Nezavisimaia gazeta* 20 February 1999: 5.

[3] "Okonchatel'noe slovo: za prezidentami," *Nezavisimaia gazeta* 17 May 1997: 3.

[4] Viacheslav Nikonov, "Belorussiia vo vneshnei politike Rossii," in *Belorussiia na pereput'e: v poiskakh mezhdunarodnoi identichnosti* (Moscow, 1998), p. 63.

[5] *Belarus' segodnia* 7 (November 1998): 58.

consciousness is the source of a no-less-contradictory mandate for Lukashenka.[6] When dealing with Russia, he must simultaneously emphasize "full integration" and "full sovereignty." Thus sovereignty was put forward by Lukashenka as the number-one precondition for any union with Russia.[7] But such a policy becomes a political and legal impediment if integration is taken seriously. Only a combination of both approaches in rhetoric and, when possible, in bilateral documents allows Lukashenka to keep the idea of integration popular within Belarus.

Thus the main goal of Lukashenka's policy seems to be power in Belarus. This is the prism through which all of his steps in Russia and elsewhere should be observed. Knowing well what is useful and what is detrimental for reaching this goal, the Belarusian president exercises, from his point of view, a consistent strategy—notwithstanding the contradiction described above.

Lukashenka's second goal is the preservation of the existing post-socialist Belarusian economic model. He apparently assumes that it will provide a basis for sustainable economic growth, a result that will also increase his domestic popularity. To keep this model running, it is necessary to establish a mechanism for direct and indirect subsidies from Russia. Thus, preferential treatment of Belarus by Russia becomes another imperative of Lukashenka's Russia policy. Short-term success of this policy has been accomplished, but its long-term sustainability has justifiably been questioned. The Belarusian "economic miracle" was made possible to a large extent by indirect Russian subsidies, which, as of 1997, amounted to an estimated $1.5 billion to $2 billion.[8] The issue is not well researched and the whole problem remains complicated.[9] Naturally, there is no such item as

[6]   On this issue see Yuri Drakokhrust and Dmitri [Dmitrii] Furman, "Peripetii inte-gratsii," in *Belorussiia i Rossiia: obshchestva i gosudarstva*, ed. Dmitri Furman (Moscow, 1998), pp. 356–59.

[7]   "Lukashenko nazval printsipy integratsii," *Segodnia* 23 January 1997: 1.

[8]   Estimate of Andrei Illarionov, Director of the Institute for Economic Analysis. Quoted in Alexander Ivanter and Iuri Shevtsov, "Ėffektivnaia diktatura," *Expert* 41 (October): 319–27.

[9]   Some details can be found in Irina Selivanova, "Ėkonomicheskaia integratsia Rossii i Belorussii i ee vliianie na razvitie narodnogo khoziaistva Belorussii," in Furman, ed. *Belorussiia i Rossiia*, pp. 319–27.

"subsidies to Belarus" in the Russian state budget. Neither state credits (rare in the second half of the 1990s and usually tied to purchases of Russian equipment) nor Russia's share in the union's budget can be treated as subsidies either legally or practically. Nevertheless, at least three points provide grounds for asserting that subsidization does take place. First, in 1996, by means of a special agreement, Russia wrote off $470 million in state debt in exchange for Minsk dropping its financial claims ($300 million that it could have charged Russia for withdrawal of nuclear weapons, military pensions, rent for military bases).[10] Estimates exist that in 1996–97, Russia "forgave" about $1 billion of Belarusian debt.[11] Second, Russia sells gas to Belarus at preferential prices ($30 per 1,000 cubic meters in 1999, and $27.90 since February 2000[12]) that are half those charged to Ukraine. Lower prices, to be fair, are provided not only for political reasons—for example, Belarusian transit tariffs are half those of Ukraine's and Belarusian industries are contributors to the Russian production process, which makes minimization of Belarusian costs logical. But whatever the rationale, preferential energy prices strongly stimulate Belarusian exports, especially to Russia.[13] In addition, although no clear evidence has been found, it is suspected that Minsk reexports Russian energy sources at world prices. Third, the customs union, because of discrepancies in tariffs on different goods in Russia and Belarus, provides a "hole" for smuggling goods into Russia. Alcohol is particularly noteworthy in this regard. Russia's losses from customs union activity in the first year of its existence, beginning in April 1995, reportedly reached $4 billion.[14] Since that time, Moscow has taken some measures that may have decreased that number, but

[10]   "Boris Iel'tsin i Aleksandr Lukashenko prostili drug drugu dolgi svoikh stran," *Segodnia* 28 February 1996: 1.

[11]   Ivanter and Shevtsov, "Ėffektivnaia diktatura," p. 26.

[12]   "Vse idet svoim cheredom," *Nezavisimaia gazeta* 5 February 2000: 5.

[13]   From the mid-1990s to 1998 Belarus' share of Russian foreign trade doubled—from 4 percent to 8 percent (approximately equal to Russian-Ukrainian and slightly less than Russian-U.S. trade). Belarus' exports to Russia grew from $1.957 billion in 1995 to $4.626 billion in 1997. Goskomstat, *Rossia v tsifrakh. 1998* (Moscow, 1998), p. 372. In 1999 Belarusian exports fell as a result of the Russian economic crisis, but in 2000 growth renewed.

[14]   Ivanter and Shevtsov, "Ėffektivnaia diktatura," p. 27.

Russian concerns remain serious. In spring 2000, to Minsk's dismay, Russia reintroduced selective control over goods imported from Belarus to check their origin, and Russian duties will be imposed on those not originating from Belarus.

Since 1996, Belarusian workers in Russia have not been categorized as foreign laborers. Their freedom of movement has been established and they have been granted equal rights to education, medical treatment, and social insurance. All this is very important for people who frequently travel to Russia, such as "shuttle traders," construction workers, and the like. They receive more than symbolic safeguards against border corruption and abuses of the law enforcement system in Russia. Their competitiveness in the Russian market compared with workers from Ukraine and the other former Soviet states has grown. This has resulted in increased positive ratings for Lukashenka.

Only the third goal of Lukashenka's Russian policy appears to be directly targeted at Russian politics itself. The Belarusian president was often suspected of having ambitions for top leadership in Russia, and, in fact, spoke in favor of the equal right of Russians and Belarusians to become president of the united state.[15] Such equal rights would be a logical consequence of the creation of a single (but not a union) state. Officially, however, Lukashenka has always denied such ambitions. He most likely assumed that the chance of his achieving such power in Russia was at most a distant possibility. His immediate goal, however, is well known. He wants to influence Russian politics from the outside, thus harvesting the results, but avoiding the risk, of too close an involvement. In an interview for a Russian newspaper, Lukashenka admitted, "Yes, Lukashenka becomes a certain factor of Russian politics . . . Since you agreed to sign the treaty [on the Russian-Belarusian Union in 1997], the Russian Federation, Russia's politicians, and the Russian president should take into account the factor of Lukashenka . . . But I won't make you glad by getting engaged in a political quarrel and pretending to rule Russia in the year 2000. You have more than enough of your own contenders . . . Of course, I could exercise certain influence . . . "[16]

[15] *Segodnia* 24 December 1997: 1.

[16] "Shapka Monomakha ostanetsa v Rossii, ia na nee ne pretenduiu," interview with Aliaksandr Lukashenka, *Nezavisimaia gazeta* 29 May 1997: 1, 5.

"Influence" is the key word. Influence, when necessary, can easily be exchanged for economic concessions and political support. Direct involvement, on the other hand, could only irritate potential counterparts.

Political Tactics

To achieve his political aims, Lukashenka must deal directly with official Moscow while simultaneously developing instruments for putting pressure on it. Within this paradigm he relies on a variety of tactics, including using his relationships with leading actors from all parts of the Russian political spectrum, appealing to Russian public opinion, and, less directly, using some of his CIS connections for influencing policymaking in Moscow.

The central element of these tactics is relations with the Kremlin and, before the March 2000 election, with President Yeltsin personally. Publicly, Lukashenka always expressed his complete respect for the Russian president, especially when the two leaders shared an opinion on an issue. He pointed out that he could "talk only with the president of Russia."[17] In addition to being pragmatic—dealing directly with the Russian leader was one of the quickest ways to achieve his own goals—he hoped that such rhetoric would raise his status in Russia. All his criticism of Russian inefficiency in the process of integration or the shortcomings of integration itself are deliberately targeted against the Russian central bureaucracy, which according to Lukashenka, openly sabotages presidential decisions. A characteristic example of this language was the undoubtedly authorized statement by the Belarusian First Deputy Prime Minister Vasil Daŭhalioŭ [Dolgolev], made shortly before Lukashenka's trip to Moscow in December 1998, that Yeltsin was surrounded by enemies of integration.[18]

In rare cases, Lukashenka has allowed his true emotions to be revealed. One such occasion occurred during the ongoing investigation of the case of journalists Pavel Sheremet and Dmitrii Zavadskii,[19] when personal relations between Lukashenka and Yeltsin

[17]   Ibid.

[18]   "Rossiia i Belorussiia gotovy k sozdaniiu konfederatsii," *Nezavisimaia gazeta* 26 December 1998: 1.

[19]   Two Russian TV journalists produced a story in which they exposed the absence

deteriorated openly. Having received severe admonishments from Yeltsin who denied Lukashenka an air corridor to fly to one of the Russian regions, Lukashenka, on 4 October 1997, made the following charged statement: "I am forty, [Yeltsin] is eighty."[20] Again, in the fall of 1999, when the momentum for preparing the treaty on creating the union was lost, Lukashenka said, "If we don't sign [the treaty] with Yeltsin, I am sorry, I have time to sign it with somebody else."[21]

Lukashenka's views of the Left and nationalist opposition in Russia are not well articulated publicly. On the surface there are no pretexts for controversies between these two actors. Lukashenka carefully uses his audience, especially when he has an opportunity to address the Russian parliament or the Parliamentary Assembly of the union, to criticize the policies of the executive power in Moscow, but when dealing directly with this part of the Russian political spectrum, Lukashenka must take into account many factors. First, under Yelstin there was open antagonism between Russian Communists and the Kremlin. To be too close to the Left would mean jeopardizing economic and political benefits. Second, Lukashenka and the Russian Communists are rivals as far as "integration" is concerned. If it ever comes to chasing the same voter, no doubts should exist as to who is the integration leader. Third, as long as one part of the Communist movement in Belarus is in opposition to Lukashenka, he should be careful not to give them additional points by strengthening the Communists in Russia. Fourth, the role of Russian Communists in formulating foreign policy is rather small. The only powerful instrument they had for many years was the parliamentary ratification of international treaties, which was absolutely guaranteed in the case

---

of proper control of the Belarusian-Lithuanian border. The story clearly contradicted, even mocked, speeches by Lukashenka that were full of rhetoric about the reliability of Belarusian border service. The journalists were put on trial, which provoked a negative reaction and a strong campaign of solidarity in Russia; according to a poll conducted by the "Public Opinion" Foundation, only 10 percent of Russians approved of this action of the Belarusian leadership. Viacheslav Nikonov, *Belorussiia na pereput'e,* p. 71. Lukashenka's popularity fell correspondingly. The sentence was rather mild—especially considering possible charges of espionage—and both were allowed to leave Belarus for Russia.

20 Quoted in Drakokhrust and Furman, *Peripetii,* p. 354.

21 "Skandal vokrug Soiuza," *Nezavisimaia gazeta* 2 October 1999: 5.

of Russian-Belarusian treaties. All this makes a rapprochement between Lukashenka and the Left at best unnecessary, if not openly disadvantageous for him, although to have an open conflict with the Russian Communists should not be a part of his plans either.

Building a relationship with the right liberal opposition in Russia is apparently not part of Lukashenka's tactics. Most likely he does not think this relationship would be useful or even possible. Russian liberals and democrats are either openly against any integration with Belarus (such as Yegor Gaidar and Anatoly Chubais) or against integration with Lukashenka's Belarus (such as Grigory Yavlinsky). Lukashenka has further neglected this part of the Russian political spectrum in the wake of the collapse of the liberal economic reforms in August 1998.

Direct contacts with the Russian regions, on the other hand, are very important for Lukashenka. It is much easier to lobby for the economic interests of Belarus with local leaders who are more interested in and more attentive to details than with the leader in Moscow. In this respect, Lukashenka was not deceptive in answering criticism that his trips to Russia's regions resembled an electoral campaign when he said that he visited those places where he saw the interests of his state.[22] As of the summer of 1999, 79 of Russia's 89 regions had trade links with Belarus, and 67 had concluded bilateral cooperation aggreements.[23] Moreover, regional contacts provide an instrument to influence Moscow, given the federal structure of Russia and the number of "red" governors. Addressing the session of the union's Parliamentary Assembly (the Russian deputation includes members of the upper chamber, which represents the Russian territories) in Homel in May 1998, Lukashenka openly blamed Moscow for stagnation in the integration process and praised the regions for having saved it: "If we hadn't found this form of cooperation, we would have surely died."[24] In a later interview, he added, "Not Moscow–Minsk, but Russian regions–Belarus is the foundation on which our union has been built and is getting

---

[22]   "V Minske pobyval vitse-premier RF," *Nezavisimaia gazeta* 1 October 1997: 3.

[23]   *Nezavisimaia gazeta* 6 August 1999: 5.

[24]   *Belarus' segodnia* 2 (1 June 1998): 16.

stronger."[25] Finally, for Lukashenka, whose visits abroad are very rare given the international isolation of Belarus, trips to the Russian regions are an opportunity for him to feel like a sovereign leader.

All of these reasons are equally applicable to Lukashenka's visits to the capitals of the CIS states. In the context of relations between Minsk and Moscow, and for Lukashenka's image as the main integrator of the post-Soviet space, trips to Ukraine and Kazakhstan are especially noteworthy. It is undoubtedly an element of his tactics vis-à-vis Moscow, and a part of his political ammunition. Otherwise, the coincidences of the timing of crucial events in Russia and Lukashenka's meetings with CIS leaders or visits to their capitals would be difficult to explain.

In this regard, 1997—the busiest year in terms of bilateral relations—was especially characteristic. On 13 January, Yeltsin, still recovering from heart surgery, proposed a set of integration initiatives that looked too far-reaching for Lukashenka and that Lukashenka criticized as potentially undermining Belarus' sovereignty and his own power. On 17 January, a meeting between Lukashenka and Ukraine's President Leonid Kuchma took place in Homel. On the eve of Lukashenka's visit to Moscow the following March to discuss the content of the treaty on the union of Russia and Belarus, Belarusian Foreign Minister Ivan Antanovich in Kyiv said that Belarus' independence was a supreme value for Belarusian people and there were no grounds for all the talk about a political Russian-Belarusian union.[26] In May, before signing the union's charter,[27] Lukashenka paid an official visit to Kyiv to sign a border treaty. Moscow, however, at approximately the same time, decided only to delimit, but

---

[25]   *Nezavisimaia gazeta* 21 April 1999: 5.

[26]   *Nezavisimaia gazeta* 4 March 1997: 3.

[27]   The final version of the Charter, signed on 23 May 1997, looks very similar to the Treaty on the Union of Belarus and Russia of 2 April 1997, which makes it to a large extent redundant. Both documents were ratified and entered into force together. The Charter was recognized as a part of the treaty. *Diplomaticheskii vestnik* 6 June 1997: 30. Initially there was a risk that if the Charter were a separate document (as is the case with the CIS Statute), the opponents of integration would limit Belarus' influence in the Union bodies by means of relevant provisions of the Charter. Therefore, Lukashenka wanted to sign both documents together and later tried to make sure the Charter would not contradict the treaty.

not to demarcate, the border with Ukraine (that is, to draw border lines on maps only, not to set markers on the ground). In another example of coincidence, Lukashenka visited Almaty in September 1997 to receive the public support of Kazakhstan President Nursultan Nazarbaev in the conflict with the Russian media and Yeltsin over the Sheremet case. Nazarbaev even jokingly asked Lukashenka whether they should stop broadcasting the Russian Public Television, ORT [Obshchestvennoe russkoe televidenie], in Kazakhstan and Belarus.[28]

Along with diplomatic and political activity, Lukashenka seemed to welcome the idea of direct appeal to Russian public opinion, first and foremost by the use of referenda on integration questions. Proposals to hold such referenda, including those on reunification, have been debated periodically in Russia since 1995. The initiative has usually come from Russian actors—such as the Duma, the Federation Council, and the ultra-integrationist "People's Unity" group led by Duma member Nikolai Gonchar—and no unambiguous linkage to Lukashenka has ever been revealed. The only partial exception is a December 1998 agreement between Yeltsin and Lukashenka to hold a referendum on the new union treaty to be drawn up in the first half of 1999. However, any treaty of this kind would require introducing changes in the Russian constitution, and Russian legislation prohibits the adoption of constitutional changes by referendum. That is why, most likely, politically non-binding discussions are held instead of referenda.

Despite the lack of access to debates regarding referenda in Russia regarding political integration, Lukashenko appears to be interested in finding a legal opportunity to mobilize Russian public opinion in his support. He has absolute confidence in his ability to use Russian public opinion effectively, as he believes he has a very good reputation there. Indeed, after the 1996 Russian presidential election, Lukashenka stated that Yeltsin's luck was that Yeltsin's rival had been Gennady Zyuganov and not himself, because had he been Yeltsin's opponent the result would have been 75 percent for Lukashenka and only 25 percent for Yeltsin.[29] Speaking to the

---

[28]   "V Alma-Ate i Minske ne liubiat rossiiskie SMI," *Nezavisimaia gazeta* 24 September 1997: 3.

[29]   Quoted in Drakokhrust and Furman, *Peripetii*, p. 364.

Parliamentary Assembly in January 1999, he estimated that his support by Russians was 90 percent.[30] Also, he believes that it would be no more difficult to win a referendum in Russia than in Belarus, where he has done it twice. Nevertheless, this component of Lukashenka's tactics has always been the least developed, and his real capacity to influence Russian public opinion remains limited.

Mistakes

In his approach to Russia, Lukashenka has underestimated the role of three important sectors of Russian political life: the media, the bureaucracy, and the liberals. Bad relations with the democratic media was a critical mistake that undermined Lukashenka's potential achievements not only in Russia, but also in Belarus, because the Russian electronic media are dominant in Belarus. Top Russian television stations and several leading newspapers were openly anti-Lukashenka from the moment he came to power. Getting involved in an open conflict with Russian journalists was completely self-defeating if Lukashenka wanted to maintain a positive image in Russia. Yet Alexander Stupnikov, an NTV correspondent, was expelled from Belarus. Later on, as mentioned above, correspondents of ORT, Belarusian citizens Sheremet and Zavadskii, were prosecuted and convicted of illegally crossing the state border with Lithuania. After that, a large segment of the Russian media continued to report events concerning Lukashenka, although not necessarily concerning Belarus, in a negative and even openly humiliating manner. Lukashenka has irreversibly lost the campaign for the media.

Lukashenka's underestimation of the role of the *apparat* in Russia is probably based on his experience with the Belarus bureaucracy. Lukashenka rather effectively controls the central bureaucracy in Minsk, and it has taken him time to understand that in Russia, agreements at the presidential level would not be implemented if they clashed with the corporate interests of Russian bureaucrats.

Lukashenka's feelings toward the liberal end of the Russian political spectrum is a mixture of negative attitudes and neglect. Both components are natural for him. He believes that his policy is correct and Russian reforms are not, and that by criticizing the liberals'

---

[30] "Staryi biudget provalen," *Nezavisimaia gazeta* 23 January 1999: 5.

undoubtedly impoverishing course, he will get extra points from the general population. This assumption might be correct, but the impact of the liberals on Yeltsin's policy during the years of Lukashenka's tenure was greater than their electoral support would imply. The liberals were responsible for Sergei Kiriyenko's appointment as Russia's prime minister. Also, Chubais' role in effectively counter-balancing the integrationists is well known.

Russia's Response

On the surface it may look as if Lukashenka's policy toward Russia has been successful. To the extent that economic donorship and political support of the present Belarusian regime are concerned, this is true, but in reality the situation is more nuanced. The reactions of Russia's political actors to the "Lukashenka's challenge" is at best mixed. Furthermore, it can be assumed that negative attitudes, caused by different and sometimes totally incompatible reasons, actually prevailed across the political spectrum.

Official Moscow in the Yelstin Era

The official response to the problem of integration with Lukashenka's Belarus and to relations with Lukashenka personally consisted of two elements: the political attitudes of the president, and the practical approaches of the government. The rationale behind these two components was not necessarily the same.

Yeltsin's attitudes were determined by the following factors. First, his political goals with regard to integration with Belarus never corresponded to those of Lukashenka, and sometimes were even on the verge of collision. Both Yeltsin and Lukashenka sought to use the popular card of integration to stay in power. In fact, Yeltsin needed it even more than Lukashenka, because his power, unlike Lukashenka's, was seriously at risk in 1996 and again in August 1998. The economic crisis ruled out a third term for the incumbent Russian leader and even brought his powers during the rest of his constitutional term into question. It is not accidental, therefore, that, both in the spring of 1996 and at the end of 1998, Yeltsin became active in the integration field. In 1996, unification with Belarus could have allowed Yeltsin to cancel the election in Russia. In January 1999, the possibility of a "Yugoslav scenario" which would have made Yeltsin president of the new union state was aired by Ivan Rybkin, the personal representative of the Russian president to the CIS states.[31] Lukashenka was a major obstacle to such a plan.

Domestically, Yeltsin tried to use the issue of integration for large-scale demonstrations aimed mostly at taking the initiative from and weakening the Communists, but also at enhancing his own role as a policymaker and deflecting public attention from politically damaging issues. In February 1995, facing the growing unpopularity of the war in Chechnya, Yeltsin visited Belarus, where he had not been since 1991 for purposes other than CIS summits, to sign a Treaty on Friendship, Good Neighborliness, and Cooperation. In March 1996, during the presidential race, when the Communist-dominated Duma adopted a nonbinding resolution on the repeal of the Belavezhskaia Pushcha Agreements which had dissolved the Soviet Union, Yeltsin responded by signing a Treaty on the Commonwealth of Russia and Belarus. In April 1997, as mentioned above, Yeltsin based his return to active political life on another set of integration issues, which resulted in the conclusion of the Treaty on the Union of Belarus and Russia. On 25 December 1998, when the Duma ratified a long-awaited political treaty with Ukraine, Yeltsin and Lukashenka signed a document declaring the intention to create a union state in 1999. Finally, the December 1999 Treaty on Creation of a Union between Russia and Belarus, the last major initiative before Yeltsin's resignation on 31 December, seemed intended to crown his political career, to let him step down as an integrator, to compensate perhaps for his early "misdeeds." Indeed, the treaty was signed symbolically on the eighth anniversary of the Belavezhskaia Pushcha Agreements.

On the other hand, when Yeltsin saw no immediate political benefit, the whole process of integration slowed dramatically, as was the situation for most of 1998[32] and then again in 1999. Yeltsin's

---

[31] *Nezavisimaia gazeta* 11 January 1999: 3.

[32] Lukashenka complained by saying "What kind of powers are these, if the Chairman of the Supreme Council, despite his sincere wish, cannot for the whole year organize at least one meeting of this body?" *Nezavisimaia gazeta* 23 January 1999. This statement left no doubt not only as to the hierarchy of roles in relations between the two leaders, but also demonstrated that Yeltsin was not inclined to take Lukashenka's needs into account; ibid., p. 5.

rationale in taking all these actions was different from Lukashenka's and this asymmetry of purpose might also have been a source of controversy.

Another factor influencing Yeltsin's views on integration most likely was his personal antipathy toward Lukashenka. Lukashenka often emphasized not only his role in the process of integration, but also his role in opposition to the dissolution of the Soviet Union (claiming to be the only Belarusian member of Supreme Soviet who voted against the ratification of the Belavezhskaia Pushcha Agreements). Yeltsin, of course, was associated with the demise of the Soviet Union, which made it more difficult for him to pretend to encourage integration. From time to time, Lukashenka made this distinction clear. For example, he welcomed the above-mentioned Duma resolution on the repeal of Belavezhskaia Pushcha Agreements, while Yeltsin's reaction had to be the opposite. Yeltsin's feelings were also influenced by members of his entourage. Some were openly anti-Lukashenka, such as Anatoly Chubais. Others were objects of provocative statements by Lukashenka, such as Sergei Yastrzhembsky, Yeltsin's press secretary who was also responsible for foreign policy matters, of whom Lukashenka said "for me [he] is nothing."[33]

Taking into account these factors, it was hardly possible to expect that Yeltsin and Lukashenka would be reliable political allies. Their aims were different and, after all, they competed for superiority in the "integration cause." The Yeltsin-Lukashenka relationship rarely showed overt hostility (the only exception was the Sheremet case) because it would be counterproductive for the politics and policies of both, but cooperation between these two rulers had rather narrow limits.

The approach of the Russian government, the second component of Moscow's response to integration with Lukashenka's Belarus, was seemingly determined by the priorities of Russian-Belarusian relations in such spheres as economics, communications, and even the military. The need to discuss and solve practical questions brought even Prime Minister Kiriyenko, a skeptic on the issue of closer Russian-Belarusian relations, to Minsk in June 1998. In October 1998, Prime

[33]   Quoted in Drakokhrust and Furman, *Peripetii*, p. 6.

Minister Evgenii Primakov paid his first official visit abroad to Belarus not only to symbolize the importance to the new Russian government's relationship with Belarus, but also to elaborate joint measures to deal with the Russian economic crisis.

To what extent has the "Lukashenka factor" played an autonomous role is difficult to measure. On the one hand, Lukashenka probably has been a convenient partner for the Russian executive power as long as he has been able to guarantee the implementation of agreements. On the other hand, however, his politics and policies interfere with the dialogue, and sometimes create additional problems for Russia and its politicians.

The Opposition

The attitude of the Russian Communist Party toward Lukashenka and his language of integration is apparently very cautious. As long as Lukashenka remains a leader of a foreign state, the Party's attitude will probably remain rather positive. This is likely to be the case, despite the fact that Lukashenka's policy split and weakened the allies of the Russian Communist Party—the Communist movement in Belarus, which neither dominates the opposition there nor constitutes a central component of Lukashenka's power base. At the same time, Russian Communists should be very cautious lest they provide the Belarusian president with any chance of participating in Russian politics. If that were to happen, it is absolutely clear that Lukashenka would attract a large share of the traditional Communist electorate.

In a battle for the electorate, Lukashenka would have many advantages compared with the Russian Communists. First, Lukashenka could back up his populism with facts that could be perceived by the Left electorate as achievements. He could use the argument that he knows how to implement socialist economic principles because his economic model provides the social minimum. Salaries and pensions are paid on time, the state (and not the oligarchs) controls the resources, and the level of corruption is lower than in Russia. Communists cannot make this argument. Second, Lukashenka can advertise that he had convictions and positions of principle on economic matters and on forms and methods of integration, whereas Russian Communists never directly challenged Yeltsin during his administration. Moreover, Lukashenka's charisma compared with the colorless figures of the present Russian Communist Party leaders would greatly improve his chances.

All these factors have been well known to the Russian Communists, which explains why, in January 1997, Gennady Zyuganov's immediate reaction to Yeltsin's initiatives on the reunification of Russia and Belarus was cold. He called the proposals "strange."[34] In addition to his desire to prevent Yeltsin from playing the integration card, Zyuganov, unlike some of his comrades, recognized the risk in bringing Lukashenka into Russian politics. Only when Lukashenka made it clear that for him the risk of anschluss of Belarus with Russia was unacceptable did the Communists return to their traditional position of supporting integration.

The basis of the antagonism that the Russian liberal political forces feel toward Lukashenka is obvious. Although among the liberal forces attitudes toward integration vary—Gaidar-type liberals fear the economic burden that better relations with Belarus would impose on Russia, while Yavlinsky understands the positive effects of this process—a rapprochement with Lukashenka's regime is universally considered to be unacceptable because of the regime's undemocratic character. Consequently, Russian liberals are consistent opponents of Lukashenka.

Regional Elites

The list of contacts between the Belarusian leadership and the Russian regional elites is impressive. In June-December 1998, top-level delegations from Primorye, Chukotka, Kostroma, Vladimir, Stavropol, Mordovia, Orel, Smolensk, Ulianovsk, Tomsk, Vologda, Altai Krai, the Republic of Altai, and Novosibirsk visited Belarus. Belarusian delegations, including some regional delegations, visited St. Petersburg, Kaliningrad, Smolensk, Omsk, and Kemerovo. In 1999, ten heads of Russian regions came to Minsk and six Belarusian delegations visited Russia. The Russian regions' policy toward Belarus mirrors to a certain extent Lukashenka's policy. Both are interested in economic cooperation. For Russian regional leaders, contact with the head of a sovereign state is no less valuable than is recognition of his status for Lukashenka.

---

[34]   Valerii Solovei, "Nadezhdy i strakhi rossiiskikh politikov," in Furman, ed., *Belorussiia i Rossiia*, p. 3.

At the same time, there are at least two sources of friction between the regional leaders of Russia and the Belarusian president. The first one is the regional leaders' apprehension that political integration may develop into the formation of a Russian-Belarusian confederacy or the entry of Belarus into Russia as a single entity with a large deal of autonomy. In both cases, the influence of Minsk and its leader on decision-making in Moscow would be incomparably greater than that of the leaders of even the largest federation subjects, except Moscow. After all, Belarus would be the largest member of the federation in terms of population. These apprehensions in 1997 caused the influential leaders of several Russian republics (Tatarstan's President Mintimir Shaimiev, Bashkortostan's President Murtaza Rakhimov, and some others) to support the super-integrationist approach to Belarus, that is, its entry into Russia as six different federation subjects whose powers would be equal to those of each of the current 89.[35]

Another source of friction are the personal political views of the Russian governors who represent the democratic wing, and who are highly critical and suspicious of Lukashenka. In addition, regional leaders must be wary of the jealous attitude of the Kremlin toward their contacts with Lukashenka.

One regional leader with whom Lukashenka has enjoyed a positive relationship is Moscow Mayor Yuri Luzhkov. For several years, Luzhkov occupied a unique political niche. Since he was not officially a national leader, an informal coalition between him and Lukashenka was possible. With his influence and independent financial and political base, Luzhkov was an important source of moral support for Lukashenka. Indeed he was one of very few people in Moscow who openly stood on Lukashenka's side during the Sheremet case. In July 1998, when Lukashenka sent Luzhkov a letter explaining his view of the conflict with Western diplomats concerning the Drazdy [Drozdy] residential compound, again Luzhkov made a

---

[35] In December 1999, during the ratification of the Treaty on the Creation of the Union State, Prime Minister Putin had to ensure the governors in the upper chamber of the Russian parliament that the treaty did not even raise the question of Belarus' prospective entry into Russia or provide it with the rights enjoyed by current subjects of the Russian Federation. "Sovet Federatsii prinial biudzhet 2000," *Nezavisimaia gazeta* 23 December 1999: 1.

public statement of support.[36] Luzhkov's views in favor of post-Soviet integration and protection of Russians in the former Soviet Union were well known. He no doubt viewed demonstrations of an ability to establish a partnership with Lukashenka as very helpful during the period when he was assessing his own plans for a run in the presidential election.

There is a chance that Luzhkov and Lukashenka will continue to be political allies. After all, Moscow remains Belarus' leading trade partner, with thirty-five percent of Russian-Belarusian bilateral trade in 1999 with the city of Moscow alone.[37] But the defeat of Luzhkov's movement in the December 1999 parliamentary elections and the reform of the Federation Council, which deprived him of a seat in parliament and the status of a federal politician, will no doubt decrease the strength and the value of this alliance for Lukashenka.

Public Opinion

Lukashenka's lack of participation in Russian politics on a daily basis makes any analysis of the general population's attitudes toward him only tentative. Theoretically, there are a number of factors that could improve Lukashenka's image in Russian public opinion. First, he is not only a charismatic leader, but also a very rare type of a populist in that he is a practitioner who tries to be convincing to his audience. Results of the post-Soviet economic experiment in Belarus would provide a good argument for a specially targeted audience.

Second, the refusal to send Belarusian troops to participate in conflicts, a policy that Lukashenka not only inherited from his predecessor's leadership, but asserted in January 1997 as a precondition for any further political rapprochement with Russia, should have worked to the benefit of his reputation among the Russian general public between the two Chechen wars. Moreover, expressing general political support for Russian actions and a readiness to take

---

[36]   In April 1998, the Belarusian authorities announced the closing of Drazdy, the residential compound of foreign ambassadors, due to the alleged need of utility repairs. Members of the international community, including the U.S., saw this as a violation of the Vienna Convention on Diplomatic Relations. Luzhkov's statement published in *Belarus' segodnia* 3 (July 1998): 40–42.

[37]   Iu. Godin, "Konvergentsiia Rossii i Belarussii," *Sodruzhestvo NGG* 3 March 2000: 3.

part in the economic reconstruction of Chechnya after the war was sure to have a positive effect.

Third, the Belarusian opposition not only failed to present itself as an alternative to Lukashenka, but even worsened its own image in Russia. Indeed many in Russia started to perceive good relations with Belarus as synonymous with good relations only with Lukashenka. This process was begun well before the constitutional referendum of 1996. In January 1995, the opposition in the Belarusian Supreme Soviet attempted not to give the floor to Duma speaker Ivan Rybkin.[38] After Prime Minister Viktor Chernomyrdin's failure as a mediator between Lukashenka and the parliament, Russia was accused by members of the opposition of having interfered in Belarus' internal affairs on Lukashenka's behalf.[39] Whether this interpretation was correct can be debated, but in terms of influencing Russian public opinion, putting all the blame on Russia was certainly short-sighted. Another blow to the opposition's relations with Russians resulted from former Belarus President Stanislaŭ Shushkevich's statement to a democratic Moscow newspaper which equated relations with Russia with the German occupation: "We have survived the occupation, we will survive the integration."[40] Fourth, Russian public opinion does not seem to be seriously concerned with Lukashenka's authoritarian nature. After all, much of Russia's own territory is ruled by elected politicians who are very far from democratic. Moreover, according to polls conducted in spring 1997, even in Moscow, which is more democratic than the rest of Russia on average, only 18 percent of those opposed to the union between Russia and Belarus made the

[38] Former leader of Belarus Stanislaŭ Shushkevich asked Speaker Miacheslaŭ Hrib not to invite Rybkin to the Supreme Soviet but to hold separate talks with him. "Rybkin's address," he said, "would be inappropriate. Let him solve problems in Chechnya." Quoted in "Lukashenko reshil sdelat' Rybkinu priiatnoe, initsiirovav referendum," *Nezavisimaia gazeta* 7 February 1995: 2.

[39] Leader of the United Civic Party Stanislaŭ Bahdankevich [Stanislav Bogdankevich] said in an interview, "A coup d'état that took place was sponsored by Chernomyrdin, Stroev, and Seleznev. From the West, on the contrary, we have support," *Nezavisimaia gazeta* 23 April 1997: 3.

[40] Stanislav [Stanislaŭ] Shushkevich. "Perezhivshim okkupatsiiu integratsiia ne strashna," *Moskovskiie novosti* 6–13 April 1997: 5. The title of the article is even more telling than the sentence quoted: "Those who have survived the occupation should not fear the integration."

argument that such a union would hinder democratic developments in Russia (73 percent thought it would exacerbate the economic situation in Russia).[41] It is noteworthy that at that time, support for integration and even reunification of the two states was reaching 60 percent to 70 percent of the electorate nationwide.[42]

Despite all these factors, the data measuring Russian views of Lukashenka himself can be interpreted differently. On the one hand, he did not become a favorite of any large part of the Russian population. In December 1996, only 17 percent of Russian respondents expressed confidence in Lukashenka, with 23 percent expressing lack of confidence. In September 1997, during the Sheremet case, his positive rating fell to 9 percent and his negative rating increased to 54 percent.[43] In spring 1997, 63 percent of Russians negatively assessed the prospect of seeing a leader of Lukashenka's type at the head of Russia.[44] In February 1999, only every fifth Russian respondent would have liked to see Lukashenka as the head of the single union state.[45] The level of Lukashenka's rating as a potential president of Russia has ranged from 3 percent to 12 percent at different times.[46]

On the other hand, these ratings should be viewed in context. Taking into account the unfriendliness toward Lukashenka of the leading media, the ironic and arrogant attitude toward the "Belarusian kolkhozman" on the part of the ruling elites, and Lukashenka's extremely limited opportunities to address the Russian audience directly, his rating in Russia is perhaps not so poor. In fact, his is inferior only to that of the Communists. This is a good reason for many influential political forces in Russia to keep Lukashenka as far away from Russian politics as possible.

---

[41]   Solovei, "Nadezhdy," pp. 426–27.

[42]   "Rossiiskoe obshchestvennoe mnenie ob ob"edinenii s respublikoi Belarus'," *Nezavisimaia gazeta* 24 April 1997: 5.

[43]   Nikonov, *Belorussiia*, p. 71.

[44]   Solovei, "Nadezhdy," p. 424.

[45]   *Nezavisimaia gazeta* 20 February 1999: 5.

[46]   "Opredeleny lidery integratsii," *Nezavisimaia gazeta* 26 November 1999.

Postscript: The Putin Era

Hypothetically, there is a niche that Aliaksandr Lukashenka could occupy in Russian politics. Charisma and populism on the one hand, and the image of a consistent integrationist and effective ruler of a country on the other, would most probably help him mobilize the support of certain segments of the Left, people nostalgic for the Soviet Union, as well as a volatile electorate of nationalists and those in favor of a strong leader. But he has not been given the opportunity.

In March 2000, Vladimir Putin was elected president of the Russian Federation. This makes the whole intrigue of Russian-Belarusian relations much more concentrated on Russian policy towards Belarus. It also means that Moscow, in addition to having a decisive influence on the final outcome of integration negotiations, has regained the initiative.

The relationship between Putin and Lukashenka is still emerging. Regarding Belarus, Putin must, on the one hand, continue the tradition according to which Belarus is Russia's closest ally and should be treated accordingly. In line with that tradition, though most likely indicating his own views as well, the president-elect paid his first foreign visit in April 2000 to Minsk. In addition, Putin will be constrained by the institutions, decisions, and people he has inherited from the Yeltsin regime. One example of how Yeltsin people will continue to play a role is the appointment of Pavel Borodin, one of the leading members of Yeltsin's team, to serve as executive secretary of the Russian-Belarusian union.

On the other hand, Putin is a very different politician from Yeltsin, and that difference has direct implications for Belarus. In the first place, Putin is not considered responsible for the dissolution of the Soviet Union. Therefore, he does not have to maintain the image of success in the CIS or in Russian relations with CIS countries. Secondly, not surprisingly given his age, Putin seems to differ from typical post-Soviet leaders in that he is more formal and probably legalist. Reaching nonbinding "fireplace" and "no-necktie" agreements with Putin looks unlikely. Furthermore, Putin is not a public politician. He does not need to manipulate "near-abroad" issues, including Belarus, to raise domestic public support. He wins or loses on other grounds. Finally, Putin's regime, unlike the previous one, is not anti-Communist, as demonstrated in a January 2000 deal between the pro-government "Edinstvo" and Communist factions. Again, this means that policies toward the CIS will probably no longer be divisive, as the game of using the "integration" card to outplay the Left opposition is no longer required. Taken together, these factors suggest that Putin's Belarusian policy will be more pragmatic and more consistent than that of Yeltsin's.

The focus of Russian-Belarusian relations will most likely move to the sphere of economic cooperation, foreign policy coordination, and defense integration, that is, to areas where goals can be achieved independently, though within the context of overarching political goals. As far as the economy is concerned, the first actions of the new administration were suggestive of future intentions. The December 1999 Treaty on the Creation of the Union State, signed by then Prime Minister Vladimir Putin, was accompanied by the Implementation Program, which set clear deadlines for fulfilling certain legal and economic procedures and tasks as prerequisites for reunification. If the Program fails—and as of summer 2000 it was already lagging behind schedule—it will be difficult to refocus on politics again. Moreover, several deadlines in the Program are in 2005, which is beyond the current presidential term in Russia.

The February 2000 visits to Minsk by First Deputy Prime Minister Mikhail Kasyanov and Chairman of the Central Bank Viktor Gerashchenko demonstrated what Putin really cares about. During those visits, Moscow refused to give Belarus stabilization credit or to deliver an additional 2 billion cubic meters of gas. Furthermore, it insisted on having only one currency issuing center, in Moscow, after the single currency is introduced. Finally, the agreed-upon contribution of Belarus to the 2000 union budget—one-third, or 780 million rubles out of 2.2 billion—is disproportionately large, suggesting that Moscow is not ready to pay an economic price for the creation of a political union.

In the military sphere, on the other hand, concrete efforts to create integrated structures should be expected. After Poland's entry into NATO and, especially, after NATO's actions in Kosovo, which illuminate the strategic importance of the Western alliance, Russia and Belarus may well consider joint efforts to neutralize, at least partially, threats posed to their own security interests by a NATO infrastructure in Poland and in the Baltic states. Such cooperation would not, most likely, involve a military build-up or the deployment of Russian troops in Belarus, but would rather aim at increasing inter-operability and effectiveness of already deployed troops, and would likely enhance the already existing joint Russian-Belarusian Air Defense.

Bilateral military-industrial cooperation corresponds to the goal of making the military-industrial complex an "engine" of economic growth. To this end, relevant documents (such as a joint defense procurement order and an agreement on establishing a joint interstate financial-industrial group "defense system") were signed in early 2000. At a later date, the Belarusian military-industrial complex can be integrated into Russia's.

Another reason to expect closer military cooperation is that this is the one sphere of cooperation where joint actions are not expensive for Russia. In terms of joint air defense, Belarus is even the donor partner. But there is one area of potential conflict. For 25 years, Russia was given free basing rights for its antimissile station in Hantsevichi [Gantsevich]. Belarus now claims its air defense costs, which go mainly into serving Russia's interests, to be $500 million annually. Perhaps this is an item for difficult negotiations in the future, but at the moment cooperation seems beneficial for both countries.

In summary, the likelihood for a more cooperative, less competitive, relationship from Moscow's point of view seems strong. Whether this new, less-politicized cooperation will be compatible with the goals of Lukashenka's policies, however, remains to be seen.

8

Andrei Sannikov
Russia's Varied Roles in Belarus

Russia's relations with Belarus are more closely intertwined than Russia's relations with any other state of the former Soviet Union. Since the collapse of the Soviet Union, Belarus continues to be of strategic importance in the political, economic, and military spheres. Moreover, in its policies to re-exert control over members of the Commonwealth of Independent States in the wake of the collapse of the Soviet Union, Moscow has in Belarus its most willing partner. Indeed, the more that independence has been demonstrated by such states as Ukraine, Uzbekistan, Azerbaijan, Turkmenistan, and others, the more Russia has felt compelled to draw Belarus closer to itself.

For its part, Belarus has maintained a strong orientation towards Russia for a number of reasons. These include its long history of subordination to Moscow, long-standing suppression of its national identity, strong economic and military dependence of its leadership on Russia, and, especially under Lukashenka, an authoritarian and undemocratic government that has led to its international self-isolation.

Belarus has consistently received, and continues to receive, special attention from its eastern neighbor. This chapter will analyze the nature of that special attention, and the characteristics of Russia's varied roles in Belarus.

The Military Factor

From the point of view of the Russian military and military-industrial complex, Belarus has been so important that Russia has kept a watchful eye on it. In the Soviet period, it was a front echelon of the

Soviet military machine, and as such, was the most militarized republic. It had one soldier for every 43 inhabitants, or a total of 240,000 troops on its territory. Its economy was defense-oriented, and heavily dependent on supplies from all over the Soviet Union.

After the breakup of the Soviet Union, Belarus—together with Russia, Ukraine, and Kazakhstan—was faced with solving the problem of succession to the Soviet Union's nuclear treaties with the United States.[1] The position of the Russian military has always been very tough on the question of other states' rights to have a say on such nuclear issues, despite the fact that the weapons were deployed on the territories of those states. With Lukashenka in power in Minsk, Russia finally achieved a degree of control over Belarusian participation in such negotiations, and has even used this control to exert pressure on other former Soviet states, notably Ukraine.

Belarus also continues to be important to Russia vis-à-vis Moscow's policy on conventional weapons. In the Soviet period, Belarus was considered to be one of the USSR's principal bases of military operation in case of a war between NATO and the Warsaw Pact. After the breakup, Belarus' military significance increased, especially in conjunction with NATO enlargement. Belarus has a developed military infrastructure that includes airfields and missile bases. In addition, it has on its territory two important strategic facilities—a radar installation in Hantsevichi [Gantsevichi] and a naval communication unit in Vileika. The status of these two facilities was first negotiated with the then Premier Viacheslaŭ Kebich, and subsequently resolved when Lukashenka came to power. In January 1995, Belarus Prime Minister Mikhail Chyhir [Chigir] and Russian Vice Premier Aleksei Bolshakov signed an agreement on the joint use of these facilities for twenty-five years, thus providing Russia with a guarantee of its military presence in Belarus through 2020.

Subsequently, it has become a tradition to conclude agreements on military cooperation during every meeting of the presidents of Belarus and Russia. For example, on 2 April 1997, along with the Agreement on the Union, the two countries signed an agreement on further joint military activities, and declared that military development should correspond to the purposes of common defense. To that end, joint

---

[1]   See William C. Potter, "The Policy of Nuclear Renunciation: the Cases of Belarus, Kazakhstan and Ukraine," Occasional Paper 22 (April 1995), Henry L. Stimson Center.

planning of military exercises and joint use of the military infrastructure were also envisaged.[2] On the eve of the meeting of the two presidents in 1997, news was leaked of a new regional defense concept involving joint combat and reconnaissance operations, reinforcement of Belarusian air defense, joint army exercises, closer military industrial cooperation, and deployment of Russian strategic aircraft and missiles in Belarus in case of the redeployment of Pershing missiles in Europe.[3] Recently Belarus and Russia marked the fifth anniversary of joint combat duty of their air defense systems. Major General M. Savich, first deputy commander-in-chief of the Belarusian air defense, stated that the formation of a single regional air defense system of the "union" of the two states had practically been completed, and the system could start functioning that year.[4]

From the military point of view, Russia has achieved much more in Belarus than in any other former republic. Military cooperation is closely coordinated, and Belarus' military infrastructure is part of Russian strategic planning. In some cases, Russia even appears to make use of Lukashenka's aggressive behavior for its own political gains. This was the case when Lukashenka suspended the implementation of the Conventional Forces in Europe (CFE) Treaty case in February 1995, as well as when he delayed the withdrawal of SS-25s from the territory of Belarus until October 1997. In both cases, Russia intervened, for which it won public relations points as the valuable and effective mediator.

Belarus is probably attractive for Russia, or rather for the Russian military-industrial complex, from the point of view of arms exports as well. Because Belarus, unlike Russia, does not participate in such arms control regimes as the Missile Technology Control Regime or the Nuclear Suppliers Group, Russia is able to use Belarus as an outlet for the export of Russian arms and technology. As early as 1996, when it became one of the ten leading arms-exporting countries, Minsk acquired the reputation of being a very active arms exporter. Officials in Minsk do not deny that they are ready to re-export Russian

[2]   Decision No. 5 of the Supreme Soviet of the Belarus Russia Community on Common Principles of the Use of Elements of Military Infrastructure of Belarus and Russia, 2 April 1997.

[3]   Sergei Anisko, "Otsel grozit' my budem NATO." *Segodnia* 12 March 1997.

[4]   "Ogromnnoe nebo—odno na dvoikh," *Vo slavu Rodiny* 31 March 2001.

armaments.[5] Such re-exporting can be arranged through Belarusian companies which, unlike their Russian counterparts that are controlled by the state, are formally private and can get permission for arms deals. These relations apparently were formalized in the Agreement on Cooperation in Exporting Products of Military Nature to Third Countries, which was signed between the governments of Belarus and Russia on 6 July 2000. The contents of this agreement were not made public.

It is also worth noting a certain synchronization of contacts between Belarusian and Russian officials, on the one hand, and internationally problematic countries like Iraq, Cuba, Iran, and others, on the other. The latest example is Iran. On 1–2 February 2001, Iran's foreign minister visited Minsk and met with Lukashenka, after which meeting Lukashenka said that Belarus was going to trade with Iran in all goods, and nobody had the right to interfere with this. In March 2001, the Iranian president went to Russia and concluded various military agreements that caused negative international reactions. Nevertheless, during the visit of the Iranian defense minister in Minsk on 22–23 March, Lukashenka stated that "there are no closed areas of cooperation between Belarus and Iran." He meant first of all cooperation in the military area.[6]

Russia also uses Belarus to test certain policies, or to bring Belarus in line with certain Russian strategies. Lukashenka, for example, made strong statements on the relations between Yugoslavia and the Belarusian-Russian "union," an idea that was being considered at the very top levels of Russian leadership. On the eve of NATO's strike on Yugoslavia, Yugoslav foreign minister Živadin Jovanović was in Minsk on an official visit and discussed with Lukashenka and the secretary of Belarus' Security Council issues of military and technical cooperation.[7]

The Economic Factor

From the economic and economic-political point of view, Belarus offers a number of advantages from which Russia has attempted to

---

5   "Minsk priglashaet Moskvu na Balkany," *Izvestiia* 4 March 1999.

6   A. Alesin, "Po protorennoi doroge," *Belorusskii rynok* 13 (2001): 8.

7   "Minsk pomozhet Belgradu," *Nezavisimaia gazeta* 12 March 1999.

benefit with varying degrees of success. Because of its geographic situation and political orientation, Belarus is the only country that provides Russia with a secure trade and transit route to Europe. The creation of a Baltic-Black Sea corridor through Latvia and Lithuania to the Baltic Sea, and through Ukraine to the Black Sea, would separate Russia from the main oil routes for exporting Caspian oil to Europe were it not for Belarus. The Yamal pipeline through Belarus and Poland will allow Russia to exert additional pressure on Ukraine.

Russia appears to have created an excellent economic position for itself in Belarus. Belarus, having cut its ties with the rest of the world, is becoming ever more dependent on Russian energy supplies. Belarus' dependence on exports to Russia is significant, whereas Belarus' share in Russia's imports is barely 4 percent. But Russia's ability to take advantage of these economic interests in Belarus has proved difficult. The administrative model of the Belarusian economy, further strengthened by Lukashenka, does not allow Russian business to expand its influence through the normal channels of private financial flows and participation in privatization projects. The only way Lukashenka allows economic ties to develop is through state regulation of those economic activities. The conflict between the state-controlled economy of Belarus and the liberalized economy of Russia makes even this cooperation almost impossible and generates considerable tension between the two allies. Despite the numerous documents signed on economic collaboration and customs union, restrictions are constantly introduced by one side or the other, such as customs tariffs or transportation quotas.[8] As was stated by Vikentii Makarevich, chairman of the Belarusian Customs Committee, the Russian customs service fully controls the border between the two countries. At times, this results in lines of automobiles up to 16 kilometers.[9] These problems usually have to be resolved on the

---

[8]   On 17 January 1999, for example, the Russian side introduced quotas for Belarusian cargo transport in violation of the bilateral agreement. As a result, hundreds of heavy trucks were stopped at the border of the Smolensk region, and the conflict was resolved only after the intervention of the Belarusian president. There are other cases of non-compliance with existing agreements. For example, Minsk still holds back a part of the customs payment that is due to Russia in accordance with the Customs Union between the two countries. "Vsem stoiat'-skomandoval chinovnik," *Rossiiskaia gazeta* 5 March 1999.

[9]   *Belorusskaia gazeta* 2 April 2001: 11.

highest political level, which means that Russia has to pay a price for its economic advantages. This price is rather steep, estimated to be as high as $1.5–$2 billion a year.[10]

Under President Putin, Russia seems to have become tougher on economic questions. When Lukashenka last year initiated agreement on a single currency wishing to use it for propaganda purposes in his presidential campaign, Russia signed the agreement but set the dates for its practical implementation in 2005 and 2008. In November 2000, Russia offered a so-called stabilization credit of $100 million to support the Belarusian currency before a single currency is introduced. This credit was badly needed by Lukashenka to support his promise to raise the average salary to $100 per month before the next presidential election in Belarus. The first tranche of $30 million was to be provided in December 2000. However, in April 2001 Belarusian authorities were still fighting to get it while Russia kept putting forward new conditions. It now appears that Moscow tried to use the politics surrounding the presidential elections in Belarus to exert more pressure on Lukashenka in order to pursue its (Russia's) own economic interests. These included, first and foremost, the privatization of the Belarusian economy with active participation of Russian capital and companies.

The Political Factor

Belarus is today the only country in the post-Soviet sphere where Russia can pursue a policy of reintegrating the empire. This is why, despite the problems that Lukashenka presents by his unpredictability and even despite blackmail he occasionally uses against Russia, Belarus is seen as the strongest ally of Russian policy among the entire CIS. Russia appears to continue to believe that its relations with Belarus can serve the purpose of reinforcing Russia's role both within the CIS and internationally. Within the CIS, the Belarusian-Russian union is said to be serving as a model for future relations, for bringing

---

[10] Irina Selivanova, "Ėkonomicheskaia integratsiia Rossii i Belorussii i ee vliianie na razvitie narodnogo khoziaistva Belorussii," in D. E. Furman, *Belorussiia i Rossiia: Obshchestva i gosudarstva* (Moscow, 1998), p. 324. In a recent interview with a Belarusian paper, Boris Nemtsov said that friendship with Belarus costs Russia $100 million per month; *Imia* 28 December 1998.

more countries into Russia's orbit. Such a strategy is dangerous, given its potential to influence certain regional leaders—such as Tatarstan's Mintimir Shaimiev and Ingushetia's Ruslan Aushev—to renegotiate their relations with Moscow along the lines of the federal union of Belarus with Russia. Moscow's wish to restore its former sphere of domination is so strong, however, that it overlooks this potentially negative impact.

Internationally, Russia is cooling its relations with the West at a precarious moment, the very moment when it must rely on Western money to sustain its faltering economy. Its policy of confrontation requires allies that are even more aggressive toward the West. Belarus fits that role, since Lukashenka, through his rejection of liberal-democratic development, has placed himself in a position of isolation from the West, with no ally but Russia.

Moscow's political relations with Belarus have been confined, for the most part, to policies of Communist and ultra-nationalist forces, advocates of so-called reintegration. Official Moscow does not have any relations with democratic forces in Belarus, since those forces are not regarded as a possible alternative to Lukashenka's regime, and are even perceived as dangerous to Russian interests. For his part, Lukashenka has supported those forces that dominate the political scene in Russia, at times demonstrating a readiness to have the most radical Russian politicians as his allies. The model of the so-called union initiated by Lukashenka and accepted by Yeltsin is supported mostly by opponents of reform both in Russia and in Belarus. The role of Moscow during the political crisis in Belarus in November 1996 serves to illustrate Russia's policy in Belarus. On the eve of the notorious referendum that month, a group of high-ranking Russian officials—including Prime Minister Viktor Chernomyrdin and Speakers of the Federal Assembly Yegor Stroev and Gennady Seleznev—came to Moscow as mediators, but, in fact, helped Lukashenka organize what is today called a coup d'état, resulting in the concentration of almost absolute power in the hands of the Belarusian president. As an ironic aside, Yeltsin, by supporting Lukashenka, considerably strengthened his opponents in the Communist-dominated Duma and in the government.

In general, all of Russia's political forces, despite sometimes differing attitudes toward Lukashenka himself, do not regard Belarus as a separate country and advocate some form of union. Even the liberal Yabloko movement, for example, on the eve of the signing of the Union Treaty in April 1997, argued that unification with Belarus might well benefit Russian interests if it is done gradually and if Belarus undergoes democratic changes. During the ratification process of the Union Treaty of Belarus and Russia, two-thirds of Yabloko's members in the Russian Duma voted in favor of it. In an interview with a Belarusian independent paper, Yabloko leader Boris Nemtsov, an acknowledged Russian democrat and reformer, spoke favorably of the unification.[11]

For Belarusian democratic forces, the issue of the so-called integration has clearly become a political one. The majority of the Supreme Soviet, including those members who were in opposition to Lukashenka, voted for ratification of the 1996 Treaty on the Formation of a Commonwealth of Russia and Belarus. Since the referendum in Belarus giving Lukashenka almost dictatorial powers, however, the issue of Belarusian independence has become closely connected with that of democratization, and integration with Russia is perceived as an obstacle to the democratic processes in Belarus.

Recently, the democratic forces in Russia have shown more understanding of, and sensitivity to, the attitude of the Belarusian opposition towards the issue of Belarusian independence. During public hearings on issues related to Belarusian-Russian integration organized in Moscow by the Right Cause coalition and involving the participation of Belarusian democrats, it was acknowledged that state sovereignty and the territorial inviolability of Russia and Belarus are of the highest priority, and the integration plans of the authorities in the two countries were denounced.[12]

Conclusion

Relations between Belarus and Russia are still mired in a transitional period. On one hand, the two nations have signed numerous documents in which they both act as independent states. On the other, the authorities in both Minsk and Moscow cling desperately to what is left of the Soviet Union and are guided in their relations by the illusion of the reversibility of history. By playing the Belarusian card, Russia has assumed the role of supporter of an authoritarian regime in

[11]   *Imia* 28 December 1998.

[12]   Memorandum of the Public Hearings on the Problems of Integration of Russia and Belarus, 18 March 1999, Moscow.

Belarus, a role that clearly undermines its position among the democratic forces in Belarus and internationally, with such organizations as the Organization for Security and Cooperation in Europe (OSCE), the European Union, and the Council of Europe. From the point of view of pressuring neighbors such as Ukraine, the Baltic States, and even Poland, Russia seems to have gained from its alliance with Belarus. Continued Russian confrontation with the West will have further impact in strengthening Belarusian-Russian relations, with potentially dangerous consequences for the West. An example of such a development can be seen in a statement by the Russian defense minister on the possibility of redeployment of nuclear weapons in Belarus.

As for the long-term prospects for Belarus' integration in Russia, public support in Belarus for such a union is already beginning to wane. In 1997, more than 55 percent of the respondents to a poll conducted by IISEPS (the Independent Institute for Socioeconomic and Political Studies) supported integration with Russia. In a poll taken in February 1999 by the "NOVAK" Sociological Laboratory, this figure had already dropped to approximately 43 percent. Moreover, signs of anti-Russian sentiments in Belarus are beginning to surface. One Belarusian human rights activist concluded in 1999 that "a negative attitude towards Russia unites the active part of Belarusian society that is in opposition to Lukashenka." Political analysts from the Institute of CIS Countries headed by Konstantin Zatulin warned Russian politicians in 1999 that all opposition parties in Belarus had "finally shown their true identity," that of being pro-West and anti-Russia.[13]

For Russia, it may seem that, by playing the intermediary in different international forums and trying to support or protect the troublemaker Lukashenka, it fulfils an important international function. But by associating itself with a dictatorial regime, it cannot but further harm its own reputation among Western democracies with whom relations should be more important for Russia.

Since Vladimir Putin became president of Russia, relations between the two countries have undergone changes. It appears that Moscow has taken a more pragmatic approach toward Lukashenka. The strategic goal of Russia remains the same—to have Belarus under its political and economic control. However, Putin seems to be more

---

[13]   "Troianskii kon' oppozitsii," *Nezavisimaia gazeta* 3 March 1999.

conscious of Lukashenka's negative international reputation and of its consequences for Russia's policy. Lukashenka faced a presidential election in 2001, which afforded Moscow the perfect opportunity to demonstrate its dominant role in Belarusian politics. The failure of Lukashenka to get international recognition of his regime through parliamentary elections held in October 2000 prompted Putin to put more distance between the Kremlin and Lukashenka. Instead of supporting the results of the falsified elections, Putin said simply that the elections were the internal affair of Belarus. Lukashenka is no longer allowed to travel freely to Russian provinces, which he did under Yeltsin, and which he would have done during the next presidential campaign. Even on the day of the fifth anniversary of the so-called union between Russia and Belarus, on 2 April 2001, Putin did not show much support for Lukashenka, who came to Moscow in order to get Moscow's blessing for the elections. Instead Putin spoke of the necessity of building democratic societies in both countries. Putin apparently is facing a dilemma of how to keep Belarus obedient with or without Lukashenka. The solution will depend on what policies, or which individual(s), will better serve Russia's economic and strategic interests.

9

Yuri Drakokhrust and Dmitri Furman
Belarus and Russia:
The Game of Virtual Integration

The majority of the Russian and Belarusian people did not desire the dissolution of the Soviet Union, and after the collapse, they sincerely hoped to restore the lost unity. This desire was confirmed by the results of the 1991 referendum that determined the fate of the Soviet Union, and by the findings of many polls conducted in both Russia and Belarus. Thus it would seem that the task of unification between Russia and Belarus would not be a difficult one. After all, it concerns the unification of territories that always have been parts of the same whole. Russians and Belarusians are very close culturally, linguistically, and ethnically. Most Russians and Belarusians view themselves as one nation, not as representatives of different peoples. Like the Russians, the majority of Belarusians are Orthodox, and the Belarusian Orthodox Church is subordinated to the Russian Orthodox patriarchate. Belarusians and Russians do not share any negative historical memories about each other and do not have any negative or hostile stereotypes similar to those that exist, for example, between the peoples of the Baltic States and Russia. Even during this present period of separation, Belarus and Russia are more economically interdependent than other European countries are one with the other.

The unification process that began in 1992 and continues to this day has involved enormous amounts of time and effort on both sides. It also has yielded surprisingly few results. This chapter will explore the reasons for this lack of progress, and for the substitution of real integration with what these authors characterize as a game of "virtual integration."[1]

The process of Russian-Belarusian integration has been punctuated by four specific agreements. The first was signed under Prime Minister Viacheslaŭ Kebich in 1992—the agreement on a monetary union to establish free-trade and ruble zones. The three others were under Lukashenka—the Commonwealth of the Sovereign States of Belarus and Russia in 1996; the Treaty on the Union of Belarus and Russia in 1997; and the Treaty on the Creation of the Union State in 1999. The integration process has been remarkably repetitive, with an almost predictable rhythm of negotiation leading to a basically meaningless agreement. In tracing the history of the process, this chapter will highlight the ways in which the leaders of both Russia and Belarus have used the process for their own political purposes, and why this manipulation has resulted in so few concrete results.

Integration under Kebich

In 1990 and 1991, Belarusian Prime Minister Viacheslaŭ Kebich (the chairman of the Council of Ministers) was an opponent of control by the central Soviet government and advocated economic sovereignty for Belarus. Kebich explained Belarus' difficulties as resulting from the policy conducted by the Kremlin and Belarus' lack of independence. However, after the collapse of the Soviet Union and against the background of the deepening economic crisis in Belarus, Kebich changed his position radically and became a proponent of Russian-Belarusian integration. In September 1993, he stated: "As a person who was unable to predict the situation and the one who bears the responsibility in front of my people, I will do everything not to restore the Soviet Union as it was before, but to create it in a new form," making an indirect reference to the Belavezhskaia Pushcha Agreements.[2] Kebich portrayed the union with Russia as the solution to all the economic problems in Belarus and took steps towards integration with Russia, most of which were directed towards the

---

[1] On this topic, see also Margarita M. Balmaceda, "Myth and Reality in the Belarusian-Russian Relationship: What the West Must Know," *Problems of Post-Communism* May–June 1999: 3–14.

[2] *Nezavisimaia gazeta* 21 September 1993: 3.

creation of the common currency system. Kebich and Russian Prime Minister Viktor Chernomyrdin came to an agreement on that question at the end of 1993.

Kebich used the policy of unification of the two currencies as a bolster to his candidacy for election to the first Belarusian presidency, the post that had been introduced by the Supreme Soviet and specifically tailored for him. Thus he hoped that the monetary union would take place before the 1994 election. But despite the friendly relations between Kebich and Chernomyrdin, and despite the fact that a preliminary agreement on the unification of the two currencies was signed in April 1994, the ratification of the agreement was postponed and the monetary union did not take place in time for the election.

The characteristics of the history of the Kebich-Chernomyrdin negotiations for currency unification continue to exist today. The agreement that was supposed to determine the future of the two countries was prepared in a hurry, and contained a strong element of ambiguity that allowed for different interpretations. The most important question, whether Belarus was to be able to determine a general currency emission policy for the Union as a whole, remained vague.[3] The failure to achieve the much anticipated unification in the end damaged Kebich's reputation and was the primary reason for his failure to be elected president. Moreover, Aliaksandr Lukashenka, his opponent who ultimately defeated him, portrayed himself as an avid supporter of integration and argued that it was Kebich who was an obstacle to integration.

"Full Integration" and "Full Sovereignty"

After Lukashenka's victory, the integration process resumed with a fresh vigor infused by the new and energetic Belarusian president. In fact, integration was the most important slogan for Lukashenka during his first months as president: "I am not only the supporter of the unification of the two states," he declared. "I am also the supporter of the unification of all Slavic people. The union of Russia and Belarus is the core around which all other peoples of the former Soviet Union

---

[3]   "Shag vpered i dva nazad (beseda s S. Bogdankevichem)," *Belorusskii rynok* 17 (13–19 April 1994). See also, "Belorusskii zaichik poka v rublevoe pole ne prygaet," *Izvestiia* 18 November 1994: 1.

can unite."[4] Lukashenka further stated, "If we remain pragmatists, then step by step we'll come to closer ties than existed in the Soviet Union."[5]

The integration process resumed in 1995. This time, it was Russia's president Boris Yeltsin who sought to use the unification process for a political purpose, namely, to compensate for Russia's failures during the Chechen war. In February 1995, during Yeltsin's visit to Belarus, an agreement on peace and good neighborly relations was signed. According to this agreement, the two countries vowed to jointly protect state borders and to carry out a joint customs policy. This was the first time that an official statement on the necessity of political integration was made. During his speech at the Belarus Academy of Sciences, Yeltsin said: "I know that many of you here in Belarus want even closer ties than stronger integration." In his reply, Lukashenka stated: "I promised my people full integration with Russia, and I will keep my word. We'll have a people's referendum to address this issue."[6] "Closer ties than stronger integration" and "full integration" undoubtedly mean here the unification into one state. It appears that both presidents were looking to the realization of their plans in the near future.

Both sides soon appeared to scale back their aims. In a May 1995 referendum, Lukashenka introduced a more modest form of integration than the one he earlier spoke of when he asked whether people supported a policy simply aimed at economic integration with Russia. More than 80 percent of the respondents gave a positive answer.

Meanwhile, liberal circles in Russia started to see dangerous signs in the Belarusian president and his ideological proximity to Russia's Communist-nationalist opposition. Russia's integration with Belarus could potentially shift the political balance inside Russia and could also further isolate Russia from the West. Strong criticism of

---

[4]   *Sovetskaia Belorussiia* 1 September 1994.

[5]   I. Gukovskii, A. Stupnikov, "Aleksandr Lukashenko: Budem pragmatikami i, vozmozhno, pridem k eshche bolee tesnym sviaziam, chem byli v SSSR," *Respublika* 22 February 1995.

[6]   O. Gruzdilovich, "Protokolom vse nachnetsia—protokolom konchitsia," *Narodnaia gazeta* 24 February 1995.

integration by Russia's liberal circles paralleled some of the delays in official negotiations. Lukashenka's dissatisfaction with the integration negotiations as well as with Russia's indecisiveness and the criticism by Russian liberal circles was clear in his 30 August 1995 interview with Krasnoiarsk TV, in which he said that all those who signed the Belavezhskaia Pushcha Agreements would be cursed and condemned by their own people.[7]

But Lukashenka himself exhibited ambivalence and inconsistency in his attitudes. During various speeches in the summer and fall of that year, he declared himself both for and against unification with Russia. For example, during his interview with the newspaper *Izvestiia*, he said: "I have never had any problems with the idea of unification."[8] During his November 1995 interview with the German newspaper *Handelsblatt*, however, his comments concerning the possibility of integration included statements to the effect that he would never allow any integration with Russia while he is president, that Belarus is a sovereign state, and that Russia itself did not demand any unification.[9] It may appear that during 1995 Lukashenka changed his views from the idea of "full integration" and state unification with Russia to the idea of full Belarusian sovereignty. In reality, he attempted to embrace both concepts at the same time. He spoke equally firmly about both "full integration," stronger than in the USSR, and about full sovereignty. The roots of later contradictions in Lukashenka's views of, and policies toward, integration with Russia were already evident.

Commonwealth

Because the idea of integration holds popular appeal in both in Belarus and in Russia, the presidential elections have served to accelerate the process. Just as Kebich badly needed to show some concrete accomplishments in the integration process in 1994, Yeltsin, in 1996, found himself in a similar situation. In March, the Russian Duma denounced the Belavezhskaia Pushcha Agreements, causing panic among the CIS presidents. Lukashenka was the only president

---

[7]   *Belorusskii monitoring* 31 August 1995.

[8]   *Izvestiia* 29 August 1995: 5.

[9]   *Belorusskii monitoring* 24 November 1995.

who supported the Duma's decision. He even recalled that he had been the only person who initially voted against the disintegration of the Soviet Union.[10] Despite Lukashenka's attempts to take the side of the Russian opposition, however, he had to remain careful in his actions. The Belarus Supreme Soviet, primarily because of the position of the presidential faction "Zhoda," did not adopt a similar decision denouncing the Belavezhskaia Pushcha Agreements.

Yeltsin's position during that time was tenuous, as his chances for re-election were minimal. Yeltsin's advisors offered a number of plans to bolster his position, one of which involved Russia's unification with Belarus. Because Yeltsin had to respond to calls for integration of the post-Soviet space coming from the Duma opposition, Belarus was definitely a convenient means to achieve this goal. The plan would require revision of the Russian constitution and postponement of the elections.[11] Back in March, Yeltsin and Lukashenka had signed the treaty that cancelled all the mutual debts the two countries had accumulated.[12] Lukashenka visited Moscow, where he conducted, according to him, seven hours of negotiations with Yeltsin. The two leaders agreed to bring integration onto a different, higher level by creating a commonwealth of two countries.

It remained unclear, however, what exactly the two leaders were planning to sign. Lukashenka stated that the major characteristic of the agreement was the formation of a supra-national government and that the decisions of its highest organs would be mandatory for both states.[13] A day later, Yeltsin made a public statement that there were no plans to form a union state with Belarus.[14] Then on 2 April 1996, the agreement of the formation of the Commonwealth of the Sovereign States of Belarus and Russia was signed. Yet the real goals of the agreement were far from full integration. The institutions that

---

[10] *Belorusskii monitoring* 18 March 1996.

[11] *Izvestiia* 27 September 1995: 1.

[12] *Belorusskii monitoring* 25 September 1995; *Belorusskii monitoring* 4 March 1996.

[13] *Belorusskii monitoring* 25 March 1996.

[14] *Svaboda* 26 March 1996.

were created, though based on the principle of equal representation for Russia and Belarus, were merely symbolic.[15]

The Belarusian opposition protested the signing of the agreement. In Minsk, thousands of people participated in mass protests, which were violently suppressed by the special police divisions. Dozens of people were arrested and imprisoned.

From Commonwealth to Union

The period between the conclusion of the April 1996 Commonwealth Agreement and the conclusion of the April 1997 Treaty on the Union of Belarus and Russia was eventful for both Russia and Belarus. Russia held its presidential election, and Belarus underwent a bloodless coup d'état, supported by Russia, that established the de facto dictatorship of Lukashenka. All this time, the Moscow mass media and Russia's liberals continued to intensify their criticism and attacks on Lukashenka. For his part, Lukashenka promoted closer ties with the Russian opposition and tried to appeal to them in his speeches. In his 8 May 1996 speech, for example, he compared the current situation in Belarus with the that in 1941 when the country was surrounded by the enemy: "We cannot look on indifferently when a monster like NATO is approaching Belarus. We'll return to you to your integral fatherland for which you were fighting."[16] For some members of Russia's opposition, albeit marginal ones, Lukashenka became an idol and, moreover, a possible future president of a united Russia and Belarus.

Yeltsin too called for the continuation of the integration process at the beginning of 1997, and sent a special message to the Belarusian president in which he called for a "synchronization of reforms," an acceleration of the transition of Belarus towards a market economy, and the creation of joint-stock companies required by the Commonwealth Agreement. Lukashenka's reaction to these proposals was highly negative. During an extended meeting at the Belarus Ministry of Foreign Affairs, he said that he had not changed his policy

---

[15] "Dogovor o sozdanii Soobshchestva Suverennykh Respublik, podpisannyi B. El'tsinym i A. Lukashenko," *Znamia iunosti* 12 April 1996.

[16] "Rech' prezidenta Belarusi Aleksandra Lukashenko na prazdnovanii godov-shchiny Dnia Pobedy," *Belorusskii monitoring* 10 May 1996.

towards Russia and that he still believed that the people of the two countries would be reunited. But he also said that there were certain issues he could not neglect. One of them was the sovereignty of Belarus and its statehood. "Belarus cannot be incorporated into any given state in the form of a region or a district of that state," he said. "We want cooperation based on equal terms. Our citizens should not be sent to any military hot spots to fight. And, most importantly, any union should be based on mutually beneficial terms."[17]

Meanwhile, tensions arose between Russia and Belarus on the customs agreement. Russia accused Belarus of profiting from duty-free imports of foreign goods, primarily liquor. Belarus adopted several measures to distance itself from Russia, which caused displeasure in Moscow. Lukashanko met with the Ukrainian leader Leonid Kuchma, and the two leaders signed customs agreements which in some areas contradicted the Russian-Belarusian customs agreements. Later it was announced that Belarus would pursue a special agreement with NATO. At the beginning of February 1997, in an interview with the newspaper *Sovetskaia Belorussiia*, Lukashenka said that Minsk's every attempt to create closer relations with its Western partners, and also with Ukraine, evoked a very negative reaction from Moscow. Once again, Lukashenka declared, "We are not planning to incorporate ourselves into any state or organization in form of a region or province, or in any other subordinate form."[18] It is difficult to say whether this statement reflected his genuine concerns, or whether he simply wanted to exert pressure on Russia to accelerate the unification process and to establish Belarus' equal position in this union. If it was the latter, then Lukashenka succeeded to some extent.

Union

The history of the 1997 Union Treaty between Russia and Belarus is very similar to the story of the Commonwealth Agreement. The Union Treaty did not contain anything radically new. The two presidents met in Moscow on 7 March 1997 to discuss the preparation of the

---

[17] "Reportazh s zasedaniia rasshirennoi kollegii MID Belarusi," *Belorusskii monitoring* 22 January 1997.

[18] *Sovetskaia Belorussiia* 6 February 1997: 2.

integration document. Lukashenka's idea was that the commonwealth would be transformed into a union, that the governing bodies of the union would have authority over the national organs, and that the decisions of the union's organs would be binding vis-à-vis the national governments. He emphasized, however, that the union would involve two sovereign states.[19]

Integration documents were prepared at the end of March. These documents envisioned that the decisions of the Supreme Soviet of the Union, which would consist of the two presidents, prime ministers, and the speakers of the two parliaments, would be adopted by the majority of the votes of its members. These decisions would also have the force of executive authority for the governments of both states. It was only at the last moment that someone in Russian president's administration—most likely Anatoly Chubais—pointed out that the agreement would limit Russia and the Russian president's freedom of political action and would give Lukashenka, who would control the Belarus members of the Supreme Soviet, considerable control over Russia's state of affairs.

The Russian mass media started a wave of protests by suggesting a possible conspiracy against Yeltsin.[20] As a result, on 2 April only a general agreement to form a union was signed. It did not contain anything concrete or threatening. The prepared agreement was called the Treaty on the Union of Belarus and Russia (Договор о Союзе Беларуси и России), and it was supposed to undergo public discussion and a referendum. Lukashenka was very dissatisfied with Yeltsin's deviation from the original plan, which had already been coordinated by the working commissions. He also threatened not to sign the treaty if it contained significant changes from the original agreement.

Russia's foreign minister Yevgenii Primakov arrived in Minsk on 7 April. As a result of his negotiations with the Belarusian president, a new charter (called a "statute" [*ustav*] to the treaty) was formulated which differed considerably from the previous one. It prohibited the

---

[19] "Doklad prezidenta Belarusi Lukashenko na zasedanii parlamentskogo sobraniia Soobshchestva Belarusi i Rossii," *Respublika* 12 March 1997.

[20] O. Latsis, "Sud'bu Rossii reshaiut za spinoi naroda (Dogovor ili zagovor podgotovlen v koridorakh vlasti?)," *Izvestiia* 1 April 1997.

legislative and governing organs of the union from adopting decisions calling for direct action. The so-called "public discussion" of the new charter started on 9 April and continued through 15 May. During this period, many Russian politicians offered to abandon the idea of the union and to start working on a project to create a real federation, in which the Supreme Soviet would be elected directly by the people and the supreme bodies would reflect the real differences in size and power between Russia and Belarus. A referendum to address the above-mentioned issue was also recommended.[21]

Belarus reacted negatively to these statements. Lukashenka said the Russian leadership was not ready for the unification. He claimed that Russia was thinking about incorporating Belarus despite the fact that even during the years of the USSR it had not been a subordinate part of any state. It was a republic, and had no less sovereignty than it had now.[22] (As is usually the case with Lukashenka, it is difficult to say whether he really thought that Belarus had the same kind of sovereignty in the USSR as it has now, or whether his protests were for show.)

On 22 May, a day before the signing of the statute, Lukashenka traveled to Moscow to discuss some differences and to settle remaining questions. In two hours, the final version of the charter, in which it was stated that all decisions of the Supreme Soviet of the union would become legitimate only after they are approved and signed by both presidents, was signed. This organ was thus stripped of any new power and authority. On the following day, Yeltsin and Lukashenka signed the "Statute to the Treaty on the Union of Belarus and Russia of 2 April 1997."

During the preparation of the union agreement, Lukashenka mounted a campaign intended to "discipline" Russian mass media organs, which had been critical of his policies.[23] For a few days in the spring of 1997, all foreign journalists working in Belarus were prohibited from broadcasting their reports outside Belarus and the ban

---

[21]   Nikolai Gonchar, "Ob"edinenie s otkrytymi glazami," *Izvestiia* 15 April 1997: 5.

[22]   *Belorusskii monitoring* 21 April 1997.

[23]   "Prezident Belarusi Lukashenko: Massirovannaia kompaniia v rossiiskikh SMI protiv belorusskoi vlasti dolzhna byt' prekrashchena," *Belorusskii monitoring* 4 April 1997.

was lifted only after the Russian government intervened. In July 1997, ORT [Obshchestvennoe rossiiskoe televidenie] journalist Pavel Sheremet was arrested and imprisoned after he reported about a lack of security at the Belarusian-Lithuanian border. Sheremet was charged with illegally crossing that border. His arrest caused considerable protest and an anti-Lukashenka campaign by the most important Russian TV networks and newspapers. They called on the Russian authorities to stop Lukashenka from doing what not a single president of a CIS country had done before—arrest Russian journalists. Yeltsin himself issued a very harsh statement demanding explanations from Lukashenka.

On 8 September, while Lukashenka was in Moscow to participate in Moscow's 850th birthday celebration, he met with Yeltsin. Regarding discussion about the Sheremet case, Yeltsin later stated that the problem had been solved. Lukashenka, however, said that it would not be discussed on the presidential level. Even in regard to this matter, one can clearly see different interpretations provided by the two presidents. Yeltsin was undoubtedly implying that the journalist should and would be released; Lukashenka was of a different opinion. Sheremet was still in prison. On 18 September, an irate Yeltsin said that the world had never set a precedent whereby two presidents reached an agreement and that afterwards one of them did not live up to it. "This is simply impossible," he said, "and must mean that one president is not thinking far enough."[24] On 2 October, Lukashenka intended to visit the Lipetsk and Iaroslav regions. Several hours prior to his departure, however, Moscow informed Minsk that the Belarusian president's aircraft would not be granted an air corridor. Yeltsin commented that this measure was an effort to put pressure on Lukashenka to release Sheremet. On 7 October 1997, the journalist was released from preliminary confinement and, in 1998, was given a two-year suspended sentence.

Once again, union negotiations were manipulated for political purposes. In this case, they were held hostage to the settlement of other political issues.

---

[24]   S. Kalinkina, "Uchen'e—svet, a neuchen'e—t'ma," *Belorusskaia delovaia gazeta* 18 September 1997.

From Union to Union State

An integration lull continued throughout 1998. The Kremlin was probably saving the integration option for use in the parliamentary elections of 1999 and the presidential election of 2000. Meanwhile, the Russian opposition, which had a majority of seats in the Russian Duma, remained very active in this area. During 1998, it made several attempts to form a parliament of the Union of Russia and Belarus. As early as March, the working group of the parliamentary assembly of the Russia-Belarus Union prepared the draft of a law on forming the parliament. The draft discussed the formation of a two-chamber lawmaking organ. The upper chamber of this legislative organ would be formed by the national parliaments and would equally represent the electorate. The lower chamber would be elected directly by the people of Russia and Belarus.

These discussions again revealed the contradictions inherent in every Russian-Belarus negotiation process and in every scheme for the unification of the two countries. The Belarus parliamentarians were against having the representatives of the lower chamber elected proportionate to the populations of Russia and Belarus. The decisions of the union parliament, however, were only recommendations and could not become final without the approval of the presidents. It became obvious that Yeltsin would not approve such recommendations.

In 1998, another characteristic of the game of integration emerged, and that was Minsk's cooperation with Russia's regions. Since 1996, Lukashenka had personally visited more than half of Russia's regions and republics, and Russian governors frequently visited Minsk as well. Many political analysts and observers interpreted these exchanges as a part of Lukashenka's so-called pre-election campaign and as an attempt to exert pressure on the Kremlin through the governors who were members of the Federation Council, the upper chamber of the Russian parliament. Lukashenka organized a widely advertised and well-publicized visit of 40 Russian governors to Brest. However, the Kremlin most likely applied some pressure, because of the 40 who originally planned to participate, only 10 actually made the trip.

The Russian economic crisis of 17 August 1998 became the herald of another move towards integration. Right after the crisis struck Russia, Lukashenka announced that he could see newly opened opportunities for integration. At first glance, his statement seemed paradoxical. Yet it was not. The economic crisis seriously aggravated the political situation in Russia, and clashes between various political forces and shifts in the political balance have always created fertile ground for Lukashenka's initiatives. It is likewise the case that any political balance established in Russia has interfered with Lukashenka's actions.

On 25 December 1998, Lukashenka and Yeltsin signed a number of integration documents in Moscow. A declaration of unification was one of the most significant of them. This document stated that, by the end of 1999, Belarus and Russia would be united into one union state and a single currency would be introduced. The possibility of having a joint referendum in Belarus and Russia to discuss the unification process was mentioned. The declaration also mentioned the establishment of the legislative and executive organs of the union, including a bicameral parliament. It was emphasized, significantly, that despite unification, Russia and Belarus each would preserve its state sovereignty as well as its independent international status.

Lukashenka, on the one hand, stated that there was no need to hold the referendum since the new declaration did not contradict the constitutions of either Russia or Belarus. Yeltsin, on the other hand, advocated the referendum. He added that no country's constitution provides for its inclusion or incorporation into another state. Once again, it was unclear what kind of state the two sides were constructing.

Union State

As early as December 1997, in an interview with "Interfax," Lukashenka openly declared his ambition to head a unified Belarusian-Russian state. He stated that if the united state was formed, then it should be based on the principle of equality, implying that not only a Russian, but a Belarusian, could become the president of the new state.[25] After the plans to form a united state were publicly announced,

---

[25] *Belorusskii monitoring* 30 December 1997.

Lukashenka's intentions started to become real. In 1998, Mikhail Miasnikovich, head of Lukashenka's presidential administration and also head of the Belarus working group that was formulating the union agreement, supported the establishment of the presidential post in the new union state. In January 1999, Russian presidential aide Ivan Rybkin announced Yeltsin's intention to be a candidate for the not-yet-established post of the president of the union state. Judging by the tone of Rybkin's statement, it sounded as if Yeltsin's announcement was meant to test public opinion and reaction to such an initiative. Throughout 1999, however, no Kremlin official ever made any such statement.

In January 1999, Lukashenka spoke on the occasion of the 10th Session of the Parliamentary Union Assembly in Minsk. Apparently, one month since the signing of the union declaration was enough time for embraces to change into reproaches. Criticizing Russia's un-willingness to accept his suggestions, Lukashenka saw the future sovereignty of Belarus threatened by Russia's refusal to take the republic's demands into consideration. The outline of the future union state in the form of a confederation was presented by Gennady Seleznev, chairman of the Russian Duma. During the press conference held after the parliamentary assembly meeting, Seleznev said that the future union state would not need a publicly elected president and that it would make more sense for the union parliament to elect a head of the executive power.

During his February 1999 visit to Mordovia, Lukashenka once again declared the necessity of publicly electing a president for the Russian-Belarusian union state. Meanwhile, Lukashenka drastically cut his public contacts with the Russian opposition. He expressed his loyalty to Yeltsin and every new prime minister. Every time the question of impeaching the Russian president was discussed in the Russian Duma, Lukashenka declared that he was categorically against it. The Duma certainly had the legal right to include the question of impeachment on its agenda, Lukashenka said, but as for himself, he was trying to be a pragmatist. Russia was experiencing very difficult times. Why should Belarus aggravate the situation by publicly introducing the complicated issue of impeachment? Lukashenka most likely took this position because he believed that only Yeltsin was able to make key decisions in the integration process, and that the process itself was facing potential enemies.

Many in Russia were apprehensive about the chaos in power that could arise after the formation of the supernational organs. This fear was strengthened by the appearance of a policy paper by Russia's Council on Foreign and Defense Policy published in *Nezavisimaia gazeta*, which advised refraining from the formation of supernational organs until Russia's presidential election. By mid-spring, contradictions surfaced. Two union agreement projects were announced. The Russian version entailed a slight modification of the union concluded in 1997. The Belarusian proposal talked about the formation of powerful supernational organs. Lukashenka commented bitterly that the Kremlin was refusing to adopt his proposal. During his meeting with Saratov Governor Dmitrii Aiatskov, Lukashenka even threatened to put the Russian leadership on his list of enemies of integration.

At the end of April, during a personal meeting between Lukashenka and Yeltsin, however, the Russian president rejected all proposals made by his Belarusian colleague. Lukashenka said that Yeltsin even turned down a proposal according to which the Russian president would automatically become the head of the union state and Lukashenka vice-president until the official election of the govern-ment. Lukashenka complained that Russia was not yet ready to follow Belarus' radical plan for integration.[26] According to Lukashenka, Yeltsin expressed his concern that the subject constituencies of the Russian Federation would want to build their relations with Moscow similar to Moscow's relations with Belarus.[27]

Many observers were surprised at the Russian president's reaction, as Lukashenka's proposal welcomed the extension of Yeltsin's power. There are several probable reasons, however, why Yeltsin refused such a tempting offer. Lukashenka's plan did not entail reducing Belarus' status to that of one of Russia's regions, even in the case of the formation of supernational governing organs. The leaders of Russia's autonomous republics (Presidents Mintimir Shaimiev of Tatarstan, Ruslan Aushev of Ingushetia, and Murtaza

[26]   *Interfaks* (ezhednevnyi belorusskii vypusk) 28 April 1999; 29 April 1999.

[27]   *Interfaks* (ezhednevnyi belorusskii vypusk) 10 May 1999.

Rakhimov of Bashkiria), on the other hand, often stated that they would seek status similar to that of Belarus should the union state be formed. Thus, Lukashenka's unification plan could entail the threat of destabilizing Russia's federal structure. In addition to this, any real unification that did not imply Belarus' incorporation into the Russian Federation required changes in the Russian constitution. Yeltsin's aide Sergei Prikhodko, explaining why the Kremlin opposed Lukashenka's version of unification, said openly that Russia was against amending its constitution.[28] Analyzing Yeltsin's resignation on 31 December 1999, one could also assume that his efforts concerning unification coincided with his search for an acceptable successor. He may well have used his stated interest in the post of president of the union as a political means to threaten his opponents.

In an interview with the Russian TV channel ORT at the end of June 1999, Lukashenka once again revealed that he had designs on the post of union president when he stated: "If the union is formed," he said, "and the president of the union is elected by direct public vote, then I should probably contend with Yeltsin for this post."[29] In July, during the 12th Session of the Parliamentary Assembly of the Union, he decided to play his trump card by accusing Russia of failing to transform the union into a union state. The Belarusian leader also alluded to the profits that Russia could enjoy from transit trade through Belarus. In addition, Lukashenka expressed reservations concerning his own foreign policy, which had focused on the east, and subsequently directed his foreign ministry to facilitate closer relations with Belarus' western neighbors.[30]

At the beginning of August 1999, the project of the union agreement was finalized and promises were made indicating that it would be signed at the beginning of September. The agreement did not entail the establishment of the post of the president of the union, and it resembled the slightly amended union agreement of 1997. A new prime minister was installed in Russia. The new head of the cabinet, Vladimir Putin, made his traditional visit to Minsk, during which he expressed the hope that the treaty would be signed before

---

[28] *Interfaks-Vremia* 26 July 1999.

[29] *Interfaks* (ezhednevnyi belorusskii vypusk) 26 July 1999.

[30] *Belorusskaia gazeta* 26 July 1999.

Russia's presidential election. Lukashenka, said that he had wished to sign the agreement with Yeltsin himself but, after making some critical remarks concerning the contents of the agreement, consented to signing the proposed Russian version. On 24 September, Yeltsin signed the draft of the notorious agreement and moved it into public discussion. The draft was also sent to the Belarusian side for approval.

The Kremlin officials were confident that their colleagues in Minsk would not have any objections. But on 30 September, Lukashenka proved the opposite. He officially stated that his country would not discuss the draft as he found it laughable, and that he would only sign the agreement contingent upon Moscow's fulfillment of its economic obligations towards Belarus.[31] He also reiterated his insistence on a high-ranking position in the Russian political hierarchy if united. Again, he attempted to use an agreement for concrete political gains.

The draft of the new union agreement contained many contradictions as well. Just as the 1997 agreement, it declared that the Supreme Soviet was the highest authority of the union state. This organ, it said, would consist of the presidents, prime ministers, and the speakers of the two parliaments. All its decisions would be approved by the vote of the two presidents. Unlike in the agreement of 1997, the decisions of the Supreme Soviet had the force of binding decree and legally had more power over the national laws. The Supreme Soviet, however, could only adopt decisions within certain union jurisdictions, whatever that meant. In addition, Article 89 of the agreement invalidated any legal claims and legal power of the decisions of the Supreme Soviet, since it stated that any decisions that contradict the national constitutions would come into force only after the amendment of the constitutions.

On 8 December, the long-delayed agreement was finally signed, along with the program for its implementation.[32] During the ceremony, Lukashenka and the Russian president also agreed to sign one more agreement by the end of Yeltsin's presidential term that would deal with the "full" unification, that is, with the union state

---

[31]   *Interfaks* (ezhednevnyi belorusskii vypusk) 1 October 1999.

[32]   "Dogovor ob obrazovanii soiuznogo gosudarstva Belarusi i Rossii i programma mer po realizatsii dogovora," *Sovetskaia Belorussiia* 9 December 1999.

per se. Shortly after the signing ceremony, Lukashenka discovered that, despite the fact that both sides agreed to introduce a single currency by the year 2005, it had not been determined where the currency emission center was going to be located. Moscow wanted the Central Bank of Russia to become such a center; Minsk demanded that a Russian-Belarusian committee, based on parity, deal with the question in the new state. In 1994, the same argument had become the bone of contention between Russia and Belarus. On this occasion too, as in 1994, the Belarus opposition held anti-integration protests, both in Minsk and elsewhere. During one of these protests in Minsk, a Russian flag was burned.

Russian and Belarusian Mass Consciousness

One explanation why Russian-Belarus integration has turned into a farce and has not achieved its goal lies in the dichotomy between the Russian and Belarusian mass consciousness. Russian mass consciousness, which was traumatized by the collapse of the Warsaw Pact and the USSR, as well as by the decline in Russian influence, seeks to regain its lost stature and to see Russia as the center of a powerful, newly reunited state. This is exactly where the theory of Russia as a natural, grand geopolitical center of Eurasia originates. It derives from the idea that all Russians (understanding "Russians" in the old imperial sense of Great Russians [Russians], White Russians [Belarusians], and Little Russians [Ukrainians]) should unite under the aegis of counterbalancing the West. Belarus occupies a modest place in these aspirations. Russians devote much more attention to Ukraine. The Russian population would welcome the union with Belarus, but they already view Belarus as a part of Russia. Although the Russians do not have any sense of superiority over the Belarusians, neither do they view Belarus as a separate nation. Russians see Belarus' idea of equality in the unification process as either a decoy used by Lukashenka to mislead his opponents or as a bargaining chip to "sell himself" (together with Belarus) at a higher price.

It is unrealistic to believe that a country of 145 million people could be unified on equal terms with one of 10 million. That would mean that Belarus would contribute only one-tenth into the general budget of the union state, yet could claim control over half of its total budget. Any realistic solution that takes such discrepancies into consideration would entail the incorporation of Belarus into Russia.

Belarusians view unification with Russia differently. Their experience of the collapse of the USSR is more painful than that of the Russians, because the collapse came to many Belarusians as a surprise. In addition, while Russian interest is not focused primarily on Belarus, Belarus' attention is centered primarily on Russia. A minority of the Belarusian people, primarily the opposition, view Russia is a source of threat and fear Belarus will be swallowed by Russia. The majority, however, view Russia as a source of hope. Notwithstanding, Russia is at the center of attention for both groups.

Even those Belarusians who favor unification with Russia, however, envision this process differently from the way Russians do. The fact is that Belarus' sovereignty is valued equally by the country's opposition forces as well as by Lukashenka's supporters. For most Belarusians, their current aspirations to reunite with Russia represent not only a return to their historic past, but to their mythical Soviet past. Reunification would include restoring totalitarian dogmas within the context of a post-totalitarian world.

This dichotomy in public consciousness is one of the key characteristics of the integration process. But the dichotomy exists on the level of the presidents as well. And it is on this level where the process is planned and carried out. As mentioned earlier, the Russians and the Belarusians view the process of unification differently. Lukashenka would not have been elected president if he had not promised unification with capitalist Russia while at the same time preserving Belarus' sovereignty and not allowing the vices of capitalism to spread there. The Belarusian public wants union with Russia, preservation of its sovereignty, and non-proliferation of Russian laws on their territory. Lukashenka has worked hard to realize this concept, and, when his attempts have failed, he has put the blame on all sorts of "enemies of the people." Yeltsin and Lukashenka, like their respective countrymen, speak different languages when discussing integration, and it later turns out that each of them has perceived the process differently.

Dichotomy also exists on the level of the two countries' ruling elites. In Russia, the division between the opponents and supporters of unification with Belarus corresponds almost precisely to the division between Left and Right. Thus, the dramatic events of the 1997 union agreement came almost entirely as a result of the clash between the teams of Finance Minister Anatoly Chubais and that of Chernomyrdin-Primakov. It was the Russian Right that insisted on annexing Belarus (incorporating it, not uniting with it on equal terms). Many, including Lukashenka, considered such an attitude as provocation—and an attempt to sabotage the unification. But one must remember that all attempts to unite are based on Belarusian proposals and on combining two different concepts—state unity on the one hand, and sovereignty on the other. The Russian Right expresses the majority of Russian public opinion. The Russian Left welcomes any form of unification and hopes that Russia's greater territory and population will eventually swallow up Belarus' claims for sovereignty and lead to its incorporation. The Russian Left's support of any form of unification with Belarus could also be explained by the lack of responsibility on their part as a non-ruling political force. On the other hand, when they feel that the unification endangers their political plans, as in 1999, they immediately lose any interest in it.

In Belarus, there are two parties that are close to the presidential administration which have opposing views towards the union with Russia. One of them supports the idea of full integration; the other has Belarus' full sovereignty on its agenda. The group that stands for full integration propagates pan-Slavic ideology and is very close to Russian nationalists. Members of this group include State Secretary of the Security Council Viktar Sheiman and Vice-Prime Minister Uladzimir Zametalin. They hope that Lukashenka will become the head of the united state and that they will be given high positions in the new Moscow government. A considerable number of Belarusian officials, however, seem to understand that Lukashenka's chances to become the head of the new state are slim and that he will not be able to promise high posts to all of them. With the appearance of the new united state, many of these officials' positions will be lowered to the level of regional bureaucrats. Members of the party that supports Belarus' sovereignty include Foreign Minister Ural Latypaŭ; editor of the presidential newspaper *Sovetskaia Belorussiia,* Paval Iakubovich; and, to a certain extent, the head of the presidential administration,

Mikhail Miasnikovich. Clashes between these groups sometimes appear in the press.[33]

The impossibility of the union is also connected with the personalities of the two presidents themselves. Lukashenka and Yeltsin both came to power through democratic elections. They also initiated their own coups, which established authoritarian powers in their respective countries. Authoritarian rulers react to attempts to limit their power more negatively than their counterparts in democratic countries. In some exceptional cases, an authoritarian leader might even be willing to give up his power (as in Yeltsin's case at the end of 1999) in order to ensure that his place is taken by a supportive and sympathetic successor, thus guaranteeing his future safety. During his term Yeltsin resisted any legislative attempts to limit his power. The problem of distribution of power during integration becomes paramount. Leaders must do everything possible to increase their popularity, even at the expense of integration. To achieve this goal, their actions should be grandiose and attract a lot of attention, as was the case during Yeltsin's attempts to boost his popularity in 1996. Still, the actual unification may not take place, as it is impossible to establish a unified state in which the power of both presidents is preserved.

It seems obvious that countries with authoritarian regimes cannot unite into one state. Different political ideologies in Belarus and Russia also add to the impossibility of unification. For Yeltsin, any unification with Belarus, even the variant of incorporation into Russia and getting rid of Lukashenka, would have meant adding the Belarusian majority to the votes of the Russian opposition. For Lukashenka, expanding the opposition presents the same problem. In addition, Lukashenka is very apprehensive of Russia's mass media, which he considers "enemies of the people."

To increase their popularity, both Yeltsin and Lukashenka would assume postures that indicated a preference for integration. But, when it was time for serious reforms that implied limitation of power, the presidents would come to a complete or partial stop, and the

---

[33]   A. Petrov, "O 'piatoi kolonne' v Belarusi (kto pytaetsia vliiat' na prezidenta A. G. Lukashenko)," *Belorussiia* 30 April–1 May 1998: 2. See also: Nikolai Gonchar, "Lukashenko ne pustit v Kreml' minskaia nomenklatura," *Obshchaia gazeta* 9–15 October 1997: 5.

integration process would be suspended for an indefinite period. Because the main goal for both leaders has been the preservation of their individual power, it is the *struggle* for integration (and here the operative word is "struggle" and under no circumstances "integration" itself) that is necessary. Thus, some sort of integration game, the ultimate goal of which is not integration but something else, is taking place. What, then is that "something else"?

The Game of "Virtual Integration"

Normally, as an authoritarian president's power solidifies, public opinion becomes less important. Ultimately, however, these men depend on it psychologically from the standpoint of preserving their power. And because the two peoples of Russia and Belarus are striving for integration, the ratings they give their respective leaders depend on the success of that integration. Integration policy not only helped Lukashenka ascend to power, but also helped him establish an authoritarian power regime and defend himself against his enemies. Integration helped him win the 1995 referendum and then carry out the coup of 1996. The coup itself would not have been successful had a plan for integration not been on the agenda.

In Russia, the 1996 Commonwealth Agreement was an integral part of Yeltsin's campaign. The two presidents could not abandon such a popular idea even after they realized the impossibility of the unification. The contradictory notions of integration held by both countries' leaders and general public in fact served as a convenient tool for political maneuver. For example, when Lukashenka perceived himself at a dangerous juncture, he would announce that it was Russia that did not want integration. He argued that what was being offered by Russia to Belarus was not integration, but rather full subordination and absorption of Belarus. Similarly, to cool down his Belarusian counterpart, Yeltsin could always call the integration plan quite realistic, but never acceptable to Lukashenka.

There is another factor that is present in this integration game. This is a game that is difficult to lose. Indeed, one leader can theoretically win no less than the entire country of his opponent. The game is relatively safe because, in both countries, the power belongs to the presidents. Only they can determine which direction the integration should follow and they can stop at any moment. But there is always a chance that the opponent, carried along by the game, will fall into some sort of a trap and sign something he was not supposed to sign. It is clear that Lukashenka would approve Belarus' annexation to Russia if he were guaranteed the post of the president of the unified state.

The game is both safe and useful. Even as Lukashenka understood that there was no possibility of his being elected president of a united state, he continued playing the game since in the very process of striving for the unachievable, the Belarusian leader gained some concrete political and economic advantages. The advantages that either leader has obtained were valid only within the framework of the game itself. The cancellation of the considerable Belarusian debt to Russia in 1996, the state-controlled smuggling of duty-free alcohol into Russia, the obtaining of cheap energy from Russia, and the sale of Russian weaponry would not have been possible without the integration game.

Meanwhile, Lukashenka avoids adopting any laws that would allow Russian industrialists to privatize Belarusian enterprises and bring Russian capital into Belarus. He perfectly understands that if Russian oligarchs become a political force in Belarus, they will be more dangerous than the Belarusian opposition itself. As he has stated: "Why would we give away ownership of the two oil-processing plants? Property means power."[34] Barring any extraordinary circumstances, integration moves will encounter clearly defined limits. As soon as integration threatens the president's power, the process will be called to a halt. As long as authoritarian power is not possible without sovereignty, the presidents will safeguard the independence of Belarus and Russia.

Integration after Yeltsin

The integration game has continued after Yeltsin's resignation. Most Russians support the idea of unifying with (or, as most of them see it, annexing) Belarus. Even those Russian politicians who think that no real unification will ever take place will find it difficult to deviate

[34] *Belorusskii monitoring* 31 August 1995.

from such a popular policy. Just as in 1996–1999, the integration campaigns will intensify on the eve of each election. It should also be mentioned that regular attempts to unite Russia and Belarus never bear real fruit, but instead achieve the more limited, but pragmatic, goal of keeping Belarus in Russia's sphere of influence.

Yeltsin's successors could change the course of the integration process. Most likely Vladimir Putin does not suffer from the "Belovezh complex," the feeling of guilt and responsibility for the collapse of the USSR. In addition, less political feuding can be expected in a less ideological post-Yeltsin administration. As a result, the window of opportunity for Lukashenka will become narrower, and it will be more and more difficult for him to use differences between Russia's various political elite groups for his political games. On the other hand, the absence of the "Belovezh syndrome" could cause a shift among the members of a post-Yeltsin administration away from a policy of integration to one of incorporation (annexation) of Belarus into Russia. It seems that Lukashenka's integration game will be less effective, and more risky, after Yeltsin, and his hopes of becoming president of the union state less achievable. A Lukashenka candidacy in the 2004 Russian elections is likely to be deemed too risky.

The question remains whether unification will continue after Lukashenka leaves office. Looking back over the Kebich years, one sees evidence that Lukashenka was not the first leader of Belarus to invent the integration game. However, adherence to Belarus sovereignty has become the political platform of basically all the opposition groups and parties in the country, including the oppositionist Communists and the liberal democrats. If indeed the integration game continues after Lukashenka leaves office, it will no doubt take less risky forms than today and will be less binding on the parties involved.

10

John C. Reppert
The Security Dimension in the Future of Belarus

On 26 January 2000, Acting President Vladmir Putin of Russia and President Aliaksandr Lukashenka of Belarus met in Moscow to celebrate the entry into force of a new union treaty designed to increase the gradual integration of the two states. The union treaty covered several security issues, such as the agreement to "form a single defense space," among its many provisions.

For the defense establishments of Russia and Belarus, this is but one more in a series of agreements, understandings, and actual programs that have defined their evolving security relationship since the breakup of the Soviet Union at the end of 1991. However, the events of 1999, including the formal expansion of NATO to the Belarus border, the NATO decision to intervene militarily in the Yugoslav province of Kosovo against the explicit wishes and interests of both Belarus and Russia, and the renewal of Russian warfare in Chechnya make the defense relationship between these two states more urgent and relevant than at any time since Belarus gave up the nuclear weapons it inherited from the Soviet Union.

This chapter will review briefly the evolution of that relationship, and the prospects and international security consequences of full integration of the two countries' defense establishments.

Background

Though Belarus formally declared its independence on 25 August 1991, and was instrumental in the events leading up to the final collapse of the Soviet Union on 25 December of that year, its enthusiasm for an independent security policy was limited. Even as Belarus head of state Stanislaŭ Shushkevich was pledging his nation to a security policy that would be "neutral and nuclear free,"[1] He moved forward on the reality of establishing a separate armed forces with considerable caution.

One reason for this was the lingering concern in Belarus that as a newly independent and relatively weak state, it might seem attractive to its neighbors to take advantage of this condition to raise territorial issues. Belarus' current territory has legally belonged to several different states at different periods of its history. Other reasons for caution ranged from the simple fact that Belarus' military forces were never designed for the exclusive defense of the republic's territory to the ethnic composition of the armed forces that Belarus had inherited.

As was quickly noted after the breakup of the Soviet Union, the military forces based in Belarus, which were largely to be transferred to the control of the new national government, were not there because of any assessment of threat to Belarus or requirement for the new nation.[2] As an example of the ethnic issue, by mid-1992, eight out of nine deputy ministers of defense were ethnically Russian, while only one was an ethnic Belarusian; only 30 percent of the officer corps overall were ethnic Belarusians.[3]

However, because of the geographic position that Belarus occupied within the Soviet structure as the major western military district reinforcing the East European members of the Warsaw Treaty Organization, deciding what to do with the armed forces on its territory was urgent in terms of political and economic factors. As the former route for European invasions from Napoleon to Hitler, Belarus was the most heavily militarized Soviet republic, with one soldier for every 43 citizens (the RSFSR averaged one for every 634 citizens).[4] Counting the soldiers coming home because of recent withdrawals from Eastern Europe, some 240,000 soldiers were based in the republic in early 1992, while calculations of Belarus' military needs at

---

[1]   George Sanford, "Belarus on the Road to Nationhood," *Survival* 38(1) Spring 1996: 141.

[2]   Stephen M. Meyer, "The Military," in *After the Soviet Union: From Empire to Nations,* ed. Timothy J. Colton and Robert Legvold (New York, 1992), p. 126.

[3]   Karen Dawisha and Bruce Parrott, *Russia and the New States of Eurasia* (New York, 1994), p. 250.

[4]   Sanford, "Belarus on the Road," p. 141.

the end of the Cold War and a small Belarusian national budget set the number required at 100,000 or fewer.[5]

A major economic consideration for Belarus was the impact of the Treaty on Conventional Forces in Europe (CFE Treaty), which was to enter into force on 17 July 1992. Belarus feared that the treaty would impose huge financial obligations upon them in order to achieve the reductions in conventional equipment on its territory the treaty required. Along with its two larger neighbors, Russia and Ukraine, Belarus picked up a very heavy requirement to destroy physically military equipment. Initial assessments from declarations provided in accordance with the CFE Treaty provisions required Belarus to destroy 1,657 tanks, 1,224 armored combat vehicles, and 130 combat aircraft.[6] All of this would have to be accomplished under the eyes of international inspectors hosted by the Belarus budget. Members of the Supreme Soviet viewed this as such an odious obligation that despite general enthusiasm for the outcome of the treaty, they were unable to achieve ratification by the time the treaty entered into force.[7]

Ukraine undertook its new independent security obligations while simultaneously and aggressively pushing for an oath of loyalty for all forces on its territory, but Belarus did not. Belarus even took early steps to establish provisions for Russia to maintain command and control over all "strategic forces" on its territory, including the nuclear missile forces, airborne units, and even significant mobility assets. A nonspecific bilateral treaty on military coordination between Russia and Belarus was ratified by 1993.

It appeared that even in these early and heady days of independence, Belarus understood that its security relationship with Russia would be close and continuous. While Shushkevich made only modest attempts from 1991 until 1994 to establish an independent and nonaligned security identity, Lukashenka, his successor, from 1994 until the present, has pushed hard for closer ties with Russia in all spheres, including security.

To assess the prospects and consequences of further integration, four factors weigh most heavily. These include a review of the

5   Ibid.

6   Richard A. Falkenrath, *Shaping Europe's Military Order* (Cambridge, Mass., 1995), p. 286.

7   Joseph P. Harahan and John C. Kuhn, *On-Site Inspections under the CFE Treaty* (Washington, DC, 1996), p. 155.

economic impact, an understanding of the geography, an appreciation of the demographic implications, and a review of current assets in the security field under Belarusian control.

Economic Impact

While a full economic assessment is provided elsewhere in this volume (see Chapters 5 through 7 herein), it is clear that in the defense sphere, both Belarus and Russia are currently underfunding their defense requirements to the detriment of their armed forces. According to the most recent International Institute of Strategic Studies (IISS) report, Belarus in 1998 (before the Russian economic crisis) was funding defense at $462 million, while Russia's expenditures were $55 billion (adjusted dramatically for purchasing price parity).[8] To compare, the Russian defense budget in 1999, at the legal exchange rate, not adjusted for purchasing price parity, was $5.5 billion, and this included supplements for the war in Chechnya.

In both cases, this continued a nearly decade-long trend in which neither country's military had been able to add new conventional armaments, conduct even minimal levels of training to maintain military proficiency, or even consistently meet requirements for payrolls and pensions. In addition, the separation of the previously integrated military-industrial complex caused both nations to lose markets for the production of military equipment components and to duplicate, in some cases, production capacity that already existed in the neighboring state.

In recent years, both nations have openly acknowledged the irrationality of this approach and have taken steps to achieve the economic benefits of greater integration. This has been reflected in joint training, such as the two major Russian exercises in 1999, Air Bridge 99 and West 99.[9] It has also resulted in closer cooperation in procurement of military equipment and spare parts for Belarus. For the first time since their separation in 1991, the two militaries signed a common arms procurement program for 2000. Its most recent manifestation was Russian Deputy Prime Minister Ilia Klebanov's

---

[8]   *The Military Balance, 1999–2000* (London, 1999), pp. 82 and 112.

[9]   Vladimir Mukhin, "Russia is Participating in Military Maneuvers," *Nezavisimaia gazeta* 23 September 1999: 5.

visit to Minsk on 10–11 February 2000 to sign an agreement creating a Russian-Belarusian international financial industrial group called Defense Systems.[10]

While the limited but real economic advantages mentioned above are commonly recognized, even a full integration of the armed forces and their budgets would be little more than the sum of the parts, because the budget for the combined force (adjusted for purchasing price parity) would be only slightly larger than France and Belgium combined. This is not a base from which the original Soviet superpower could be recreated in any practical way. Ironically, it is Russian concerns about assuming financial responsibility for the economically less-developed Belarus that has been one of the major brakes on further integration.

Geography

The eastward enlargement of NATO in 1999 to include Poland, Hungary, and the Czech Republic increases the strategic value of Belarus as a security partner for Russia. Belarus shares a border of more than 180 miles with Poland and is much closer to the Russian enclave of Kaliningrad than any portion of Russia proper. A union between the two states that creates a "common defense space," as has been agreed to in the latest treaty, has several important geographical implications.

First, a union would place the military forces of the Russian-Belarusian union on a border of almost two hundred miles with NATO (Poland) and along the traditional invasion route into Russia favored by Europeans for several hundred years. Second, a union would restore the traditional Soviet security border with Poland, for which the Russian (Soviet) general staff had developed defense contingencies, emplacements, and lines of supply and communication. Third, and most important from a psychological perspective, a union might permit the Russians to redeploy nuclear weapons 300 miles closer to NATO than is currently possible on Russian territory, excluding the isolated Kaliningrad region.

Though the possibility of a major war in the middle of Europe that haunted military personnel on both sides during the Cold War now

---

[10]   Vladimir Mukhin, "Russia, Belarus Unite on Air Defense," *The Russia Journal* 21 February 2000: 1.

seems quite remote, the "forward movement" of Russian forces toward the new members of NATO would assuredly cause a renewed look at NATO defense capabilities and the controversial question of stationing foreign forces in Poland. In part to avoid antagonizing Russia and Belarus, Poland has not forced the issue of stationing other NATO troops on its territory.

The integration of Belarusian and Russian defense space would offer some advantages to the union. It would help to relieve pressure on the limited Russian defense manpower that is now required to maintain some defense structure on Russia's western border with Belarus, while Belarus orients its forces toward the border with Poland. Because Russia has never initiated plans to "defend" its border with Belarus as a true external border, union would also relieve the theoretical necessity to build minimal physical defense structures, which otherwise would be required.

It is the specter of a forward march of Russian nuclear weapons that causes the greatest concern internationally, particularly in Europe. If any movement of nuclear forces were confined to restoring the strategic nuclear forces withdrawn to Russia in the early 1990s, then the impact on other countries is largely psychological from a technical military perspective. Russian ICBMs are currently capable of striking any point on the globe, and a 300-mile forward movement would mean, in the case of the United States, for example, that warning time would be reduced from 30 minutes to 29 minutes.

Shorter-range nuclear weapons, however, might be quite another matter. Under the existing Intermediate Nuclear Forces (INF) Treaty of 1987, both the United States and the Soviet Union destroyed all nuclear-capable missiles with ranges between 500 and 5,500 kilometers and pledged to build no more missiles of that type. In practical terms, this means that the remaining short-range missiles based in Russia are not capable of reaching Poland, the closest NATO territory. Moved to the western border of Belarus, however, these missiles could reach near the eastern German border, covering all of Poland and parts of Hungary.

The politics of this geography is uncertain. Polls taken in Russia as recently as November 1999 indicate an overwhelming reluctance of Russians to transfer nuclear weapons or technologies to other states. More than two-thirds of all Russians polled held this opinion.[11] At the

---

[11]   Information provided by Dr. Vladimir Orlov, PIR Center, Moscow, Russia, 16

same time, there is ambiguity within both Russia and Belarus about whether a union of the two states, as the most recent agreement specifies, would mean that Belarus would no longer be regarded as a "foreign" state. This "loss of independent identity" for Belarus has been the source of the most vocal opposition to further integration. Despite this remaining ambiguity and its treaty and political implications, a recent Russian media report stated that sources close to Lukashenka indicate that "Belarus and Russia have agreed in principle to return nuclear weapons to Belarus."[12]

In terms of plans for future NATO enlargement, this single defense space would immediately change calculations for Lithuania, which would then be caught between Kaliningrad and the new Russian-Belarusian coalition, and for its two Baltic neighbors, Estonia and Latvia, who are only slightly more removed. Their aggressive pursuit of NATO membership expresses the concern that Russia remains a likely threat, and its physical expansion through Belarus would strongly reinforce this fear.

Demographics

One of the major implications for the Russian Army of the collapse of the Soviet Union was that it was no longer able to tap into the relatively large conscription pools of the Soviet bloc countries. Records of the past decade indicate how difficult it has been for Russia to conscript enough young men to fill the ranks of its greatly reduced armed forces. With the renewed fighting in Chechnya, Russia was forced to abandon the policy put in place in November 1998, which stated that conscripts could be sent into combat zones only on a volunteer basis.[13] While integration with Belarus is no panacea for that problem, the pooled manpower of the two states and the shortened external borders would offer some relief.

Current demographic data indicate that Belarus has about 80,000 males reaching age 18—draft age—annually and a total militarily significant manpower reserve of about 2,700,000 males between ages 15 and 49.[14] Among this number are many who received their military

---

November 1999.

[12]   Radio Liberty, 7 March 2000.

[13]   "Saving Private Ivanov," *Izvestiia* 20 September 1999: 1.

[14]   *CIA World Factbook, 1999* (Washington, DC, 1999), p. 47.

training in the former Soviet Union and therefore have some degree of proficiency using the equipment that is still dominant in the Russian military inventory.

The other factor that greatly enhances the value of recruits from Belarus, even compared to other former Soviet republics, is compatibility. The relationship between Russia and Belarus has been long and close. As a representative of the U.S. Embassy in Moscow, I was visiting the capital of Minsk the week Belarus formally declared its independence in 1991. In street surveys with a number of people, the major question I posed was "What is the primary difference between Russians and Belarusians?" An academic provided the most poignant answer after pondering for several moments. He said, "the prefix." The addition of "bela-" to the name Russia did not seem to me an adequate basis for national identity. But, in practical terms, it makes sense, for the peoples of Russia and Belarus are thoroughly integrated. In the last census taken before the breakup of the Soviet Union, 1.2 million citizens of Belarus were living in Russia, while 1.3 million Russians were living in Belarus (out of a total population of 10 million there).[15] Linguistically, the citizens of Belarus who speak only one language, speak Russian, not Belarusian.

Current Assets

The current armed forces of Belarus number some 80,000, roughly equal to the combined forces of Hungary and the Czech Republic. These forces are equipped with about 1,800 modern main battle tanks, 1,500 armored combat vehicles, 1,500 pieces of artillery, and nearly 300 modern combat aircraft, including helicopters.[16] While theoretically organized for countrywide defense, they are largely emplaced on the western border with Poland and the northern border with Lithuania.

Before the breakup of the Soviet Union, the territory of Belarus had been an independent military district designed to reinforce allies to the west. For this reason, it has a fully developed, integral communications and transportation system that has been deliberately constructed to tie in directly with Russia's. Its roads, railroads, and electronic communications systems could be reintegrated with the

---

[15]   Sanford, "Belarus on the Road," p. 137.

[16]   *The Military Balance, 1999–2000*, p. 82.

larger Russian security network with virtually no modification or expansion. It is highly likely that even the old Soviet secure communications system linking Moscow to the military district headquarters in Minsk remains operational in standby mode.

The Russian Armed Forces currently operate two critical military facilities in Belarus. One is a major communications facility for Russian ships and submarines in the North Atlantic at Vileiki, and the other an early-warning air defense radar complex in Hantsevichi [Gantsevichi], near Baranavichi.[17] The Russians are still completing the latter facility to replace the large complex they formerly owned at Skrunde, Latvia, which was dismantled under funding from the United States. The facility in Hantsevichi is critical in providing a long-range warning system for the important northwest corridor extending into Western Europe.

The largest real military asset of the Belarus armed forces is effectively already integrated with the Russian forces: the air defense system. At the time of signing the most recent union agreement, the presidents noted that Belarusian and Russian air defense forces have served together for five years.[18] In February 2000, Lt. Gen. Valerii Kostenko, commander of the Belarus air defense forces, proposed that the air defense command and control be formally integrated into a single unit, citing the American-Canadian air defense system as a precedent.[19] In the aftermath of the NATO-led conflict in Kosovo, which both Russia and Belarus opposed, Lukashenka announced that he was doubling the combat potential of Belarus over a two-year period, specifically by modernizing the air defense systems with Russia's technical help.[20]

As mentioned above in the economics discussion, the reintegration of the military-industrial complex of Belarus with that of Russia offers some advantages. Belarus was a major producer of transportation vehicles, electronics, and some weapons systems. Its small, surviving research and development system managed to produce a volley-fire rocket system, reportedly improving on the

---

[17]   "The Tashkent Treaty Is Activated," *Izvestiia* 24 April 1999: 2.

[18]   Mukhin, "Russia, Belarus Unite on Air Defense," p. 1.

[19]   *ITAR-TASS* in English, 8 February 2000.

[20]   Valery Kovalev, "Belarus Gets Ambitious in Defense Sphere," *Krasnaia zvezda* 30 June 1999: 3.

"grad" system that the Russians used to pummel Chechen towns in the final months of 1999.[21]

Most importantly, from a military perspective, Belarus and Russia have already set the stage for further integration by planning a coordinated exercise schedule. As mentioned earlier, Belarus was able to participate in the two major Russian exercises last year, Air Bridge 99 and West 99. In addition, Russians participated in the largest command-post exercise in Belarus in 1999,[22] and the Belarus Ministry of Defense announced a series of tactical exercises for 2000 "to further strengthen coordination between the Belarusian and Russian Armed Forces."[23]

Consistent with integration in procurement and exercises, Belarus has acknowledged that its current doctrine is largely a derivative of the Russian military doctrine (not yet adjusted for the 2000 Russian military doctrine, which had not been finalized in Russia during the last Belarusian review of its own document).[24] In the same manner, Belarus and Russia signed a protocol on 16 February 2000 agreeing to unify their respective military laws.[25]

Conclusion

While politics by its nature is always difficult to predict, two independent and powerful forces seem to be pushing on Belarus simultaneously to conclude a meaningful security arrangement with Russia that could transform regional security in the center of Europe.

From one direction, Belarus, like Poland, is powerfully driven in its pursuit of security by its own history. As the traditional invasion route to Russia, Belarus has suffered disproportionately in past conflicts. In World War II, Belarus lost a greater percentage of its population to the conflict and suffered greater physical destruction

---

[21] "Belarus Designs Volley-Fire Launcher," *Nezavisimaia gazeta* 20 November 1999: 5.

[22] Vladimir Mukhin, "Maneuvers of CIS Member States," *Nezavisimaia gazeta 23* September 1999: 5.

[23] Colonel Yury Voistinov, "Practice and Quality Is the Priority of Battle Training," *Vo slavu Rodiny* 1 February 2000: 1.

[24] Yuri Strigelsky, "The Myth of Military Doctrine," *Belorusskaia delovaia gazeta* 2 July 1999: 2.

[25] Belarusian News Agency, *BelaPAN* in English, 1925 GMT 16 February 2000.

than any other country. It was in part in recognition of this extraordinary price that Belarus was awarded a seat in the United Nations while still a component of the Soviet Union. Yet, this suffering is marked in Belarus with a degree of pride for its role as the bulwark of defense of the Slavic peoples and the Orthodox faith against attackers from the West.

Even more recently, "security events" outside of Belarus have extracted a very high price from the Belarusian people and territory. The Chernobyl nuclear accident of April 1986 contaminated 22 percent of the arable land in Belarus and partially contaminated 70 percent of its entire territory.[26] In both these crises, Belarus quickly understood that it did not have the internal national assets to cope with the terrible consequences.

From another direction, events in 1999 created both the need and opportunity for a fundamental transformation of security relationships that was pressing and unique. The long-awaited NATO expansion became a reality, placing NATO on the Belarusian border. Within a month, this alliance was at war with a traditional ally of both Russia and Belarus—Yugoslavia, despite powerful efforts by both nations to preclude NATO military operations in defense of the Kosovar Albanians. At the time, President Lukashenka went so far as to propose to open the treaty under development between Russia and Belarus to Yugoslavia as well. Finally, the leadership of Russia passed from an aged and ailing President Yeltsin to a young and vigorous Vladimir Putin, a change of power initiated by Yeltsin's resignation on 31 December 1999 and subsequently confirmed by the Russian population in the March 2000 elections.

The practical events of 1999, such as the joint exercises and procurement in which Belarus and Russia participated, have provided a sound basis for further integration. It appeared that momentum was building even on the political front. During his visit to Belarus during the NATO campaign in Kosovo in April 1999, Russian Minister of Defense Igor Sergeev proposed that the two nations move beyond their "partnership" and become "allies."[27] In this sense, the original Tashkent Treaty of 1992, which divided the defense resources of the former Soviet Union among the republics, might realize its promise of a full and active form of defense cooperation. Though it is not likely

26   Sanford, "Belarus on the Road," p. 141.

27   "The Tashkent Agreement Is Activated," p. 2.

that anything resembling the original Commonwealth of Independent States (CIS) security merger then envisioned will become a reality, this union would be the most far-reaching manifestation of that intent to date.

As mentioned earlier, the aspect of this closer security cooperation most likely to capture world attention is the forward deployment of nuclear weapons. While the military and psychological impact have already been discussed, the political and legal consequences are no less important. Belarus acceded to the Non-Proliferation Treaty (NPT) as an independent, non-nuclear state in 1993. A decision to allow weapons once again on its territory would raise issues about its independence or its adherence to the NPT, or both.

Of course, a seriously deteriorated security relationship between the East and West could undermine the complex security treaty regime that has built up over the past 15 years. A decision by the United States to deploy a national missile defense (NMD) system without gaining Russia's agreement to amendments to the 1972 Antiballistic Missile (ABM) Treaty could lead to an unraveling of the whole structure. An abrogation of the ABM Treaty could lead to Russian withdrawal from the Strategic Arms Reduction Talks Treaty (START-I), the INF Treaty, and possibly even the provisions of the CFE Treaty. The consequences of the latter two possibilities are especially significant in defining the military importance of Belarus. If the union were formed and if Russia were outside the strictures of the INF Treaty and could fill the gap by again producing nuclear-capable missiles with a range between 500 and 5,500 kilometers, missiles based in Poland might cover most of Europe. Likewise, if Belarus and Russia in a union were no longer constrained by the CFE Treaty, there could be the threat or reality of large-scale forward deployment of conventional force capabilities. Belarus had agreed to a ceiling on military forces of 100,000 under the CFE Treaty 1A agreement.[28]

The absence of a viable network of international security treaties could greatly increase the significance of a fully integrated military regime. It would almost certainly cause defensive measures by NATO nations that would exacerbate the security concerns shared by Russia and Belarus.

---

[28] Roy Allison, "Military Forces in the Soviet Successor States," *Adelphi Paper* (International Institute for Strategic Studies) 280 (October 1993): 47.

Two major issues remain to be decided in assessing the broader security impact. The first is the internal, domestic reaction to any further integration of the two states. While public opinion polls have shown broad support, there is some measure of determined resistance in both countries. Most explicitly, the Belarusian Popular Front (BPF), a consistent opponent of Lukashenka, has threatened to "take up arms" to prevent unification with Russia.[29] In March 2000, reports came from Belarus of police roundups of BPF supporters at Lukashenka's direction.

As a subset of this, another form of internal pressure that could derail future military cooperation might come from the actions of the two governments. Lukashenka was accused of undermining key provisions of the January 2000 union by instituting new policies on taxation, customs, and transit rights for Russian goods within one month after the treaty had entered into force.[30] Following his election in March 2000, Putin promised a series of decisive moves "to strengthen the state." While these have not yet been defined, they could influence either favorably or unfavorably a more formal merger with Belarus. Decisive military moves within the new union agreement, most particularly the redistribution of nuclear weapons onto Belarusian territory, would likely draw world attention and Western condemnation.

The second factor that could affect further integration is external—the reaction of the West. NATO is still defining its own future, and its actions, which affect Belarus and Russia or their interests in important ways, will influence the emerging security relationship. Continuing discussion of further enlargement of NATO, particularly as it concerns the Baltic countries to the north of Belarus, seems a further impetus to ever-closer cooperation and integration on the part of Belarus and Russia.

In terms of NATO's activities involving Belarus interests, the Kosovo situation appears to be a huge dilemma, beyond the current capacities of NATO to resolve; it may further stress both NATO's own members and its relationship with Belarus, Russia, and other states sympathetic to the Serb population. NATO's Partnership for Peace, in contrast, includes both Belarus and Russia and could serve as a bridging vehicle to deal with potential misunderstandings with

---

[29]   *Novosti* 23 January 1999.

[30]   Vasily Verbin, "Belarus' Surprise Move," *Moscow News* 8–14 March 2000: 1.

NATO's eastern neighbors. In fact, in earlier days before Lukashenka's more strident posturing, Belarus was one of the most active former Soviet republics, having both multilateral and bilateral ties with NATO members.

A final important but independent factor that could affect further integration is the impact integration could have on Ukraine, which has the distinction of being the second largest Slavic state in the former Soviet Union and an aspiring bridge between East and West. Likewise, Ukraine has a unique opportunity to influence the relationship in both positive and negative directions. While Ukraine has largely been publicly neutral on any further integration by Belarus and Russia, a large portion of the population would consider a merger as a test case for an eventual reunification of the three states that took apart the Soviet Union in 1991.

In the security realm, a Russian-Belarusian union that produced a greater voice in international affairs and allowed more rational economic support for the armed forces would generate both interest and sympathy from Ukraine. Conversely, the first detachment of Belarus military forces ordered into one of Russia's security quagmires, such as Chechnya or even Tajikistan, would greatly encourage Ukraine's courting of the Western nations of NATO.

The celebration of the new cooperation agreement between Belarus and Russia in January 2000 was little noticed or commented upon outside of the two countries directly involved. Given the defense and security implications, it deserved greater attention.

The tenuous security relationship between East and West in Europe even a decade after the widely heralded end of the Cold War is best reflected in the fact that we remain unable to name the new epoch in which we live. Citizens of both the East and West entered the new millennium with only the "post-Cold War" label to mark international security relationships. A description for relations that defines only "what was is no more" suggests an ambiguity both about what is and, even more, about what is to be.

11
Astrid Sahm and Kirsten Westphal
Power and the Yamal Pipeline

The Yamal Pipeline is one of the largest projects in the European gas industry. Its completion will not only determine the future position of Russia's largest company, Gazprom, in the European gas markets, but will also have important implications for Russia's international position and its relations with the other states of the Commonwealth of Independent States (CIS), especially Belarus, whose territory is crossed by the Yamal pipeline. Gazprom's expenses for the construction of the pipeline represent the largest foreign investment Belarus has received for a single project since it gained independence. The key question is whether Belarus is able—and willing—to use these investments and future revenues from gas transit to free itself from the heritage of the Soviet planned economy, with its artificially low energy prices.

   Since the Soviet Union split up into energy-rich "haves" and energy-poor "have-nots,"[1] Belarus has depended almost completely on energy deliveries from Russia. The situation is aggravated by Belarus' inability to pay for its energy needs. Reducing this dependence on Russia requires market reforms in order to overcome the energy-intensive nature of the Soviet-inherited economy and to build up an efficient energy-supply system with a realistic price structure. The political consequences of the increasing energy debts of Belarus and the other "have-nots" highlight the significance of energy questions for the success of the transformation process and its importance for the process of nation building. Ensuring a stable national energy supply is therefore also a matter of national security.

---

[1]   Robert E. Ebel, *Energy Choices in the Near Abroad: The Haves and Have-nots Face the Future* (Washington, DC, 1997).

The "have-nots," such as Belarus, are dependent on Russia—and primarily on the joint-stock company Gazprom. But they are not the only ones. Russia dominates the vital export sphere and transport routes to the West for the other "haves," but nonetheless depends on its western neighbors as transit countries. Russia is also affected by the Soviet heritage of distorted price and cost structures, which leads to the problem of mutual indebtedness both in the internal Russian energy market and in inter-CIS economic relations. The energy relationship between Russia and its neighbors can therefore be described as one of asymmetrical interdependence. Asymmetrical interdependence may cause political irritations and can intensify international conflicts, but international relations in the energy sector also require cooperation, coordination, and harmonization of interests. Taking distribution into account, the problems of energy supply are at the center of political struggles and negotiations at both the international and domestic level.

The Yamal pipeline will by no means change the existing interdependence structure. To understand the different general interests and possible options of the involved actors, we will first separately analyze Belarus' energy policy and Gazprom's business strategy. Then we will focus on the significance of the Yamal pipeline project for the Belarusian-Russian relationship. Based on our interpretation of the interconnections between the Russian state and Gazprom and of the policy strategy of the Belarusian elite, we will try to explain the implications of energy questions for the Belarusian-Russian integration process. Finally, we will include the European context, because the Yamal pipeline is of concern to European consumers. Moreover, the West European countries' long-term energy supply strategy will influence both their policy toward Belarus and Russia and Belarus' and Russia's policies.

Belarus' Energy Picture and Its Foreign Policy Toward Russia

Belarus was one of the republics most completely integrated into the Soviet economic system. This was particularly obvious in the field of energy supply. As late as 1978, Belarus was able to meet 48 percent of its energy demands with its own resources; however, by the end of the 1980s, the situation had totally changed and Belarus was importing nearly 90 percent of the fuel and energy that it consumed.[2] This development was partly a result of the reduction in Belarusian production of oil and peat, the only domestic energy sources in resource-poor Belarus: in 1990, it produced 2 million tons of oil, 0.3 billion cubic meters of natural gas, and 4.5 million tons of peat, which together covered only 13 percent of the country's total annual energy consumption.[3] It was also partly a result of Soviet policies of centralized industrialization, which caused an increase in energy imports. Most significantly, gas imports increased from 4.2 billion cubic meters in 1980 to 14.1 billion cubic meters in 1990, while oil imports remained unchanged at 37 million tons per year.[4] A large part of these oil supplies went to the two large oil refineries in Mazyr [Mozyr] and Navapolatsk [Novopolotsk], the industrial centerpieces of the country. In addition, the republic became an importer of electricity, generating only 75 percent of its needs via its own thermal power stations. Consequently, at the end of the Soviet era, it was already clear that the republic's positive balance in interrepublic trade was possible only because of artificially low energy prices.[5]

Independence came, therefore, as a heavy burden to Belarus. The new state was hard hit by the rapid price rises for energy supplies after the collapse of the Soviet Union. As a result, in 1992, Belarus had to spend 25 percent of its gross domestic product on energy imports, compared with 1.7 percent in 1990. Belarusian products therefore became less competitive on CIS markets, which led to an increasing trade deficit and a dramatic decline in production. At the same time, Belarusian debts grew rapidly because the country was not able to pay for its energy imports, especially for gas. In August 1993, when the Belarusian gas debt exceeded $100 million, Gazprom cut off gas supplies to Belarus for the first time. In the face of this energy crisis, the

---

[2]   Astrid Sahm, *Transformation im Schatten von Tschernobyl. Umwelt- und Energiepolitik im gesellschaftlichen Wandel von Belarus und der Ukraine* (Münster, 1999), pp. 149ff.

[3]   Valentin Gerasimov and Alexander Mikhalevich, "Prospects for Nuclear Power Development in the Republic of Belarus," Paper for the Uranium Institute Annual Symposium (1993), p. 1.

[4]   Hermann Clement, *Die Energiewirtschaft der GUS,* Arbeiten aus dem Osteuropa-Institut München, no. 151 (March 1992), p. 55.

[5]   See Olga Abramova, *Integration zwischen Realität und Simulation. Die belarussisch-rußländischen Beziehungen seit 1991* (Mannheim, 1998), p. 9.

chairman of the Supreme Soviet, Stanislaŭ Shushkevich, characterized the republic's situation at a parliamentary session in September 1993 as hopeless.[6]

How to ensure security of energy supply was, therefore, the key question for the survival of the young, independent Belarusian state. Unfortunately, neither the ruling elite nor the population was ready to manage this task. During perestroika, national independence had been the political aim of only a small group of people, represented mainly by the Belarusian Popular Front. In 1991, the overwhelming majority of the population generally supported the ideas of independence and democracy, but was not ready to bear the social costs of a radical transformation process. Conscious of the people's mentality, the government avoided any serious economic reform program and attempted to obtain guarantees of a continued cheap energy supply and the maintenance of a single monetary system to keep Belarusian products competitive on CIS markets. In 1992, Prime Minister Kebich and the other government members still believed that the CIS could develop functioning multilateral structures that could replace those of the former Soviet Union; however, during 1993, it became clear that the CIS would have no future as an effective interstate organization and that Russian policy favored bilateral contacts with the CIS states as a more effective power instrument. At that point, the Belarusian government started to seek a special relationship with Russia, Belarus' main external supplier of energy. Under Lukashenka, elected president in July 1994, this policy was continued and even intensified because the "virtual" idea of reunification always served as an important source of popular legitimacy for Lukashenka.[7]

The question of Belarus' growing energy indebtedness remained one of the dominant problems in the Belarusian-Russian integration process during the following years. The first important agreement was the so-called "zero option" in February 1996, when the Belarusian and Russian governments agreed to cancel Belarusian energy debts totaling $1.3 billion. Belarus agreed to give up compensation for the decommissioning of nuclear missiles and for the ecological damage caused by the presence

---

[6] Astrid Sahm, "Setzt Belarus auf Atomenergie?" in *Die Folgen von Tschernobyl*, ed. Bernhard Moltmann, Astrid Sahm and Manfred Sapper (Frankfurt/Main, 1994), p. 80.

[7] Abramova, *Integration zwischen Realität und Simulation*, pp. 14ff; Astrid Sahm, "Politische Konstruktionsversuche weißrussischer Identität," *Jahrbücher für Geschichte Osteuropas* 42 (1994): 541–61.

of Russian troops on Belarusian territory. Because structural problems had not been resolved, though, the energy debts again began to increase and gas debts amounted to $200 million by the end of 1996. This occurred despite the fact that Russia accepted barter as a form of payment for the supplies and Belarus undertook intensive administrative efforts to fulfill the repayment agreements.[8]

The main cause of Belarus' growing debts was the spiral of mutual nonpayments among producers, distributors, and consumers of energy, and among different economic sectors. This problem was aggravated by the energy price structures in Belarus. After independence, Beltransgaz, the state-owned operator of the gas transmission system in Belarus and therefore the main debtor to Gazprom, and Beltopenergo, the main state-owned gas distribution company, were obliged to sell energy to end consumers for less than they paid to Gazprom.[9] As a solution to this problem, the Belarusian government sought to reach an agreement with Russia permitting Belarus to buy energy at domestic Russian prices.[10] Actually, this meant that in economic—but not in political—matters Belarus wanted to be treated as a Russian province. This was one of the most important reasons why Lukashenka signed the Union Treaty in 1997 and other bilateral integration agreements in recent years. Indeed, the establishment of a single energy system had already been proclaimed by the first treaty on the creation of a community of the two states signed in April 1996.[11]

In view of its unilateral dependency on Russian energy supplies, Belarus' advantageous geostrategic position as a transit country is its only real trump card in its relationship with Russia. At present, the transit of oil, about 90 million tons per year, is most significant, while, during the 1990s, Gazprom exported only 24.5 billion cubic meters of gas per year through Belarus. Unlike Ukraine, which is currently the main transit country for Russian gas, Belarus has not demanded high transit fees in cash from Russia. It has agreed to reduced energy prices instead. Because of this, Belarus paid about $50 per 1000 cubic meters for imported gas in 1996–1998 and about $30 in 1999–2000, while Ukraine

---

[8]   Abramova, *Integration zwischen Realität und Simulation*, p. 32; Sahm, *Transformation im Schatten von Tschernobyl*, p. 191.

[9]   "Kto zaplatit za neispol'zovannyi gaz?" *Belorusskaia gazeta* 15 June 1998.

[10]   "Ch'i v Belarusi truboprovody," *Belorusskaia gazeta* 8 June 1998.

[11]   Ustina Markus, "Energy Crisis Spurs Ukraine and Belarus to Seek Help Abroad," *Transition* 2(9) 3 May 1996: 14–18.

had to pay about $80 in previous—and $50 in recent—years.[12] The national opposition has heavily criticized the government for not making correct use of Belarus' geopolitical position, accusing it of thereby selling the country's independence.

The Belarusian Energy Program

Actually, the National Program of Power Development in Belarus, adopted in October 1992 by the Belarusian government, seemed to be in accord with the demands of the national opposition to strengthen Belarusian sovereignty. The program, which covers the period up to 2010, declared its main aim to be the achievement of maximal self-sufficiency in the generation of electric power. To realize this aim, the authors of the national energy program suggested building a nuclear power plant in Belarus. "Under the existing economic and political situation, the Republic of Belarus, being an independent state, cannot manage without nuclear power in the future," they argued.[13] Nevertheless, the government did not risk open support of the nuclear option because of negative public attitudes to nuclear power in the aftermath of the Chernobyl catastrophe. The other key problem was the question of financial costs; because attempts to find foreign investors or to secure credit lines have been unsuccessful, the continued nuclear power debate seems to be an artificial dispute in the current Belarusian situation.[14]

Other possibilities for increasing domestic energy production or reducing energy demand by improving energy efficiency and modernizing thermal power stations would also require large

[12] Margarita M. Balmaceda, "Gas, Oil and the Linkages between Domestic and Foreign Policies: The Case of Ukraine," *Europe-Asia Studies* 50(2) 1998: 257–86; Aleksej Šurobovič, "Wirtschaftliche Aspekte der Union von Rußland und Belarus," *Berichte des BIOst*, 15 (2000): 21.

[13] Gerasimov and Mikhalievich, "Prospects for Nuclear Power Development," p. 5. At present Belarus has no nuclear power plant on its territory. The construction of a nuclear heating plant was stopped in 1988 due to the growing antinuclear movement in the Soviet Union in the aftermath of the Chernobyl catastrophe.

[14] According to the latest statements of V. Herasimaŭ [Gerasimov], chairman of Belenergo, the completion of the nuclear power plants before 2010 is not realistic. Cf. David Marples, *Belarus: From Soviet Rule to Nuclear Catastrophe* (New York, 1996), pp. 127ff; "Komissiia po AES—za moratorii," *Belorusskaia gazeta* 11 January 1999; "Za ėnergetikami ne zarzhaveet," *Belorusskaia gazeta* 27 December 1999.

investments. In recent years, the government has adopted some special programs on saving energy and on the development of local and nontraditional forms of energy production, but these programs have shown few results, mainly because of lack of funds. Belarus also has no large gas storage facilities, which would provide some security against supply interruption, because costs for them are too high.[15] The republic has heavy fuel oil storage capacity, which can substitute for gas at the thermal power stations because many power stations have a dual fuel capability. Detailed plans also exist for reducing demand in the event of shortages from Russian suppliers. According to these plans, businesses will suffer shortages first and private consumers last, to avoid broad social protests by the population. This shows clearly the political priorities of the government.[16]

The national energy program also mentioned diversification as a way of increasing the security of supply; however, for financial and technical reasons, while the diversification of oil supplies is easy to manage, the same is not true of gas and other energy supplies. During 1992, the Belarusian government entered into negotiations with some Arab countries on the possibility of oil deliveries. It also sought to import fuel from such countries as Poland, Australia, Turkmenistan, and Norway;[17] however, these plans failed to materialize because Belarus was not able to pay for the imports in hard currency. Belarus is also deeply in debt for the electricity it imports from the Ignalina nuclear power station in Lithuania. The idea of an oil pipeline from the Black Sea to the Baltic, which was favored by the Belarusian Popular Front, did not gain the support of the government. The government's rejection of the plan was motivated by the high costs of the project and by the political implications of what seemed to be an anti-Russian corridor of the western post-Soviet states.[18] It is very likely that Russia threatened to

---

[15]   In November 1999, the first part of the Pribug gas storage facility, with a final active capacity of 1.4 billion cubic meters, was opened. The costs of the construction, which was begun in 1992, amounts to $90 million. Until then, Belarus had only one small gas storage facility near Orsha. In comparison, Ukraine has 14 gas storage facilities. See "Gaz pro zapas," *Belorusskii rynok* 46 (1999); "Realizovan superproekt," *Belorusskaia gazeta* 22 November 1999.

[16]   London Economics, *Global Energy Strategy for the Republic of Belarus*, Final Report, August 1995, pp. 30ff, 40.

[17]   Clement, *Die Energiewirtschaft der GUS*, p. 55; Helen Fedor, ed., *Belarus and Moldova: Country Studies* (Washington, DC, 1995), pp. 53ff.

[18]   In the Baltic States, Poland, and especially in Ukraine, the idea of a community from

cancel privileges regarding prices for Belarusian energy imports should Belarus diversify suppliers.[19]

To sum up, during the 1990s Belarus was unable to achieve the main goals of its national energy program because of a lack of funds and the weakness of the efforts of the ruling elites. There have not been any serious reforms in the Belarusian energy sector, which has maintained its centralized structure. Former Energy Minister Valiantsyn Herasimaŭ [Valentin Gerasimov], who until 2000 headed the state-owned company Belenergo, stated in 1998 that gas should not become the dominant energy form used in Belarus.[20] Nonetheless, the role of gas in the Belarusian energy system is likely to increase in the future. According to the National Energy Program, Belarus' gas consumption will double to 27 billion cubic meters by 2010. A large program of gasification is being carried out in the Chernobyl contaminated areas to avoid secondary contamination by burning wood. Without the construction of a nuclear power plant, it is planned that 80 or 90 percent of electricity will be produced with gas.[21] Therefore, Belarusian dependency on Russian gas and on Gazprom will increase.

Gazprom's Strategy of Becoming a Big Player in the World's Energy Markets

Gazprom's strategy is directed toward expanding its markets and increasing its export volume to become a big player in the world's energy markets. This aim is facilitated by the fact that the Soviet Union started its first non–Eastern Bloc deliveries more than 30 years ago to Austria, then in 1973 to Germany. Consequently, the Russian gas industry already has the reputation of being a reliable supplier. In contrast to the Soviet era, Gazprom now seeks to deepen its value-added chain by becoming more involved in the marketing and distribution of its gas instead of simply delivering it to the border of the client country. In accordance with this target, it is pursuing a well-balanced enterprise policy by establishing trading and transport firms in those countries to

---

the Black Sea to the Baltic receives more support from government structures, but no concrete steps have been taken because of the high costs of the project. See Sahm, *Transformation im Schatten von Tschernobyl*, p. 198

[19] Abramova, *Integration zwischen Realität und Simulation*, p. 12.

[20] "Gaz nel'zia prevrashchat' v monopoliiu," *Belorusskaia gazeta* 18 May 1998.

[21] Sahm, *Transformation im Schatten von Tschernobyl*, p. 383.

which it delivers gas.[22] Gazprom has built up a network of transit and trading companies in joint ventures with domestic gas companies throughout the EU and Eastern and Southeastern Europe, and is entering Middle Eastern and Asia-Pacific markets and China.

This strategy of "downstreaming'" is accompanied by a calculated and well-targeted entrance into other markets. Gazprom, therefore, constantly pursues ambitious plans to expand its pipeline network. In addition to the Yamal pipeline, the Blue Stream Project, an underwater pipeline on the bottom of the Black Sea to open up the Turkish and Middle Eastern markets, is of special importance. A trans-Balkan Pipeline from Burgas, on Bulgaria's Black Sea coast, to the Greek Mediterranean port of Alexandroupolis is under study. A Gazprom joint venture with the Finnish company Neste Oy was set up and a feasibility study has been completed for a North European gas line to continental Europe via the Scandinavian countries. Gazprom also is participating in the Interconnector from Bacton (UK) to Zeebrugge (Belgium), which will put an end to the United Kingdom's isolation from the European markets.[23] Regarding these plans, one can conclude that Gazprom's business strategy is targeted toward emerging as a transnational company with its roots in Russia.

Gazprom's main interest is to increase its foreign currency earnings (which it badly needs because of serious nonpayment problems at home and in neighboring countries), to exploit additional reserves, to upgrade and repair its facilities, and to complete huge projects like the Yamal Pipeline. Since the early 1990s, when Gazprom started to expand into the European market (relying on long-term supply contracts), nearly 100 percent of hard currency earnings have come from Europe. These assets secure credits and loans for future projects or projects in progress.[24] Increasing these exports is achieved by reducing gas deliveries to neighboring countries. According to official sources, exports to other

---

[22] Katharina Preuss-Neudorf, *Die Erdgaswirtschaft in Rußland: Merkmale, Probleme und Perspektiven unter besonderer Berücksichtigung der Integration der russischen und der europäischen Erdgaswirtschaft* (Köln, 1996).

[23] Neftegazovaia Vertikal', *Gazprom: Vchera, segodnia, zavtra* (Moscow, 1998), pp. 185–224; Stepan Dereschow, "Ziele und Wege der energiewirtschaftlichen Kooperation zwischen Deutschland und Rußland," in *Deutsch-russische Energiekooperation unter Globalisierungsdruck* ed. Andrei Kuxenko and Friedemann Müller (Ebenhausen, 1998), pp. 85–90.

[24] Price Waterhouse, *RAO Gazprom, IAS Consolidated Financial Statements* (Moscow, 31 December 1997).

successor states fell dramatically between 1990 and 1994—by 54 percent. This trend has continued, but to a smaller extent.[25] Deliveries to Belarus were subject to variations because of temporary shortages due to the country's growing gas debts, and ranged between approximately 14 billion and 17 billion cubic meters of gas from 1994 to 2000.[26]

Nonetheless, deliveries to Belarus were generally consistent with requirements. The Russian monopolist Gazprom was forced to manage increasing Belarusian energy indebtedness with great flexibility, because Belarus was not and is not in the position to pay its debts in cash. Gazprom itself sees Belarus as a stepping-stone to the European market. In addition, Belarus is an attractive future market. However, there is another reason for the apparently tolerant handling of debt management by Gazprom—its special relationship with the Russian government, which, according to most observers, always tries to increase its influence on the neighboring CIS states by playing the energy debt card.[27]

Gazprom: A State Agency or a Strong Corporate Player?

The instrumentalization of energy dependence for Russian foreign policy purposes was especially obvious during the Russian-Ukrainian negotiations on the Black Sea Fleet.[28] Generally, the Russian government has built its policy of reintegration of the post-Soviet space on the dependence of the other CIS members on Russian energy supplies and has instrumentalized Gazprom's deliveries by turning the gas tap on and off.[29] But there is another way to look at the situation. It is equally

---

[25]   Ebel, *Energy Choices in the Near Abroad*, pp. 24ff; Matthew J. Sager, "The Russian Natural Gas Industry in the Mid-1990s," *Post-Soviet Geography* 1995 (9): 521–64; *Belorusskaia delovaia gazeta* 20 October 1999; *Belorusskii rynok* 28 (2000): 17.

[26]   Neftegazovaia Vertikal', *Gazprom*, p. 184; Ebel, p. 230.

[27]   For an overview see Heiko Pleines and Kirsten Westphal, "Rußlands Gazprom. Teil I: Die Rolle des Gaskonzerns in der russischen Politik und Wirtschaft," *Bericht des BIOst* 33 (1999).

[28]   See Ole Diehl and Kirsten Westphal, "Ende einer Beziehungskrise? Aktuelle Entwicklungen der russisch-ukrainischen Beziehungen," *Truppenpraxis* 1993 (6): 594–99.

[29]   Kirsten Westphal, *Hegemon statt Partner: Rußlands Politik gegenüber dem "nahen Ausland"* (Münster, 1995); Jakov Pappe, "Neftianaia i gazovaia diplomatiia Rossii," *Pro et Contra* 2 (1997) 3: 55–71.

plausible to argue that Gazprom uses the Russian government as an instrument of its own policies, especially because the policy of reintegration includes the possibility of low transit costs and easy achievement of property rights in the CIS countries.[30] In reality, the relationship between the state and the gas industry monopolist is much more complicated and multifaceted than those two ways of viewing it would suggest. Gazprom began its life as a state company but over time its policies have become more and more business oriented, which has at times put it on a conflict course with the government, especially where the interests of the Central Asian states are concerned. Gazprom is a company in transition: simultaneously a monopoly with a major federal state share and an international corporation. The company's operations have both market and monopoly features. On the one hand, the company is inextricably locked into the pattern of inter-enterprise debts and tax delinquency that plagues the Russian economy, while, on the other hand, it acquires its own credits and foreign loans on the international capital market and acts as an international player.

Gazprom holds an extraordinary position. It is the world's largest producer and supplier of gas. It controls more than one-fourth of proven world gas reserves and is, with 30 percent, Western Europe's most important gas supplier.[31] Gazprom contributes 25 percent of Russia's total internal revenues and 20 percent to 25 percent of its hard currency receipts. Furthermore, the gas industry, which is up to 94 percent dominated by Gazprom, generates approximately 10 percent of the Russian gross national product.[32] The main asset of and basis for Gazprom expansion is the Russian United Gas Supply System, including production sites, main gas pipelines, and underground storage facilities, which functions as a single technical and economic mechanism and preserves a so-called natural monopoly. Gazprom is active in other sectors, such as heavy industry and telecommunications, to reduce its

---

[30]   On 26 December 1994, for example, the government adopted a resolution promising Gazprom a state contribution of $30 per 1000 cubic meters of gas the company exported in accordance with state interests. Additionally, Gazprom was to receive compensation for the transit fees it must pay to Ukraine, Belarus, and Moldova. See Valery Krjukov and Arild Moe, *The New Russian Corporation? A Case Study of Gazprom* (London, 1996), p. 29.

[31]   Neftegazovaia Vertikal', *Gazprom*, p. 135.

[32]   E. Mueller-Elschner, *Die russische Energiewirtschaft im Umbruch, unveröffentlichtes Positionspapier* (Magdeburg, 1998).

dependence on Western imports of equipment. The company also owns assets in the banking and media sectors.[33] These equities contribute to the emergence of the company as a so-called financial industrial group. The financial industrial groups have dominated the Russian privatization process and Russian economic policy in recent years. Unlike the other financial industrial groups dominated by big players like Vladimir Potanin, Mikhail Khodorovsky, and Boris Berezovsky, Rem Viakhirev's Gazprom emerged from the financial crisis in August 1998 in comparatively good shape, because Viakhirev had concentrated on developing the company's business, flanked by a long-term strategy built around the core business of production, distribution, and processing, and last but not least around the export of Russian gas.

The Russian natural gas company has been called a state within a state. Despite efforts to divest itself of unrelated subsidiaries and to make the financial and corporate structure more transparent, Gazprom has been, because of its network of farms, factories, and social welfare measures, more than a monopoly concentrating on its primary business. This is because of the geographical and climatic conditions with which Gazprom has to deal. Working in remote areas, Gazprom has had to build entire cities, where it must ensure the urban infrastructure and socio-cultural opportunities. Gazprom employs about 370,000 persons, but it is estimated that the company indirectly supports six million people, making it an important social and political actor.[34] Many observers therefore have been less disturbed by its financial and corporate structure than by the company's political position.

The Gazprom Group was the alma mater of politicians such as former Prime Minister Chernomyrdin, former Energy Minister Petr Rodionov, and former Chief of the Russian Central Bank Sergei Dubinin, who moved from positions in the government to Gazprom and back, thereby establishing close contacts between the two. There has also been personnel overlap through the Board of Directors and the Committee of State Representatives, where state authorities and ministries, such as the Ministries of Finance, Economics, and State Property, are represented.[35] Additionally, the Russian state holds 38 percent of the

---

[33]   See, for example, *Pipeline News* 28 (7–13 September 1996); Neftegazovaia Vertikal', *Gazprom*, pp. 137ff, 171–78 [jdelay@new-europe.gr].

[34]   *AKM*, 3 February 1999; *Petroleum Economist*, May 1996, p. 38.

[35]   Salomon Brothers, *Gazprom: Leveraged to European Growth* (London, 1998); RAO Gazprom, *Godovoi otchet* (Moscow, 1998), pp. 42ff.

company's share capital. Nevertheless, the rights of disposal and control belong to the management of Gazprom, because, in 1992, the state agencies passed 35 percent of the share capital to Gazprom's chief executive, Viakhirev, in the form of a trusteeship. Taking into account that the company itself holds 8 percent and its subsidiaries around 7 percent of the shares, the management under Viakhirev controls at least 50 percent of the votes. This puts him in a position to determine the company's strategy autonomously, because the remaining shares are widely dispersed between Russian natural persons and legal entities.[36] These connections were the basis for strengthening the position of the monopolist, although the so-called young reformers and the IMF challenged its existence in 1997 and 1998. Nevertheless, Gazprom management, which wants to preserve the company's integrity, its monopoly, and its extraordinary position as a production and transport company with expansionistic plans to foreign markets, succeeded in defeating this demand by reorganizing its financial, corporate, and management structures.[37] After the election of President Vladimir Putin in March 2000, the administration's attempts to increase its control over Gazprom intensified once again. In 2000, these attempts were successful insofar as, at the shareholder's meeting in June 2000, the state kept 5 of 11 representatives on the board of directors and the vice-chairman of the presidential administration, Dmitrii Medvedev, replaced Victor Chernomyrdin as head of the board. Furthermore, a former government member, Boris Fedorov, represents the small shareholders. Only four board members come from management, and one from the biggest foreign shareholder, Ruhrgas; however, the main aim of Putin's government was not really to touch the extraordinary position and monopoly of the company, but to achieve more transparency in its financial transactions.[38]

The solidification of Gazprom's position within Russia was accompanied by, and probably would not have been possible without, the fulfillment of some basic requirements, such as the steady and cheap

[36] Pleines and Westphal, Rußlands Gazprom, pp. 9–10; Kirsten Westphal, *Russische Energiepolitik, Ent- oder Neuverflechtung von Staat und Wirtschaft* (Baden-Baden, 2000).

[37] See: V. A. Kriukov, "Gazovaia promyshlennost' Rossii," *Problemy prognozirovaniia* 1998 (1): 55–65.

[38] *Reuters* 30 June 2000; *Kommersant* 1 July 2000; *Vremia i novosti* 3 July 2000; "Starye novye," *Belorusskaia delovaia gazeta* 5 July 2000.

supply of energy to the Russian population, to the public sector, and to strategic economic branches, as well a significant contribution to the Russian budget, especially when money was badly needed. The relationship between the Russian state and Gazprom is, therefore, one of mutual concessions and benefits. Whenever possible, Gazprom has attempted to eliminate the gas debts of neighboring countries via asset and equity swaps, as well as by taking over property belonging to ancillary industries and to the energy sector. The chronology of permanent shortages and growth of deliveries to CIS countries like Belarus must also be seen within this context.

To summarize, during the 1990s, Gazprom has managed to come out of the ongoing transformation process as a very strong economic and political actor that not only has close relations and interconnections with the Russian state, but also enjoys a great deal of autonomy because it has immunized itself against state interventions during the struggle of restructuring the natural monopolies. During recent years, Gazprom has developed a more business-oriented strategy, which it cannot, however, pursue in the CIS as long as the problems of mutual debts are still unsolved.

The Yamal Pipeline in the Strategy of Gazprom

The Yamal Pipeline will permit the doubling of Russian exports to Europe and is therefore a top priority project for Gazprom. The entire two-thread Yamal pipeline system will have an initial capacity of 83 billion cubic meters per year, including around 52 billion cubic meters to Western Europe. Gazprom hopes to be sending 65 to 80 billion cubic meters per year or more through the pipeline by 2010. It will stretch over 4,107 kilometers and "will unite Europe's entire energy system from Poland to Spain," stated chief executive Viakhirev in November 1996.[39] The cost of the Yamal Europe project is estimated at $40 billion. Gazprom's engagement in Germany, which is not only an important market but also the gatekeeper to other countries, is one of the cornerstones on which the Yamal pipeline rests. The German sections built by Wingas JV, a joint venture of Gazprom and Wintershall, will connect the Yamal pipeline to Western and Southern Europe through the JAGAL pipeline system and become fully integrated in the European

---

[39] *Pipeline News* 35 (covering 22 October–1 November 1996), p. 8 [from jdelay@new-europe.gr].

network through the MIDAL-STEGAL and WEDAL systems.[40]

The name of the pipeline refers to the important reserves of the "supergiant" category on the Yamal Peninsula. The reserves were already known in Soviet times and their development was one of the largest Soviet economic projects. These reserves are important for meeting the expected growth in demand, but their exploitation is a real challenge in terms of techniques and equipment because of the difficult geographical and climatic conditions of the permafrost. The exploitation of these reserves requires the construction of a pipeline, but, because of the high costs involved, a certain price must be obtained for the gas upon completion of the project to ensure its profitability. The Yamal reserves would enable Gazprom to supply Europe well into the twenty-first century, because the production of gas is expected to peak at a level of 200 billion to 250 billion cubic meters per year.[41] Gazprom has won financing from European banks for the European part of the trunkline system, but has had difficulties finding capital for the Russian section, as well as fully tapping Yamal's reserves. Its completion, therefore, depends on the international discussion of concrete plans and negotiations. Consequently, in 2000, estimated completion of the total Yamal project extended beyond 2010.[42]

According to the original plans, the first line of the 4,200-kilometer Yamal pipeline, which was begun in 1995 and has links to existing pipelines in some places, was to be finished in 1998. Its different stages are not necessarily connected to the exploitation of the Yamal fields. It is possible to use the 575-kilometer Belarusian and 866-kilometer Polish sections for export before the whole pipeline is completed. Therefore, they must be seen as a key section of the future pipeline. Three hundred and sixty-five kilometers of the Belarusian part follow the same route as the already operating three-thread pipeline network, Torzhok-Minsk-Ivatsevichy. The pipeline hooks into this existing Belarusian pipeline and then into the Polish grid. According to Beltransgaz, the pipeline goes across 200 kilometers of swamps and crosses 75 rivers, 10 railroads, 42

[40]   Stepan R. Dereschow, "Ziele und Wege der energiewirtschaftlichen Kooperation zwischen Deutschland und Rußland," in *Deutsch-russische Energiekooperation unter Globalisierungsdruck, SWP - S 425*, ed. Andrei Kuxenko and Friedemann Müller, (Berlin: Stiftung Wissenschaft und Politik, Sept. 1998), pp. 85–90, esp. pp. 85–86.

[41]   E+Russia AG, *RAO Gazprom*, (Vladivostok, 1997); *Oil & Gas Journal,* Gazprom Special 1993, p. 34.

[42]   *Tribuna* 24 May 2000.

roads, 3 high-voltage lines, 11 pipelines, and 5 cables. Moreover, the project entails clearing 257 kilometers of forest and recultivating land along the trunk line. There are plans to build five compressor stations, in Orsha, Krupki, Minsk, Niasvizh [Nesvizh], and Slonim, with a total capacity of 752,000 kW, on the Belarusian section. Using all compressors, the total capacity of the two-thread Belarusian section will be 68 billion cubic meters a year.[43]

The Policy toward Belarus

The construction of a pipeline, and especially of such a giant project as the Yamal-Europe pipeline, is of great strategic concern because it fixes long-term earnings, costs, and relationships. Consequently, the choice of the pipeline route is an extremely important decision, which to a large extent determines Gazprom's further potential to supply the European market with Siberian gas, to earn valuable foreign currency, and to support its entrance into the European distribution market. In addition to the Belarusian option, Gazprom considered four other options—through Lithuania, Latvia, Ukraine, and the Baltic Sea—as possible pipeline routes. In view of the well-known conflicts with Ukraine over transit questions, it was clear that the pipeline should not cross Ukraine. Rather, one function of the new pipeline is to sidestep Ukraine and break up the Ukrainian monopoly as the gatekeeper of Russian gas exports to Western Europe. Another argument in favor of Belarus was that the route through Belarus is the shortest one. Therefore, construction costs were expected to be lower and, after the completion of the pipeline, transport costs for gas would also be lower than through Ukraine. Finally, Belarusian transit fees are a fraction of those of neighboring countries. Consequently, Belarus represented the best alternative for an export route to the European market.[44]

Despite the allegedly good Belarusian-Russian relationship, confirmed by the signing of the treaty on the union of the two states in April 1996, negotiations on the conditions for construction of the Belarusian part of the Yamal pipeline did not go easily. Gazprom even periodically threatened to re-route the pipeline through either Lithuania or Latvia because of Belarus' failure to meet Gazprom's conditions of

---

[43] *New Europe* 27 October–2 November 1996: 21.

[44] "Po vole 'Gazproma' Belarus' stanet blizhe k Evrope," *Belorusskii rynok* 43 (28 October–3 November 1996).

repayment.[45] In fact, Belarusian lack of funds was the main problem in the negotiations. Gazprom agreed to raise $2.5 billion for the construction of the Belarusian part on its own using a syndicated loan from Western banks, led by Germany's Dresdner Bank.[46] For the transfer of the construction funds, Gazprom suggested founding a Russian bank on Belarusian territory in August 1995. After the Belarusian government rejected this suggestion in September 1995, the two sides agreed on the foundation of a joint bank, which was to become the successor of the existing Belarusian bank Olymp. The official registration of the joint Belgazprombank, however, was delayed until the autumn of 1996, mainly because of internal Belarusian power conflicts. Gazprom and Gazprombank received 70 percent of the shares of the new bank, Beltransgaz 15 percent, and other Belarusian organizations 15 percent.[47] Because of the protracted negotiations, construction of the Belarusian portion of the pipeline, which was to have begun in the fourth quarter of 1995, with completion scheduled for the first quarter of 1997, was not begun until the fourth quarter of 1996.

According to the 1996 agreement signed by Gazprom and the state-owned Beltransgaz, the Belarusian company was responsible for building the Belarusian section. Despite the fact that Gazprom financed the construction, Beltransgaz was also to become the operator and formal owner of the functioning pipeline, but Gazprom did not intend simply to provide a grant of $2.5 billion to Beltransgaz; Gazprom demanded the privatization of Beltransgaz in order to receive a controlling majority of shares. As the monopolist owner of the Belarusian pipeline system and thus the only enterprise of this kind within the CIS, Beltransgaz was especially attractive to Gazprom. Indeed, when construction on the Yamal pipeline started, the privatization of Beltransgaz seemed to be only a matter of time. Its privatization also seemed to be in accordance with the interests of Beltransgaz, which expected to obtain more business opportunities. One of the options considered was that Beltransgaz would receive Gazprom shares in exchange for the transfer of Beltransgaz' shares to Gazprom.[48]

45   Fedor, *Belarus and Moldova*, pp. 53ff.

46   *Energy & Politics* 19 (28 May 1998) [from jdelay@new-europe.gr]: 21–22.

47   "Obmanet li prezident Gazprom?" *Belorusskaia delovaia gazeta* 31 October 1996; "Stanet li Belgazprombank rukoi Gazproma v Belarusi?" *Beloruskaia gazeta* 18 May 1998.

48   "Aktsionirovanie 'Beltransgaza': po gazam!" *Belorusskaia delovaia gazeta* 4

The fact that Beltransgaz's president Mikalai Macharniuk [Nikolai Mocherniuk] temporarily became a member of Gazprom's board of directors in 1996 could have been considered as a first step toward such an agreement.[49] Nonetheless, the privatization of Beltransgaz eventually failed, mainly because of its rejection by the Belarusian president. In 1998, Macherniuk was forced to resign and was replaced by Piotr Piatukh [Petukh], a loyal ally of Lukashenka who had never before worked in the energy sector.[50]

This was already Gazprom's second attempt to take over the Belarusian gas transport company. Gazprom had also demanded the privatization of Beltransgaz in 1994 to achieve a settlement of Belarusian gas debts; however, after initially agreeing, the Belarusian side refused to privatize the company. In 1995, President Lukashenka made a list of enterprises belonging to the "golden state reserve," which was not to be privatized. This list included Beltransgaz and other Belarusian companies in which Gazprom was interested. In fact, the only case in which shares were actually transferred to Gazprom took place in 1995 in connection with the Brest gas equipment enterprise.[51] One can explain this by the general "fear of privatization" characteristic of the Belarusian government and especially of President Lukashenka. This seems to be connected with a hidden "fear of Russia," because privatization would reduce the influence of the Belarusian ruling elites.[52] Giving up the energy infrastructure would mean losing Belarus' only trump card other than its position as a transit state, and thus appearing empty handed in its relationship with Russia. Therefore, privatization was only acceptable for the Belarusian government in cases where privatization would bring large government-controlled investments to the country. This was quite obvious during the lengthy negotiations in 1995 concerning the privatization of the Azot enterprise, Belarus' largest producer of chemical fertilizers and one of the largest gas consumers in the country. Belarus rejected the privatization after Gazprom refused to

October 1996.

[49] "Belorusskoe grazhdanstvo v obmen na rossiiskii gaz," *Belorusskaia delovaia gazeta* 28 October 1996.

[50] "Reveransy Gazproma," *Belorusskaia delovaia gazeta* 19 March 1999.

[51] "Khozhdenie Gazproma za Beltransgazom," *Belorusskaia gazeta* 11 May 1998.

[52] Balmaceda has stated a link between "fear of privatization" and "fear of Russia" in the case of Ukraine, but this link seems to be a broader phenomenon which emerges in different forms. See Balmaceda, *Gas, Oil and the Linkages*, p. 286.

invest hard currency in the modernization of the enterprise.[53]

The privatization issue was not the only problem that arose between Belarus and Gazprom. When construction on the Belarusian part of the Yamal pipeline was eventually begun in 1996, the deadline for its completion was scheduled for the end of 1998. Gazprom wanted to transport 28 billion cubic meters of gas along the first 977-kilometer stage of the gas pipeline between Belostok and Torzhok by 1999, but, in September 1997, one of Gazprom's German suppliers suspended delivery of pipes and valves for use on the 209-kilometer section between Niasvizh and Kandratki on the Polish border because Gazprom was not able to pay for its supplies.[54] Nonetheless, Belarusian Deputy Prime Minister Prakapovich [Prokopovich] still promised at the beginning of 1998 that work on the Belarusian part would be finished as scheduled. He also denied that Gazprom expressed discontent with the work of Belarusian construction firms.[55] However, construction continued to go very slowly during 1998, partly because Gazprom diverted funds meant for Minsk to Warsaw to speed construction on the Polish trunks. Construction on the Belarusian part began again on a large scale only in 1999.[56] At last, in autumn 1999, the first line of the pipeline became operational along the 209-kilometer-long section between Niasvizh and the Polish border. This allowed Gazprom to increase its gas exports through Belarus by about 1.5 billion cubic meters until the end of 1999. During the official opening ceremony on 21 September 1999, President Lukashenka spoke enthusiastically about the future prospects of the pipeline, while Gazprom chief Viakhirev was more cautious and confessed openly that construction of the pipeline went through so many difficulties that he preferred not to remember its history.[57] His position

---

[53] The situation in the oil sector was somewhat different. In this case the Belarusian side agreed to the foundation of different Belarusian-Russian joint ventures such as Slavneft and Rosbelneft because otherwise the country's large oil refineries would have had to stop their work. Nonetheless, the Belarusian side tried to preserve control over the enterprises concerned.

[54] "Unfinished Business," *Russia Today* 22 May 1998.

[55] "Gazprom obeshchal restrukturizatsiiu dolga Belarusi," *Belorusskaia gazeta* 9 February 1998.

[56] "Iamal'skii gaz pridet s opozdaniem," *Belorusskaia delovaia gazeta* 23 February 1998; *Belorussiia: Obzor tsentral'noi pressy* 1–6 February 1999 [from: hright@glasnet.ru].

[57] The first trunk line across Poland with a capacity of 32 billion cubic meters was also inaugurated only in September 1999 and, therefore, just as much behind schedule.

was confirmed by the fact that, because of the lack of money, neither side realized its plans to finish the second section of the Belarusian pipeline, from Niasvizh to the Russian border, in 2000.[58]

Gazprom's financial problems, which were mainly caused by falling gas prices and the necessity of paying taxes in cash, also gave rise to the company's stricter course concerning energy debts in 1998.[59] Gazprom's key demand was that Belarus should increase its share of cash payments for gas supplies to 74 percent, with only 26 percent being covered by barter deals. During the previous year, the two sides had agreed on a reversed proportion of barter and cash payments, and in 1997, Belarus paid in hard currency for only 8 percent of Russian gas supplies.[60] Negotiations became even more complicated because of disagreements on the amount of Belarusian total indebtedness, including debts from past years and fines for delayed payments.[61] In May 1998, these sums amounted to $220 million for deliveries since 1997. After lengthy negotiations, Gazprom surprisingly accepted the old payment system at the beginning of August 1998, with only 26 percent of energy supplies to be paid in hard currency. Thus, the amount to be paid in cash by Belarus was again at the same level as what Russian customers pay in cash for gas. In reality, Belarusian hard currency payments in 1998 did not exceed the 8 percent share of 1997. Therefore, in 1999, both sides agreed on a fixed sum of $200 million—later reduced to $120 million—to be paid in hard currency, but in 2000 they returned to the share solution, with 20 percent to be paid in cash.[62]

Gazprom also did not insist on the complete fulfillment of its demands concerning the $200 million debt Beltransgaz still owed it

---

Additionally, in the same month, the Iagal-North pipeline, connecting German cities with the Yamal pipeline was completed. Cf. "Truba kak zalog blagopoluchiia," *Belorusskii rynok* 38 (27 September–3 October 1999); *Financial Times Energy Country Report: Ukraine & Belarus*, London, forthcoming.

[58] "Oblako v shtanakh," *Belorusskaia gazeta* 26 December 2000.

[59] "Skandal s Gazpromom," *Belorusskaia gazeta* 6 June 1998.

[60] *RFE/RL Newsline* No. 10, 15 January 1999.

[61] Hermann Clement, *Das "Great Game" am Kaspischen Meer und die russische Integrationspolitik. Stand und Perspektiven der wirtschaftlichen Integration in Ostmitteleuropa und der GUS,* Arbeiten aus dem Osteuropa-Institut München, No. 216, December 1998, p. 63.

[62] Šurobovič, *Wirtschaftliche Aspekte der Union*, p. 24.

(according to Gazprom) for deliveries received before 1997.[63] Initially, in 1998, Gazprom wanted the debts to be repaid in state certificates backed by shares in key Belarusian companies, especially in construction firms that would be involved in laying the second line of the Yamal pipeline. The company was also interested in ownership of the land tracts along the gas pipeline. Because the Belarusian government agreed to issue bonds only on the condition that they could not be transferred to third parties, Gazprom decided once again to pull back its property-related demands. The debt reconstruction agreement signed between Belarus and Russia in the beginning of 1999 allowed Belarus to reduce its current debts to Gazprom from $232 million on 1 January 1999 to $159 million on 1 January 2000;[64] however, by October 2000, Belarusian debts had again risen to $244 million. In December 2000, after 18 months of negotiations, the Russian Central Bank finally agreed to grant Belarus a $100 million credit, two-thirds of which had to be used for the repayment of gas debts.[65]

In general, Belarus seems to be the short-term winner in the negotiations of recent years. Gazprom and the Russian government seemed to be acting in accordance with Lukashenka's arguments that Russia should show more understanding for Belarus because of the country's friendly policy toward Russia, its position as the best transit route, and because Minsk, as "the only outlet" for Russian exporters, "was not stealing oil and gas from the Russians."[66] However, it seems more likely that Gazprom simply had no other choice, because Belarus is not able to pay more than it is currently paying. Consequently, Gazprom must finish the Belarusian part of the pipeline with its own funds to save the money already invested, because, as one observer stated, "A pipeline with a gap in it is worth nothing."[67]

---

[63] Gazprom demanded that Beltransgaz pay its old debts of $200 million incurred prior to 1997 because the zero option of 1996 covered only debts on the government level, but not on the company level. Cf. "Belarussian leaders resist proposal to swap property for Russian gas," *Jamestown Foundation Monitor* 7 August 1998.

[64] "Gazprom soglasoval ob″emy, kak poschital nuzhnym," *Belorusskaia gazeta* 18 January 1999; "Krutye mery," *Belorusskaia gazeta* 6 December 1999.

[65] Šurobovič, *Wirtschaftliche Aspekte der Union*, pp. 24, 28; "Viakhirev toropitsia na Zapad," *Belorusskii rynok* 43 (30 October–5 November 2000); "Zhizn′ vzaimy, ili pochem nynche vlast′," *Belorusskaia delovaia gazeta* 20 November 2000.

[66] *Interfax* 12 April 1998.

[67] "Unfinished Business," *Russia Today* 22 May 1998.

The Impact of the Yamal Pipeline on the
Belarusian-Russian Relationship

The construction of the Belarusian part of the Yamal pipeline began just when the struggle between President Lukashenka and the Supreme Soviet over a new constitution was at its peak in Belarus. The Russian government offered to mediate a compromise solution in the Belarusian political crisis. In the end, the agreement reached on 22 November 1996 between the conflicting sides during a visit to Minsk by Prime Minister Chernomyrdin of Russia favored the position of the Belarusian president and helped him win the controversial referendum on 24 November 1996. Russia was also the only member of the OSCE that recognized the results of the referendum, by means of which Lukashenka established an authoritarian regime and extended his presidential term to 2001. Most opposition members and many independent observers used one word to explain the Russian position: "truba" (pipe). According to them, the Russian government's support for Lukashenka was largely motivated by Russian strategic military interests and by the fear that the national opposition would demand much higher transit fees for gas exports after coming to power. Therefore, a power change in Belarus could endanger the construction process of the Yamal pipeline—a risk neither Gazprom nor the Russian government was ready to take.[68]

Although this assessment may be an exaggeration, the construction of the Yamal pipeline strengthened Lukashenka's domestic political position and gave Belarus additional bargaining power to resist Gazprom's demands to agree on debt-for-share swaps. Belarus succeeded in keeping energy prices low and preserving ownership of its energy sector. In fact, the Russian state and Gazprom were permanently subsidizing Belarus. According to Russian economists, grants to Belarus and Russian losses from its customs union with Belarus amounted to $3 billion between 1996 and 1999.[69] These losses were exacerbated by the artificially low exchange rate used by the Belarusian National Bank in the Belarusian-Russian agreements on debt settlements.[70]

---

[68] Otto Latsis, "Bespokoinaia druzhba," *Izvestiia* 18 December 1996; "Interesy 'Gazproma' prevyshe vsego," *Svaboda* 16 April 1997.

[69] "Kak belorusskoe pravitel'stvo doit énergoresursy," *Belorusskaia gazeta* 19 October 1998.

[70] Clement, *Das "Great Game,"* p. 64.

Nevertheless, the construction of the pipeline did not help Belarus obtain hard currency for the modernization of its economy, because, to a large extent, the construction work performed by the Belarusian side was used to repay debts for Gazprom's gas deliveries. Thus, from the $240 million the country paid in the first half of 1998 for $384 million worth of gas received, $203.5 million, or 84 percent, was paid for by construction work on the Yamal pipeline and other Gazprom projects.[71] Nonetheless, Gazprom's investments in the construction of the Yamal pipeline constituted a large share of total foreign investments in Belarus, which slipped to $115 million in 1998 from $172 million in 1997.[72] Therefore, it is fair to conclude that cheap energy helped Belarus to survive but not to develop after independence.

The worsening economic and financial situation and heightened international isolation make the republic still more dependent on Russia. Russia's share of Belarus' trade has consistently increased during recent years, reaching about 60 percent in 1998, although the absolute trade volume began to fall after the Russian financial crisis in August 1998. Trade between the two countries is largely characterized by a chronic Belarusian deficit and by barter deals to which countries with a developed market economy would hardly agree.[73] The advantages Belarus received from the Yamal project are also likely to increase its energy dependence on Russia. In accordance with the Gazprom-Beltransgaz agreement, the Russian company must fund the construction of a gas-fired power generation station near Minsk. After completion of the pipeline, Belarus expects to double its gas imports from Russia and gas consumption may exceed the 30 billion cubic meters for which the Belarusian national energy program of 1992 provided.

Gazprom seems ready to accept the above-mentioned losses to support this increasing Belarusian dependence, because the company is interested in avoiding the emergence of other gas companies in Belarus as potential competitors. This has already happened, for example, in Lithuania and Ukraine, where the ruling elites invited Western investors to take part in different energy projects, among them the construction of pipelines. Therefore, one reason for Gazprom's interest in integration

---

[71]   "Poka Gazprom ne kliunet," *Belorusskaia gazeta* 27 July 1998.

[72]   "Foreign Investment in Belarus Falls in 1998," *Reuters* 13 January 1999.

[73]   "Politicheskaia èkonomiia na gaze," *Izvestiia* 17 December 1998.

between Belarus and Russia is that it would help Gazprom secure the future Belarusian market.

Additionally, Gazprom hopes that integration will help the company take over the Belarusian gas industry and especially the Belarusian pipeline system to finally solve the property question. Accordingly, the new union treaty signed on December 1999 by President Yeltsin and President Lukashenka provides for a united gas transport system that includes "the entry of the Belarusian gas transport infrastructure into Gazprom" by 2000. This was Gazprom's third large attempt to take over Beltransgaz, as also confirmed by the measures taken to strengthen the position of Belgazprombank (a joint Russian-Belarusian bank dominated by Gazprom and Gazprombank) in 2001. In addition, the treaty provides for the creation of a united electricity system in which the Russian electric company EES, led by the well-known reformer Anatoly Chubais, is interested.[74]

Gazprom's interest in Russian-Belarusian integration can also be explained by the fact that, under present conditions, the supply of gas to Belarus can only be regulated by close cooperation between Gazprom and the Russian government. Parallel energy-related negotiations are often conducted on company and government levels. Debt agreements are also signed on both government and company levels. Indeed, the technical realization of debt settlements is a very complicated mechanism involving several interactions. For the restructuring of $70 million of Belarusian debt in 1999, for example, Beltransgaz borrowed money from Gazprombank to pay Gazprom, which passed the money to the Russian budget, thus partly fulfilling the company's tax obligations. The Russian Finance Ministry, for its part, used the money to purchase Belarusian products, especially agricultural machinery; so the money was returned to Belarus. All the participants gained something from these arrangements, but the Russian participants are not completely content with these mechanisms. Prime Minister Sergei Stepashin blocked the $70 million deal for several months because the Russian government wanted to avoid barter agreements via the Russian budget. Only after Vladimir Putin became prime minister was a green light given to the second part of the debt reconstruction agreement. In accordance with its new, more independent business strategy,

---

[74] *Programma deistvii Respubliki Belarus' i Rossiiskoi Federatsii po realizatsii polozhenii Dogovora o sozdanii Soiuznogo gosudarstva*, Article 9.8 and 9.9; "Sektor gaza," *Belorusskaia delovaia gazeta* 5 August 2000.

Gazprom seeks to act more autonomously in the debt question, too.[75] In addition, Lukashenka's attempt to reach an agreement with President Yeltsin on the prices for gas supplies to Belarus and thus to sidestep Gazprom failed in March 1999. In reaction, Gazprom temporarily reduced gas supplies more significantly than ever before.[76]

Despite its general support for Belarusian-Russian integration, Gazprom does not want a concrete integration model, mainly because the Belarusian and Russian governments have no common interests regarding the political integration of their countries, as evidenced by the fact that only a few concrete steps toward integration have been taken during past years. The Belarusian demand for equal rights within a real Belarusian-Russian union is not acceptable for Moscow because it would cause too many problems with the territorial subjects of the Russian Federation. For Russia, the most likely option for integration is, therefore, complete incorporation and even this could be too cost intensive for the Russian state; however, Lukashenka does not want to lose power during the integration process. Incorporation for him would therefore only be acceptable if he had some chance of becoming president of Russia or at least of obtaining a leadership post in the Russian establishment, but that is unlikely to happen, especially after President Yeltsin's resignation and the election of Vladimir Putin as president. Integration, therefore, is more virtual than real, and both sides seem to use it mostly as an instrument of symbolic policy within their own domestic political struggles. (On this topic, see the chapter by Yuri Drakokhrust and Dmitri Furman in this volume.) This strategy of virtual integration will probably continue—unless the Belarusian leadership changes its policy course or has no other choice but to agree to political incorporation (as, for instance, in the case of a complete economic collapse in Belarus).[77] For Gazprom, either of the two possible options of incorporation or a continued close relationship without real unification seems to be equally tolerable at the moment because both options are in accordance with the above-mentioned company interests and do not threaten the company's monopoly.

[75] "Gazprom soglasoval ob″emy, kak poschital nuzhnym," *Belorusskaia gazeta* 18 January 1999.

[76] "Lukashenko pridumal novuiu model′ mirovogo poriadka," *Belorusskaia delovaia gazeta* 1 March 1999.

[77] Clement, *Das "Great Game,"* p. 135.

The completion of the Yamal pipeline will probably not change the character of the Belarusian-Russian integration process, but will slightly change the relationship of asymmetrical interdependence between the two countries. In contrast to most observers, we do not believe that the completion of the Yamal pipeline will strengthen the Belarusian position. The completed pipeline will give more bargaining power to Belarus, because the country will be able to block important Russian gas exports, but Belarus will not achieve the current Ukrainian position because, after completion of the Yamal pipeline, there will no longer be a monopolistic gatekeeper of Russian gas exports to the Western countries, which Ukraine has been.

Belarus will probably not be able to demand high transit fees because it did not take part in financing the pipeline and it will not have the right to re-export gas. Although transit fees increased from $0.296 to $0.4 per 1,000 cubic meters per 100 kilometers during recent years, total Belarusian transit revenue for the transport of 26 billion cubic meters of gas amounted to $40 million in 2000. This corresponds to the price of 8.2 percent of gas imported by Belarus. Only by 2005 is transit expected to exceed 30 billion cubic meters. Transit fees will continue to be paid not in cash, but rather to be taken into account via the discount Belarus receives on energy prices.[78] During a period of falling world gas prices this situation is less advantageous for Belarus. Therefore, in 1999, the Belarusian government intensified its efforts to obtain gas at the domestic Russian price (which is now $15 per 1,000 cubic meters) but only achieved a reduction to $30 per 1,000 cubic meters, which was later reduced to $27 per 1,000 cubic meters as the amount of gas transiting Belarus increased with the completion of the first section of the Yamal pipeline. According to the 2000 agreement between Belarus and Gazprom, Belarus received 16.8 billion cubic meters in that year, although Belarus wanted 20 billion cubic meters in order to reduce more expensive oil imports.[79] One-quarter of the agreed gas deliveries to Belarus were to be supplied by the relatively new Russian gas company Itera, which started its activity as gas supplier and agent for

---

[78]   "I opiat' o trube," *Belorusskii rynok* 50 (18–24 December 2000); "Rossiia reshila uporiadochit' tseny na gaz," *Belorusskaia delovaia gazeta* 17 January 2001.

[79]   "Reveransy Gazproma," *Belorusskaia delovaia gazeta* 19 March 1999; "O dolge zabyt'!," *Belorusskaia delovaia gazeta* 1 February 2000.

the realization of barter payment agreements in Belarus in 1997.[80]

Nevertheless, even the guarantee of continued cheap energy supplies and rising transit earnings will not help the country solve its economic crisis and cost structure problems as long as it continues its present domestic policy. Thus, in October 1999, Belarusian consumers paid Beltransgaz for only 13.8 percent of the gas they received, and in October 2000 for only 6.8 percent.[81] Belarus badly needs investments for the reconstruction of its energy sector, especially for the modernization of its power plants and of the old Torzhok-Minsk-Ivatsevichy gas pipeline, which will now serve only for domestic gas supplies. Therefore, the Belarusian energy sector is very interested in ways to earn real money, which the existing gas pipeline projects do not achieve, for the above-mentioned reasons. So far, the joint project with Russia's United Energy Systems, signed in November 1999, of exporting electricity to Poland seems to be more promising in this regard. The precondition of such projects, however, is the privatization of the energy sector. It seems unlikely that Belarus will be able to refuse Russian property claims in the near future.[82]

International Impact

Viewed from a broader context, energy relations are closely connected to security and foreign policies and therefore constitute an important policy field in international relations, because the asymmetrical nature of the interdependence leads to both conflict and cooperation.

---

[80] It is interesting that the former Belarusian presidential executive chief Ivan Titenkov started to work in the Moscow's office of Itera in 2000. Šurobovič, *Wirtschaftliche Aspekte der Union*, p. 24; "Indul'gentsiia dlia 'Itery,'" *Belorusskaia delovaia gazeta* 5 February 2000.

[81] This can be partly explained by the fact that domestic gas prices remained at $69 per 1000 billion cubic meters in order to reduce the existing debts to Gazprom. See "Pravitel'stvo pytaetsia sokratit' dolg," *Belorusskii rynok* 51 (27 December 1999–2 January 2000); "O dolge zabyt'!," *Belorusskaia delovaia gazeta* 1 February 2000; "Pristrelka diskontov," *Belorusskaia gazeta* 27 November 2000; "Rossiia reshila uporiadochit' tseny na gaz," *Belorusskaia delovaia gazeta* 17 January 2001.

[82] The strategy of EES is to export electricity produced in the Brest power plant with Russian gas to Poland. See "Ob"edinili ènergosistemy," *Belorusskaia gazeta* 29 November 1999. For the Belarusian privatization plans in the energy sector for 2000, see "Belarus' pristupaet k èksportu èlektroènergii," *Belorusskii rynok* 51 (27 December 1999–2 January 2000).

Coordination is necessary because the energy producers want to sell their products, while consumers must secure their demands through purchases. Establishing gas supplies requires long-term treaties owing to the natural monopoly of gas transport, which can only happen via pipelines. Trade, then, is an important production factor, since energy transfers establish steady contacts and institutionalize bilateral negotiations. Belarus is one of the most important transit countries because the Yamal pipeline goes through it. Theoretically, this should have a stabilizing effect, because it calls for adoption of international customs. With integration into the European energy system, involvement in processes of negotiations and coordination is made easier. Through the institutionalization of this platform, Belarus would have the chance to take some steps toward its so-far totally unrealized plans for energy diversification and to become involved in cooperation in other policy areas as well.

However, Belarus' international political situation, resulting from President Lukashenka's domestic policies, does not create an encouraging framework for the cooperation required for energy relations. If Belarus pursues and intensifies its political course as a wrong-way driver, it will feel pressure from both sides—from European consumers and from Russia. The first results of the internal reorganization Gazprom has undertaken in its business strategy have underlined the importance of a good company image. Therefore, Gazprom will probably not support Lukashenka if his regime's bad reputation hinders the company's export chances. In addition, because cash payments are also becoming more important for Gazprom within the CIS, an economically reformed and developed Belarus being a reliable and liquid customer would be more advantageous than an annex that requires constant subsidies. Consequently, it may be expected that this will encourage Belarus to accept international norms and to leave the path of a so-called "rough state," on which it has already embarked.

To prevent the further isolation of Belarus, the West should pursue a well balanced de-escalation policy with the Belarusian establishment and with the opposition. In the energy policy field, Western strategy could be oriented toward implementing the norms and rules fixed in the European Energy Charter Treaty, which was signed by Belarus and Russia in 1996. The European Energy Charter Treaty includes the obligation of states to facilitate, and not to impede, the transport of energy through pipelines.[83]

---

[83] Rainer Liesen, "Transit Under the 1994 Energy Charter Treaty," *CEPMLP On-*

The Charter could introduce international norms and habits through the back door and be a first step into the "European house." The Western countries have instruments to pressure Russia and Belarus to implement the norms of the Charter, because both states must raise financial resources in the West.[84] Gazprom has been successful in this so far, and there are clear signals that it is beginning to act like an economic rather than a semi-political player, which indicates progress in the company's institutional reforms. Gazprom is currently opening itself to foreign companies—an act that had been previously unthinkable and a taboo because of patriotic and nationalistic fears of selling Russia's land and resources to foreigners. Foreign ownership of Gazprom will be allowed to increase to 20 percent, as was determined in 1999.[85]

Germany plays a role of extreme importance in all these energy-related questions because it is one of the main consumers of Russian gas and the main pillar of Gazprom's engagement in Europe. Thus, Gazprom has founded several joint ventures in Germany and German gas companies are interested in participating in the Russian gas industry to increase the security of Germany's gas supply. The Ruhrgas company had been holding a 3.5 percent stake in Gazprom itself and another 0.5 percent through its joint venture with Gazeksport (Gazprom's subsidiary that deals with gas exports).[86] Its total share grew to 5 percent in December 2000.[87] A representative of Ruhrgas was elected to Gazprom's Board of Directors on 30 June 2000.[88] The participation of foreign companies and their representation in management could be one way to influence Gazprom's policy. Because of its position as a guarantor of internal and external gas supply, the company could play a substantial role in establishing a realistic price and cost structure in Russia, which is the main foundation for a functioning market economy in the country. Western cooperation with Gazprom should involve

---

Line Journal 3(7) [http://www.dundee.ac.uk/cepmlp/html/article3–7.htm].

[84] Thus, the European bank for reconstruction and development has asked for detailed information about the financial interconnections between the gas companies Gazprom and Itera in order to reach a decision about a $250 million credit for Gazprom. "Na zapakh gazovykh sverkhpribylei," *Nasha svaboda* 21 November 2000.

[85] "O gazosnabzhenii v Rossiiskoi Federatsii," *Sobranie zakonodatel'stva Rossiiskoi Federatsii* 1999, No. 14, article 1667.

[86] *The Financial Times* 25 May 1999: 27

[87] *Vedomosti* 9 December 2000.

[88] *Reuters* 30 June 2000; *Kommersant* 1 July 2000; *Vremia i novosti* 3 July 2000.

creating institutional incentives that would help the company achieve this goal. A partnership between Western companies and Gazprom to achieve economic reforms could therefore be of mutual advantage for all involved actors. Gazprom's ability to compete in Western markets could function as an importer of rational market behavior and thereby generate a strong interest in creating a reliable income structure in the CIS countries while disposing of its semipolitical attitudes.

Despite the positive signals in international energy relations mentioned above, we also see some opposing tendencies. Although, on the eve of the deregulation of Europe's gas market, Gazprom seems to be in the comfortable position of having undertaken strategic investments in the European market, this may not necessarily be the case because of the growing competition on the international gas market. Although the slowly growing demand for gas in Europe cannot be met by producers in the United Kingdom, the Netherlands, and Norway, Russia must compete with other producers such as Algeria, which could put remote Russia, with its arctic production sites, in a challenging position. The other problem that Gazprom is even more concerned about is fluctuating gas prices and the use of short-term contracts and spot transactions, which will bring down both wholesale and retail gas prices. With gas prices falling, especially in 1998 and 1999, Gazprom's export income has decreased, by approximately $1 billion in 1999. In turn, in 2000, rising gas prices have increased Gazprom's income enormously.[89] Gazprom's management is aware that these ups and downs might cause an imbalance between the capacities of exporters to invest and growing consumer demand, thus sparking a real energy crisis. This perception could lead Gazprom to change its business strategy by orienting itself toward less developed gas markets, such as in Northern and Southeastern Europe, the Middle East, and Asia Pacific, while still maintaining Western Europe as a major consumer market.[90]

These developments could also affect the future of the Yamal pipeline. At the beginning of 2001, it seems realistic that the entire first Yamal line will be operational by the end of the year. Because of the lack of funds and the existing construction difficulties, the construction of the second line, which would double transit capacity

[89]   *Neftegazovaia Vertikal'* 13 December 2000.

[90]   "Gazprom Frets over Gas Prices amid Expansion," *Oil & Gas Journal* 8 November 1999: 28; "Gazprom optimiziruet éksportnye marshruty," *Belorusskii rynok* 50 (20–26 December 1999): 12.

into Western Europe, has been questioned. Nevertheless, because of the announcement made in September 2000 by Romano Prodi, president of the European Commission, about the intentions of the EU to double its gas imports from Russia to 240 billion cubic meters, Gazprom needs to continue the extension of its pipeline system. As a short-term solution to meet increased EU gas needs, on 18 October 2000 Gazprom and the large West European gas companies agreed on a feasibility study on a branch-line pipeline from Belarus via Poland to Slovakia. This pipeline, with a capacity of 30 billion cubic meters and a total length of 370 kilometers, would branch off the existing Belarusian pipeline system. The total cost amounts to $2 billion; construction time will be two years.[91] This plan, which must be confirmed in summer 2001, evoked loud protests in Ukraine and Poland, but Russia managed to calm these emotions by promising in December 2000 not to reduce gas transit via Ukraine, while Ukraine agreed to stop its illegal gas usage. President Kuchma of Ukraine even suggested increasing the transit volume from 120 billion to 150–170 billion cubic meters.[92]

Gazprom must diversify its export routes, as it has been trying to do by intensifying talks on a Scandinavian pipeline system,[93] but the financing of this strategy will depend on continued high gas prices and international credits. Consequently, the EU-Russian agreement on increased gas transport volumes does not necessarily mean the realization of the expansive Yamal project, although it makes it more likely. If Gazprom really were to cancel the second section of the Yamal pipeline—for example, in favor of other, less expensive and possibly not-European pipeline projects—the Yamal pipeline could lose its strategic significance for Gazprom as the main route of Russian natural gas into Europe. Changes of that kind would coincide with existing anti-Western elements in Russia. In fact, Russia's present foreign policy can be characterized as an ambivalent strategy of "antagonistic cooperation"[94] aimed at retaining Russia's world-

---

[91]   See, for example, *FSU Oil and Gas Monitor (NewsBase)* 3 March 2000, 18 July 2000, 22 August 2000, 5 September 2000; *RFE/RL Newsline* 24 October 2000; and "Oblako v shtanakh," *Belorusskaia gazeta* 26 December 2000.

[92]   "I opiat′ o trube," *Belorusskii rynok* 50 (18–24 December 2000).

[93]   WPS – CIS Oil & Gas Report, 15 January 2001.

[94]   Manfred Sapper, *Großmachtpolitik ohne Großmachtressourcen. Rußlands Irak- und Nahostpolitik,* HSFK-Report (Frankfurt 1999), p. II, 12.

power status. If European integration and the enlargement of NATO are perceived in Russia as leaving the states east of the Polish border in an isolated position, the union with Belarus could be an instrument to threaten the West. In this case, Russian-Belarusian integration would be contradictory, if not antagonistic, to the integration taking place in Europe and the West.

Western Europe, therefore, should be interested in supporting a decision in favor of the construction of the second stage of the Yamal pipeline, because this could force a further integration of Russia into Europe and thus moderate the country's antagonistic ambitions. The West must also pay more attention to Belarus, which lies between the two poles of supplier and consumer and could be marginalized in its role as a transit country if Western consumers only deal directly with Gazprom. For Belarus, the completion of the Yamal project is of high importance because only the exploitation of two lines will ensure that Belarus can profit from transit costs to pay off its debts to Gazprom.[95] The completion of the Yamal pipeline is, therefore, of common interest to Belarus and Western Europe, and could serve as a starting point for the improvement of their mutual relationship. In this regard, Germany, as Belarus' most-important Western trade partner, could also play a crucial role.

The Yamal policy is a very interesting example of the interconnections and amalgamations of political and economic actors and interests in Russia and Europe. The Yamal pipeline is also a prism for the difficult Belarusian-Russian relationship. We believe that the Yamal pipeline is becoming a litmus test for future relations, because it will show whether Belarus is able to assert its position as an important transit country and realize its own interests, or whether it will become an annex of Russia. Until now Belarus has not managed to divest itself of its Soviet heritage.

---

[95] "Strategicheskaia opasnost'. Proekt 'Gazproma' v obkhod Belarusi," *Belorusskaia gazeta* 29 November 1999.

12

Hrihoriy Perepelytsia
The Belarus Factor in the European Policy of Ukraine

The emergence of an independent Belarus has brought about significant geopolitical changes in Europe. Belarus has become an object of military and political interest of neighboring countries and other key European states. At the same time, due to its geopolitical and geostrategic position, Belarus has considerable influence on politics in neighboring countries and in general on the balance of power in Eastern Europe. At the crossroads of emerging regional coalitions, Belarus can make or break how these coalitions will be configured. Belarus' relations with one of its most important neighbors, Ukraine, largely reflect its general geopolitical orientation.

Trends in the Development of Belarusian-Ukrainian Relations

Belarus' and Ukraine's differing geopolitical orientations are a major factor in their bilateral relationship. Ukraine's foreign policy is oriented toward integration with Europe, but the integration process is one with many steps. Ukraine is currently a member of the Organization for Security and Cooperation in Europe (OSCE) and the Council of Europe. The primary concerns of Ukrainian foreign policy are enhancing cooperation with the European Union (EU) and the North Atlantic Treaty Organization (NATO) and practical implementation of the Agreement on Cooperation and Partnership between Ukraine and the EU and of the NATO-Ukraine Charter. Ukraine's immediate goals are to attain associate membership in the Western EU (WEU) and the EU, and full-fledged membership in the EU in the long term.

Belarus' foreign policy, on the other hand, is pro-Russian, promotes CIS integration within the Belarus-Russia-Ukraine triangle, and favors isolation from Europe. Russia, for its part, prefers to remain an independent player in Europe, with undivided influence over Eurasia.

In this regard, Belarus and Ukraine are very important to Russia's policy, although they have different roles to play. Belarus' part is that of an obedient "junior partner," serving as a training ground for the military and political integration of the countries of the Commonwealth of Independent States (CIS), especially Ukraine, into the sphere of Russian national interests. Russia is trying to keep a tight grip on Ukraine, thereby isolating it from European integration. Sensitive to Russia's interests, Belarus has attempted to keep Ukraine out of Europe and incorporate it into the Belarusian-Russian partnership. Ever since Ukraine chose to develop its foreign policy strategy as that of a "bridge" between Russia and the West, Belarus has been trying to be a "bridge" between Ukraine and Russia. Just as Ukraine is viewed as a key element of European stability, so is Belarus seen as a key factor in CIS integration. There is an even bigger controversy between Ukraine and Belarus in the sphere of military policy, particularly on the issues of nonaligned status, NATO, and the Tashkent Treaty on Collective Security (CIS, 1992).

As a rule, only countries whose independence and sovereignty are already very solid seek neutral non-bloc status. Formal non-bloc status ratifies existing conditions, which helps the neutral country achieve national security. To the CIS nations, neutral non-bloc status has become a way to achieve sovereignty with little more than a declaration. It cannot be viewed as a mature statement of national security and foreign policy strategy. Initially, Ukraine and Belarus differed in their respective approaches to neutrality and the avoidance of military blocs.

From the beginning, Ukraine's embrace of neutrality and non-bloc status was an expression of its policy toward Russia, and not of its policy toward NATO. Kyiv assumed that Russia, being the legal successor to the Soviet Union, would not easily give up its military-political claims to Ukraine. Russia has regularly sought Ukraine's adherence to the Tashkent Treaty and to bilateral agreements on military cooperation. Ukraine's non-bloc status has enabled it to avoid all such entanglements with Russia and the CIS. In addition, non-bloc status, better than any other, finesses the domestic political situation in Ukraine, in which different regions still harbor distinctive geopolitical inclinations. Non-bloc status thus also serves the interests of internal political stability.

For Belarus, on the contrary, non-bloc neutral status was of a narrower, more transient, and tactical nature. Belarusian leaders saw the declaration of neutrality and non-affiliation with military blocs as a way to constrain NATO and prevent pro-Western and pro-NATO sentiments from gaining ground among the Belarusian public.[1] Belarus' Communist elite also used non-bloc status to insulate themselves from the democratic processes underway in Russia; however, quite soon after independence, strong pro-Russian sentiments among the Belarusian public forced its national leaders to abandon their neutral non-bloc status and move quickly toward a closer relationship with Russia.

Ukrainian and Belarusian differences on NATO are also diametrically in opposition. As put by President Leonid Kuchma, Ukraine seeks to have friendly, mutually beneficial relations with NATO. Unlike Belarus, Ukraine sees NATO expansion as an element of adapting the European security structure for new conditions and not as a threat to its national security. Ukraine also believes that while NATO expansion will not happen overnight, the expansion process should continue after the admission of the early candidates. NATO's openness to cooperation with other countries and to incorporating new members should remain one of its defining principles. The fostering of relations and deepening of cooperation between the new European democracies will likely play an important role in the European integration process, with NATO expansion as one of the key components of that process.

Belarus has followed Russia's foreign policy lead in choosing a more confrontational model for its relationship with NATO. Minsk has expressed its complete disagreement with NATO's expansion to the east. President Aliaksandr Lukashenka emphasized Belarus'

---

[1]   George Sanford, "Belarus on the Road to Nationhood," *Survival* 38(1) Spring 1996: 147.

opposition by saying that "it is not only the view of the leadership of this country but, above all, the position of the Belarusian public, 90 percent of whom strongly reject the expansion of the North Atlantic bloc."[2]

Unlike its Belarusian ally, Russia, at the same time it was counteracting NATO, was busy bargaining for a special military and political role in Europe. Moscow created a mechanism of influencing NATO decision-making that would enable it to uphold Russia's interests, including legitimization of a military presence in the CIS. Belarus adopted a stance that rejected NATO expansion, which left it in an uncertain relationship with NATO and without any international security guarantees whatsoever. As a further step in its anti-NATO policy, Belarus acceded to the Tashkent Treaty.

The different geopolitical orientations of Ukraine and Belarus thus explain the relative isolationism that characterizes their relations. Over the years since independence, Ukrainian relations with Minsk have grown steadily colder as Ukraine has further deviated from the Belarusian foreign policy course. The tendency was especially apparent when, having become president, Aliaksandr Lukashenka dissolved Belarus' Supreme Soviet; in this way he destroyed the opposition and fully seized power in the country. At the same time, Belarusian authorities arrested Ukrainian citizens who represented Right-wing political organizations and took part in the Belarusian Popular Front protests in Minsk.

This isolationist tendency also manifested itself when Belarus would not support Ukraine in resolving their common issue of nuclear disarmament. Ukraine held talks on its own with Moscow and Washington on security guarantees and financial assistance for nuclear disarmament. However, after Ukraine made some progress in discussions on the issue, Belarus took advantage of its results; for example, it was also granted financial assistance. At the same time, Ukraine was the first to support Belarus' initiative to create a nuclear-free zone in Central and Eastern Europe. Belarusian Minister for Foreign Affairs Uladzimir Sianko [Senko] introduced this initiative on

---

[2] "Glavy gosudarstv Ukrainy i Belarusi podpisali dogovor o gosudarstvennoi granitse," *Vseukrainskie vedomosti* 14 May 1997: 2.

18 April 1995 at the Nuclear Non-Proliferation Treaty extension conference.[3] President Leonid Kuchma of Ukraine further elaborated Belarus' initiative at the spring session of the Parliamentary Assembly of the Council of Europe in 1996. He then brought up the idea of a nuclear-weapon-free "zone" in Central and Eastern Europe.[4]

As Ukraine sought stronger sovereignty, isolationism in Belarusian-Ukrainian relations intensified. The Belarusian government and people attached less importance to sovereignty and independence than did the Ukrainians.[5] Therefore, Minsk regarded Ukraine's attempts to strengthen its sovereignty as a display of Ukrainian nationalism, which the Belarusian political elite and much of the population treated negatively.

Russian-Ukrainian disputes over territory and the Black Sea Fleet also fostered strained relations between Belarus and Ukraine. Belarus' pro-Russian foreign policy implied solidarity with Moscow on every issue, leaving Ukraine with no hope for support or mediation from Minsk in Ukrainian-Russian disputes.

By and large, Ukraine's policy toward Belarus lacked any overall political strategy, which resulted in an uncoordinated series of limited accomplishments. The legal securing of international state borders was one of those accomplishments, and was also a manifestation of Ukraine's stronger emphasis on state sovereignty.[6]

The intensification of Belarusian-Russian integration—most notable after Minsk and Moscow concluded the Treaty of Union between Belarus and Russia on 2 April 1997, which was ratified by both parliaments in June 1998—brought about a new phase in their relationship. Tangible interests of both states drove Russian-Belarusian integration. Unlike Moscow, which pursued integration for mostly political and geopolitical reasons, economic interests guided Minsk. Nevertheless, rigid obligations in the foreign policy, military, and political spheres accompanied the economic benefits for Belarus.

---

[3]   Document NPT/CONF. 1995/SR.3 §10 (New York, 1995).

[4]   Hennadii Udovenko "U strany dolzhny byt′ ne postoiannye druz′ia i vragi, a postoiannye interesy," *Vseukrainskie vedomosti* 4 January 1997: 3.

[5]   Sanford, "Belarus on the Road," pp. 149–50.

[6]   "Glavy gosudarstv Ukrainy i Belarusi," p. 2.

Under Article 16 of the Treaty of Union, Belarus was obliged to coordinate its foreign policy and collective security decisions with Russia.[7] Thus, Russian interests began to dominate Belarus' foreign policy. These interests also shaped Belarus' attitude toward Ukraine, and drawing Ukraine into the Belarusian-Russian union became a grand goal. Implementation of Minsk's strategy, however, ran counter to the interests of Ukraine because of the loss of sovereignty that integration necessarily entailed. Ukrainian President Kuchma disapproved of the Belarusian-Russian union, saying "Creating unions within the CIS is nonsense. It is a path to the disintegration of the CIS," and adding, "Belarus and Russia are differently developing countries and their governments have different visions, therefore the unification will be purely mechanical."[8] Most Ukrainians dislike Belarusian-Russian unification. Polls indicate that more than 41 percent of Kyivans believe that Ukraine should not join the union between Russia and Belarus. Twenty-four percent feel that Ukraine should join the union when conditions are right, 21 percent favor joining the union immediately, and 14 percent gave no answer.[9]

Despite its negative attitude, the Ukrainian government realized that Belarusian foreign policy had undergone substantial changes after the Union Treaty. According to Sherman Garnett, "This change in status of Belarus may affect the regional balance of power,"[10] and indeed it has. This change was especially evident in bilateral relations. Contacts with Minsk demonstrated that the Belarusian foreign policy community relied completely on the power and authority of Moscow, essentially reducing them to another instrument of Russian foreign policy. Lukashenka even said that top Ministry of Foreign Affairs officials often had to interpret various statements and actions of their

---

[7]   "Ustav Soiuza Belarusi i Rossii, St. 11," *Rossiiskaia gazeta* 24 May 1997: 2.

[8]   Leonid Kuchma 'Ob"edineniia vnutri SNG: ėto put' k razvalu vsego Sodruzhestva," *Vseukrainskie vedomosti* 2 April 1997.

[9]   Protsent kievlian protiv prisoedineniia Ukrainy k Soiuzu Rossii i Belarusi— opros, INTERFAX Ukraina 21 May 1997, Kyiv.

[10]   Sherman W. Garnett, *Keystone in the Arch: Ukraine in the Emerging Security Environment of Central and Eastern Europe* (Washington, DC, 1997): 106.

Moscow counterparts.[11] Belarusian attitudes toward Ukraine became more aggressive after integration with Russia as the chief strategic goal of Belarusian foreign policy focused on getting Ukraine to join the Belarusian-Russian union.

Ukraine was forced to consider all of these new factors. Its former policy of isolationism toward Belarus could not be effective in relation to a Belarus so closely tied to Russia. Ukraine's new strategy towards Belarus shifted toward one of "limited cooperation." The essence of such cooperation was a separation of Belarus' national interests from Russia's and a build-up of relations based on the common interests of Ukraine and Belarus. Those interests were found in the economic sphere and in the sphere of international regional cooperation. Thus, in its relations with Belarus, Ukraine sought to develop a bilateral political dialogue with Minsk and simultaneously enhance regional political cooperation within the Warsaw-Kyiv-Vilnius-Minsk quadrangle. Ukrainian foreign policy has recently been focused on this task.

On Ukraine's initiative, Lukashenka was invited to participate in the Vilnius International Conference on "Co-existence of States and Good-Neighbor Relations as a Guarantee of Security and Stability in Europe." President Kuchma invited Lukashenka to participate in the summit of Heads of States and Governments of the countries of the Baltic Sea region to be held in Yalta in 1999.[12] Through these dialogues Ukraine intended to slow down Belarusian-Russian integration. Having a keen interest in Belarus' sovereignty, Ukraine tried not to abandon Minsk to Moscow. Intending to engage Belarus in regional political cooperation, Ukraine wanted to demonstrate to Minsk alternative foreign policy orientations. By encouraging economic cooperation, Ukraine is striving to maintain its traditional market in Belarus and offer Ukraine's market to Belarus as an alternative to Russia's. The purpose of economic cooperation was the same as the purpose of the political dialogue—Ukraine was trying to change Belarus' one-sided, pro-Russian orientation not only in foreign

---

[11]   *Sovetskaia Belorussiia* 6 February 1997.

[12]   "Kuchma ob itogakh Vilniusskoi konferentsii," INTERFAX Ukraina 5 September 1997 (Vilnius).

policy, but also in terms of the economy. To that end the presidents of Belarus and Ukraine met twice, in Homel and Kyiv. The Treaty on Economic Cooperation from 1998 to 2000 and 12 other intergovernmental agreements were concluded.[13] This legal basis enabled an increase in trade between the countries to 1997. (See Figure 1.) The decrease in trade volume after 1997 was a result of Ukraine trying to sell exports for hard currency, instead of barter.

Figure 1
Ukrainian Foreign Trade in Goods with Belarus (1995–1999; US$ million)

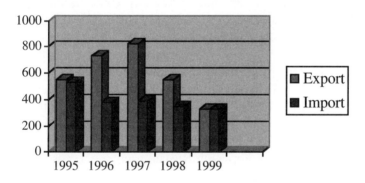

Ukraine plans to develop regional industrial cooperation by concluding and fulfilling bilateral agreements with its neighbors, including Belarus. Mutually beneficial agreements on the border regions in the context of the Bug River Euroregion are being prepared. Ukraine and Belarus cooperated to coordinate their cleanup efforts in the aftermath of Chernobyl. Ukraine has invested in Belarus' economy; there are 150 Ukrainian enterprises in Belarus (investments amount to $500,000), while in Ukraine there are 40 Belarusian enterprises (investments amount to $17 million.)[14] Nevertheless, for several reasons, even economic cooperation is limited.

---

[13] "V Kiev pribyl prezident Belarusi," *Vseukrainskie vedomosti* 13 May 1997.

[14] L. Haidiukhov and L. Chekhalenko, "SND v ekonomichnomu i politychnomu prostori Ukraïny," *Viche* 3 (1998): 35.

First, Belarus' and Ukraine's narrow interests account for limited economic cooperation. Belarus' share of Ukrainian exports ranges from 4.6 percent to 5.8 percent; Belarus' share of Ukrainian imports is 2.3 percent.[15] Belarus prefers the Russian market because of its greater capacity and the fact that Belarusian enterprises are more dependent on Russian parts and energy.

Second, opportunities for economic cooperation between Belarus and Ukraine were constrained after Belarus joined the union with Russia. Now Belarus must comply with the Ukrainian/Russian trade regime, common customs tariffs, and nontariff trade regulations. When Russia waged an economic war against Ukraine, imposing a 23 percent tax on Ukrainian goods, Belarus was compelled to join the discriminating measures against Ukraine.

Third, political priorities still dominate economic priorities. Both Russia and Belarus prioritize their political interests in relations with Ukraine. Lukashenka, on the one hand, takes advantage of cooperation with Ukraine to secure his position in relations with Moscow and improve his status in the union.[16] On the other hand, he makes economic cooperation with Ukraine conditional on Ukrainian accession to various unions with Russia, such as the customs union and the political union.

Moreover, Lukashenka is actively exploiting cooperation with Ukrainian regions to affect the political situation in Ukraine. By shaping attitudes in the region and playing on regional differences in Ukraine, he is seeking to force Ukraine to join the Belarusian-Russian union. Lukashenka has first targeted Crimea, the east and southeast regions of Ukraine, where pro-Russian and pro-Soviet tendencies are strong and the population is nostalgic for a unified Slavic state. Under the pretense of spreading regional cooperation through a local mass media controlled by the Left political forces, Lukashenka's regime ideologically influences the population of these regions of Ukraine, aiming to form a "socialist paradise" in Belarus and thereby inducing

[15]   "Vneshniaia torgovlia Ukrainy tovaramy," *Expressinform* 561 (9 December 1998).

[16]   E. Nesterenko, "Ukrainsko-belorusskii alians ne nameren vystupat' protiv Rossii," *Vseukrainskie vedomosti* 4 March 1997.

Ukraine to follow "the Belarusian model" of development. Lukashenka has achieved considerable success in carrying out this task. Exploiting the political instability in Ukraine, the differing geopolitical orientations of its regions, and the considerable influence of the Left, Lukashenka has managed to bring Ukraine closer to the Belarusian-Russian union. This began to become evident after the 1998 elections, when the Left forces won the majority of seats in Ukraine's parliament, the Verkhovna Rada. This outcome is one of several possible future directions for the Belarusian-Ukrainian relationship.

Belarusian-Ukrainian Relations and Plausible Integration Scenarios

Belarusian-Ukrainian relations will likely evolve toward one of several possible integration scenarios: Ukraine and Belarus join a restored Soviet Union or a new Slavic union with Russia; one or both countries join the European Union; or one or both countries undertake regional integration with other neighboring countries along the Baltic–Black Sea axis. It is highly unlikely any time soon that Belarusian-Ukrainian relations will be based on purely bilateral interests and will not be affected by broader regional influences.

Restoration of the Soviet Union Scenario

In this scenario Belarusian-Ukrainian relations will resemble relations between republics within one entity rather than relations between independent states. This scenario is only viable if the following conditions are met: orthodox Communists come to power in Russia, Belarus, and Ukraine, and a single Soviet-style Communist Party is created; domination of Communist ideology is unquestioned; an authoritarian regime is restored; and the countries comprising the union give up their sovereignty. Strange though it may appear, the most promising prerequisites are in Ukraine. The Ukrainian Communists, headed by their hard-line leader Petro Symonenko, have remained faithful to the former Soviet Communist Party's program goals. In addition, they are the most powerful political party in Ukraine. Nevertheless, polls show that the Communists cannot win more than 30 percent of the vote or gain more than 30–35 percent of seats in the Verkhovna Rada. Moreover, only 14 percent of

Ukrainians back the idea of restoration of the Soviet Union.[17] The main guarantor against revival of the Soviet Union, however, is the Communist Party of the Russian Federation. Following national-patriotic ideology, the Russian Communists are seeking to restore the great Eurasian Russia within the former Soviet borders.[18] The growing imperial thinking of the Russian political elite facilitates attainment of this aim. Lukashenka's authoritarian regime in Belarus has deprived the Belarusian Communists of almost any hope of coming to power. This scenario is thus much less likely to come to pass because Lukashenka is opposed to revival of the Soviet Union—instead he has made Belarus' primary foreign policy task the building of a "Slavic Union."

Slavic Union Scenario

According to this scenario, an ideology based on Panslavism, Orthodoxy, and Eurasianism will unite Ukraine, Belarus, and Russia within one entity. Panslavism is attractive because it exploits the ethnic and racial kinship of Ukrainians, Russians, and Belarusians. Panslavism gained Lukashenka considerable popularity in Ukraine. Indeed, belonging to the Slavic people is what unites not only the three countries but also Russians and Ukrainians in Ukraine. That 65 percent of ethnic Ukrainians as well as 75 percent of Russians in Ukraine associate themselves first and foremost as Slavs[19] accounts for considerable support of the idea of Slavic unification, especially among ethnic Russians in Ukraine. Only 19 percent of Ukrainians overall favor a Ukrainian-Russian-Belarusian confederation total,[20] while 80 percent of ethnic Russians, 62 percent of people over 50, 88 percent of the Crimean population, and 87 percent of people in eastern

---

[17]   "Politychnyi portret Ukraïny," Bulletin of the Demokratychni initsiiatyvy Foundation, 1997 (18): 112.

[18]   A. P. Tsygankov and P. A. Tsygankov, "Pluralism ili obosoblenie tsivilizatsii? Tezis Hantingtona o budushchem mirovoi politiky v vospriiatii rossiiskogo vneshnepoliticheskogo soobshchestva," *Voprosy filosofii* 1998 (2): 18–34.

[19]   "Growing Pains in Ukraine's Political Culture," USIA Opinion Analysis 14 March 1996 (M-48–96): 3.

[20]   "Politychnyi portret Ukraïny," p. 112.

Ukraine favor the confederation.[21] All told, 62 percent to 68 percent of the Ukrainian population advocates Ukrainian sovereignty. Only 3 percent of the Ukrainian population[22] and 16.5 percent in Belarus say "yes" when the ultimate goal of the "Slavic Union" is defined as joining Ukraine and Russia. In Russia, however, there is wide support for this idea as the way of restoring a "Greater Russia" by incorporating the territories and resources of Ukraine and Belarus. This idea also fulfills Lukashenka's purpose, because he intends to become the leader of the unified Slavic state. In reality, however, an ideology based on the premises of Panslavism, Orthodoxy, and Eurasianism is problematic in serving as a unify force.

Whereas Belarus and Ukraine are more purely Slavic countries, Russia is a multinational country. If Russia appeals to Slavism as its official ideology, the result might be internal conflict between Slavs and non-Slavs in Russia and the consequent disintegration of the Russian Federation. Orthodoxy cannot be a uniting force, either, because in Ukraine there are three Orthodox Churches that are hostile to one another and only 78 percent of Belarusians are members of the Orthodox Church.[23]

Even the traditional concept of Eurasianism is problematic in that it does not correspond to current democratic/humanist norms.[24] It is a combination of overgrown government centralism, cult of the ruler, and government's irresponsible and occupation-like treatment of its people.[25] In this regard, Eurasianism fits earlier historical patterns of leadership in Russia. It also fits Lukashenka's style, which is heavily based on a cult of personality. If the Slavic Union scenario is realized in form of the Russian-Belarusian-Ukrainian union, it may result in

---

[21] "Ukraine Opinion of US, Russia, Foreign Aid," USIA Opinion Analysis 14 March 1996 [=M-52–96].

[22] "Politychnyi portret Ukraïny," p. 112.

[23] S. V. Pavlov, K. B. Meezentsev, and O. O. Liubitsev, "Geografiia religii," *Artek* (Kyiv) 1988: 383.

[24] A. Korol′ev, "Tataro-mongol′skoe nashestvie v istorii russkogo gosudarstva," *Obozrevatel′* 8(91) 1997: 55–63.

[25] N. Rozov, "Natsional′naia ideia kak imperativ razuma (èskiz geoèkonomicheskoi i sotsio-kul′turnoi strategii Rossii dlia XX veka)" *Voprosy filosofii* 10 (1997): 13–28.

either collapse of the Russian Federation or creation of a unified Russian state with a rigid, totalitarian regime.

Ukraine and Belarus join the EU and NATO Scenario

This scenario could provide a very strong impetus for bilateral relations between Ukraine and Belarus. However, while 37 percent of Ukrainians and 34 percent of Belarusians advocate integration with the West, this scenario seems unlikely. Belarus currently has neither the economic nor the political prerequisites for developing its relations with Ukraine according to this scenario. Moreover, Belarusian official policy is in opposition both the EU and NATO.

Although Ukraine has officially requested to join the EU and Euroatlantic security institutions, it (unlike Central European countries) has many obstacles on its way to integration with Europe. Ukraine still maintains its orientation to the CIS and Russia. Unlike in the Central European countries, in Ukraine the goal of integration with the EU is neither to unite the political elite nor the natural continuation of Ukrainian reforms. Cooperation with Belarus will produce even more complications for Ukraine on its way to the EU.

If Ukraine is successful in European integration, and the present political regime in Belarus remains, isolationism between Belarus and Ukraine will grow. Ukraine will have to impose a tight visa regime on Belarusian citizens in compliance with EU demands and to comply with other EU regulations.

The Subregional European Integration Scenario

While Ukraine faces tough requirements for, and obstacles to, joining the EU, Russia's current struggles to exercise authority over its large territory make a Slavic Union unlikely; therefore, a subregional integration scenario seems the most promising. One form such an integration might take would be realized along north-south lines in Central-Eastern Europe.[26] Theoretically, this scenario would be embodied in the Baltic–Black Sea alliance. Belarus and Ukraine could be the central link in this alliance, providing a transport, service, and communication infrastructure. This is the only alternative to a pro-

---

[26]   *Security Dialogue* 28(3) September 1999: 351.

Russian orientation by Belarus; however, if Belarus welcomes this opportunity, it must prioritize cooperation with north European and Black Sea countries. Poland, Lithuania, Turkey, Moldova, Romania, and Ukraine must in turn promote a Belarusian policy shift in their direction. The regional nature of Belarus' external economic and foreign policy activities and its trade with neighboring Russian and Ukrainian regions could facilitate this change of orientation.

The Diverse Integration Scenario

A diverse integration scenario can be represented as the integration of Ukraine and Belarus in different security systems and civilizations—Ukraine, realizing its strategic purpose, joins the economical, political, and defense structures of the West and Belarus integrates with Russia. Variations of that scenario can be as follows: Ukrainian membership in NATO or in the EU, or a united Belarusian-Russian state or a military union of Belarus and Russia.

Actually, this scenario is becoming more likely. Belarus, after concluding the latest accord with Russia on 8 December 1999, essentially agreed to transfer key defense functions to a future allied state—integration of the Belarusian army units with the Moscow Military District is already in progress. Although Kuchma declared in his inaugural speech that the issue of Ukraine entering NATO is not urgent, he sees the long-term future of his country as joining the structures of European security, especially the EU.[27] The majority of Ukraine's population supports Ukrainian membership in the EU; however, taking into account that the EU is not only a political-economic union, but also a defense structure, Ukraine's entry into the EU in the context of the diverse integration scenario would differ little from its entry into NATO.

In the post Cold War era, two political poles have emerged on the European continent, one centered in the European Union and one centered on the Russian Federation. Those countries that are included neither in the process of European integration nor in Russia's reintegration policy will become a zone of fierce geopolitical and

---

[27] "Vystup Prezydenta Ukraïny Leonida Kuchmy na rozshyrennomu zasidanni kolehiï Ministerstva oborony Ukraïny 23 lystopada 1999 roku," *Narodna armiia* 25 November 1999.

political-military rivalry in the periphery between these two force centers. In this event, Ukraine will likely have to give up its non-bloc status and join one side or the other. If Ukraine joins the European structure of collective security, it will be protected from external threats and the conditions for dynamic political economic development will be created. However, one of negative consequences of European integration will be intensified political, economic, and military confrontation with Belarus and Russia. But if Ukraine does not move in this direction, one of the integration scenarios involving Belarus and Russia will likely occur, and Ukraine's sovereignty will be lost.

Conclusion

Ukraine's relations with Belarus are overshadowed by the larger integrative movements in the region. Ukraine's current policy of limited cooperation arises from Belarus' ever closer relationship to Russia. As Ukraine tries to move closer to the European Union—and as Belarus moves in the opposite direction toward Russia—it is unlikely that even this limited cooperation between the two countries will continue. A better long-term alternative for both countries, however, would be to pursue a strategy of subregional cooperation. Combining the efforts of neighboring countries such as Poland, Lithuania, Turkey, and other countries of the Baltic and Black Sea regions, Ukraine and its neighbors may one day be able to control collectively their own fates, even in the shadow of more powerful political forces.

Appendix. *History of the Belarusian-Ukrainian Relationship*
(1991–1999)

8 December 1991	Meeting of the heads of state of Belarus, Ukraine, and the Russian Federation. Signing of the agreement on creation of the Commonwealth of Independent States.
10 December 1991	Ratification of the agreement on the Commonwealth of Independent States by Ukraine's Verhovna Rada.
11 December 1991	Enactment by the Presidium of the Verhovna Rada of "About the Establishment of Diplomatic Relations with the Member-states of the Former Soviet Union"
13 March 1992	Meeting in Kyiv of the heads of the member-states of the CIS, at which the "Agreement on the Protection of State Borders and Marine Economic Zones of the Commonwealth of Independent States" is signed.
22 January 1993	Visit of Ukrainian President Leonid Kravchuk to Minsk for participation in a Council Meeting of the heads of state and governments of the member states of the CIS.
13 June 1993	Agreement between the Belarusian, Russian, and Ukrainian governments for urgent measures on increasing economic integration.
2 June 1994	Visit of Ukrainian Prime Minister Vitaly Masol in Minsk for participation in celebrations for the 50th anniversary of the liberation of Belarus from German occupation.
15–16 December 1994	Official visit of Ukrainian Prime Minister Vitaly Masol in Belarus and signing of agreements on cooperation in environmental protection.
27 December 1994	Visit to Ukraine of a Belarusian parliamentary delegation led by the President of the Supreme Soviet of Belarus, Miacheslaŭ Hryb [Grib].
16–17 June 1995	Official visit of President Leonid Kuchma of Ukraine to Belarus and the signing by the

	presidents of Ukraine and Belarus of a treaty of friendship and cooperation between Ukraine and Belarus.
14 December 1995	Official visit of a Belarusian government delegation led by Prime Minister Mikhail′ Chyhir, during which a provision on the intergovernmental agreements on the mutual protection of the investments and guarantees of human rights concerning pensions is signed.
17 January 1997	Meeting of Aliaksandr Lukashenka and Leonid Kuchma in Homel (Belarus), during which a treaty on economic cooperation between Belarus and Ukraine for 1998–2000 and 12 intergovernmental agreements are signed.
12 May 1997	Official visit of Lukashenka to Kyiv, during which the presidents of the two countries sign a treaty on state borders.
5 February 1998	Negotiations of Ukrainian Prime Minister Valerii Pustovoitenko in Minsk with Lukashenka on the immediate resolution of the problem of double taxation and the essential increase of mutual commodity circulation.
26–27 August 1998	Meeting between Lukashenka and Kuchma in Crimea.
11–12 December 1998	Visit to Belarus of Kuchma. Signing of the Ukrainian-Belarusian intergovernmental agreement on the simplified border transit regime for citizens living along the Ukrainian-Belarusian border.
27 January 1999	Official visit to Belarus of the chairman of the Verkhovna Rada of Ukraine, Oleksandr Tkachenko, during which he declares the necessity of the reconstruction of the commonwealth of Ukraine, Belarus, and Russia and of the strengthening of political cooperation.
12–13 March 1999	Visit of Lukashenka to Ukraine, during which Belarusian business leaders from the Zaporizhzhia and Donetsk areas meet and the governors of some Belarusian regions negotiate with the administrators of some Ukrainian regions.

	Lukashenka confirms Ukraine's proposal to join the union of Russia and Belarus.
3 June 1999	Visit to Kyiv of a Belarusian military delegation led by the chief of the anti-aircraft defense troops, Lieutenant-General Valery Kostenko, during which prospects for cooperation between Belarusian and Ukrainian anti-aircraft defense troops are considered.
10–11 June 1999	An interparliamentary conference, "Belarus, Russia, Ukraine: Experience and Problems of Integration," is held in Kyiv. In addition to the Belarusian, Russian, and Ukrainian members of parliament, the deputies of Yugoslavia and a delegation from the interparliamentary assembly of the CIS take part in the meeting.
23 July 1999	An agreement between Ukraine and Belarus on cooperation in the field of national minorities' rights is signed in Kyiv.
16 November 1999	Russian, Belarusian, and Ukrainian businesses begin work on a project to modernize the Tu-134 passenger plane.
30 November 1999	Participation of Lukashenka in Kuchma's inauguration.

13

Algirdas Gricius
Lithuania and Belarus: Different Paths on the Way Back to the Future

The Soviet empire, created in December 1922, existed for 69 years. It disintegrated in 1991, also in December, when the leaders of Russia, Ukraine, and Belarus—Boris Yeltsin, Leonid Kravchuk, and Stanislaŭ Shushkevich—met in Belavezhskaia Pushcha, Belarus, and decided to create the Commonwealth of Independent States (CIS) in place of the Soviet Union. Although the cooperation between the democratic movements in Lithuania and Belarus (the Lithuanian Restructuring Movement "Sajudis" and the Belarusian Popular Front, respectively) began in the perestroika period of Mikhail Gorbachev, real interstate relations began to develop only after the unsuccessful putsch in Moscow in August 1991 and the two countries' recognition of each other's independence in December of the same year. Diplomatic relations between Lithuania and Belarus began in December 1992.

In the period between the unsuccessful Moscow putsch and the disintegration of the Soviet Union at the end of 1991, the so-called "sovereignty parade" of former republics of the Soviet Union took place. (The Baltic States had already declared the restoration of their statehood in 1990.) At that time, it was difficult to predict what path the other (non-Baltic) former Soviet republics would take in establishing their sovereignty. Even now this is not easy to predict. The paths these states will take are primarily tied to the development perspectives of the CIS. Whether the CIS will be used as a mechanism for civilized divorce (the interpretation of most Ukrainian politicians) or as a new way to integrate half-sovereign states (the understanding of the Belarusian political elite) will depend to a great extent not only on the former Soviet republics that declared their sovereignty, but also on the aims and priorities of the internal and foreign policy of the Russian Federation.

Belarus, one of the four republics that formed the basis of the Soviet Union in 1922, now clearly supports the restoration of strong federal ties with Russia and the creation of a new Slavic state entity, which it feels that Ukraine also should join.[1] This current attitude of the leaders of Belarus (which is now supported by the majority of the inhabitants of Belarus) can in great part be explained by the complicated economic situation in the state. Belarus was confronted with economic problems—as were many of the other former republics of the Soviet Union after its disintegration—that it was unable to and most likely did not want to resolve by using the principles of a market economy to implement economic reforms. All this allowed a deputy of the Belarusian Supreme Soviet, the little-known former collective farm chairman Aliaksandr Lukashenka, cleverly using populist promises, to win the election for president and begin to implement policies of restricting democracy and returning to a planned economy, from which Belarus had not strayed very far.[2]

After Lithuania reestablished its statehood, it began to implement policies to create a free market and strengthen democracy. It fortified this decision at the end of 1992 by adopting its state constitution in a referendum. During the referendum, the voters also approved a constitutional act that prohibited the Republic of Lithuania from joining any interstate structures that would be created on the basis of the former Soviet Union.[3] In the field of internal affairs, despite the considerable difficulties encountered in restoring the rights of citizens to their former property that had been nationalized when the Soviet Union occupied Lithuania, and the social tensions that arose when privatizing state property and implementing economic restructuring, Lithuania has not given up its chosen path. Rather, it has tried to

---

[1]   Kathleen J. Mihalisko, "Belarus: Retreat to Authoritarianism," in *Democratic Changes and Authoritarian Reactions in Russia, Ukraine, Belarus and Moldova*, eds. Karen Dawisha and Bruce Parrott (Cambridge, 1997), pp. 223–81.

[2]   Ibid.

[3]   *Constitution of the Republic of Lithuania, 1992* (Vilnius, 1993), p. 133.

accelerate it. Lithuania's foreign policy priorities are integration as quickly as possible into Western and trans-Atlantic political, economic, and security structures, including membership in the EU and NATO. In addition to other foreign policy priorities, Lithuania wants to maintain good, friendly relations with all neighboring states. Thus, relations between Lithuania and Belarus, despite all the complicated and differing attitudes about many international problems, hold an important position in Lithuania's foreign policy. In an interview with the present author, the president of the Republic of Lithuania, Valdas Adamkus, said that a different political orientation of the states must not affect neighborly relations. "It looks like this principle is more and more taking root in our cooperation with Russia and Belarus."[4] Not only the political and economic interests of the two countries, but also Lithuania's and the entire Baltic region's security determine the importance of these relations.

Historical Influences on the Internal and Foreign Policies of the States of Central and Eastern Europe

Twentieth-century European history, with its complicated political changes and large loss of human life and material goods, left deep marks in the consciousness of its inhabitants, particularly in Central and Eastern Europe. After the end of the Cold War and the collapse of the Soviet Union, most of the countries and nations that had been part of the Soviet Union tried to understand and evaluate their recent past and to find their place in the Europe of the twenty-first century. The Baltic States, including Lithuania, have a clear understanding of the

---

[4]   An exclusive interview was granted to the present author on 15 March 1999. Answering the question, "What policy should the EU, the U.S., and other Western countries pursue in striving to integrate Belarus into the community of European countries?" the Lithuanian president said: "Lithuania welcomes positive changes in the dialogue between Belarus and Western countries. We see in them a part of our own work. Lithuania has supported in every possible way the dialogue with Belarus and worked to open up all possible channels for contacts and cooperation. Our efforts have been supported by Western countries, which also favor resuming and maintaining the dialogue with Belarus. Undoubtedly, further relations between Belarus and the West will depend to a large extent on the developments in Belarus. I am sure, however, that Western countries should maintain the dialogue with Belarus, rather than isolate it."

Molotov-Ribbentrop Pact and its secret protocols, which led to their forced incorporation into the Soviet Union, an incorporation that the partisan movement in Lithuania opposed with arms for more than five years after World War II.[5] Most current political figures, the majority of the citizens in Lithuania, and a large part of those who emigrated, including postwar refugees (more than 500,000), who primarily moved to the U.S., Western Europe, and Australia, view the period between the wars (1918–1940) as the period of the successful creation of an independent and democratic state. In Belarus, on the other hand, both the current political elite and the citizens have a totally different understanding and evaluation of the former Soviet Union and World War II and of their consequences for Central and Eastern Europe. Most people in Belarus view their almost seventy-year history in the totalitarian Soviet state, disregarding the Stalinist repression and cruelties, as the period of building socialism, fighting fascism, and constant, if meager, social guarantees provided by a planned economy and party nomenclature rule. Such a perception makes it difficult to plant and develop the principles of democracy, and even more difficult to make the transition from a planned to a market economy, inevitably increasing social tension for a certain period of time. The fact that the Belarusian population during the Soviet period never developed a strong sense of national identity has also considerably influenced the formation of such a perception.[6]

These different perceptions of history have had a considerable influence on the formation and implementation of the foreign policies of Lithuania and Belarus. Lithuania's foreign policy priorities have remained practically unchanged since the parliamentary elections at the end of 1996 and the presidential elections at the beginning of 1998. Lithuania, in its foreign policy, seeks:

---

[5]   Romuald J. Misiunas and Rein Taagepera, *The Baltic States: Years of Dependence, 1940–1980* (Berkeley and Los Angeles, translated edition 1992); idem, *Baltijos valstybes: priklausomybes metai 1940–1980* (Vilnius, 1983), pp. 92–103.

[6]   Antanas Kulakauskas, "European Dimension, Good Neighborly Relations and Lithuanian Society," *The Texts of Vilnius Conference '97* (Vilnius, 1997). Also, Stephen R. Burant, "Foreign Policy and National Identity: A Comparison of Ukraine and Belarus," *Europe-Asia Studies* 47(7) 1995: 1132–33.

- integration into Euro-Atlantic political, economic, and security structures,
- the development of good and constructive relations with neighboring countries,
- mutually beneficial cooperation with all democratic and friendly countries, and
- comprehensive and multilateral regional cooperation.

At least two of the four main foreign policy priorities are directly connected with bilateral Lithuanian-Belarusian relations. An analysis of these relations cannot ignore Russia's relations with Lithuania and, to an even greater extent, with Belarus. Even though there have been some difficulties in economic matters, Lithuania's relations with Russia have developed normally. In 1997, Lithuania made an agreement with Russia delimiting the state borders in the Kaliningrad district and thus completed the legitimization of all of its land borders with neighboring countries. One can hope that good relations with Russia and the determination of legal borders with neighboring countries will have a positive influence on Lithuania's efforts to gain membership in the EU and NATO.

In spite of repeated assertions by state officials about the multidirectional, balanced character of Belarus' foreign policy, it has a clearly defined eastern orientation. The orientation to the east, or more accurately to Russia, arose even before Lukashenka became Belarus' president; in practical terms, it had never been directed in a different direction. Stephen R. Burant writes, "Belarusian political elites have demonstrated little willingness to try to establish a European, or Central European, identity for their country to distance it from Russia."[7] Former Belarusian Prime Minister Viacheslaŭ Kebich's point of view on Belarusian-Russian relations, expressed in 1994, supports this opinion. In a speech to the Belarusian Supreme Soviet, he said that Belarusian-Russian relations were Minsk's basic foreign policy priority, "owing to the community of Belarusian-Russian culture, the identical interests of two fraternal peoples."[8] All the leaders of Belarus, from Shushkevich to Lukashenka, have pursued a policy of closer relations with Russia and broader integration in the

[7] Burant, "Foreign Policy and National Identity," p. 1133.

[8] Ibid., p. 1136.

CIS. One can consider Lukashenka only as a more active supporter of this policy and of deeper integration into Russia.

Despite different priorities and orientations in internal and foreign policies, Lithuania maintains quite active bilateral relations with its eastern neighbor. Explaining the necessity of maintaining active bilateral relations with Belarus, Adamkus, in the above-mentioned interview, said:

> Different orientation of states should not have a negative impact on neighborly relations . . . We exchange views with our neighbors on our integration into Western security and economic structures, emphasizing at the same time that this process is not an obstacle on the way to further cooperation. On the contrary, new possibilities arise, for example, to implement joint cross-border projects by using EU funds under EU programs. Apart from problematic issues, Lithuania shares a considerable load of work with Belarus: demarcation of the border, improvement of the capacity of border-crossing posts and border control, and implementation of joint projects in energy and transport sectors. Many possibilities are provided by direct contacts between the border districts of Lithuania and Belarus, and activities of the Euroregions established at the border of both the states. Cultural exchange is not active so far.

Cultural relations might be enlivened with the establishment of the Frantishek Skaryna fund that has been initiated by both presidents.

Later in this chapter we will examine the economic ties between Lithuania and Belarus (and between these two countries and other countries), their cooperation in developing democracy, their security policies, and the influence of their bilateral relations on the security of Lithuania and the Baltic region.

Economic Cooperation

In spite of substantial efforts by the state to change their direction, to a great extent Lithuania's economic relations with foreign countries, especially in matters of trade, remain tied to the east—that is, to Russia and other CIS countries. According to statistics for the first nine months of 1998, trade relations with other CIS countries exceeded 30 percent of Lithuania's foreign trade, of which 65 percent (20 percent of Lithuania's total foreign trade) was with Russia. Although levels of trade with Western countries, especially the EU, increase each year (according to statistics for the first three-quarters of 1998 they constituted 42 percent of total foreign trade), the huge trade imbalance nevertheless creates considerable worries for the Lithuanian government. In the area of investments, capital from Western countries exceeds by many times investments from CIS countries. According to preliminary statistics for 1998, foreign direct investments in Lithuania reached $1,600 million, or $432 per capita.[9]

Recent statistics about the Belarusian economy and its relations with other countries are quite scant and often not very reliable.[10] According to the World Bank, Belarus' foreign trade deficit after 1996 had grown considerably and its trade with non-CIS states was quite small.[11] Privatization recently has slowed significantly. Similar findings are also reported by the International Monetary Fund,[12] which indicated that in 1996 barter trade became dominant with many countries, especially with Russia. Per capita foreign investments in 1995–1996 were only $4.[13] According to unofficial statistics, trade with CIS countries accounted for 80 percent of Belarus' total trade.[14]

Despite quite different orientations and priorities in foreign economic relations, Lithuanian-Belarusian foreign trade developed quite dynamically and, in 1997, exceeded $500 million. Lithuanian-Belarusian foreign trade in 1995–1998 is shown in Table 1. Belarus is Lithuania's fourth-largest export market (after Russia, Germany, and Latvia). In 1998, approximately 8 percent of Lithuania's total foreign trade volume will have been with Belarus.

---

[9]   Department of Statistics, Government of the Republic of Lithuania.

[10]   *Belarus Monitor,* NTsSI Vostok-Zapad and ATs Stretegiia, 1999, p. 41.

[11]   International Bank for Reconstruction and Development, *Country Study: Belarus* (Washington, DC, 1997), pp. 15, 39.

[12]   International Monetary Fund, *Belarus: Recent Economic Developments,* November 1997, p. 50.

[13]   Ibid., p. 53.

[14]   These figures were provided at the end of 1998 in Minsk at a meeting of lecturers and students from the Institute of International Relations and Political Science (Vilnius University) with lecturers and students from the European Humanitarian University (Minsk).

Table 1
Lithuanian-Belarusian Foreign trade (million US$)

	1995	1996	1997	1998 (January–September)
Total	424.2	450.3	532.6	369.4
Exports	291.0	342.0	396.6	270.4
Imports	133.1	108.2	136.0	99.0

Source: Department of Statistics, Government of the Republic of Lithuania.

In 1997, 10.3 percent of Lithuania's total exports went to Belarus (3rd place among trading countries) and 2.4 percent of imports (13th place) came from there. Lithuania's exports to Belarus were mostly products of the chemical and allied industries, mineral fuels, mineral oils and products of their distillation, vehicles other than railway or tramway rolling stock, and electrical machinery and equipment with parts. Belarusian exports to Lithuania included textiles and textile articles, products of the chemical and allied industries, mineral fuels, mineral oils and products of their distillation, bitumen products, and mineral waxes. These levels of trade were reached even though the Lithuanian-Belarusian Government Agreement on Free Trade signed in 1993 had not yet gone into effect. The tariff union that Belarus formed with Russia has hindered its implementation. The complicated way the two countries make settlements for electricity is also worth mentioning. Lithuania provides Belarus with about 25 percent of the electricity that it consumes. It is not paid for primarily in hard currency, but in various goods, about whose selection and price disagreements frequently arise. In March 1999, the Belarusian debt to Lithuania reached $100 million. Quarrels and Lithuania's threats to stop providing electricity have begun. Knowing that Lithuania cannot deliver its excess electric energy, produced at the very powerful (2.6 MWe) Ignalina Nuclear Power Plant, to other countries without making new agreements and investments, Belarus has not hurried to resolve problems of paying for the electricity. The governments have temporarily succeeded in resolving the conflict, but there is no guarantee that it will not occur again. Belarus' trade with the Baltic States for 1995–1998 is shown in Table 2.

Table 2
Belarus' Trade with Baltic States (in million US$)

	Lithuania	Latvia	Estonia
1995			
Total	264.2	253.5	34.8
Exports	146.4	195.7	19.0
Imports	117.8	57.8	15.8
1996			
Total	298.8	188.3	25.3
Exports	145.4	139.3	15.1
Imports	153.4	49.0	10.1
1997			
Total	329.7	139.6	28.3
Exports	137.8	72.5	16.4
Imports	191.9	67.1	11.8
1998	*January-September*	*January-May*	*January-March*
Total	267.2	99.5	3.9
Exports	103.0	57.1	2.1
Imports	164.2	42.3	1.8

Note: The amounts in Tables 1 and 2 differ because the Republic of Belarus Ministry of Foreign Economic Relations does not include the costs of Lithuania's electricity exports and uses a different method for calculating the costs of exported (as barter trade) production.

Source: Baltiiskii kurs Fall/Winter 1998: 12 (according to the data provided by the Ministry of Foreign Economical Relations of the Republic of Belarus).

From the two tables, one can see that the volume of Lithuania's trade with Belarus, especially in 1997 and 1998, is significantly higher than that with Latvia or Estonia. The difference becomes even greater when the costs of Lithuanian electricity exports are added. This can be explained by the fact that Estonia and Latvia consider Belarus mainly as a transit country for their exports to Ukraine and Central European countries, while Lithuania tries to expand bilateral trade, which is closely tied to the settlements for providing electricity to Belarus. Belarusian investments in Lithuania are very small; according to the Lithuanian Statistics Department, on 1 October 1998, they amounted to only $900,000.[15] These investments make up only 0.06 percent of all investments in Lithuania's economy. There is a similar situation with Lithuanian investments in the Belarusian economy, which do not exceed $1 million.[16]

For Belarus, the Baltic States, especially Lithuania and Latvia, are important not only as trade partners, but even more as transit routes for trade with the West. Because of the current low trade levels with the West, this question is not particularly urgent for Belarus, but if it decides in the future to expand its trade ties with Western countries, the shortest route to the only nonfreezing seaport in the Baltic States, Klaipėda, might become quite important. Currently, about 10 percent of cargoes handled in Klaipėda's port are in one way or another connected with Belarus.[17] For several years, Lithuania and Belarus have been conducting negotiations for a long-term agreement "On Providing Transport and Other Services for Shipping Cargoes through the Klaipėda State Sea Port." Belarus has suggested that the draft of this agreement be supplemented by the articles of the United Nations Convention on transit trade for internal continental states, which provide for the free transit of cargoes through the territory of neighboring states that have access to sea waters.

On the other hand, Belarus is important for Lithuania as a transit state in its trade with the east, especially with Russia and Ukraine. There are also numerous unresolved problems in this field. Belarus limits the issuance of free permits to Lithuanian shippers transporting cargo by trucks. Russian shippers traveling through Belarusian territory to Lithuania make unlimited use of such permits, which limits Lithuanian shippers' ability to compete with Russian shippers in transporting goods to Russia, Ukraine, and other CIS countries, and from those countries to Lithuania. One way for Belarus, Russia, and Lithuania to expand economic relations might be to use a shuttle-type train from Mukran (Germany) to Klaipėda (Lithuania) to Minsk (Belarus) to Moscow (Russia). The implementation of this project has been hindered by the difficulties that arise in coordinating transit

---

[15] Department of Statistics, Government of the Republic of Lithuania.

[16] Ibid.

[17] *Baltiiskii kurs* Fall/Winter 1998: 12.

tariffs and quotas. The projected beginning of the shuttle train route in 1998 was postponed until 1999.

A problem that remains in resolving transit questions is the capacity of the existing border-crossing posts. At times, long lines of cargo automobiles form at the border posts. President Adamkus of Lithuania raised this question with the Belarusian president in a telephone conversation in March 1998 and during the Medininkai-Kamenyi Log border post meeting in November of that year.[18] The Lithuanian side at this time can inspect and pass 2,000 vehicles per day through the main transit trade post at Medininkai-Kamenyi Log, while the capabilities of the Belarusian side are a fraction of this. As part of the TACIS Program, the EU has granted Belarus 3 million ECU for the reconstruction of this border post. One might expect that Belarus' border-crossing capacity would also be increased at other Lithuanian-Belarusian border-crossing posts.

To summarize the problems of Lithuanian-Belarusian economic development and foreign economic relations, both countries face large, although different, problems. While Lithuania is striving for a free market economy and hopes to hasten privatization by trying to attract more investments from the West, Belarus has essentially stopped privatization, is trying to preserve the collective and state farms, and does not seek to restructure its industry or attract foreign investments. Belarus' state-subsidized inward-oriented industry limits the possibility of expanding export markets, and increases its dependence on Russia. All this, no doubt, creates additional problems for expanding further economic cooperation between Lithuania and Belarus.

Cooperation on Human Rights and Democracy Inititiatives

In spite of major economic difficulties and shortages and restrictions on democratic rights, the internal political situation in Belarus is relatively stable, indicating that the patience of many former Soviet Union nations and especially of Belarus is indeed very great. Numerous politicians from foreign countries and international organizations, including the Organization for Security and

---

[18] *Izvestiia* 14 November 1998: 3. Also, *Belorusskaia gazeta* 11 May 1998: 14.

Cooperation in Europe (OSCE) and the EU, have expressed their opinion on the restrictions on the independent press, the questionable legitimacy of the current Supreme Soviet (parliament), and the limitations on the activities of opposition organizations. The scientific coordinator of the Belarus Analytical Center "Strategy," Valerii Karbalevich, in his article "Going into a Crisis," has provided a comprehensive analysis of the internal political situation and foreign policy of Belarus.[19] The internal political and economic situation in Belarus undoubtedly influences its foreign policy and relations with neighboring countries, including Lithuania. Lithuania is interested in political stability, improvement in the economic situation, and the development of democracy in Belarus because these have a direct influence not only on Lithuania's security, but also on the general stability of the Baltic region. The citizens of every state and their legitimate authorities have the right to select the form and methods of ruling the state, to make decisions on how to solve internal political and economic questions, and to determine foreign policy priorities; however, Lithuanian political figures, including representatives at the highest level, have more than once declared that the problems of Belarus must be decided according to universally recognized principles of democracy and a legitimate state, strictly adhering to the principles of human rights and freedoms.

In an interview in the newspaper *Belorusskaia gazeta,* a former Lithuanian ambassador to Belarus, Victor Baublis, perhaps being too candid, said:

> We declare openly: Lithuania is interested that a civil society be formed more quickly in Belarus, that all the democratic forces be allowed to express themselves more freely, that all human rights and freedoms be guaranteed more firmly. We are interested in a democratic and stable Belarusian government that would carry out economic reorganizations.[20]

In holding to this view, Lithuania tries to maintain ties as broad as possible with Belarusian social organizations, science and educational institutions, media representatives, and the Belarusian community in Lithuania. Contacts between the universities and youth organizations

[19] *Belarus Monitor* 1998: 3.

[20] *Beloruskaia gazeta* 11 May 1998: 14.

of Lithuania and Belarus recently have become more active.

In December 1997 in Minsk, the Lithuanian Ministry of Education and Science signed an agreement for cooperation in the field of education for 1998–1999. At the end of 1998, the University of Vilnius and the Belarus State University signed a broad bilateral treaty that provides for the exchange of instructors and students, general projects for scientific research, and cooperation between student organizations, among other things. The International Relations and Political Science Institute (Vilnius University) established ties with the European Humanities University in Minsk. In October 1998, a group of lecturers and students (30 persons) from the European Humanitarian University visited Vilnius. During the visit, they held talks with their University of Vilnius colleagues, met with the heads of various universities in Vilnius, visited the Lithuanian parliament, and had a meeting with the parliament chairman. In December, some Lithuanian students made a similar visit to Minsk. Seminars for instructors and students, in which lecturers and known political figures from both countries will give speeches, are planned for once a month in Vilnius and Minsk. OSCE Advisory and Monitoring Group Head Ambassador Hans-George Wieck has promised to support the implementation of this project. The Council of Lithuanian Youth Organizations is planning a cooperative project with some Belarusian youth organizations. The project envisions acquainting Belarusian youth with the principles of activities of nongovernmental organizations and holding courses of instruction for the leaders of Belarusian youth organizations.

The Lithuanian government, limited by its financial situation, supports the activities of the Belarusian community (55,000 people) in Lithuania. The state radio in Lithuania transmits programs every day in Belarusian. The state television also has a weekly half-hour-long program. Two newspapers, one of which receives government support, are printed in Belarusian. There is a Belarusian high school in Vilnius, Belarusian classes in a Russian school in Visaginas, and Belarusian Sunday schools in Kaunas and Shiauliai. Vilnius Pedagogical University has a department of Belarusian language, literature, and ethnology.

In Belarus, there are two Lithuanian schools, which were constructed with Lithuanian funds. The Belarusian government maintains one of them, while the maintenance and service costs of the other are fully financed from the Lithuanian budget.

The Belarusian president, in a September 1997 interview with the Lithuanian daily *Respublika,* responding to the question of when the opposition press in Belarus will be able to publish in their homeland, answered: "We are living in Europe and everyone has the right to publish their newspapers where they want to." He added that if they found it cheaper to publish them in Lithuania, they could publish them there.[21] Of course, he "forgot" to mention the different price scales at home for the press supporting the government and for that opposing it. In recent times, it seems that there are no problems sending publications printed in Lithuania to Belarus.

At the beginning of 1999 another kind of problem arose that may introduce friction in Lithuanian-Belarusian relations. Former Lithuanian Minister of Communications and Information Sciences, Seimas deputy Rimantas Pleikys, announced his intention to form a radio station "Baltic Waves," which would transmit programs to Belarus. One of the aims of this station would be to provide objective information about events to the inhabitants of Belarus. Belarusian Ambassador to Lithuania Uladzimir Harkun [Vladimir Garkun], in commenting about the transmission of such programs, declared them to be interference in the internal affairs of the sovereign Belarusian state, saying, "If the radio station headed by Seimas deputy R. Pleikys begins broadcasting, I think that it would have some influence on the relations of our states and the treaties that are being prepared."[22] The idea of creating the radio station is supported by some influential Seimas deputies and one of the journalists' organizations backing the ruling Conservative Party—the Lithuanian Journalists' Association—but members of the Seimas Foreign Affairs Committee, after its meeting in February 1999, declared that the Lithuanian state does not support "Baltic Waves" radio, that the Seimas has nothing to do with it, and that creating it was a private undertaking.[23] The Lithuanian Government has not officially expressed its opinion on the matter. In the interest of promoting better relations, it has suggested

21   *Respublika* (Lithuanian daily) 6 September 1997: 6.

22   *Respublika* 23 January 1999: 9

23   *Atgimimas* (Lithuanian weekly) 5 February 1999: 11.

that the Belarusian state institutions make an agreement on a parity
basis to transmit radio and television programs in Lithuanian
(prepared in Belarus) over Belarusian radio and television. Analogous
programs could be also transmitted in Belarusian over Lithuanian state
radio and television. The Lithuanian state institutions have also asked
for facilities for Lithuanian Sunday schools, with their teachers
receiving pay for their work, as has been done for a long time in the
corresponding Belarusian schools in Lithuania. Since 1994, there have
also been discussions with Belarusian representatives on the request
by Lithuanian Catholics in Minsk to be allowed to have masses in
Lithuanian in one of the churches in the city.

It is well known that trust in political parties in post-communist
states is not very high but it is strangely paradoxical that trust in
political parties by both the Lithuanian and Belarusian people, in spite
of their state structures having different principles of formation and
representation, is similar (7 and 5 percent, respectively, demonstrate
trust in political parties as independent political actors).[24] The political
organizations in the Lithuanian Seimas are parties that existed in the
prewar period or were established after the restoration of
independence (except for the Democratic Labor Party, which was
formed on the basis of a reformed Communist Party) and function as
social-political institutions strengthening democracy. In Belarus, the
political parties and organizations in the Supreme Soviet
(Communists, Agrarian, Liberal Democratic, Movement for Social
Progress and Justice, and others) are not a real opposition to the
totalitarian regime of Lukashenka and do not assist in the creation of a
democratic society. From time to time, some of them, especially the
Belarusian Communist Party, stage a protest or organize picketing in
front of the Lithuanian Embassy in Minsk. Such protests target, for
example, the court proceedings in Lithuania against former Lithuanian
Communist Party activists Mykolas Burokevichius and Juozas
Jarmalavichius, who are accused of trying to overthrow by force the
legitimate state authorities and of active participation in the events of
13 January 1991.[25] It is thus easy to understand why Lithuanian

---

[24]   *Lietuvos rytas* (Lithuanian daily) 27 February 1999: 3. Also, Oleg Manaev,
"Nezavisimye issledovaniia i obshchestvenoe razvitie: Beloruskii variant,"
Analiticheskii biulleten' 3 (October–December 1998): 7.

[25]   During the October 1998 protest in front of the Lithuanian embassy in Minsk,

parties and political organizations do not maintain ties with the Belarusian political parties that are in power. It is more difficult to understand why Lithuanian parties and political organizations do not maintain more active ties with the social-political organizations (Belarus Popular Front, United Citizens Party, Social-Democratic "Hramada" [Gromada] of Belarus, and others) in the Belarusian opposition. The splintering of the Belarusian opposition forces, the very low popularity of their leaders in the eyes of the public,[26] and the neutral position of most Lithuanian political party leaders to the political processes in Belarus may, perhaps, explain this.

Examples of the efforts to enliven these relations include the visit to Lithuania by a group of former Belarusian Supreme Soviet deputies, headed by Stanislaŭ Bahdankevich [Bogdankevich], who met with the leaders of the Seimas in early 1998, and the participation of two Lithuanian Seimas deputies, members of the Conservative Party, at the Belarusian Democratic Forces Congress in Minsk in January 1999. In both cases, the Belarusian Ambassador in Lithuania, in meetings with high officials of the Lithuanian Foreign Affairs Ministry, expressed his country's displeasure with such political contacts, declaring that they do not help develop friendly relations between the states.[27] In Lithuania, in turn, governmental and nongovernmental institutions are concerned with the restriction of democracy in Belarus and support the declarations of the EU, the OSCE, and the European Council that the 24 November 1996 referendum results are not legitimate. Thus, Lithuanian political parties and organizations ought to maintain contacts and cooperate more actively with related political organizations and thereby assist the development of democracy in Belarus. The current low popularity among the Belarusian population

---

which was organized by the movement "For Social Progress and Justice" and the Belarusian Communist Party, an appeal was presented to Lithuanian President Valdas Adamkus to release immediately the allegedly political prisoners who were being tried in Vilnius. On 13 January 1991, Soviet Armed Forces stationed in Lithuania seized the Radio and Television Building and television tower in Vilnius. During encounters with unarmed defenders of the television tower, 13 people were killed. The leaders of the Lithuanian Communist Party (CPSU), including M. Burokevichius and J. Jarmalavichius, were active organizers and participants in these activities.

[26]   *Navini* 30 December 1998: 4.

[27]   *Atgimimas* 5 February 1999: 11; *Belorusskaia delovaia gazeta* 5 March 1998: 2.

of not only the political organizations in opposition, but also those represented in the parliament and their leaders, allows Lukashenka to maintain his high rating in public opinion polls.

Lithuanian-Belarusian Bilateral Relations and their Influence on the Security of the Baltic Region

In discussing official interstate relations between Lithuania and Belarus, which began less than 10 years ago, one should note that they were never strained or full of conflict. This is probably in part due to the moderate policies toward Belarus of former President Algirdas Brazauskas of Lithuania (1993–1998). It appears that Valdas Adamkus, the current president, maintains a similar policy. One of the most important events in Lithuanian-Belarusian relations was Lukashenka's 1995 visit to Lithuania, during which a good neighbor and cooperation treaty and a treaty marking the state borders were signed. In 1993–1997, Lithuania and Belarus also signed agreements on international cargo transport by trucks, pension guarantees, simplified border crossing for residents of the border area, and others. One of the most urgent questions for Lithuania is the signing of a readmission treaty with Belarus. After long negotiations, including a further review of the draft treaty in 1998 (after which, at the request of Belarus, the treaty was corrected so that it would go into effect only after ratification by the parliaments), Belarus continues to refuse to sign the treaty. Belarus explains its inability to sign the agreement by noting its obligations to the CIS, which plans to prepare a single readmission policy for all the states belonging to the confederation. Belarus' failure to sign the readmission treaty is but one example of how Moscow influences Belarusian foreign policy.[28]

The Lithuanian National Security Statute mentions the following risk factors that might influence the country's security: obstacles for Lithuania to obtain international security guarantees, the stationing of armed forces of other states along the Lithuanian border, the military transit of foreign countries through Lithuania, and illegal migration, among others.[29] Thus, the movement of refugees who seek asylum in

---

[28]   *Belorusskaia gazeta* 21 September 1998: 6.

[29]   A. Gricius, "Vliianie 'Beloruskogo faktora' na vneshniuiu politiku Litvy i

the West through Belarus to Lithuania, the slow pace of completing the demarcation of the state border with Belarus, environmental protection questions in border areas, and especially the size of the Belarusian armed forces and their location are directly connected to state security. The recent, more active efforts by Belarus to speed up the process of integration, including military integration, with Russia raises the potential danger to the security and stability of Lithuania and the Baltic region considerably. Polish political scientist Antoni Kamiński correctly observes that, for the neighboring states, the very existence of a union between Belarus and Russia is not as important as the circumstances under which it develops.[30] Adamkus, expressing his position on Belarusian integration with Russia, said that foreign policy orientation and choice of allies and alliances was a matter for each state to decide, but he added that such a choice must be based on consensus within society,[31] meaning that Lithuania, just like other countries, including Belarus, has the right to freely choose defense alliances. The frequent and unexpected changes in the Russian government, the poor health of then President Yeltsin, the strain in relations between Russia and Ukraine, and the prolonged financial-economic crisis hardly have helped to serve the successful creation of a union of states. In addition, it is not the democratic, but rather the conservative forces in Russia that most actively support the rapid, total integration of Russia and Belarus. Their leaders, such as Gennady Zyuganov, Vladimir Zhirinovsky, and Albert Makashov, have more than once declared that Russia should seek the reestablishment of the CIS within the territorial borders of the former Soviet Union.

In its "Declaration on State Sovereignty" (in 1990), Belarus declared that it would seek the status of a neutral state, not joining any blocs, but this declaration was only of a declaratory nature, and Belarus has never based its security policies on it.[32] In 1997,

---

stabil'nost' v Baltiiskom regione," in *Belorussiia na pereput'e: v poiskakh mezhdunarodnoi identichnosti,* ed. Sherman Garnett and Robert Legvold (Moscow, 1998), p. 157.

[30] Garnett and Legvold, eds., *Belorussiia na pereput'e,* p. 133.

[31] This position was expressed during an interview of the president of Lithuania by the author on 15 March 1999.

[32] Hrihoriy Perepelytsia, military policy specialist at the Ukrainian National

Lukashenka once again avowed that Belarus needed a military alliance with Russia.[33] Although Belarus formally participates in the "Partnership for Peace Program," the state leadership, and especially Lukashenka, opposes NATO expansion eastward. Speaking at the plenary session of the 52nd United Nations General Assembly on 26 September 1997, Belarusian Foreign Affairs Minister Ivan Antanovich declared that if NATO ever advanced to the Belarusian borders (a reference to Poland), Minsk would have "to analyze in a serious manner ways to ensure the security of the state." In the same speech, Antanovich also stated that in recent times "internal changes" were occurring in NATO that indicate that the organization could become a council of Euro-Atlantic partnership. In unofficial conversations, Belarusian state representatives admit the inevitability of NATO expansion eastward, but never fail to stress that Belarus still considers such expansion to the east a "historical mistake."[34]

In bilateral meetings with Lithuanian representatives, Belarusian state officials have recognized Lithuania's right to join international defense unions and security structures. This assertion is in the joint statement that the Lithuanian and Belarusian presidents made after their meeting at the end of 1998 at the Lithuanian-Belarusian border post of Medininkai. As the Russian newspaper *Izvestiia* notes, during the meeting the position of the Belarusian president on the question of Lithuania joining NATO was considerably more moderate than that of his Russian colleague.[35] Although Belarus often expresses active support for the creation of a nuclear free zone in Central and Eastern Europe, Lithuania cannot ignore the considerably larger Belarusian armed forces (about 100,000 soldiers), their restored close cooperation with Russia's armed forces, and their expressed hints that nuclear

---

Strategic Studies Institute, analyzes in detail the military-political integration of Belarus and Russia and changes in Belarusian security policies and Belarus' position in regard to the expansion of NATO: see *Belarusiia na pereput'e*, p. 87. He asserts that the 1990 Belarusian statement on its status as a neutral state, not joining any blocs, was only a transitional tactical maneuver.

[33]   ITAR-TASS, 22 May 1997.

[34]   The present author obtained this information during unofficial discussions with representatives of the state institutions.

[35]   *Izvestiia* 14 November 1998: 3.

weapons would come in handy.[36] The military land and sea forces stationed in the Kaliningrad district, which, according to the Lithuanian-Russian agreement, have the right of military transit through Lithuanian territory, also create a danger to the security not only of Lithuania but of the whole Baltic region.[37] Thus, the April 1999 NATO summit meeting in Washington and the decisions on the further expansion of the alliance taken there will be very important for Lithuania and for the other Baltic States.

Lithuania is interested in the development of democracy, stability, and economic growth in Belarus. This has a direct effect on the security of Lithuania and the general stability of the region. The Lithuanian and Belarusian presidents, during their meeting at Medininkai, reaffirmed the goal of their states to develop relations on the basis of the Good Neighbor and Cooperation Treaty signed in 1995. The heads of state recognized the importance of the local governments and the determination to respect the values of mankind, human rights, and fundamental freedoms.[38] It was decided to cooperate in the preparation and implementation of programs for training state officials. The presidents also expressed support for personal contacts between citizens and the development of cooperation between nongovernmental organizations and the mass media. Also discussed during the meeting were trade, economic, and regional cooperation; the passage through border posts; illegal migration; and other issues. Lithuania clearly is trying to maintain an active dialogue with Belarus. It believes that the international isolation of Belarus would have negative effects on its political and economic development and on its relations with neighboring countries. Lithuanian Presidential Advisor on National Security and Foreign Policy Questions Albinas Janushka said that Lithuania held a slightly

---

[36] *Respublika* 27 February 1999: 10.

[37] The Polish weekly newspaper *Czas* (BNS, 26 October 1997) wrote about the dangers for Lithuania and Poland from the Kaliningrad district.

[38] The leaders of Lithuanian state institutions, including former and current presidents Brazauskas and Adamkus, have more than once declared that Belarusian internal problems must be resolved in accordance with universally recognized principles of democracy and a legal state, strictly observing human rights and freedoms.

different position than EU countries on its relations with Belarus.[39] He noted, "In all conceivable circumstances we will always remain neighbors with Belarus and that means that we have to maintain friendly relations and cooperate. It is pleasant that, despite certain contradictions, both sides understand this."

U.S. Ambassador to Lithuania Keith Smith views very favorably Lithuania's efforts to maintain a dialogue with Belarus and especially the last meeting at Medininkai. He declared, "Washington welcomed the 12 November summit of the presidents of Lithuania and Belarus, hoping it will help promote democracy in the region."[40] The ambassador also noted that the U.S. strongly supports the formation of closer ties between Lithuania and Belarus and the efforts of state institutions aimed at strengthening the values of democracy and human rights. This statement by the ambassador is noteworthy in that it shows that the U.S. government hopes that Adamkus, as an ardent supporter of democracy, can positively influence the development of political events in a neighboring country. The future will show how realistic these hopes of U.S. and Lithuanian politicians are.

In pursuing bilateral Lithuanian-Belarusian cooperation, Lithuania also supports the activities of the OSCE mission in Belarus and by concrete methods and events supports the fulfillment of the recommendations of this organization. In November and December 1998, Lithuanian experts participated in seminars organized by the OSCE Advisory Monitoring Group for training Belarusian election observers and invited Belarusian representatives to observe elections in one of Lithuania's voting districts (November 1998). The election observers from Belarus were acquainted with how elections in Lithuania are carried out. It is regrettable that Belarus' neighbors, Poland and Ukraine, do not maintain active contacts with Belarus. The same can also be said of Latvia, which views the political and economic developments of its neighboring state in a quite passive manner.

Lithuania views positively the restoration of EU-Belarusian negotiations that provide the opportunity to conclude the process of ratifying the partnership and cooperation treaty between the EU and

---

[39] *Belorusskaia gazeta* 21 September 1998: 6.

[40] *Minsk News* 24–30 November 1998: 1

Belarus. These relations were made even more complicated by the conflict that arose after the eviction of the ambassadors from their residencies in the Drazdy area of Minsk as a result of which most of them were recalled to their countries for consultations. Lithuania behaved in a different manner than the other countries of Western and Central Europe and its ambassador returned home for unlimited vacation. With the resolution of the conflict at the beginning of 1999, the Baltic States hope that renewed contacts between Belarus and the EU and Western states will not only help the process of successful EU expansion, but will also strengthen the stability of the Baltic region. This stability and Lithuanian security would increase even more if the Baltic States were accepted into the EU in the next five years. This would speed up the development of their economies and provide the so-called "soft security" that would provide the opportunity to influence the development of democracy in Belarus more actively.

Conclusion

There can never be too much democracy. All the states that have chosen the path of developing democracy constantly confront questions on how to preserve and develop it. This question, without doubt, is especially urgent for post-communist countries. In the analysis of relations between states, primary attention is not always directed at the perfection of the political system or violations of human rights, but discussions about Belarus and its relations with other states usually mention its president, Lukashenka, his authoritarian rule, and the weakness of democracy in the country. This is probably because, for many Western democratic states, Belarus' neighbors, such as Poland, Lithuania, Latvia—and even Ukraine—are states that, in spite of their socialist heritage, differ, to a greater or smaller degree, from Belarus with respect to their political systems, the beliefs of their inhabitants, and their chosen path for development. At the same time, all of them are in transition. Belarus is in last place in this process in many respects. One cannot assert that a consolidated democracy has already been established in Lithuania and other post-communist states, but basic democratic principles are maintained, market economies are being implemented more rapidly, and efforts are being made to eliminate the one-party methods of rule used in the past.

In talking about Lithuanian-Belarusian relations, one should first pay attention to the factors that influence them. If Russia is still capable of influencing the course of Lithuania's economy and foreign trade, then this influence is much greater on Belarus not only in economic policy, but also in foreign and security policies and in internal political affairs. Lithuania is expanding its bilateral relations with many democratic states and international organizations, while Belarus' recent bilateral relations have been limited to trips to several not-very-democratic foreign countries and the CIS states. This international isolation of Belarus may have a negative effect on Lithuanian-Belarusian relations. Lithuania's relations with Belarus are also influenced not only by a different attitude toward democratic values, but also by different foreign policy priorities and opposing vectors of geopolitical orientation.

Summarizing Lithuania's relations with Belarus, relations between Belarus and Lithuania are more advanced than Belarus' relations with Poland and Latvia. In spite of certain restrictions that arise because Belarus is a member of the CIS and has difficulty paying Lithuania for providing electric power, the volume of trade and established economic ties allow one to expect growth, even if limited, in the future. Even though most problems that arise between Belarus and Lithuania concern cooperation on questions of developing democracy, these disagreements are not severe and will not damage bilateral relations. The absence of interparliamentary relations is explained by the fact that the EU and the European Council at this time do not recognize the legitimacy of the Belarusian Supreme Soviet. It is unfortunate that the states have not developed interparty relations that could more actively promote the formation of a democratic multiparty system in Belarus.

The current political regime in Belarus and its foreign and security policy create many problems—first of all, for the security of the Baltic States and the stability of the Baltic region. This question could become quite acute if the political situation in Russia becomes worse or if social disturbances develop in Belarus. Lithuanian state institutions believe that this problem can be solved not by isolating Belarus from democratic Europe, but by expanding contacts and dialogue with government institutions and various levels of society, especially with youth and nongovernmental organizations. As one can see from this chapter, this task is being carried out quite successfully. In conclusion. One can only wish that other states would also participate in this difficult dialogue, the results of which might not be felt very soon.

14

Agnieszka Magdziak-Miszewska
Belarus: Poland's Strange Neighbor

By way of introduction, I would like to emphasize that I am not a political scientist, but a commentator who has been involved for several years now in the practical and theoretical study of the areas situated to the east of Poland—strictly speaking, the European part of the Commonwealth of Independent States (CIS). Although the temperament of a commentator does not diverge significantly from that of an academic, the tools used in research as well as the nature of the commentary are slightly different. This paper will attempt to connect both methods in order to allow for an analysis of Polish policy towards Belarus and to evaluate the prospects for its development.

One cannot write about Polish-Belarusian relations without taking into account four important variables: history; Belarus' current internal situation; the existence of a significant Polish minority in Belarus and a Belarusian minority in Poland; and, last but not least, the Russian factor.

The Historical Legacy

It is impossible to define Belarus as either a "totally West European" or "totally East European" country. Indeed, in both a geographical and more geopolitical sense, Belarus connects the Baltic and Black Sea areas. This role of "connector" found its fullest expression in the form of the Grand Duchy of Lithuania, "within which Belarus, for over four hundred years, together with the Polish crown jointly formed the

Polish-Lithuanian Commonwealth (*Rzeczpospolita Obojga Narodów*, literally 'Republic of Two Nations')."[1]

The ideas surrounding the rebirth of the Grand Duchy proved particularly lively around the period of the anti-Russian uprisings of 1831 and 1863, leading to the emergence of the Confederation of the Grand Duchy of Lithuania in 1915, which was replaced shortly thereafter by the Bolshevik Lithuanian-Belarusian Socialist Republic. Yet the idea of a Baltic-Black Sea Alliance lives on today in the manifestos of many opposition parties in Belarus.[2] For a long time, in fact, the leader of the Belarusian Popular Front saw a Baltic-Black Sea Alliance as an alternative to an eastward NATO expansion.[3]

In contrast to the Lithuanians, who view the Polish-Lithuanian Commonwealth as a significant obstacle, which for more than a hundred years prevented the creation of an independent Lithuanian state, historically conscious Belarusians regard this period with a degree of nostalgia. The state that united Poles, Lithuanians, Belarusians, and Ukrainians reflects, in their opinion, a period when Belarus fully participated in the political and cultural life of Europe, the effect of which—if it had not ended in the Commonwealth's demise—would have been the formation of a modern state that could have become an integral part of Central Europe. This, of course, is a non-productive, ahistorical analysis; it does, however, lay a positive foundation for Polish-Belarusian dialogue, despite the fact that there are very few political groups in Poland who see any sense in the recreation of such a multinational entity in any form other than at the level of multi-lateral cultural, regional, and economic cooperation.

Yet the impact of history on Belarusian-Polish relations is not only positive. There is another historical legacy that has a rather negative influence on the bilateral relations between the two countries,

[1]   Sergei Dubovets [Siarhei Dubavets], 'Tsentral'naia Evropa: pochemu nas tam net?" *Beloruskie klimaty* 4 (1997).

[2]   The idea of the rebirth of the Polish-Lithuanian Commonwealth also finds a following within Lithuanian and Ukrainian political movements; in Poland, the concept was propagated by the Confederation for Polish Independence led by Leszek Moczulski.

[3]   See Materials from the Euro-Atlantic Association Conference: "*Białoruś – Polska – Ukraina. Bezpieczny region w bezpiecznej Europie*" (Warsaw, 1997).

namely the legacy of the twentieth century's interwar period. In 1918, after two hundred years of partition, Poland regained its independence. However, as a result of the Riga Peace Treaty (1921), which brought the Polish-Bolshevik war to an end, Belarus was divided between Poland and Soviet Russia (into so-called "Eastern" and "Western" Belarus). The nationality policies of the new Polish state were aimed at the polonization of the eastern territories (*Kresy*) by means of settling ethnic Poles (usually families connected with the military) and forced assimilation of minorities. This led to bitter conflicts, at times taking the form of armed exchanges initiated by the Belarusian Popular Association (*Belaruskaia narodnaia hramada*) and the Moscow-controlled Communist Party of Western Belarus. Belarus' territorial reunification came as a result of the Ribbentrop-Molotov Pact of August 1939.

On 17 September 1939, Soviet forces invaded Poland. This is remembered as a day of national tragedy for the Poles, while in Belarus it is a public holiday celebrating the day when the nation was united and regained its independence. The Poles saw the entry of German forces into the eastern territories as a second occupation. After the initial Soviet attack, it was the appropriate time in their minds to form their own underground armed resistance movement. For many patriotic Belarusians, however, this represented a period of liberation from both Polish and Soviet occupation, and, for this reason, many welcomed the Germans as liberators. For Poles, this was a betrayal and collaborationism. For the Belarusians, the Polish Home Army was an anti-Belarusian movement opposed to the principles of Belarusian independence. This dramatic period in both nations' histories, supported by aggressive Soviet-inspired anti-Polish propaganda, left an indelible imprint on the collective consciousness of the majority of Belarusian society and created the stereotype of a "Gentry Poland" (*Pańska Polska*) that threatened Belarusian national aspirations. Indeed, this negative imprint proved to be more powerful than the superficial propaganda of Socialist Internationalism during the period 1945–1989.

This negative stereotype resurfaced once again between 1989 and 1991 with such force as to form the basis for the stance of the democratic opposition in Belarus: the first visit of the Polish Minister for Foreign Affairs, Krzysztof Skubiszewski, to Minsk, was met with opposition by the leader of the Popular Front, Zianon Pazniak [Zenon Pozniak]. Consequently, a declaration on Polish-Belarusian cooperation was not signed. And still today, Aliaksandr Lukashenka, the Belarusian president, when talking of external enemies, often refers to negative stereotypes of Poland and Poles.[4]

Belarus' Internal Situation[5]

For some years after Belarus' de facto independence in 1991, the country was hardly noticed against the background of the crisis-ridden other former republics. Indeed, "there were no internal armed conflicts, or inter-ethnic and inter-confessional disputes. All remained virtually dormant during the collapse of the Soviet Union. Relations with neighboring states, as well as with Russia evolved evenly and without difficulty. Nobody in Minsk even considered playing the "nuclear card."[6] It is, therefore, sometimes difficult to comprehend what happened afterwards, why Belarus was left behind in the general trends towards democratization and real independence from Russia that were taking shape in the region.

Yet if one looks more deeply, some of the roots of this situation can be discerned. While the Baltic States and Ukraine "seized their independence when that opportunity first presented itself, Belarus was in no rush to achieve its sovereignty."[7] Indeed, the way independence "fell" upon Belarus was very different from the way independence was achieved and struggled for in the Baltics, and may be more reminiscent of the way events developed in Central Asia. More than the elites responding to their nation's striving for a sovereign state, politicians in Belarus were moved first and foremost by the desire to

[4] On the mutual stereotypes held by Poles and Belarusians, see Uladzimir Padhol: "W oczach sowka," and Ryszard Radzik: "Ruski i Pan—asymetria stereotypu," both in *Więź* September 1997.

[5] In this part, questions concerning national identity and the self-identification of Belarusians have been omitted, as well as those related to events that led to the current political and economic situation in Belarus. Attention is given only to those aspects that are seen as the main subject of this paper.

[6] Introduction to Sherman W. Garnett and Robert Legvold, eds., *Belorussiia na pereput'e. V poiskakh mezhdunarodnoi identichnosti* (Moscow, 1998).

[7] Garnett and Legvold, introduction to *Belorussiia na pereput'e,* pp. 14–15.

"preserve their own authority and to save the conservative life-style, based on Soviet principles, against encroaching liberal ideals, first manifested through Gorbachev's perestroika, and later, more threateningly, through Yeltsin's Russia."[8] This conservatism also limited the real policy options open to Belarus in the first years of independence.

In the years 1991–1994, the activities of the Belarusian government nomenklatura and the Communist-dominated Supreme Soviet made it impossible to carry out any serious economic reform and put an effective halt to the development of private enterprise or civil society institutions (e.g., a free media, especially in the realm of electronic media). As forcefully shown by Polish authors Sarhiej Owsiannik and Jelena Striełkowa,[9] the Belarusian opposition, though having some authority in the state, was nevertheless very weak and proved itself unable to exert any impact on key decisions or upon an increasingly frustrated society becoming alienated from the country's political elite. The logical consequence of this alienation is that the political options come down to choosing "one of us," namely an "ordinary person" who is seen to be freeing an increasingly impoverished population from the corruption of bureaucrats and the loud and opaque messages of political rabble-rousers. Lukashenka turned out to be just that "ordinary person." I am in agreement with those analysts and commentators who maintain that Lukashenka's authoritarian government is, paradoxically, accelerating the processes of nation-building in Belarus, which, in its short period of independence (especially giving a national characteristic to the education system and allowing free travel abroad)—now manifests itself by way of a growing, albeit passive, opposition to Lukashenka's politics. Yet this does not make things easier for Poland. Whatever the long-term effects of Lukashenka's policies, Poland has as its neighbor a state that will, in the nearest future, remain authoritarian, with a command economy and with investment and trade policies, which, controlled single-handedly by Lukashenka, remain difficult to predict. Belarus maintains a position of virtual isolation with regard to the

---

[8]   Ibid.

[9]   Sarhiej Owsiannik and Jelena Striełkowa, *Wladza i społeczeństwo: Białoruś 1991–1998* (Warsaw, 1998).

outside world (except for Russia, with whom the notion of integration, especially military, is advocated) and is hostile towards European and Euro-Atlantic institutions. The economic and social chasm between Poland and Belarus (which, during the 1980s, had a comparable standard of living) deepens each year. Belarus' economic conditions may prove to be the most significant barrier in their inter-state relations, even after a change in the political situation within Belarus. This is particularly true if one takes into account the fact that, within the growing number of opponents to Lukashenka, proponents of radical governmental and economic reform still represent a minority.

In December 1997, Lukashenka could count on 45.5 percent of the votes in the entire country, and, in May of that year, 62.9 percent of the population claimed to support integration with Russia.[10] Simultaneously, 64 percent of Belarusians said they were in favor of independence. Further investigation into this question, carried out by the Independent Institute for Socioeconomic and Political Studies (IISEPS) in Minsk, showed that Belarusians understood integration to mean an absence of borders and customs on the one hand, and the establishment a currency union with Russia on the other.[11] Furthermore, according to the same study, adherents of a market economy and closer cooperation with the West represent less than half of those who would not vote for Lukashenka and two-thirds of those who are staunch opponents of integration with Russia (about 20 percent of Belarusian society). That 20 percent (that is, the group of people who are interested in both independence *and* in market reforms) is the fundamental group upon which a future Belarusian democratic and market-oriented state may be based and a platform from which to develop Polish-Belarusian relations.[12]

[10] Opinion Poll conducted by the Novak Institution May–December 1997.

[11] *Bulletin'*, NISEPI, 1996 (1).

[12] On this topic, see also Chapter 1, by Timothy Colton, in this volume.

Minorities

The number of ethnic Poles who are citizens of Belarus is estimated at between 420,000 and 550,000.[13] Most ethnic Poles live in the peripheral areas surrounding Hrodna [Grodno] (where they make up 25 percent of the population), Brest, Minsk, Vitsebsk [Vitebsk], Homel [Gomel], and Mahilioŭ [Mogilev], as well as in Minsk itself. The Polish community in Belarus is significantly different from that in Russia and Lithuania. In contrast to the Polish minority in the Russian Federation, ethnic Poles in Belarus have maintained their feelings of national identity and, for the most part, retain a very good command of the Polish language. In 1990, the Union of Poles in Belarus, which has its own Polish language newspaper, *"Głos znad Niemna"* ("Voice from the Niemen [Neman]"), was established. Unlike their counterparts in Lithuania, ethnic Poles in Belarus actively supported (and continue to support) the idea of Belarusian independence, and, in 1992, the Union of Poles in Belarus and the Belarusian National Front prepared a joint list of candidates for various elections. After 1990, thirty schools with Polish language instruction as either compulsory or an extra subject were established. In September 1996, a Polish school with Polish as the main language of instruction opened in Hrodna. This project was supported with funds from the "Polish Commonwealth," a Polish state organization concerned with supporting cultural development and education worldwide. Until very recently, the Polish minority in Belarus was not the subject of any open attacks by the Lukashenka regime. Problems of this nature emerged during the last days of February 2000, following protests by Poles from the city of Lida, who demanded the fulfillment of promises to create a Polish-language school. In mid-March, Lukashenka accused the leadership of the Union of Poles in Belarus of acting in a way that was at odds with the state constitution and threatened to "reconsider the statutes of the Union in this respect." This might have been a first step in the outlawing of the Union, which, of course, would have an adverse effect on Polish-Belarusian relations. Half a million ethnic

---

[13]   See Elżbieta Smułkowska: "Wokół problemów narodowej identyfikacji mieszkańców Białorusi,'" *Przegląd Wschodni* 4(3)15 1997. Marek Ziółkowski: "Relations with Belarus," *Yearbook of Polish Foreign Policy* (Warsaw) 1997.

Poles in Belarus undoubtedly represent an important element in the inter-state relations between the two countries, and the fear at present is that they may, so to speak, become Lukashenka's hostages. This makes it necessary for the Polish government to exercise great caution in its relations with Minsk.

A separate problem pertains to Polish Catholic priests working in Belarus (70 percent of the priests in Belarus are Polish citizens). In spite of the fact that the vast majority of them know Belarusian or Russian and conduct religious services in these languages, there are numerous accusations by government officials of attempts at a policy of polonization by these priests. Moreover, official regulations governing residence permits for foreign clergymen are quite strict and can be used to withdraw such permits from priests whose activities are seen as inconvenient.[14]

Around 250,000 ethnic Belarusians live in Poland, above all in Białystok and surrounding areas. The largest Belarusian organization (and one that was also active in the Communist period) is the Belarusian Socio-Cultural Association (BTSK), which is linked ideologically to the Polish post-communists (the leader of the

---

[14]   For example, "on 3 July 1995, the Cabinet of Ministers of the Republic of Belarus issued an Executive Order establishing the procedure for inviting foreign clergymen to the Republic and regulating their performance of duties within its borders. This piece of legislation has imposed a number of substantial obligations on religious organizations that invite foreign priests. The leader of a religious body inviting a priest is duty-bound to have him registered with the appropriate local administration authorities. The registration will be valid for one year, with the priest remaining assigned to one specific religious congregation without the right to move on to another one. Priests who fail to abide by the provisions of the Executive Order may have their registration withdrawn, which would be tantamount to a cessation of their right to perform their pastoral duties. A refusal of registration or its withdrawal makes the chief of the church administration, such as a bishop, bound by duty to transfer the clergyman in question to another post. It is not quite clear what the state authorities would do if the bishop refused to comply with this provision. It is quite possible that the priest would then be expelled from the country. Regulating the number of foreign priests working in Belarus is the general intention of the said piece of legislation. The country's authorities have made known their intention to withdraw registration from Polish passport-holding Catholic priests and, in some cases, have started the actual withdrawal procedures. Expulsion signals received from Belarus have so far, however, been proved to be premature." Ziółkowski, "Relations with Belarus," p. 166.

Association, Leon Syczewski, is a parliamentarian affiliated with the Union of the Democratic Left [SLD, *Sojusz Lewicy Demokratycznej*]). As members, the Association counts those Polish Belarusians who openly sympathize with the Lukashenka regime. In July 1996, at a worldwide congress of Belarusians, I attended a speech delivered by Suczewski, the president of the Association's delegation, addressed to the Belarusian president. At the meeting, as well as on Belarusian state television, he repeatedly and publicly criticized Polish policy towards the current Belarusian authorities, claiming Lukashenka's support for his organization. Such pronouncements, of course, do nothing to assist relations between Poles and Belarusians in the Białystok region, where, as is understandable, a degree of antipathy towards the BTSK and its leaders can be felt. This, in turn, is transferred onto the whole Belarusian minority, even when they represent a totally different political outlook.

Those Belarusian minority organizations in Poland that are proponents of a sovereign, democratic Belarusian state are usually those that came into being after the demise of communism. They are mainly Belarusian and students' unions. Taking into account their activities as well as those of the Center for Citizenship Education (*Centrum Edukacji Obywatelskiej*), a foundation bringing together Poles and Belarusians, it can be said that they support the Belarusian opposition. Based on this, Białystok has often been referred to as the "Belarusian Piedmont." The activities of these organizations have frequently been the cause of more or less official disapproval by the Belarusian authorities.

The Perpetual Partner—Russia

The Polish-Russian relationship has been radically altered by the emergence of Belarus and Ukraine as independent states.[15] "One of the components of this situation is a zero-sum game in Polish-Russian relations, with the aim of weakening the other side's influence on Belarus and Ukraine. There also is the strategic orientation of Poland

---

[15] On this topic, see also Marek Calka, "The Warsaw-Kyiv-Moscow Security Triangle," in Margarita M. Balmaceda, ed., *On the Edge: The Ukrainian-Central European-Russian Security Triangle* (Budapest, 2000).

(earlier, Russia, too) towards the West, stating a real reason for the avoidance of intense rivalry between Warsaw and Moscow over these states."[16]

The situation has not led to intense rivalry—and in no way can rivalry be considered an element of Polish foreign policy. Poland's Belarusian activities on this front, however, are treated in Moscow with the utmost suspicion. For example, former Polish Prime Minister Hanna Suchocka, during a visit to Minsk in 1992, said that she hoped that close relations, like those between Belarus and Moscow, soon would be the order of the day with Poland. In reaction to this statement, Maksim Iusin, writing in *Izvestiia,* attacked Poland, claiming that Warsaw was trying to dominate Belarus and inculcate it with the instruments of its own anti-Russian orientation. Suchocka was accused of being incompetent and of showing a lack of tact and political culture.[17] Similarly, Moscow's activities in the territories of Ukraine and Belarus are seen in Poland as a symbol of Russian imperialism or neo-imperialism.

The problem, I fear, has to do with a real and objective conflict of interests and of political aims between Poland and Russia vis-à-vis Belarus and Ukraine. Arkady Moshes writes that it has to do with the centuries-old feeling of injury, which still, with uncanny force, is supported by the negative stereotypes of the "*Liakh*" and the "*Moskal.*" The areas that make up contemporary Belarus and Ukraine have been the subjects of rivalry between the two states since the seventeenth century. Even a few decades after the victory of the Russian elite (and the third partition of Poland), the notion that all Poles dreamed of a retaking of the lands of the Great Lithuanian Kingdom at the moment Poland regained its independence, was hard to dispel. In the nineteenth century, questions surrounding the future of those lands made it impossible to reach a final understanding between Polish conspirators and Russian Decembrists, despite their having a common goal of overthrowing the tsar. As is justifiably

---

[16] Arkadij Moszez [Arkady Moshes], "Ukraina i Białorus jako współczynnik stosunków polsko-rosyjskich," in *Polska i Rosja. Strategizcne sprzeczności i możliwości dialogu,* ed. Angieszka Magdziak-Miszewska (Warsaw, 1997), p. 177.

[17] Artur Michałski, "Obraz Polski w rosyjskich mediach," in *Polska i Rosja, Strategizcne sprzeczności,* p. 60.

argued by Aleksei Miller, the territories of an "ideal" Polish homeland
(*"Ojczyzna"*) and of the Russian political elite found themselves in an
insoluble conflict:

> In Russia, during the nineteenth century, there was the conviction of
> there being a great Russian nation, embracing Great Russians
> (*Wielkorusinów*), Ukrainians (*Małorusinów*), and White Russians
> (*Białorusinów*). Against this backdrop, the result was the gaining of
> momentum of the mechanisms of suspicion and antipathy towards
> Poland. On both sides, the idea was formulated that the conflict was
> of a never-ending character and thus impossible to solve.[18]

These mutual perceptions and suspicions, on the part of the Poles
and Russians, fed by aggressive Bolshevik propaganda, have survived
to the present. The extent to which this manifests itself in Poland,
relating to exaggerated fears concerning the possibility of Belarus'
becoming absorbed by Russia, and containing in itself elements of
territorial claims (still to be encountered in the statements of former
Polish inhabitants of Vilnius, Hrodna, and Lviv), is comparable to
periodic comments in the Russian press regarding plans to recreate the
Republic of Two Nations, which supposedly clearly shows that
Poland wants "that which is ours" (*"nashe"*). It is only in the last few
years that proposals have emerged that nongovernmental groups
organize three-way seminars on the subject of Polish-Russian-
Ukrainian or Polish-Russian Belarusian relations in order to break the
spell of suspicion.[19]

Poland is equally concerned with the support that Lukashenka's
authoritarian regime receives from the Russian ruling class, as well as
with both states' declared desire for deep integration. Polish fears
relate not only to the desire for integration (which is frequently
emphasized by Polish politicians), but to its military and political
consequences, which are loaded with the notion of integration as
serving the function of opposing—rather than supporting—someone
or something.

---

[18]   Alieksei Miller, "Historia jako czynnik współczesnych stosunków polsko-
rosyjskich," in *Polska i Rosja. Strategizcne sprzeczności*, p. 46.

[19]   See Vyacheslav Nikonov, "Belorussiia vo vneshnei politike Rossii," in Garnett
and Legvold, *Belorussiia na pereput'e,* pp. 105–130.

One of the reasons that Yegor Gaidar was dismissed from his post as premier of Russia was his opposition to integration with Belarus, which, in his view, had no economic rationale and could result in slowing down the pace of reform within Russia. Most of today's Russian political elite have rejected this argument in the same way that they have been indifferent toward the fears voiced by representatives of the democratic parties concerned with the consequences of Lukashenka's encroachment on the Russian political scene. The views of this elite, which the Russian political scientist Aleksander Tsypko calls the "Moscow imperialist intelligentsia," find their best expression in reports and commentaries by public members of the Council for Foreign Policy and Defense Policy, especially Sergei Karaganov and Viacheslav Nikonov. They see Belarus as falling exclusively within the sphere of Russian influence, and, together with the Russian Communists, they promote the idea of integration.

Considerably fewer adherents can be claimed by Irina Kobrinskaja, in whose words

> In order to avoid processes of integration with Belarus being turned into an instrument of anti-Western politics (what threatens seriously is the danger of isolation), it is essential to find a European direction—both political and economic. Given its geopolitical positioning, Belarus can and should perform a specific role in the normalization and improving of relations with Russia, and potential partners in Central Eastern Europe, above all Poland, but also the Baltic States, especially Lithuania and Germany. The joint and coordinated efforts of Minsk and Moscow can, in this respect, prove to be much more effective than an independent and not always consistent policy of Russia, especially vis-à-vis Central Europe.[20]

Such a vision of the role and place of Belarus in the region is close to the hearts of many politicians in Warsaw. It is hard to imagine, however, that the Belarus of Aliaksandr Lukashenka would want to, or would be in a position, to realize it. It is, therefore, difficult to imagine that Belarus will be able to change its direction according to the vision of Kobrinskaja.

---

[20] Irina Kobrinskaja, "Nowe spojrzenie na stosunki rosyjsko-polski," in *Polska i Rosja, Strategizcne sprzeczności,* p. 99.

Opportunities and Barriers in Belarusian-Polish Relations

Some authors have focused attention on the tremendous contradiction stemming from the fact that Poland seems to have at its disposal many positive elements that should help in the development of a proactive and forward-looking policy towards Belarus—four hundred years of shared struggle against external domination by Tsarist Russia and a common predisposition for peace and distaste for conflict, which make the Belarusians closer to Poland than to an expansionist Russia. Considering these factors, it would be both logical and absolutely justifiable for Polish politicians to take into account the historical weaknesses of Belarusian national self-consciousness and the resulting weaknesses of the country's democracy, and for the Poles to undertake all efforts (in the political, economic, and cultural arenas) to help put Belarus on the European track of democratic development.

So what kept Poland from developing a more constructive policy towards Belarus, especially in the period 1991–1994 when conditions seemed most conducive to such a course? Developing policy along these lines would have been extremely beneficial, not only to Belarus, but to Poland as well: Poland could have had the chance to help create a neutral and democratic state to the east of its borders and, in this way, "at the same time prevent direct danger close to its Russian border, with its overtones of bloody conflict."[21]

How do we explain this paradox? Why would Polish politicians neglect this historic chance? Some Polish commentators such as Natalla Piatrowicz have attributed this shortsightedness to what they saw as Poland's excessive fixation on the West, which led to a neglect of its eastern neighbors. (A similar situation could be observed in terms of Polish policy towards Ukraine.)[22] Yet this neglect led to tragic consequences, as it allowed Belarus to "fall into the orbit of a pro-imperial Russia and its supporters, who have brought a collectivist-fascist style dictator to power. As a result, Poland now has an anti-democratic neighbor with a desperate economic situation and

---

[21]   Natalla Piatrowicz, "Drobne uwagi o polskiej polityce zagranicznej," *Wież* September 1997.

[22]   On this topic, see Calka, "The Warsaw-Kyiv-Moscow Security Triangle."

universal poverty."[23] It was not until 1996, after Lukashenka's reform of the constitution along authoritarian lines following a well-orchestrated referendum that Poles woke up with a delayed cry of "the Russians are coming."[24]

Are these commentators right? Has Poland missed a great once-in-a-lifetime opportunity of helping to bring about a democratic and independent Belarus? Did such a chance ever exist? Was there ever really a shadow of a chance of realizing this by a class of politicians fixated on the West and not noticing what was going on to the East? It is doubtful that this could have happened, although there is a grain of truth in the emotional objections of commentators such as Piatrowicz.

Created in 1990, the doctrine of a multileveled (*"wielopozio-mowe"*) Polish foreign policy vis-à-vis the USSR was geared toward maintaining equidistant political and economic contacts with the Soviet Kremlin and the capitals of states that were establishing their sovereignty at that time, in particular, the Baltic states, the Russian Federation, Ukraine, and Belarus. The most spectacular manifestation of this policy came during the tour by then Minister of Foreign Affairs, Krzysztof Skubiszewski to the Soviet Union (Russia, Belarus, and Ukraine) in 1990. In Moscow, Skubiszewski met Mikhail Gorbachev, president of the Soviet Union, and Boris Yeltsin, head of the Supreme Soviet of the Russian Federation. During the course of the latter meeting, a declaration of mutual cooperation and friendship was signed. A similar declaration was signed in Kyiv, where, after the official session, a secondary meeting with the Ukrainian opposition was held. The visit to Minsk, however, ended in disaster: the idea of such a joint Polish-Belarusian declaration was not welcomed by the Communist authorities in Belarus, and, with the unexpected assistance of Pazniak, the leader of the Belarusian Popular Front, opposition was lodged against the idea of any friendship or cooperation agreement. (An agreement was finally signed in April 1991 after protracted negotiations.) By looking at the reasons for this "disaster," we can get a sense of some of the factors that would have interfered with improved relations, even if Polish policy had been more far-sighted and constructive.

[23] Piatrowicz, "Drobne uwagi."

[24] Ibid.

The historical underpinnings of Pazniak's position were discussed at the beginning of this paper. Yet above and beyond any historical factors, another reason for the cool reception given to Polish initiatives can be identified, namely the political. The strategy of the Belarusian Popular Front (BPF) was to find the quickest possible means of recreating a sense of national self-consciousness among Belarusians—through their use of opposition to the state's historical neighbors. And here they had half a century of Soviet propaganda to pave the way. Although Soviet censorship had, without distinction, blunted all manifestations of anti-Russian feeling, it did not prevent criticism of Poland, and Belarusian democrats turned to popular anti-Polish stereotypes from the 1920s and 1930s: Belarus must defend itself in the face of a Polish threat aimed at plundering and destroying Belarusian independence. This stereotype continued in force up to the actual collapse of the Soviet Union. My own numerous visits to Belarus during this period and discussions with the leader of the BNF as well as the Belarusian Catholic Association (*Belarusskaia Katalitskaia Hramada*) confirmed the fears with regard to widespread Belarusian perceptions of a so-called "Polish imperialism." Similar experiences during the first years of contact with Belarus had a paralyzing effect upon those Polish politicians who wanted to become more deeply involved with that country.

The burden of history required Polish politicians responsible for shaping Poland's foreign policy towards its eastern neighbors— especially Belarus, Ukraine and Lithuania—to use an unusually careful approach in order to avoid at all costs the impression that Poland might be trying to return to a dominant position in the region. Another important factor is that Belarus' Communist nomenklatura of the first post-independence years did not have the full political authority to respond favorably to the Polish efforts.

After the collapse of the USSR, Belarusian democrats for the first time had the opportunity to develop contacts with the Western world, and Poland was a country through which the road to European capitals lay. Today, objections to Poland voiced by leaders of the Belarusian opposition in the first years after independence (Pazniak himself now sees Poland now as a defender of Belarusian interests in Europe) seem simply ahistorical and unreal.

This does not, however, change the fact that the multi-level and, later, multi-vector Polish eastern policy became, in practice, a russocentric policy. The declarative recognition of the strategic importance of Ukrainian independence for the realization of Poland's *raison d'état* remained, for a long time, a catchy slogan. From the Polish perspective, Vilnius was a more important partner than Minsk, and its importance led to the reluctant development of bilateral relations with Vilnius. Moscow, however, always remained center stage for the Polish political class. The old principle postulated by the Polish historian, political activist, and publicist Juliusz Mieroszewski, namely that relations between Poland and Russia were, above all, dependent on Poland's position in Kyiv, Minsk, and Vilnius, was only remembered relatively late in the game. This does not mean that Belarus was completely forgotten. Poland recognized Belarusian independence, which was announced on 24 August 1991, four months later.

The year 1992 was exceptionally fruitful for Belarusian-Polish relations. In March, during a visit to Warsaw by the Belarusian foreign minister, Piotr Kraŭchanka [Kravchenko], official diplomatic relations were established. The first Polish ambassador to Belarus was Professor Elżbieta Smulkowa, a scholar of Belarusian language and literature and an authority on Belarusian history and nationality issues. Smulkowa's nomination was a clear sign of Poland's intention to view Belarusian independence as here to stay and Belarus as a nation capable of developing relations and building its national self-identity. From the very beginning, all official documentation going through Warsaw to the seats of authority in Minsk was prepared in Belarusian.

The Belarusian ambassador in Warsaw at the time was deputy minister of foreign affairs, Uladzimir Sianko [Vladimir Senko]. The ambassador's high rank was supposed to demonstrate the relative importance that Belarus placed on the successful evolution of the bilateral relationship with Poland.

In June 1992, during a visit to Warsaw by the head of the Belarusian Supreme Council, Stanislaŭ Shushkevich, a treaty pledging good neighborliness, friendliness, and cooperation was signed. The agreement obliged both countries, among other things, to build their bilateral relations on the principles of partnership and good neighborliness, and to confirm that neither side would undertake acts that might disturb the existing borders. Both sides also promised to support and protect investments, to ease the flow of capital, goods, services and labor, to promote cooperation around borderland areas, and to establish a wide range of contacts between political parties and civil institutions.

The following principles were adopted concerning policies towards ethnic minorities: observance of international principles and standards; ensuring the freedom to use one's mother tongue; and support for ethnic education and the freedom to form social and cultural organizations. Prime Minister Suchocka paid an official visit to Minsk in November 1992. Several agreements were signed during this visit: agreements on the avoidance of double taxation and on technical cooperation, as well as a declaration on cultural and scientific cooperation. Furthermore, it was declared that a Polish-Belarusian commercial bank should be established.

Consultations at the deputy foreign minister level were held for the first time in December 1992. During these talks, Poland undertook to lend its support to Belarusian efforts to gain membership in European organizations (above all, the Council on Security and Cooperation in Europe, the Council of Europe, and associate membership in the European Community). A preliminary agreement was concluded with respect to the use of Polish ports by a Belarusian merchant fleet that Minsk intended to establish. During a visit to Warsaw several days later, Paval Kazloŭski [Pavel Kozlovskii], Belarus' minister of national defense, and Janusz Onyszkiewicz, Poland's minister of defense, signed a declaration on the establishment of permanent working contacts between their ministries and on cooperation in the area of personnel training. An agreement on military cooperation was signed in March 1993.

Poland also rapidly became Belarus' most important economic partner (apart from the CIS, of course), with trade between the two countries reaching around $306 million in 1992. During this time, various organizations were formed for the purpose of promoting the development of bilateral economic relations: the Belarus-Poland Society, the Poland-Belarus Association, and a Chamber of Trade and Industry, as well as numerous regional associations. The same year saw the registration of more than three hundred joint ventures and about forty Polish enterprises operating on Belarusian territory. These represented about 40 percent of all Belarusian joint ventures, and Polish capital accounted for more than 20 percent of foreign investment in Belarus. What was achieved in that year can be considered impressive. It was, however, an exceptional time for bilateral relations.

Problems soon arose in the economic arena. They were based in the lack of free market reforms in Belarus, the absence of clear-cut legislation governing economic activity, and the restriction of trade to barter transactions (as a result of a shortage of financial resources). The development of relations between Polish and Belarusian social organizations was hindered by problems related to the failure of the Minsk authorities to respect the rights of the Polish ethnic minority: Belarus began to level accusations that Polish priests were engaging in a policy of polonization and that children—Chernobyl victims—were being subjected to polonization during their recuperative/rehabilitation stays in Poland.

At the same time, once the most important elements of a legal and treaty framework were in place, the interest in maintaining regular contacts with Minsk on the part of the Polish Foreign Ministry declined. It became increasingly clear that the focus of the attention of the Polish political class had shifted to Moscow and Kyiv. President Lech Walesa's visit to Minsk also failed to provide any new impetus to the development of a dialogue between Minsk and Warsaw. Cooperation within the framework of the Bug and Neman [Niemen] River Euroregions, which was discussed at the time, was never fully realized in practice. Subsequent meetings between ministers and prime ministers of the two countries never exceeded the bounds of political convention. Belarus became increasingly relegated to the sidelines of Polish foreign policy. The authoritative Polish Foreign Policy Annual, for example, devoted less and less space to Belarus and it received almost no mention at all in the Polish mass media. A symbolic expression of this state of affairs was the appointment of Ewa Spychalska, former leader of the post-communist trade union movement and a marginal figure in Polish political life who lacked any experience in international affairs, as ambassador to Minsk.

The efforts made by Polish President Aleksander Kwaśniewski to improve this situation failed. His decision to be on first-name terms with Lukashenka met with considerable criticism in Poland.

The dissolution of the Supreme Soviet of the 13th Session in 1996, the constitutional referendum, and the proclamation of a new constitution by Lukashenka also encountered widespread condemnation in Poland. Poland, like the United States and members of the EU, did not recognize the new status quo: Warsaw regards the dissolved supreme soviet as the legal source of authority in Belarus and considers the 1994 Constitution to be still valid. The increasing authoritarianism displayed by the Lukashenka regime has revived Warsaw's interest in Belarus, which has once again begun to make headlines in Polish newspapers and magazines. One response to the events in Minsk has been the attempt to establish a common regional policy toward Belarus. In November 1996, the presidents of Poland, Lithuania, and Ukraine issued a joint declaration in which they voiced their deep concern about the course of events in Belarus and called on the Belarusian president to resolve the constitutional conflict in accordance with democratic norms and the principles of respect for human rights. This joint declaration remains the only manifestation of a common policy toward Minsk by the states of the region. Nevertheless, it ushered in a new era of bilateral relations that could be defined as a "cold peace," which has been punctuated by periods of intense, but short-lived, tension prompted by aggressive statements from Lukashenka directed at Warsaw and repeated press campaigns in which Poland is accused of pursuing a policy course that threatens Belarus' security and of engaging in espionage and subversion (together with the CIA) against the country.

On 6 March 1998, Mariusz Maszkiewicz (previously Poland's consul general in Hrodna) became the new Polish ambassador to Minsk, only to leave the country a few weeks later—along with his counterparts from Western states—following the conflict over the Drazdy diplomatic residences. At the same time, Poland lowered the status of its contacts with representatives of Belarus' state administration to the level of under-secretary of state. There has been, however, no suspension of inter-parliamentary contacts or exchanges of economic experts.

Since 1998, the key principles underlying Poland's foreign policy toward Belarus has been seeking to avoid freezing bilateral contacts at the working level, preventing Belarus' complete isolation in the international arena, as well as promoting all nongovernmental organizations that maintain contacts with the Belarus opposition, conduct educational activities, and support Belarusian social organizations. On the one hand, this policy is dictated by the need to retain instruments for protecting the Polish minority and on the other hand, by the belief that the complete isolation of Belarus will not have any impact on Lukashenka's policies or on his position within the state and might, in fact, prevent the development of democratic organizations and opposition parties, which are already weak.

Since 1997, the Belarusian opposition has viewed Poland as its most important ally in the struggle with the Lukashenka regime and as an advocate of its interests before the West. Yet the absence of unambiguous gestures of support on the part of the Polish government sometimes prompts accusations of opportunism and appeasement toward Lukashenka. The degree of restraint displayed by official Warsaw, however, is motivated above all by the need to protect the ethnic Poles living in Belarus and to maintain good relations with Moscow. (The latter was particularly important when Poland was seeking NATO membership and when one of the goals of Russian diplomacy was to depict Warsaw as suffering from "incurable Russophobia" that, in the light of Warsaw's inability to conduct a rational policy toward Russia, posed a threat to relations between Russia and NATO.)

A clearer position has been adopted by the Polish Sejm, which has been giving its unambiguous support to the Belarusian democratic opposition. Polish deputies have hosted numerous visits by representatives of the Supreme Soviet of the 13th Session, and are involved in the activities of Polish nongovernmental organizations engaged in all kinds of training activities for political leaders, independent journalists, social activists, economists, and entre-preneurs, as well as seminars on international affairs.

In a message to the Belarusian nation issued by the Sejm of the Republic of Poland on 15 January 1999, Polish parliamentarians wrote:

> We express our profound support and respect for all democratic forces in Belarus—patriots who are concerned about the future of their nation, the observance of human rights, and the establishment of a just and effective economic system. The Sejm of the Republic of Poland lends its moral support to the deputies of the Supreme Soviet of the 13th Session, who are being denied the possibility of

exercising their mandate . . . We express our solidarity with all those
who are being subjected to repression in Belarus because of their
beliefs and their activities in support of freedom . . . Poland has an
interest in the restoration of democratic institutions, [and] the
strengthening of the national identity and sovereignty of the
Belarusian state. The existence of a democratic, sovereign, and
stable Belarus is in the interest of Europe.

As could be expected, this message gave rise to another round of
accusations from Minsk, where it was seen as further proof of
Poland's hostile disposition toward Belarus and indicating that, on
joining NATO, Poland might become a genuine threat to the peace-
loving Belarusians.

Another field of Polish activity is the involvement of many Polish
NGOs working in Belarus or with Belarusians. Their main goal is to
support the very weak (but still existing, and in some places actually
growing) civil society organizations and NGOs, providing them with
such equipment as fax machines, computers, and printers; subsidizing
the free press and media; and organizing various workshops,
conferences and schools for young leaders, journalists, economists,
sociologists and future farmers. The topics of such training seminars
range from "Key Rules of Civil Society" and "Self-Government in
Contemporary Democratic States" to "Privatization," "Budgeting for
Small Private Business," "EU and NATO in the World Security
System," and "The Nature of the Russian Oligarchy." It is worth
mentioning that according to a variety of sources almost 15,000 young
Belarusians participated in these programs in 1999 alone.

Of course, one may ask whether this interest in Belarus and such
involvement in the problems of the state have come too late. There is
no doubt that Poland was in a position to have paid more attention to
its neighbor's problems and could have done so. For example,
thousands of young Belarusians should have taken part in Polish NGO
programs at least several years earlier. Poland also should have used
every available means of promoting Belarus in the world. Would this
have had a fundamental impact, however, on the way in which the
situation in the country has developed? The answer is undoubtedly no.

On the other hand, Poland's integration into European and Euro-
Atlantic structures requires the country to formulate a clear eastern
policy within the framework of those structures. (Indeed, Washington
expressly expects Poland, as a member of NATO, to have such a

concept.) One of the key elements of a policy of this kind must become—and this lies in our own interest—a policy toward Belarus. The destabilization of our Eastern neighbors threatens to force us into the position of becoming a front-line state, a role that is definitely far from attractive.

At the same time, as Antoni Kamiński has rightly argued:

> Today, the area comprised by Poland and Belarus should be described as a "region between a united Europe and Russia." With Poland's entry into NATO and the EU, this region will contract to consist of Belarus. A union of Russia and Belarus, if it becomes a fact, will move Russia to the West—the buffer zone will disappear and the Polish-Belarus border will become the border between the CIS and a united Europe. This border, in view of Russia's role in the region, may become an arena for tensions. Today, the "Belarus problem" possesses not just regional, but pan-European dimensions.[25]

---

[25] See Antonii Kaminskii [Antoni Kamiński], "Polozhenie v Belorussii kak ugroza bezopastnosti Pol'shi," in Garnett and Legvold, *Belorussiia na pereput'e,* p. 56.

15

Hans-Georg Wieck
The Role of International Organizations in Belarus

Introduction

The independent Belarus news agency BelaPAN conducts public opinion polls on a regular basis. Asked about the trustworthiness of national and international organizations (20 organizations were listed), Minsk citizens put—according to polls conducted in March 1999—the Organization for Security and Cooperation in Europe (OSCE) behind the churches, the United Nations third, followed by the army and the president.[1] Citizens of Minsk, more so than the population in the countryside, take the international environment into account when discussing their own future. Nevertheless, connections with the outside world—except for those with Russia—are very limited at this point.

On the international stage, Belarus is a largely unknown country situated on the Western border of the former Soviet Union. It is a country that is either ignored internationally or considered to be essentially an appendix of the Russian Federation. Although he had been voted into the office of the presidency in 1994 in a democratic election, in November 1996 President Aliaksandr Lukashenka maneuvered to enhance his power and subdue the opposition by way of a questionable referendum. This, in turn, earned for Belarus the dubious reputation of an untrustworthy, autocratic regime with a very poor human rights record and ideologically rooted anti-Western policies.

[1]   BelaPAN "Zerkalo" March 1999: 15–17.

Belarus is a country in which, among the intellectual and political leaderships, traditionally pro- and anti-Russian sentiments, pro- and anti-Polish sentiments, and a militant Belarusian-language-based nationalism are driving forces behind the formulation of political strategies.[2] These are conflicting and competing political forces within a country whose outer boundaries have undergone many changes in history. It is a country from which Russia deported two million or more Poles and from which Germany deported and killed the Jews, who were significant both in number and in terms of their accomplishments and contributions to the country.

In World War II, Belarus was a major battlefield and suffered enormously. Over two million of its 10 million inhabitants perished in the war. Many cities and villages were completely destroyed. Belarus, before gaining its independence in the aftermath of the dissolution of the Soviet Union in 1991, had enjoyed the status of an independent country only once and only for a very short period of time, from 25 March 1918 until early 1919, when it was under German protection.

The white-red-white flag of that short-lived state derived its existence from the Grand Duchy of Lithuania in the 13th century, with Vilnius as its capital and the Belarusian language the official language of the court, until 1696. The flag regained its function as the national symbol in 1991, but Lukashenka replaced it again with a Soviet-style flag. The flag continues to be the emblem, fostered and blessed by the Belarusian Popular Front after the 1996 constitutional crisis which made Lukashenka the ruler of an autocratically structured state.

Belarus is a corporate state with a powerful presidency and a kind of parliamentary assembly, nominated by the president after the constitutional coup d'état in November 1996, and composed of members taken from the Supreme Soviet of the 13th Session. Parliamentarians were in large numbers proposed as candidates in the 1995–1996 elections by the farm and labor collectives, that is, employees of state-owned or stated-controlled enterprises and agricultural collectives. These bodies have a privileged position in the nomination process of candidates for elections. Once elected, members of parliament can be recalled by their collective constituencies if they are performing "badly." Representatives elected in this way call themselves "independent." In reality, however, they are the representatives of the "Party of Power."

---

[2]   Paola Baril, *L'identité nationale de la Bielorussie* (Lyon, 1998).

The state-run enterprises and agricultural collectives receive highly subsidized credits and financial support. To move in the direction of a market economy would mean to undermine the two pillars on which the power of the presidency is based—collective farms and collective labor in state-run enterprises. A change could occur if this "social contract" were to be put into question by labor itself (that is, by official trade unions). It is more probable that this will happen than will an uprising of farmers against the presidency, although many of them live in miserable conditions.

In March 1999, according to the "Zerkalo" opinion polls, the president enjoyed the full confidence of 10 percent of the population in Minsk and of 22 percent of the countryside. He was distrusted completely by 42 percent of the Minsk population, but only by 24 percent in the countryside. Thirty-four percent of the people of Minsk and 20 percent of the population in the countryside trust him partially.[3] His approval rating as president declined from 20 percent in July 1998 to 13 percent in March 1999. The opposition, being very much divided and not "above party rivalry," however, is not a real challenge to the presidency at this juncture. It is not reaching out to the very large part of the population that feels negatively affected by presidential policies, but would likely rally only in support of a nationwide reform program "above the party lines."

Because of its historical complexity and, especially, because of the backward-looking orientation of the current elites, it is necessary to recapitulate a bit of the country's history. Belarus, then called Ruthenium or Belo Russiia, was at one time united with the Kingdom of Poland and the Grand Duchy of Lithuania (united after the 1569 Union of Lublin as the Polish-Lithuanian Commonwealth). The Belarusian language, part of the East Slavic family, at times was the official language in the Lithuanian Court. At other times, Poland supported the spread of Polish in Belarus. In 1696, Polish replaced Belarusian in official documents and the Latin alphabet replaced the Cyrillic alphabet. This was changed again after the incorporation of the territory of Belarus into the Russian Empire in connection with the partition of Poland between 1772 and 1795. Seventy-five percent of the population still claims to speak Belarusian as their mother tongue. In 1991, Belarusian was made the official language of the country.

---

[3]   BelaPAN "Zerkalo" March 1999: 15–17.

Lukashenka introduced Russian as a second official language, and in cities, it is de facto used more than Belarusian.

Under the Russian Empire, Belarusian self-government was abolished. A more or less forced conversion to Russian Orthodoxy took place, which explains why today only a small fraction of the population still adheres to the Greek Catholic Church, which had been created in 1596 through the Union of Brest.

After the establishment of the Belarusian independent state in 1991, the handling of the nuclear arms of the former Soviet Union attracted to Belarus the interest of the United States and of Western Europe. The withdrawal and dismantling of these nuclear weapons and their missile systems and the reduction of former Red Army conventional forces concentrated in large numbers in this important Soviet military district were accomplished through international agreements (in 1993) and through Belarus' accession to the Nuclear Non-Proliferation Treaty (in February 1993). Reductions on the basis of the Conventional Forces in Europe (CFE) agreements (in 1990 and 1992) were implemented. While Lukashenka hails the high standards of the Belarus armed forces' equipment and capabilities, however, most of the officers look to Moscow for help, rather than to the empty pockets of President Lukashenka. There is a joint missile defense radar station at Hantsevichi [Gantsevichi], southwest of Baranavichi in Minsk Oblast.

These complex historical roots and the country's difficult economic and social conditions must be taken into account when addressing the role of international organizations in Belarus today. The temptation is great to address these issues in a way that is guided by the spirit of the Cold War—a temptation reinforced by the backward-looking orientation of the regime. Such an approach, however, would end up in a dead end, even more so for the West than for Lukashenka. After all, Lukashenka has the option of returning with his bankrupt country into Russia's fold, which should hardly be an objective of Western strategy.

Belarus at the Crossroads

Although declaring its sovereignty as early as 27 July 1990, the actual establishment of an independent Belarus did not occur until 25 August 1991, and was not confirmed until the dissolution of the Soviet Union in December 1991 by an agreement signed on 7 December at Viskuli, in western Belarus, near the Polish border. On that date, Boris Yeltsin of the Russian Federation, Leonid Kravchuk of Ukraine, and Stanislaŭ Shushkevich of Belarus declared the dissolution of the Soviet Union and the establishment of a kind of confederation of successor states to the Soviet Union. Together with the other successor states, they gained international recognition and committed themselves to recognize international obligations entered into by the Soviet Union, in particular, recognition of frontiers, agreements on disarmament and arms control, and the commitment to peaceful settlement of issues. Their commitment to democratic structures, the rule of law, and the observance of human rights technically was ensured by virtue of Soviet commitments to the Conference on Security and Cooperation in Europe (CSCE) in Copenhagen on 29 June 1990 (in the Document on the Conference of the Human Dimension), and the Paris Charter, on 21 November 1990.

Following the dissolution of the Soviet Union, countries of the Commonwealth of Independent States (CIS) continued to be run on the basis of the constitutions adopted in 1977 and structured according to the so-called Brezhnev Constitution of 1977. While Yeltsin had been elected president of the Russian Federation in May 1992 by a nationwide presidential election, with Alexander Rutskoi and Vladimir Zhirinovsky as rival candidates, in Ukraine and in Belarus the leaders were renominated or elected by parliament. (Shushkevich and Kravchuk technically were speakers—chairmen of the presidiums—of their respective parliaments; they also acted as formal heads of state). The supreme soviets (often referred to as "parliaments" after 1991) constituted an element of continuity in the period after the dissolution of the Soviet Union. This continuity also turned out to be an obstacle for meaningful reform. Only on 15 March 1994 did Belarus adopt a new, democratic constitution, on the basis of which presidential elections were held in July 1994. Lukashenka, the chairman of the anti-mafia and anti-corruption committee, won the contest in a run-off, soundly defeating Prime Minister Viacheslaŭ Kebich.

The political basis of the Lukashenka camp was formed by the generation of political "elites" rooted in the collective labor and farmer structures. They ran as "independent" candidates—and still do so. This turns elections that are designed, in a democratic society, to determine the composition of parliament and, in most cases, the political fabric of the government into a political campaign to rally public support for the state structures and the holders of office.[4]

The law on local elections, which was adopted in December 1998, emerged from consultations between the OSCE Advisory and Monitoring Group (AMG) with Belarusian authorities (including the National Assembly and Ministry of the Interior). In the end, however, it did not reflect the substance of the OSCE suggestions. In analyzing the new law, the AMG came to the conclusion that the law could not guarantee free and fair elections.[5] The opposition political parties and nongovernmental organizations boycotted the elections, which had an official turnout of 67 percent of the registered voters. Spot checks by international and domestic observers determined that in many polling stations the 50 percent participation threshold was not met.

In 1990, the country was hardly prepared for political and economic independence. It faced great difficulties in the privatization of its industrial complexes and in establishing a genuine democratic foundation for the state. The collapse of the Soviet Union had occurred at the top, not at the bottom. At the grass roots level, the country continued to function as it always had—awaiting orders, as well as living supplies, from the center.

In November 1996, a referendum on amendments to the 1994 Constitution was held. After the results were manipulated, the president declared this plebiscite binding for the country, even though it had been indicated on the ballot sheets that the results would not be binding. Forcing a controversial decision through the Constitutional Court, Lukashenka went on to shape the state structure by selecting 110 of his followers (mostly independent members of parliament) from the Supreme Soviet of the 13th Session and establishing by nomination the "independent" National Assembly. The Supreme Soviet of the 13th Session, elected in 1995 and 1996, was dissolved. The Russian Federation accepted this result in spite of earlier attempts at mediation between the opposing forces. The European Union (EU), the Council of Europe, and the U.S. all rejected recognition of the unconstitutional actions by Lukashenka. After an ill-fated mediation attempt by the European Union and the Council of Europe on 15

---

[4]   OSCE Advisory and Monitoring Group on Belarus (OSCE-AMG), *Preliminary Assessment of Local Elections on April 4, 1999* (Press release) Minsk, 5 April 1999.

[5]   *OSCE Assessment of the New Election Law on Local Elections in Belarus*, OSCE Advisory and Monitoring Group in Belarus press release (Minsk, 15 January 1999).

September 1997, the Council of Europe suspended the guest status of Belarus, and the European Union suspended high-level political contacts and the continuation of the ratification of the Partnership for Cooperation Agreement with Belarus. The Parliamentary Assembly of the OSCE continues to recognize the Supreme Soviet of the 13th Session as the democratically elected parliamentary body in Belarus.

The democratic transformation process was delayed by Lukashenka's constitutional manipulation. He also extended the duration of his presidency by imposing in 1996 a new version of the 1994 Constitution, and then restarting his term of office in November 1996. The opposition rejected this and called for presidential elections on the basis of the Supreme Soviet of the 13th Session.

Instead of using this "golden opportunity" to rally the discontented segments of the population behind this motion, the opposition presented two rival candidates: Zianon Pazniak [Zenon Pozniak], the leader of the nationalists, who was living in Poland after having won asylum from the U.S., and Mikhail Chyhir [Chigir], Luka-shenka's prime minister from 1994 to 1996, who resigned in 1996 because of disagreements with Lukashenka. As a candidate, Chyhir enjoyed some sympathy in Moscow and could be considered there a successor candidate to Lukashenka. Pazniak organized a highly political defamation campaign against Chyhir, which may have cost Chyhir his chance as a nationwide choice to replace Lukashenka in an open, free, and fair contest. It is doubtful whether, under existing conditions and with a rivalry between two "party candidates," the wide range of discontent with Lukashenka and his system of govern-ment could be exploited. In addition, any attempt to organize elections against the existing state machinery would be risky.

The strategists who designed this campaign sought to undermine Lukashenka's official status on the international stage and thus bring him down. This confrontational strategy assumed that the outside world would disrupt official relations with Belarus if Lukashenka did not step down at the end of his term of office as based on the 1994 Constitution. Certainly Russia would not do so. The already poor relations between Western OSCE countries and Belarus would be further downgraded, without offering any alternative.

The dangers of a coup d'état if pursued by the strategists were fully recognized by genuinely democratic forces, which held a nationwide Congress of Democratic Forces on 29 January 1999, under the chairmanship of Henadz Karpenka [Gennadii Karpenko], the presidential candidate of the liberal Civic Union Party. Unfortunately, he passed away under questionable circumstances (during surgery following a stroke) on 6 April 1999. His death was a great loss for those who sought to generate a broad-based Movement for the Renewal of Belarus, which could have gained momentum had it succeeded in mobilizing the discontent of the people in the country who were not ready to join political parties. Such a movement would have followed the examples of Poland and East Germany in the 1980s, leading to roundtables and constitutional compromises.

Given the choice for Belarus between a balanced relationship with Russia and with the West (represented by the EU), and an unbalanced relationship (either 90 percent relationship with Russia and 10 percent relationship with the West, or the reverse), the overwhelming majority of the population would opt for the balanced one.

International Organizations—Their Roles in Belarus

The Belorussian Soviet Socialist Republic was a founding member of the United Nations. For this reason Belarus has had relations with many agencies of the UN since the 1950s. Belarus has been a partner in many of its special programs, and the UN enjoys high prestige in Belarus. Nevertheless, the number of projects adopted for Belarus has declined so greatly that in 1998 the outgoing director in charge of projects in Belarus was replaced not by a representative from a third country but by a local representative. This is indicative of the decline in Belarus' significance within the UN.

The World Bank, the International Monetary Fund, and the European Bank for Reconstruction and Development have all withdrawn personnel, and all their Belarusian programs are on hold. The International Monetary Fund had signed two agreements for special drawing rights for Belarus in 1993 and 1995—each amounting to about $200 million. Of the latter one, only one tranche was utilized ($70 million). As a result of the financial crises that erupted in Belarus in March 1998 and in Moscow in August 1998, a technical assistance program was discussed to help reduce the social burdens of these crises. To date, no concrete results have come of those negotiations.

The EU did not renew technical assistance programs after the decision taken by the Ministerial Council in 1997 to disrupt political contacts with, and technical assistance programs for, Belarus—with a few exceptions in the humanitarian, social, and democratization fields.

A new program designed to support the development of civil society has not yet been finalized with the Belarusian government.

The $5 million EU Council project was examined by both sides with a great deal of ideological bias. It was eventually put into effect at the end of 1999. Some projects from earlier times (on democratization, economic research, and border-crossing facilities) are still being implemented.

Early in 1997, very shortly after the political developments in Minsk in November 1996, the EU Council adopted on 24 February "Conclusions" regarding Belarus, which were based on the fact-finding mission by a high level Dutch official.[6] In these conclusions, the Council made a number of recommendations to the authorities in Belarus, namely to restore the principles of the separation of power, to establish a dialogue between the administration and the Supreme Soviet of the 13th session, to remedy the flaws that caused the confrontation in the country, and to restore the freedom of the media. The Council also recommended to EU member states not to render support for Belarus' application for membership into the Council of Europe pending changes toward democracy in Belarus, not to proceed with the interim agreement or the Partnership and Cooperation Agreement, to undertake bilateral political contacts on a case-by-case basis only, and to review the Community and the National Technical Assistance Programs with the objective of continuing only those supportive of the reform process.

The EU Council expressed its readiness to render support for a dialogue between Belarus and the EU, the OSCE, and the Council of Europe, and to enter into a comprehensive dialogue with the authorities and the opposition to assist Belarus in embarking on democratic and economic reforms. In light of the failure of the ensuing initiatives, in particular the failure of the trilateral dialogue between the EU, the government, and the opposition, the matter was again under discussion in the EU Council on 15 September 1997.[7] On that occasion, the EU confirmed its recognition of the 1994 Constitution and of the Supreme Soviet of the 13th Session. It

---

[6]   DAP-PRR/Inf (97)98, 9 April 1997, circular to the members of the Council of Europe, EU Council Conclusions adopted on 24 February 1997 [Council of Europe Press Service, Luxembourg].

[7]   DAP-PR/Inf(97)287, 23 September 1998, Conclusions of the EU Council Meeting on 15 September 1997 [Council of Europe Press Service, Luxembourg].

reminded the authorities in Belarus that relations between the EU and Belarus will not improve as long as Belarus fails to move toward respect for human rights and fundamental freedoms, and to observe the constitutional principles inherent in a democratic state governed by the rule of law. The Council decided that the tripartite working group would resume its discussions when the EU determines that the necessary conditions for achieving results in line with the working party's terms of reference have been met; that EU member states would not support Belarus' membership application to the Council of Europe; that the European Communities and their member states would conclude neither the interim agreement nor the Partnership and Cooperation Agreement; that bilateral ministerial contacts between the European Union and Belarus would, in principle, be established only through the presidency or the Troika; that the implementation of Community technical assistance programs would be halted, except in the case of humanitarian or regional projects or those that directly support the democratization process; and that the member states would look at their technical assistance programs in Belarus with a view to their cessation, except in the case of humanitarian and regional projects or those that directly support the democratization process. Finally, these conclusions would be reviewed when and if Belarus reconsiders its position.

The Council of Europe, for its part, suspended Belarus' guest status but maintained Belarus' participation in some technical and cultural areas. In January 1999, it was decided to have the political committee establish hearings and meetings with representatives from the two parliamentary bodies in Belarus. The first meeting of this type took place on 27 April 1999. Otherwise, the political positions of the Council of Europe, the Parliamentary Assembly of the OSCE, the EU Council, and the European Parliament remained unchanged in substance, but opened some avenues for more dialogue.

The Parliamentary Assembly of the OSCE established an ad hoc Belarus Working Group in 1998 under the chairmanship of former Romanian Foreign Minister Adrian Severin. Other members of the group come from Finland, Germany, Georgia, and Ukraine. They visited Minsk and Moscow on several occasions. They organized a roundtable in Bucharest with parliamentarians from both sides and with independent personalities to discuss the requirements that must be met if free and fair elections were to be implemented. According to the constitution of 1994 and the amended one of 1996, parliamentary elections were required to take place in 2000.

The relationship of the EU and its member states with Belarus has been reduced to the maintenance of relations as such, without initiating any new bilateral projects. The Council of Europe is not considering Belarus' application for membership. The Parliamentary Assembly of the OSCE continues to have relations only with the democratically elected Supreme Soviet of the 13th Session of Belarus. The OSCE, however, has adopted a policy of dialogue based on the requirement that Belarus comply with the OSCE commitments that it has entered into, namely the commitments under the Document of the Copenhagen Meeting of the Conference on the Human Dimension of the CSCE, dated 29 June 1990, and the Charter of Paris for a New Europe, dated 21 November 1990. In these documents, OSCE member states committed themselves to introducing and defending pluralistic democracy, the rule of law, and market economies. On the recommendation of the 1997 report of the special representative of the Danish Chairman-in-Office, Niels Helveg Petersen, the Council established the Advisory and Monitoring Group of the OSCE in Belarus, as mandated by Decision No. 185, dated 18 September 1997, and adopted with the agreement of the Belarusian government. The AMG was established "to assist the Belarusian authorities in promoting democratic institutions and in complying with other OSCE commitments; and [to] monitor and report on this process."

On the basis of this decision, the office of the AMG includes the head of the group and a team of four experts from other international institutions and organizations (or member states). After protracted negotiations between OSCE Secretary General Giancarlo Aragona and Belarusian Foreign Minister Ivan Antanovich [Antonovich], a Memorandum of Understanding (MoU) was signed on 18 December 1997. The MoU provided for AMG diplomatic status, the right to invite foreign and national experts, and access to everyone in the country, as well as access by everyone in the country to the AMG (according to the Text of Decision No. 185, dated 18 September 1997, and of the MoU, dated 18 December 1997, Annex).

In complying with the guidelines issued by the Danish Chairman-in-Office, the activities of the AMG concentrated in the first phase on efforts to contribute to the development of legislation for democratic institutions (such as elections, ombudsman, media, penal code and penal code procedures, and a parliamentary law-making process). In response to the first AMG working paper, the government set up a number of working groups (on legislation for democratic institutions; on the implementation of laws establishing institutions, such as the media; on human rights observance; and on education). A great deal of work was undertaken in the course of 1998, notably on a law on elections, including local elections; a law on the establishment of an ombudsman; consultations in connection with the parliamentary review of the penal code and penal code procedures; proposals for the development of new legislature for mass media; and the review of the existing governmental control on printed media.

The AMG also engaged in a dialogue with the opposition, notably with the presidium of the Supreme Soviet of the 13th Session (including Siamion Sharetski and others); members of the political parties, such as the Communist Party, the Belarusian Popular Front, the social democratic parties, and the United Civil Party, as well as with the Belarus Group IABLOKO; and many nongovernmental organizations, in particular Charter-97 (headed by Andrei Sannikaŭ [Sannikov]), the Belarus Helsinki Committee, "Viasna" (also known as Viasna-96, headed by Tatiana Protka), the Center for the Rights of the Press (headed by Mikhail Pastukhaŭ [Pastukhov]), and the Belarusian Association of Journalists (headed by Zhana Litsvina [Litvina]). Contacts were also established with a number of foreign foundations working in Belarus, such as Ebert Stiftung, Stresemann-Stiftung, United States foundations representing both the Republican and Democratic political parties, and British and Scandinavian organizations. The AMG engaged in programs with academic institutions in the area of human rights education and compliance. Communication was established between Belarusian institutions and specialists in other countries for the purpose of translating up-to-date legal texts.

The AMG established a section for the handling of cases of administrative harassment and human rights violations. The Group would study the cases and discuss them with the respective state institutions. Local lawyers recruited by AMG support this work. To advance the concept of dialogue as the major instrument for any solution of the ongoing constitutional crisis (a term not accepted by the government), the AMG initiated a number of internationally attended seminars on crucial issues in the transition process, such as those on "Free and Fair Elections," "Democracy, Social Security, and Market Economy," "Information Society," and, in Minsk and all the provincial capitals, on the training of domestic election observers. The

AMG also prepared five regional conferences on "Self-Government, Rule of Law, and Regional Economic Development," a conference series that involved regions in neighboring countries.

The AMG has also engaged in analytical work. It provides "activity reports" on a by-weekly basis that are circulated to all delegations of the Permanent Council and, through the OSCE Secretariat, to international organizations such as the EU, the Council of Europe, the Parliamentary Assembly of the OSCE, and the parliamentary bodies of the European institutions. In-depth analyses have covered the human rights situation, Lukashenka's political strategy, political parties and the opposition, nongovernmental organizations, the mass media, and economic options for Belarus. These analyses are reviewed periodically.

The AMG undertook a political assessment of the local elections in Belarus organized on 4 and 16 April 1999. It had previously analyzed the Law on Local Elections, which was adopted in December 1998, a law that failed—according to the AMG statement made public on 15 January 1999—to meet OSCE standards, in spite of months of substantive consultations between official institutions and the AMG. One day after the elections held on 4 April 1999, the AMG presented its assessment at a press conference. It characterized the elections as a campaign of the government to register public support for the state institutions and their leaders. As such, they were not genuinely democratic elections, designed to bring about public debate on issues of the state and to seek in a competitive effort the election of representatives from rival political forces to the parliamentary bodies and, indirectly, to the respective government. The press statement also noted the types of manipulation that had been undertaken in the election process by state institutions, including the electoral commissions, to pass the 50 percent threshold. The opposition political parties boycotted the elections.

On the basis of its mandate and the MoU, the AMG has, in principle, access to all citizens. In reality, however, this access is often blocked. For example, it was not able to gain access to detained opposition leaders Viktar Hanchar [Gonchar] and Chyhir in March and April 1999, although, as a general rule, the AMG has access to all prisons and to all prisoners and detained citizens. It does have access from time to time to Lukashenka, and maintains close links with political parties, nongovernmental organizations, and the media. The opposition criticizes the AMG for serving as a fig leaf of the government. The government criticizes it for nonobjective reporting.

The AMG stands for dialogue and for a peaceful solution to underlying political and constitutional conflict, a concept that has not yet been adopted by either the government or the opposition. This dialogue could, however, come about in the case of a further decline of the economy, under Russian pressure, or if public support for Lukashenka slips significantly.

It is important that institutions such as the AMG exist in Belarus to improve democratic awareness in Minsk and in the provinces, and thus offer an alternative to the inherited political spirit of deadly enmity between political rivals. This state of mind dominates Lukashenka and therefore also dominates his opponents. The spirit of the Cold War very often determines the language chosen abroad about this country. While there is the slogan in the case of human rights violations of "silent diplomacy versus public exposure," in reality, in the aftermath of the Cold War, communication has taken on quite a different quality. It can be said that the methods of "direct substantive talk" and "public debate" are complementary. It would be wrong to say that only one of the two approaches can alter the course of the government in particular cases, but it would also be highly counterproductive to compromise one or the other approach as being futile.

In Belarus, the AMG raises with the government and the courts any issue or human rights case that falls within its broadly defined mandate. Although its advice may not be followed in each case, the AMG helps these institutions understand the real dimension of the issues. It is able to do this because the discussion does not take place in a confrontational climate. The "Party of the Power" may decide not to change course now, but reflection within the system will take its course.

Confrontation or Dialogue

In 1999, political discussion in Belarus focused on the question of presidential elections, which were required to take place that year, but which had been postponed by a decision of Lukashenka and the "National Assembly." According to that decision, as stated earlier, Lukashenka's term of office was recalculated to start anew in 1996 (instead of 1994), using the 1996 amended Constitution as a justification for the determination.

The Supreme Soviet of the 13th Session entered into a political coalition with the Belarusian Popular Front (Pazniak) and with Mikhail Chyhir, the former prime minister under Lukashenka, to call for a presidential election on the basis of the 1994 Constitution. It was argued that the election must be announced by Parliament, which also nominated the Central Electoral Commission. This was done on 10 January 1999. Under the chairmanship of Viktar Hanchar, the Central Electoral Commission called for an election on 16 May 1999. It invited nominations of candidates, who were required to collect 100,000 signatures. Accordingly, Pazniak and Chyhir were recognized as candidates on 31 March 1999. Pazniak was residing in the U.S. and Poland. Chyhir had been arrested at the end of March on charges of embezzlement and abuse of power. Hanchar had already been jailed for ten days for an unauthorized demonstration. Preparations for the election continued, and it was held between 6 and 16 May 1999, with the use of mobile ballot boxes. Most of the observers had doubted whether the election could in fact be implemented in the face of the declared intentions of the government. Therefore, the election effort was viewed primarily as a demonstration of public protest against the Lukashenka regime. The election turned out to be a failure. Pazniak withdrew before election day, and collection of ballots took place only symbolically. Rivalry broke out between the two candidates. Pazniak characterized Chyhir as a representative of Russian interests. Given the political apathy of more than 50 percent of the population, only a candidate who was promoted by a movement uniting all parties and other interested groups, and who gathered visible public support from all corners, including from groups hitherto tied to the presidential system through the trade unions and labor collectives, could bring about a new, non-Lukashenka majority. Lech Wałęsa had been able to create such a majority in Poland under conditions of martial law, even in spite of the dissolution of Solidarity by the authorities.

If the election did not take place on 16 May, the Supreme Soviet of the 13th Session intended to meet on 21 July 1999 to declare the Chairman of the Presidium to be Head of State. It was assumed that the Supreme Soviet of the 13th Session would comprise a quorum (the majority of the 195 members elected in 1995–1996), and thus be in a position to make such a decision.

The strategy of the opposition was geared toward disavowing Lukashenka at home and abroad and to seeking the termination of official relations of the West with Lukashenka. Under such circumstances, the opposition suspected that the political climate in the country would change in their favor. The opposition had been able to gather support from Moscow in only a very limited way. Chyhir was being looked upon in some quarters of Moscow as a possible and acceptable successor to Lukashenka. On the other hand, Moscow was trying to live with Lukashenka, not because it agreed with his political strategy and philosophy, but because of the advantages Russia derived under his leadership, such as in the areas of military cooperation and arms exports to strategically important countries. Moscow has also been afraid of political instability and of anti-Russian tendencies in a post-Lukashenka environment.

Under the conditions of the political confrontation between the two camps in Belarus, that of Lukashenka and the opposition (itself divided between Communists, nationalists, and democrats), the AMG seemed to be the defender of a lost cause, that of dialogue, roundtable discussions, peaceful solutions, and new constitutional compromises. Following a defeat in one or all of its attempts for power, the opposition groups had to review their strategies.

Should OSCE member states continue to deal with Lukashenka along non-compromising lines after the end of his constitutionally legitimized term on 20 July 1999, while also renewing and even intensifying the call for reform and adherence to the constitution and OSCE commitments, the opposition will be forced to reshape its attitudes toward the OSCE. It will discover that the road to success will be through rallying those layers of the population that are beginning to feel the decline of the economy and those who were supportive of the president until now on the basis of a platform of "Renewal of Belarus." It will, however, be a difficult task for the opposition to unite on the basis of such a strategy. The AMG could be helpful.

The government has begun anew consultations with the AMG on a law for the parliamentary elections. Before engaging in this effort, they will have to discuss by what means the political basis for such a law could be enlarged—that is, by roundtable, public hearings with the opposition, or by nationwide debate in the mass media on the principles of such a law and of the accompanying issues (the media, financial support, functions of parliament, and separation of power).

The "Union" between Russia and Belarus

Strictly speaking, the issue of the Union between Russia and Belarus is not within the purview of the AMG. It is also not something that needs to be discussed when talking about international organizations in Belarus. Nevertheless, it is of such importance to Belarus that it cannot be ignored. The subject has various layers. It entails issues of economic ties as a heritage of the industrial and economic web of the Soviet Union, as well as a consequence of economic and social policy pursued by Lukashenka. It also entails political ties, based on the concept of a "Slavic Union," or based on the imperial concept of Moscow as a component in the development (or negligence) of the CIS as a concept to prevent the slippage of Belarus into Central Europe.

At different times, "Union" means different things to different people. For Lukashenka, the Union represents a means to fulfill his desire to contain Western influence in Moscow and Kyiv, and to enlarge the scope of influence of his state and economic model (a planned economy based on state-run enterprises and state-run farms, with a political base recruited from the cadres of the collective farms and collective labor organizations). It would allow Belarus and the countries of the Slavic Union to defend more effectively their interests in dealing with the West, and to do so more successfully than done by Moscow today.

To maintain the momentum of this political goal, a new Union treaty must be signed every year. In substance, however, very little is added to the already existing cooperation between the two countries, be it in the military and intelligence fields, or in the sphere of economics as a result of the customs union.[8]

Preferential treatment of Belarus by Russia is of vital importance for Belarus' economic policy. The economy of Belarus is managed in such a way that payment for gas and oil deliveries from Russia (the energy equivalent of about 15 million tons of oil) can be made by way of barter with goods manufactured at subsidized conditions in the giant former Soviet factories. Up to 70 percent of the gas bill is "paid

---

[8]   See annex with the English translation of the documents signed in Moscow on 25 December 1998 by Lukashenka and Yeltsin on the creation of a union in 1999: http://www.president.gov.by/rus/parliament_assembly/souz/proekt.htm. The final document is located at http://194.226.121.66/webnpa/text.asp?NR=H19900343.

for" this way: with tractors, television sets, refrigerators, heavy equipment, trucks, and foodstuffs. In addition, because of the notion of the "Union," Lukashenka is insisting on a gas price at the domestic Russian level ($21 per 1,000 cubic meters, as of this writing) in contrast to the international price for Russian gas of $50. Currently he has obtained a price of $30 to $40 per 1,000 cubic meters. Because such concessions cannot be granted by Russia to all CIS member states, there must be a special relationship between Russia and Belarus to justify such a concession.

The notion of becoming in the end the 90th subject within the Russian Federation does not suit Lukashenka, nor is it acceptable to Belarus, as is clearly shown by the opinion polls. Support for an all-embracing Union has dropped sharply, from 47 percent in 1996 to 21 percent in 1999. Opposition to such a union has grown from 20 to 33 percent of the population. Economic ties, however, are considered important. The strengthening of ties with Western countries is regarded with some apprehension in Belarus, because a loss of jobs is anticipated, jobs that are artificially maintained at the cost of galloping inflation. (In January 1998, $1 was worth 38,000 Belarusian rubles; one year later the Belarusian ruble had devalued to 380,000 Belarusian ruble per $1.) Western countries absent from the scene in Belarus cannot expect to be trusted as prospective partners.

For obvious reasons, it is not possible for Russia to enter into a treaty with Belarus for the establishment of a "confederation" between the two states. Such a treaty would probably cause the disintegration of the Russian Federation.

In the end, all the institutions engaged in the process of unification have agreed to try to harmonize the legislatures on critical issues between the two countries, for instance on the legal structures of joint ventures, of economic enterprises, and the like. At times, the notion of the Slavic Union still flares up, as it did during the crisis over Kosovo and the tension between Yugoslavia and the West.

The Road to Negotiations and Their Collapse

The attempt of the Central Electoral Commission of the Supreme Soviet of the 13th Session in May 1999 to implement an alternative presidential election, and thus lay the groundwork for the discontinuation of the cooperation of the Western world with the Lukashenka government, collapsed. The AMG, supported by the

Belarus ad hoc Group of the OSCE Parliamentary Assembly under its chairman, former Romanian Foreign Minister Adrian Severin, reinforced its efforts to bring about a meaningful dialogue between the government and the political opposition for a new national consensus on key issues of democratic reform. In Bucharest in June 1999, an informal gathering of politicians from the opposition, representatives of nongovernmental organizations, and members of trade unions, organized and conducted by the AMG and the Belarus ad hoc Working Group of the OSCE Parliamentary Assembly, took place. On that occasion, a concept evolved for negotiations between government and opposition political parties with the participation of the "third sector." The concept constituted the basis of a discussion on 15 July 2000 between Severin and this author on the one hand, and Lukashenka on the other. The government had been invited to the Bucharest meeting, but it declined at the last minute on the grounds that it did not want to discuss Belarus issues outside the country. However, agreement was reached with the president on the framework of the negotiations and on the agenda. He designated his trusted assistant Mikhail Sazonaŭ [Sazonov] as chairman of the governmental delegation.

The concept envisaged negotiations on "Free and Fair Parliamentary Elections in 2000" between representatives of the government nominated by the president and representatives from the eight opposition parties that had formed a Consultative Council. The negotiations would take place under the aegis of the AMG, and would also be attended by representatives of a number of nongovernmental organizations, trade unions and academic institutes, who would take part by invitation of one of the three other participating groups—the government, the opposition, or the OSCE. The following agenda items were agreed upon: an electoral code, access of the opposition to the state-controlled mass media, the functions of the new parliament, and confidence-building measures, which in a preliminary round of consultations would have to be identified in order to create a climate conducive to meaningful negotiations.

The following opposition parties took part:

- the Belarusian Popular Front (Liavon Barshcheŭski, later Vintsuk Viachorka)
- Social Democratic Hramada (Stanislaŭ Shushkevich)

- Social Democratic Party National Hramada (Mikalai Statkevich)
- United Civil Party (Stanislaŭ Bahdankevich; Anatol Liabedzka since early 2000)
- Communist Party of Belarusians (Siarhei Kaliakin)
- Liberal Democratic Party (Siarhei Haidukevich).[9]
- Labor Party (Aliaksandr Bukhvostaŭ)
- Women's Party (Valiantsina Palevikova)

In the course of 1999 and 2000, the Belarusian Popular Front (BPF) split in two parts. The majority elected Viachorka as the new chairman. Pazniak, the founding father of the BPF, and his representative in Belarus, Iuri Belenki, established the "Christian Conservative Party of the Belarusian Popular Front." The party suspended its role in the negotiation process and kept as its chairman Pazniak, who lives in Poland. The party also engaged in a disinformation campaign against the activities of the OSCE mission in Belarus.

In July 1999, the Annual Session of the OSCE Parliamentary Assembly adopted a Belarus Resolution urging the government and opposition to conduct negotiations on the concept of free and fair elections, and urged the government to give the opposition access to the state-controlled mass media. The operative paragraph of the resolution, dated 10 July 1999, reads as follows: "[The Parliamentary Assembly] calls upon the Government of Belarus to agree to elections procedures and the conduct of the elections in accordance with OSCE Commitments, and to provide political parties and opposition groups with access to time on the [Belarus National] Television and Radio."

The Parliamentary Assembly also appealed to OSCE governments and international organizations to express their support for the development of a democratic process in Belarus, and to provide assistance as appropriate and necessary. This resolution was adopted unanimously. The following year, such unanimity could not be achieved with regard to the Belarus Resolution adopted by the Bucharest Session of the OSCE Parliamentary Assembly.

President Lukashenka nominated Mikhail Sazonaŭ, one of his closest and most trusted advisors, who had been in charge of the negotiations with the Russian Federation on the Union Treaty and its

---

[9] The Liberal Democratic Party did not recognize any role for the Supreme Soviet of the 13th Session and left the roundtable at one point.

implementation, as chairman of the working group for the public dialogue. Sazonaŭ explained to the diplomatic corps in a briefing session held at the Ministry of Foreign Affairs in early September 1999 that the negotiations would take place on the three issues agreed upon, and that confidence-building measures would be discussed. On the basis of proposals worked out by the AMG, "consultations" were conducted between experts from both sides for arrangements on access by the political parties to the state-controlled electronic and printed mass media. The results were the general agreement, the "Protocol of Agreement on Conditions of Political Opposition Access to the State Mass Media for the Period Prior to the Negotiations between the Government and the Opposition Political Parties," signed on 29 October 1999, and the "Protocol on the Organizational and Technical Conditions of Political Parties' Access to State Controlled Media," as initialed on 5 November 1999.

Shortly afterwards, the political winds changed again in the power center of the country. State-paid journalists revolted against agreements, which they considered impositions on their freedom as editors. Patriotic politicians revolted against negotiations with opponents. Perhaps there was also opposition from those who feared public debate without governmental guidance on critical issues in the relationship between Russia and Belarus. Indications received from Sazonaŭ even prior to the Istanbul Summit of OSCE countries on 18–19 November 1999 were alarming, because they suggested the end to the negotiation path just underway. Although Sazonaŭ had enjoyed the trust and encouragement of the president, the positions taken were not discussed and agreed upon between members of the close circle of advisors of the president. These positions brought down Sazonaŭ, who was released from his functions, and with him the concept of genuine negotiations between the government and the opposition. For weeks and months afterwards, the nomination of a successor was promised. The process of negotiations was to be maintained. However, in the end, a concept emerged on the part of the president which eliminated direct negotiations on the basis of equal status for both sides.

The new concept, presented by the president on 22 February 2000, established a broad framework of public political dialogue with all social forces in a forum, in which government officials would participate. However, the recommendations that would emerge on the various issues under consideration would only be recommendations addressed to the government for further consideration. The president nominated Uladzimir [Vladimir] Rusakevich as the new chairman of the presidential administration's working group, also in charge of management of the Public Political Dialogue.

On the issue of the election law, only a very few recommendations were adopted for governmental consideration, and only a few of those were actually introduced into the legislation. It was clear that the political parties cooperating in the Advisory Council could not accept the presidential framework and concept of dialogue. The AMG again initiated proposals for direct talks between the government and the opposition in order to settle the "constitutional controversy." Such talks would be needed, according to the Belarus statement in the OSCE Istanbul Summit Declaration, in connection with a meaningful dialogue on free and democratic elections, including media access and the respect for human rights. The Belarus paragraph in the Summit Declaration reads as follows:

> We strongly support the work of the Advisory and Monitoring Group in Belarus, which has worked closely with the Belarusian authorities as well as with opposition parties and leaders and NGOs in promoting democratic institutions and compliance with OSCE commitments, thus facilitating a resolution of the constitutional controversy in Belarus. We emphasize that only a real political dialogue in Belarus can pave the way for free and democratic elections through which the foundations for real democracy can be developed. We would welcome early progress in this political dialogue with OSCE participation, in close cooperation with the OSCE Parliamentary Assembly. We stress the necessity of removing all remaining obstacles to this dialogue by respecting the principles of the rule of law and the freedom of the media.

These initiatives by the AMG failed to bring about meaningful negotiations. Even worse, Uladzimir Rusakevich, who supported the initiation of direct negotiations between the government and the opposition, was relieved of his duties and named ambassador to China. The attempt to move towards democratic rule by way of negotiations between the opponents had failed.

Framework for Conditions of Parliamentary Election, October 2000

By the end of August, the Public Political Dialogue and the repeated appeals by OSCE, the European Union, and the Council of Europe through their visits to Minsk brought about some improvements in the electoral code. However, these measures did not affect in any way the position of the opposition parties. Five out of the eight political parties cooperating in the Advisory Council decided to boycott the elections since the four criteria had not been met and the parliament to be elected did not have any genuine power. They decided, however, to take part in the presidential election, thus downgrading the earlier principal rejection of anything related to the operative constitution. The Communists, opposed to Lukashenka, and the Liberal Democratic Party decided to run in the election, but their candidates barely survived the registration, not to mention the election.

The democratic parties underwent a critical phase, because the boycott was not strictly observed. The Social Democratic Party National Movement, under the chairmanship of Mikalai Statkevich, left it to the members to run in the election. This was done by Statkevich himself and others. The result was devastating for them, as well as for almost all candidates from other political parties of the opposition who had defied the boycott. Volha Abramava [Olga Abramova], the representative of the Belarusian branch of the Russian Political Party "Yabloko," could make it as an independent candidate, as did one of the United Civil Party activists.

The elimination of independent and democratic candidates took place in the registration procedure, which permitted eliminating candidates supported by initiative groups that were required to deliver 1,000 valid signatures. By establishing that 15 percent of the 350 signatures were invalid, every one could be eliminated. This was the fate of most of the independent and democratic candidates. Indeed, 220 out of 750 candidatures were rejected. Although 180 complaints and appeals were submitted, only a few were successful. At no time did the government hesitate to interfere in the proceedings if this was deemed politically necessary.

Thus the elections changed from being a competitive exercise into a state-run event. This could be proven on the basis of the results of a countrywide independent election observation organized by six registered nongovernmental organizations, including, the Belarus Helsinki Committee, the Voters' Association, the L. Sapieha Foundation, the Belarus Initiative, and the Association of Free Trade Unions. The AMG supported this project financially and with professional advice. The European Commission, Germany, and Great Britain provided voluntary contributions. Five thousand observers followed events in 3,000 polling stations. Five thousand violations of the election law and of the by-laws were registered and were subject of complaint. Eighty different modes of manipulation in the handling of the ballot sheets were established. The government acknowledged that 13 constituencies did not achieve the participation of 50 percent of the registered voters. However, on the basis of the original protocols, the Central Coordination Council established that the 50 percent threshold was not reached in 30 additional constituencies. Thus in 43 constituencies, more than a third of the 110 constituencies, the 50 percent threshold was not reached. This meant that the new parliament did not achieve the required number of two-thirds elected deputies. Of course, the complaints and appeals were rejected in the juridical bodies of the country.

In order to properly prepare the decision on the dispatch of international observers, the European institutions held three technical conferences in the course of 2000. During the first conference, in April 2000, they adopted a position paper identifying the benchmarks, also called criteria, according to which the European institutions—the European Union, the OSCE, and the Council of Europe—would eventually decide. In light of the lack of progress made in the four critical areas (that of the electoral code, access of political parties to the media, functions of parliament, and human rights observance in relations with political opponents), they rejected the idea of organizing genuine international observation. Instead they established a Technical Assessment Mission of the Office for Democratic Institutions and Human Rights (ODIHR), and asked the Parliamentary Troika (the European Parliament, the Parliamentary Assemblies of the Council of Europe, and the OSCE) to continue their advisory and monitoring activities, and therefore be in Belarus on election day as observers in their institutional capacity.

On the eve of the elections, the ODIHR Technical Assessment Mission submitted an analysis of the framework, which was described as falling short of European standards and not able to ensure free, fair, equitable elections. The analysis stated:

> The 15 October parliamentary elections in Belarus failed to meet minimum international standards for democratic elections, including those formulated in the 1990 Copenhagen Document of the OSCE. In particular, these elections fell short of meeting the commitments for free, fair, equal, accountable, and transparent election. Despite some improvements since previous elections, the process remained flawed.

The Parliamentary Troika, which was composed of Severin as president of the Parliamentary Assembly of OSCE, Jan Wiersma from the European Parliament, and Wolfgang Behrendt from the Council of Europe, published a political situation assessment of the country in connection with the elections. It came to the following conclusions:

> The Troika took note in its report dated October 16, 2000, of the findings of the ODIHR Technical Assessment Mission. It welcomed efforts of the authorities to satisfy the democratic demands of the European Institutions, but concluded that insufficient progress had been made in the four critical areas (Electoral Code, Access to state controlled electronic media, functions of parliament, and human rights respect in dealing with political opponents). It deplored that the authorities did not recognize the desire for democratic change expressed by significant parts of the Belarus population. The troika stated that under such circumstances it could only recommend at this stage that a decision concerning the normalization of relations with the relevant institutions in Belarus should be taken at a later stage on the basis of progress made on the "four criteria" including the democratic practices of the parliamentary entity which emerges from the elections. The Troika committed itself to continue its engagement in Belarus.

Thus, in the opinion of the European institutions, the elections did not bring about meaningful progress in democratization. However, the process of dialogue and evolution would proceed for the very reason that a desire for a change of direction was emerging in Belarusian society. The Parliamentary Troika stated that they remained ready to continue their cooperative engagement in Belarus in favor of the democratic processes in the country.

The president committed himself on several occasions, including in an interview in Lida on 11 August 2000, to enhance the functions of parliament, possibly in a substantive manner, only after the presidential election, by way of a referendum-based constitutional amendment.

There was a chance for substantive change in favor of democratic rule, but it was missed. Nevertheless, the "winds are changing" and the European institutions must stay engaged.

On the Eve of the Presidential Election

According to the operational constitution, by September 2001 the presidential election must take place. The parliamentary elections have provided valuable insight into the working of the vertical system in the case of elections. There is no independent election commission, and governmental interference is the rule.

There is a need for the establishment of fully-fledged independent election observation, from the very first stage of establishing initiative groups, through the registration process and the work of the election commissions, and finally through election day and the counting process. The agenda of the AMG for 2001 is amply filled, and includes achieving improvements in all four areas of the international agenda for Belarus: the electoral code and regulations, media access, the functions of parliament, and the respect of human rights in dealing with political opponents.

It is assumed that the European institutions will again use the mechanism of the Technical Conference to measure progress and determine the kind of international observation of the election. But there is also the issue that the opposition is facing. In order to gain the support of 50 percent and more of the voters, there has to be a candidate who is able to swing the opinion of the voters and gain their confidence. Unity is needed and so is a sense of responsibility for the whole. Undoubtedly, international support will come, but will it come in the right way and for the right candidate? It must, if it comes, contribute to unity and to a jointly-supported candidate. If it is divisive, which could be the case, it will be decisive for bringing about the defeat of the challenger(s) in the presidential election. It appears that a broad centrist coalition of four to five candidates will establish a common platform strategy. After the registration process, the coalition is likely to stay together and determine the most suitable candidate for change.

Conclusion

Given the lack of political stability that is expected to become dominant after the end of the Yeltsin era, Lukashenka and his goals for Russia, Belarus, and Ukraine should not be overlooked. The Lukashenka concept could infect other successor states of the Soviet Union, including Russia.

At present, there is hardly any Western industrial, economic, or financial activity in Belarus, although such activity would probably help Belarus perform in the Russian and Western markets by raising the level of infrastructure, labor, and manufacturing in Belarus. Nor is there much in the way of cultural or intellectual input. The only Western organization with access everywhere in Belarus is the OSCE, with the limited capacities of the AMG. The activity of Western embassies in Belarus is reduced to that of low-key dialogue and the management of official relations, with little engagement in any direct high-level political dialogue. Outside the country, Western dialogue is carried on primarily with opposition leaders and nongovernmental organizations. In the absence of any meaningful ties with Western markets, Belarus' economy is slipping more deeply into the Russian fold. Reunification with Russia may occur by default. Democratic forces in the country have little to offer to the population as a credible economic alternative. A challenge to Lukashenka could emerge in the form of a broadly based centrist coalition.

Belarus can survive in its present autocratic structure and with its command economy with Russia as virtually its sole important partner. Without the West, however, it cannot develop its industrial potential into a real competitive one. Belarus is in need of an open door policy toward both Moscow and the West. For its part, the West is in need of a new policy of "carrots and sticks," different from the currently prevailing one. Belarus is part of a region that should be seen as one area in which the struggle for democratization, market economies, and the rule of law requires active Western participation.

16

Sherman Garnett
The Belarusian Policy Dilemma[1]

The United States and its allies have a Belarusian policy dilemma, though they are largely unaware of it. This dilemma has three basic sources, the first of which defines the dilemma itself. Belarus is simply too strategically important a state, not because of what it has accomplished or might accomplish, but for where it sits physically on the map and the impact it could have on Europe. It stands at a vital crossroads where the post-Soviet space meets an expanding Europe. It shares this special geopolitical significance with other such crossroads between the former USSR and the outside world—Ukraine, parts of the Caucasus, Central Asia, and the Russian Far East.[2]

These places inevitably become a test of the political, economic, and geopolitical processes that are creating new regional configurations from parts of the former USSR and adjoining states. Belarus occupies crucial territory between Poland and Russia. Poland's eastern border is already the dividing line between the North Atlantic Treaty Organization and non-NATO Europe, and will likely become the dividing line between the European Union (EU) and non-member states in the region over the next several years. The character of the Polish-Belarusian border will determine in no small measure the relationship between this institutionalized Europe and the rest of the continent that stretches to the Urals and beyond. Geography alone

---

[1] This essay draws upon analysis and policy recommendations from Sherman Garnett and Robert Legvold, "Policy Options for Europe's 'Reluctant Participant,'" in *Belarus at the Crossroads*, ed. Sherman Garnett and Robert Legvold (Washington, DC, 2000).

[2] For an overview of the larger region of the western borderlands in which Belarus plays a crucial role, see Sherman Garnett, "Europe's Crossroads: Russia and the West in the New Borderlands," *The New Russian Foreign Policy*, ed. Michael Mandelbaum (New York, 1998), pp. 64–99.

makes it difficult to isolate Belarus or to see it somehow as a non-European country, even if it shows little inclination for democracy and free markets. Belarus will help define Europe–particularly the stability of institutionalized Europe's new borderlands–simply because of where it is and what it will become.

Two other sources of this policy dilemma are Belarus itself and the West. Belarus was taken by surprise by its newfound independence, and still is nostalgic for the halcyon Soviet era. It is a country not altogether comfortable with change. Its leaders, drawn largely from the old nomenklatura, watch warily for evidence of political or economic reform in Belarus. With the rise of its current president, Aliaksandr Lukashenka, their suspicions have turned to outright hostility. Lukashenka wants no part in the democratic and free market processes that define most of the rest of the continent. He seems in fact to revel in Belarusian exceptionalism, applying a firm hand at home and focusing foreign policy almost exclusively on Moscow and the world's outcasts.

The third factor contributing to this policy dilemma is the West, which sees Belarus as a stagnant place, one of the last bastions of the old ways, a kind of socialist theme park. The West has largely placed Belarus in the category of states to be neglected and isolated, unless some dramatic change in behavior is forthcoming from Minsk itself. Together with Belarusian exceptionalism, these two additional sources—Belarus and Lukashenka's leadership, and the perceptions of the West—serve to accentuate the policy dilemma.

This chapter will examine in detail the ways in which Belarus could play a significant—and largely destabilizing—role in the region, and in Europe as a whole. The seriousness of the Belarusian policy dilemma will emerge after the stakes themselves are made clearer. In addition, it will suggest policies that could create incentives for Belarus to end its exceptionalism. These policies would not fully overcome the impediment created by Lukashenka's desire to use any Western engagement to legitimate his own rule. However, they do take more seriously Belarus' potential destabilizing role than the current U.S. and Western policies do.

The Potential Stakes

There are at least two ways in which Belarus could become a destabilizing force in the region. The first is through integration with Russia, particularly through an integration that would feature significant melding with the Russian military and renewed forward deployment of Russian military assets in the country. This possibility has to be taken more seriously since Vladimir Putin has come to power in Russia. Boris Yeltsin encouraged a high level of pro-integration rhetoric, but neither he nor his key aides saw the issue as central to Russia's foreign policy agenda. Putin, however, is clearly aiming at a more hands-on approach, though he too faces both a wide range of potentially competitive priorities and a narrow resource base with which to pursue them. Over time, such an integrated military structure could significantly reverse the gains already made in the region and in Europe as a whole, gains toward smaller, more stable conventional and nuclear forces.

The second way Belarus could destabilize the region would arise from developments within Belarus alone. It depends upon President Lukashenka's regime experiencing a crisis. If the current regime in Belarus unraveled, it would export instabilities into neighboring Lithuania, Poland, Ukraine, and Russia. Russia, in particular, would feel compelled to intervene in the event of serious internal chaos in Belarus, but other neighbors could not remain indifferent. These states would fear the impact of political and economic chaos or the flow of short- and long-term migrants into their own countries.

Both of these potential paths for Belarus becoming a source of instability and concern need further consideration and analysis.

Russian-Belarusian Integration

Analysis of Belarus often begins and ends with the inevitability of Russian-Belarusian integration. Belarusian statehood and a sense of national identity among the Belarusian people are seen to be weak. General support for integration has been strong within both countries. Yet, the two leaders have vacillated between making a commitment to integration and signing broad, sweeping agreements, and alternately disagreeing on levels of incorporation and military involvement. This attempt at bilateral integration has been no more successful than numerous other attempts among the Commonwealth of Independent

States (CIS) or among subsets of the CIS. It is time to recognize the limits and constraints on this process. At least three deserve special mention.

The first constraint is structural. The two governments are "out of sync" politically and economically. Even after the August 1998 Russian financial collapse and the appointment as prime minister of Yevgeniy Primakov, a strong supporter of Russian-Belarusian integration, Russia remained a far more open society than Belarus. Putin may have narrowed the distance somewhat, given fears that he is moving toward greater control over media and regional political structures, but there is still a vast gulf between Putin's Russia and Lukashenka's Belarus. As proof of this continued gulf, the two sides have regularly clashed over human rights issues, especially over the shape of the Belarusian Constitution in 1996, the treatment of Russian ORT [Obshchestvennoe rossiiskoe televidenie] journalists in 1997, and the disappearance of a Russian cameraman in July 2000.

There is an additional structural problem, namely the political and economic shortcomings of both sides. Neither Russia nor Belarus has the political and economic advantages that fuel West European integration. Weak governments and contracting economies lack the means to carry out planned integration. They are a key source of the gap between paper commitments and implementation. Monetary union might provide Russia control over some important assets in Belarus, but such control would be a sustained burden on the still struggling Russian economy.

The second limitation lies in the profound differences among integration's supporters. Polls regularly show the idea of Russian-Belarusian integration as a popular one, but even its supporters bicker over the motivations and goals of the plan. Lukashenka has at times seen a bilateral union as his ticket to a larger political stage, whether directly or indirectly, as the co-leader of the union. Since the rise of Putin, however, the Russian stage must look less attractive, since Putin in large measure is trying to occupy the political space Lukashenka would covet. The most impoverished Belarusian people want the union to produce old-fashioned, Soviet-style social and economic benefits. Russian energy interests want concessions for the pipeline through Belarus, connecting to the European market. But perhaps the most important group of supporters—Russian nationalists, Communists, and those focusing on geopolitical advantages of the union—see integration as a means to traditional great power for

Russia. They care very little for Belarusian sovereignty or the preservation of Minsk's autonomy in a new commonwealth. Sergei Karaganov, a leading Russian foreign policy commentator, admitted that most Russians think of integration with Belarus as "absorption."[3] While former President Yeltsin himself had spoken on national television on the eve of signing the Union Charter in early 1997 of creating "a unified state," President Putin has refused to sign the accord that would create even a joint, defensive military force. Speaking to his parliament in February 1997, Lukashenka vowed Belarus would never become part of a merged state with Russia. In sum, the differences that divide the idea's supporters are serious and unlikely to be easily overcome.

The third constraint to Russian-Belarusian integration is the opposition in both countries. Though a group in political retreat, Russian reformers have little interest in adding the contracting Belarus economy to Russia's economic burdens. They see little appeal in adding a region to the political mix likely to support Communist and nationalist tendencies. In Belarus, the political and economic elites that support Lukashenka and benefit from sovereignty are jealous of their privileges. They want help from Russia, but they do not want stronger Russian political and economic groups to supplant them. The elite have insisted on equality in the union and the sovereignty of its two state members. Most Belarusians want to limit the military obligations such a union might impose. They do not want Belarusian youth to die in a future Chechnya or Tajikistan. Belarusian national and political opposition groups have openly rallied against the union, risking arrest and physical harm. It is also clear that the leaders of the two countries do not see eye to eye. Both Yeltsin and Putin have had frequent, public disagreements with Lukashenka over key issues.

These constraints, not the widespread enthusiasm for integration in both countries, will determine how far this process can go. It is unlikely ever to reach the union proclaimed by so many in both countries as their goal and reaffirmed in December 1998. Below the surface, the declared interests of the key actors are too divergent. Each day strengthens the sense of national consciousness among Belarusians–particularly among the young, the intellectuals, and those who hold the reigns of power and see the advantages that

---

[3] *RFE/RL Newsline* 4 February 1999.

independence has brought. Russia's continuing internal troubles make it reluctant to pay the price integration demands.

Though union is unlikely, the two countries are and will remain strong partners, with Belarus especially dependent on continuing Russian economic support in the form of direct subsidies, acceptance of barter, and toleration of late payments on energy and other debts. In private conversations, Belarusian officials, journalists, analysts, and even members of the opposition stress their country's continued economic dependence on Russia, as well as the strong and deep cultural, linguistic, and historical ties binding the two countries. Neighboring states and the West in general must begin their approach to Russian-Belarusian relations by recognizing this link, yet not exaggerating the ability of Belarus' ties with Russia to destroy Belarusian independence.

What matters to the West in the near term is the bilateral security relationship. This relationship has the potential to alter the emerging security environment in the region and in Europe as a whole. The two countries have made headway in linking their militaries. They see eye to eye on most developments in Europe, especially the undesirability of NATO's further enlargement and of NATO bombing in Kosovo. Voices in both Minsk and Moscow, including Lukashenka himself, have regularly characterized Russian-Belarusian security relations as providing the basis for an ambitious set of countermeasures to the emerging NATO and EU-based systems. At times, analysts, opposition figures, and Lukashenka himself have spoken of the potential for new Russian nuclear and conventional deployments.

Certainly, the rhetorical claims of Lukashenka and senior Russian officials often portray military cooperation as an ambitious and assertive counterweight to what they perceive as negative security developments in Europe. But, the actual pattern of cooperation is more limited and less ominous. Still it needs to be monitored over the long term.

The two sides have signed a series of military agreements that commit themselves to regular staff talks on key defense issues. The air defense systems of the two countries have conducted joint exercises and are becoming more integrated. Russia is training key elements of Belarus' future officer corps. Russia also appears to have substantial influence over the personnel policies of the Belarusian Ministry of Defense and other key power ministries. Belarusian air defense assets, early warning radar, and other military infrastructure are already a part of long-term Russian planning and joint use.

Belarus, however, still insists on keeping its forces at home. Lukashenka is as opposed to deploying his soldiers to the far-flung reaches of the old Soviet Union as any other leader in the CIS. He has insisted on keeping this long-standing restriction on out-of-country deployment as part of any future bilateral integration agreement. He made this plain as recently as August 1998, when he said he would not send Belarusian troops to defend CIS borders in Central Asia in the event of a Taliban attack. Lukashenka stressed that Belarus will defend CIS interests "in the western direction, from Kiev to Riga."[4] The staffing levels of Russian personnel at early warning and submarine communications facilities within Belarus are strictly capped and regulated by treaty. Cooperation among the border guards of the two countries has deepened, but Belarus has insisted that only its own forces guard the national borders with Ukraine, Poland, Lithuania, and Latvia.

Senior Russian and Belarusian officials have made it plain that they do not want to deploy Russian ground or nuclear forces into Belarus, though the idea regularly resurfaces as a trial balloon or rhetorical gesture from the Russian side and even occasionally from Lukashenka himself. The West has an obvious interest in encouraging a reciprocal pattern of restraint between NATO-Poland and Russia-Belarus. The Russian-Belarusian relationship itself has not crossed the line of conventional or nuclear deployments. In fact, there is a rough parallelism between NATO's restraint regarding Poland and Russia's regarding Belarus. Moreover, U.S. and NATO officials have a cadre of willing interlocutors in both Minsk and Moscow to help ensure that the pattern of restraint continues.

---

[4] Lukashenka made the remarks on Belarusian television, 23 August 1998. They were reported in *RFE/RL Newsline* on 25 August 1998. In a speech to the Belarusian Supreme Soviet in March 1996, Lukashenka said: "Not a single Belarusian citizen will ever be engaged in warfare outside our territory." See *FBIS Daily Report: Central Eurasia*, 27 March 1996 [originally carried on Minsk Radio, 27 March 1996]. Lukashenka softened this stance by joining a collective security council whose members include Armenia, Kazakhstan, Kyrgyzstan, Russia, and Tajikistan. Members agree to send military units only upon request and only to repulse military aggression, and to hold joint anti-terrorist operations and maneuvers. However, Lukashenka maintains that Belarusian troops will be kept out of "hotspots." Reported in *Belarus Today* 13 October 2000.

Belarusian Stability

This leaves the problem of Belarusian internal stability. Here conventional wisdom sees a country surprised by independence, ruled initially by a local nomenklatura unwilling to reform either political or economic life, and now by a would-be dictator whose base of support is an aging rural population. These judgments are not wrong. Lukashenka's regime is oppressive and likely to be long-lived, but it is not all there is to Belarusian politics.

First, Lukashenka has created a strongly authoritarian state on a weak base. The kind of political isolation he hopes to impose on his country cannot be sustained. He may remain an unchallenged political figure within Belarus, but his state has already been brought willy-nilly into a burgeoning East-West trade. A new gas pipeline is being built through the country. Lukashenka's internal security apparatus may well be strong enough to frustrate his own people, but it cannot shut out the rest of the world. On many key issues of human rights and democratic process, Russia stands closer to the outside world than to the Lukashenka regime, though the post-Yeltsin Russian leadership may well erode this imperfect Russian-Western convergence.

Second, despite the leadership's prideful claims of economic success, its resort to Soviet-style techniques—price controls, state-guided trade, heavily subsidized industry, exchange-rate manipulation, and the curtailing of imports—leads to a dead end. Growth has come at the expense of soaring inflation, controls have produced long lines and food shortages reminiscent of an earlier period, and the reorientation of trade toward Russia puts the Belarusian economy increasingly at the mercy of trends buffeting the Russian economy.[5] As became apparent during the Belarusian ruble crisis in March 1998, the Belarusian authorities can insulate their economy from the world outside only to a degree. Sooner or later—sooner if Russia cannot or will not provide the magic bouquet of subsidized energy prices, congenial markets, and currency support—they will come face to face with the unforgiving discipline of modern international economics.

Third, Belarus is changing. The current population is markedly old and rural, precisely the groups most nostalgic for Soviet times and

[5]   See Sam Glebov, "Where Has All the Food Gone?" *Minsk News* 12–18 May 1998, and Alexander Vasilevich, "IMF, Concerning Belarus's Economy," *Minsk News* 23 February–2 March 1998.

most responsive to Lukashenka's mix of populism and discipline. The active opposition in Minsk or in other large cities remains small, but tenacious. The future, however, could well belong to the young, especially as Lukashenka's economic illiteracy comes face to face with global economic realities. The elderly collective farm workers who embrace Lukashenka today are slowly being replaced by a generation that has seen Europe, if only through the mirror of Russian television. They know what they are missing. Lukashenka may well successfully delay this generation's encounter with greater political freedom, but he cannot afford to leave them totally outside Europe's prosperity. They want a better life than that offered by the discipline of the collective farm or state factory. They see themselves increasingly as Belarusian and citizens of the Belarusian state. It will take time, but Lukashenka and his successors will have to deal with their political and economic demands.

Finally, the ruling elite that support Lukashenka have interests of their own that they do not necessarily share with him. Many have gained their current prominence through long-standing positions in the nomenklatura and more recent fealty to Lukashenka himself. Yet, their long-term interests are not necessarily those of their president. The current generation of Belarusian business and political leaders does not want competition from anywhere, particularly from the new Russian business and political leadership. This difference among the Belarusian leadership is a serious chink in Lukashenka's armor, certainly more serious in the short run than that posed by the opposition in the streets.

Despite this list, the basic fact is that Lukashenka dominates both internal and foreign policy. His figure looms large indeed over every aspect of current political life. No real political opposition has developed that could openly defeat him. Beneath the inflated results of his corrupt referenda lies a solid political majority, the same majority that brought him to power in a fair election in 1994. Any policy that seeks to engage this troubled nation will have to reckon with a politically strong and formidable president. It is wrong to underestimate him or to dismiss his odd reports. They do not sound so odd inside Belarus, especially among Lukashenka's core supporters who want order, state intervention, and the benefits of the old system.

A Preference for Inclusion

The dark and backward side of Belarusian internal and foreign policies are obvious, but the nation and its people are more than the current regime imagines or allows. Belarus' neighbors, the U.S., Western Europe, and Belarus itself need to imagine policies that do not ignore or excuse the current stagnation and repression, but are not stymied by them either. In particular, these policies need to be guided by a preference for inclusion of Belarus within Europe as a whole, though this inclusion must have modest goals in the beginning and long-term staying power to overcome Lukashenka's inclination to oppose it or use it to strengthen his own legitimacy.

Such a strategy cannot give Lukashenka a free pass. It will continually be challenged by the tension between the near-term desire to keep him at arms length and the long-term danger of an isolated and unstable Belarus. This tension is inherent in the current situation. Dealing with it is preferable to ignoring it or pretending that it does not exist. The recommendations below do not quarrel with the wisdom of refusing direct political support to the Lukashenka regime and of pressing for a dialogue between the regime and its opposition. However, they stress no less the need to remain involved in the country, to foster a serious exchange of views with Belarusian leaders, particularly on issues of European security, and to look for the broadest possible consensus among Belarus' neighbors in formulating a productive policy toward the country.

End Belarusian Security Isolation

Belarus is at a crucial turning point in defining its long-term security orientation. Given the still uncertain nature of the Russian-Belarusian union and the West's interest in ensuring that any future bilateral relationship takes a course conducive to stability in the region, a policy of isolating Belarus from the larger security environment in Europe is counterproductive. Moreover, it cannot be in the interest of either the U.S. or Europe to see Belarus rally to the Irans, Syrias, Libyas, and Cubas of the world, as Lukashenka has increasingly done. Lukashenka has strengthened ties with Libya by the appointment of an ambassador and a proposed two-day visit; he hopes to set up a Joint Commission on Economic, Trade, Scientific and Technical Cooperation, all in the space of one year (2000). The more he is reviled by the Western democracies, the more he revels in the pomp and praise he receives from these states. Lukashenka treats acceptance of this sort as proof that his Western critics, not Belarus, stand alone. The danger is not merely that he will come to see this set of states as his country's natural friends, but that he will sanction a broadening military cooperation with them. Thus, a secondary and indirect reason for pursuing an earnest security dialogue with Belarus is to give its leadership a stake in playing by the rules that regulate the transfer of military technology to states seen by the West as potential troublemakers.

Lukashenka may spurn a serious discussion of security issues or make himself a dubious interlocutor on most subjects, but this scarcely justifies isolating the Belarusian military, particularly at a time when it is formulating the terms of a long-term security relationship with Russia. On this crucial question, the U.S. and the major European powers should think twice before forfeiting their influence. The range of bilateral and NATO-sponsored military-to-military programs, coupled with NATO's announced posture of military restraint in Poland, provides a sound basis for a modest yet sustained security dialogue with Belarus. Belarusian diplomats discovered rather late that they too would like a special agreement with NATO. Pursuing such an agreement is in Western interests, though celebrating its completion by a summit—as long as the politics of Belarus remains repressive—is not.

The West's security interest in Belarus did not end when the last nuclear weapon left in November 1996. Significant portions of the old Soviet military industrial complex remain in Belarus. Economic decline has inspired a series of arms sales or attempted sales to Sudan, Yemen, Iran, Iraq, China, and Vietnam. The temptation for a rogue regime to export these and other important technologies will remain. Shutting off discussion, technical advice, and material assistance on export controls makes little sense.

The dialogue between the Belarusian and Western militaries must be considerably strengthened. These programs need not be thought of as conferring legitimacy on Lukashenka. While various police and intelligence agencies are part of his program to suppress the population, the Belarusian military to date is not. Efforts to bring the emerging Belarusian military leadership into contact with normal Western practices is especially important at a time when the only voice on security matters many hear are Lukashenka's or that of their Russian counterparts.

Speaking face to face with Belarusian military and defense officials is a matter of common sense. Even if high level contacts are to remain limited, lower level ones should continue. The visits of deputy assistant secretaries of state or defense to Minsk are not signs of support for the regime. Yet, they matter profoundly for maintaining normal dialogue with an emerging military and foreign policy leadership and for accurately gauging conditions in the country. Small programs aimed at the aftereffects of denuclearization or securing and disarming neglected stockpiles of Soviet conventional munitions will have a wider impact on both the military and the population at large.

Encourage Regional Initiatives with Belarus

Belarus is too important to isolate and engagement must begin in the neighborhood. The conclusion of a Belarusian-Ukrainian border treaty in 1997 was a positive start. Lithuania, too, has taken a positive step in inviting Belarusian representation to the Vilnius meeting of East European states in 1997. Warsaw will continue its policy towards Belarus. Polish Foreign Ministry Spokesman Pawel Dobrowolski has stated, "[O]n the one hand, we criticize President Lukashenka's policy and violations of the law committed by him, but on the other, we will not break relations with Belarus. Now, we will maintain them more on a social than a political level."[6] Yet, these efforts must be sustained. There is no greater challenge to the stability of Poland's eastern border than Belarus. The whole question of Polish-Belarusian relations is a historically sensitive one, but nothing like that Poland has already overcome with Ukraine.

Efforts designed to strengthen regional cooperation, such as the Baltic Sea Council or ongoing programs between Poland and Ukraine, should invite positive contributions from Belarus. Working-level delegations and observers should be invited to meetings. Belarusian cooperation should be actively sought on issues such as regional crime, migration, and drug trafficking. There must be NATO and European support for this kind of engagement. Often, in the past several years, Polish officials were left to wonder whether dynamic eastern policy initiatives helped or hindered their country's chances for membership in Western institutions. These institutions should send a strong signal that such initiatives are encouraged.

---

[6]   Dobrowolski was quoted in *RFE/RL Newsline* 21 July 1999.

Engage Russia

Helping to get Belarus back on track should be a broad-based effort that brings together the U.S., Western Europe, Russia, and Belarus' neighbors. Precedents for such a cooperative effort already exist in the negotiating structures that produced the soft landings negotiated on Baltic troop withdrawal and Ukrainian denuclearization. These structures brought together the states of the region, Russia, and the outside world for a common purpose. The structures themselves did not eliminate deep disagreements often over basic issues. They did, however, bring together the key players at a single table.

Russia is just such a key player. It is the driving force in creating a bilateral military and security relationship with Minsk, though this issue seems largely ignored by NATO countries in their bilateral and multilateral discussions with Russia on security matters. There are no fora in which discussions could take place with Belarus on this issue. Russia is also vitally concerned about Belarusian stability, as evidenced by its intervention—though to little avail—in Belarus' November 1996 constitutional crisis. At various times, Russian representatives have pushed Lukashenka to hold early parliamentary and presidential elections, a goal sought by the Western community, and the Russian foreign minister supposedly played a key role in persuading the Belarusians to accept the establishment in Minsk of the Organization for Security and Cooperation in Europe (OSCE) monitoring group in early 1998. Though many in Russia want nothing to do with encouraging reforms in Belarus, and define Russian interests in purely geopolitical terms, others see the importance of change there. A reforming Belarus automatically makes Russian-Belarusian integration more open to European influence.

Any effort with Russia requires Western countries to acknowledge the strategic link between Minsk and Moscow. It requires including a Russia that is unlikely to see eye-to-eye with the West on many key issues. However, it will also require both Russia and Belarus to face certain facts. In particular, it would force both parties to admit that integration is unlikely to resolve the problems faced by both countries. The two nations are not—nor can they be—building an eastern version of the European Union. Russia and Belarus can derive the maximum benefits both seek from close ties that fall well short of integration. These ties would be nothing to fear for Belarus' neighbors or Europe as a whole, provided they do not lead to the redeployment of Russian nuclear or combat forces in Belarus. Both sides have to work hard to see that the restraint on military deployments in the region continues.

The West needs to understand that, along with continued fragmentation and the failure of the Commonwealth of Independent States as a whole, a variety of forms of cooperation are likely to emerge in the former USSR. Western policy must reflect an understanding of the trends and distinguish the good from the bad. The West also has to think about policies that increase the transparency and interaction between both halves of Europe. The last thing needed is the construction of a new wall in Europe.

Create Incentives in Favor of Europe

The free flow of people and goods between Belarus and the outside world needs encouragement. The current obstacle is, of course, Lukashenka himself. In the long run, the problem will also be complicated by EU enlargement. Poland is already under pressure by its future partners to put in place greater restrictions on its eastern borders.

The long-term enlargement of Europe's great institutions will create dilemmas for Belarus and its neighbors. NATO has succeeded in defusing the most obvious security tensions arising from enlargement. Its voluntary military restraint on the deployment of nuclear weapons and large-scale conventional forces in Poland and the creation of a special forum with Russia appear to have called forth in turn a restraint from Belarus and Russia. Time is needed for both sides to live with the new arrangement.

The European Union must devise the economic and political equivalent of this NATO policy, keeping the border between EU and non-EU countries in the region as soft as possible. This is a tall order, because Belarus (and other states, like Ukraine) must exercise sufficient control on its side of the border to create EU confidence in a relaxed regime. Yet, without efforts to think through the parameters for future borders in this region from the European Union itself, there is the very real likelihood that the region will be redivided into haves and have-nots. Such a division would have deep and enduring security consequences, helping to underscore the notion that a stable, secure, and prosperous Europe is coterminous with membership in NATO and the European Union.

Lend Support for an Internal Trigger for Reform

Obviously, these policies need some kind of trigger within Belarus. Even with the best of intentions on the part of the outside world in general and Belarus' neighbors in particular, all that has been suggested above to stimulate a more productive relationship with Minsk stands or falls on whether Belarus begins to move internally away from the isolation the current regime has imposed upon the country. Belarus cannot remain a state bent on building "socialism in one country" and still be a full participant in Europe. It is not possible in this Europe. The fate of such a political strategy is not to occupy center stage in Europe, as the ominous other, but to be marginalized, with harmful consequences for Belarus and for Europe as a whole.

The conditions for such a trigger are, in part, already present. Economic stagnation, generational change, the limits of what Russia can provide, the example of markets working in Poland and Russia, and fissures within the leadership itself are already constraining Lukashenka's political options. Western policies designed to deny Lukashenka legitimacy and recognition have had an impact, though a limited one. The October 2000 election in Belarus is but the most recent example of Lukashenka turning a deaf ear to such efforts, yet the European Union and OSCE must continue to try to mediate between Lukashenka and the opposition. The West has to be a voice for human rights, pluralism, and democratic reform. Much more thought needs to be given to ways in which Russia could be included as an additional lever for change within Belarus.

No one can or should expect Lukashenka's conversion to Western-style political and economic reform, for he currently has genuine support among the broad populace. Yet, while he personally shares few of the West's core values, other elements in society do understand and respect the advantages of democratic practice, and still others, less preoccupied with political principles, recognize the importance of integrating Belarus into the larger European economic setting. The outside world can and should have a serious conversation with these groups. Meanwhile, Belarus' neighbors, the U.S., and the West Europeans should continue to press for a state that operates within the law and heeds the voice of a democratic opposition. They should continue to back the efforts of those who want to promote economic and political reform. But the outside world should also invest more in long-term changes that no dictator can control. These investments should aim at supporting core elements of a still weak civil society. Support for the everyday activities of labor, religious, and social organizations—without a direct link to today's demonstration or tomorrow's election—are important. Improving the basic health and education infrastructures of Belarus should also be a goal.

Outside help can only provide a small fraction of what Belarus itself needs, but scholarships, exchanges, training, and material assistance to target institutions would demonstrate the outside world's continued concern about the country and its people. Lukashenka will obviously oppose many of these programs. He will try to use others to end the isolation imposed upon him. Yet, his resistance need not be the last word, unless the prevailing indifference of the major Western powers, in effect, makes it so. Lukashenka would find it difficult to oppose a concerted and coordinated external effort to help Belarus and its people, particularly as the shortcomings of the Belarusian economy become more apparent.

Outside observers need to remember not only Belarus' importance to the long-term health and stability of the region and Europe as a whole. They also need to remember that allies within the country are seeking a change of orientation. This change would imply neither simply favoring Europe nor rejecting Russia. It would accord with Belarus' deepest interests, creating more leverage for constructing a Russian-Belarusian relationship open to Europe and one more in keeping with the needs of Belarus itself. It would appeal to the rising generation, which is looking for something beyond the conservatism of the collective farm.

Conclusion

None of the above can ignore the very real obstacles that keep Belarus a reluctant participant in Europe. Lukashenka is a comparatively young man, seemingly in firm control of his country, who believes that his and his country's future lies to the east. The slow progress made by Belarus has justified its isolation in the minds of many Western policymakers. Some of these same policymakers assume that Belarus is part of Russia's geopolitical space and thus is Russia's problem.

Yet, such conclusions ignore the structure of international relations in the region. This structure is "multipolar," though not in the ideological sense Primakov has used the term. The collapse of the old order in this part of Europe—Russia's weakening and transformation, the creation of new states, and the increased activity of the outside world—creates a new pattern of diplomacy. Small- and medium-sized states have the "breathing space" to make their weight felt. Long-term stability in the region no longer depends solely on Moscow or Brussels, but on the interaction of these capitals with Warsaw, Kyiv, Stockholm, Vilnius, Minsk, and others.

The defection of Belarus from the region, either by direct challenge to the emerging order or by its isolation from it, would affect the stability of its neighbors and of Europe as a whole. What happens in Belarus is not just a curious sideshow or a socialist holdover. Contrary to the expectations of many Western observers and policymakers, the stakes in Belarus are high. Now is the time for those who understand to act.

17

Elaine M. Conkievich
The NGO Approach: Possibilities for Positive Engagement in Belarus

The information coming out of Belarus about conditions there—political, economic, and otherwise—continues to be discouraging, with little or no relief in sight. Belarus is not following the path of transition of its neighbors, or even of other former Soviet republics. For those working on Belarus, the question inevitably arises as to how to best become involved in Belarus to promote democratic change. Which inroads will reap positive results? This chapter makes the case for involvement in Belarus through domestic nongovernmental organizations (NGOs). It addresses how to support NGOs, what can be expected by working through them, what their impact on the country might realistically be, and gives concrete examples of NGOs' capabilities and results that have already been achieved.[1] Engagement through NGOs is an extremely difficult path, but the most effective one in light of the current political and economic situation in the country.

Brief History of NGOs in Belarus

In the early 1980s, informal student movements formed in Belarus, primarily to promote cultural objectives. With the institution of the

---

[1]   For the purposes of this paper, when specific NGOs are mentioned, it is solely with the objective of providing examples to illustrate the points made. It in no way implies that they are the only NGOs worth mentioning.

policy of perestroika, NGOs in Belarus grew in number and in their activity. They took the place of the student groups, but still focused primarily on cultural, educational, or ecological issues. In the late 1980s, however, with the revelation of the damage caused by the Chernobyl nuclear disaster and the uncovering of the Kurapaty killings of 1937, more people were drawn to public actions and organizations. In 1989, the Belarusian Popular Front (BPF), the first political organization in the country to oppose communism, was founded.

With independence in 1991, the actual establishment of a "third sector" in Belarus began, and nongovernmental organizations became legally registered entities. The goals of NGOs evolved to include the promotion of democracy, a market economy, and the rule of law. With the political events of 1996, particularly the highly questionable referendum in November, NGOs in Belarus became even more involved in political affairs as the legitimacy of their ruling government came into question. These developments led to the establishment, in early 1997, of the Assembly of Belarusian Pro-Democratic Nongovernmental Organizations, an umbrella organization that serves as a focal point for NGOs across the country and seeks to contribute to the democratic transformation of Belarus.[2]

Legislation Regulating NGOs

For the purposes of developing legislation to govern them, NGOs in Belarus come under the broad term "public associations." The 1994 law (with amendments in 1995), "On Public Associations,"[3] regulates the existence of NGOs and other public groups, such as political parties and trade unions.

In order to understand better the situation of NGOs in Belarus, it is useful to take a closer look at the law governing their existence. The purpose is not to analyze the law in depth, but rather to note some

---

[2] Vladimir Rovda, "Annual Report of the Executive Bureau," *Analytical Bulletin* (Executive Bureau of the Assembly of Belarusian Pro-Democratic NGOs) 2 (1998): 4–6.

[3] "On Public Associations," Law of the Republic of Belarus of 4 October 1994, No. 3254-XII (with an addition made by the Law of the Republic of Belarus of 31 January 1995, No. 3560-XII). (Unofficial translation.)

parts of the law that make the existence and functioning of NGOs in Belarus difficult, thus complicating attempts by outsiders to engage in Belarusian affairs through them.

The law "On Public Associations" is vague. In Article 2, citizens are given "the right to establish, upon their initiative, public associations and to join existing public associations." Article 3 places the only limitation on the establishment of a public association: an association is not allowed if its activities are deemed to involve the "overthrow or violently change [in] the constitutional social order, breach the unity and security of the state, propagandizing war, violence, kindling of national, religious and racial enmity." However, according to Article 5:

> The state shall ensure preservation and protection of the rights and legal interests of public associations. Interference of state bodies and officials into the operation of public associations, as well as interference of public associations into the operation of state bodies and officials, shall not be allowed, except in cases envisaged by the legislation of the Republic of Belarus.

Unfortunately, few state bodies and officials abide by this article. The state does not protect the interests of NGOs and, indeed, interferes in their activities in unacceptable ways, even if legislation seemingly is used at times to justify this interference.

Article 13 of the law gives the Ministry of Justice responsibility for registering international and republic-wide public associations. Local groups register with the department of justice of the executive committee of the regional and Minsk city councils. The decision on accepting a group's registration is to be taken within one month from the application's date of submission. In early 1999, around 2,200 associations were registered with the Ministry of Justice in Belarus. It is unclear how many of those were strictly NGOs—as opposed to hobby or sport clubs, and the like—though NGOs may have numbered half or more of the total registered associations.

Chapter 4 of the law "On Public Associations" is devoted to the "control of the activities of public associations in accordance with legislation and charter: responsibility and breaching of legislation." Article 25 of this chapter gives the procurator general control over the activities of associations with regard to ensuring compliance with the

Constitution and legislation of Belarus. This article also states that the bodies responsible for registering associations are also responsible for ensuring that they operate according to their charters. The article gives officials from the bodies registering associations "the right to take part, within their competence, in all events held by these associations, to know their documents and decisions, to request and receive information on questions of charter activities of the public association." This particular part of the article is rather troubling, as it leaves wide open the possibility of harassment in the form of controls.

The legal control of the activities of Belarusian NGOs takes place in three forms. First, their compliance with the Constitution of Belarus and Belarusian legislation is supervised by the procurator general. The 1993 law "On Prosecution of the Republic of Belarus" gives the procurator general wide powers to search, seize materials, and punish violators without due process. Second, the Ministry of Justice, or the bodies under the ministry responsible for registration, controls whether NGOs' activities are in compliance with their charters in accordance with Article 13 of the law "On Public Associations." Third, the State Revenue Service controls the financial activities of NGOs, again having broad powers to search, seize materials, and levy duties and taxes at will.[4]

Overall, the law "On Public Associations," while a good initial attempt to legislate for the public sector, is insufficient for governing NGOs in the long run. The legislation must be revised to improve and clarify registration procedures. Most importantly, the provisions on the so-called "control" of activities must be rewritten into basic principles to guide the legal functioning of the organizations and not to restrict their activities. If such amendments, at a minimum, are not made, then the establishment and functioning of the third sector will continue to be greatly hindered.[5]

---

[4] Olga Chadeeva, "Gosudarstvennyi kontrol' za deiatelnost'iu obshchestvennikh ob"edinenii," *Belorusskaia delovaia gazeta* 18 June 1998: 16.

[5] Elena Tonkacheva, "Sostoianie zakonodatel'stva o nekommercheskikh organizatsiiakh v Respublike Belarus,'" *Belorusskaia delovaia gazeta* 18 June 1998: 11.

Difficulties Facing NGOs

With the adoption of the law in 1994 and its subsequent amendment in 1995, all registered NGOs in Belarus were required to re-register. NGOs had until 1 July 1995 to re-register, otherwise they would be stricken from the register and could obtain registration later only as a new organization. NGOs faced great difficulty during and following the re-registration process. The registration procedure was long and complicated, with an extensive list of required documents to be submitted with the application. When (and if) an NGO managed to register, its activities were usually closely monitored. If it was deemed to be anti-state, the organization was subjected to various forms of harassment. Such monitoring and harassment continue today.

One of the major threats to the existence of NGOs in Belarus is administrative harassment in the form of denial of, or excessive delay in, registration, sudden and unexplained rent increases, tax audits, and denial of facilities for functions or permits for public meetings and demonstrations. The inability to acquire permits for public meetings and demonstrations forces NGOs to pursue their objectives in a way viewed as illegal by authorities. This, in turn, gets their leaders and/or adherents arrested on administrative charges of participating in an unsanctioned meeting, which may result in 3–15 days of detention, a hefty fine, or worse. On occasion, authorities mete out physical abuse as a deterrent or punishment.

These forms of harassment suggest that state authorities view NGOs not as partners, but as opponents at best, and "anti-state" at worst. To counter such anti-state activities, some "government" NGOs have been created, the so-called GONGOs. These organizations are given extensive official support, including financial, in order to give an impression of the existence of functioning, widely supported, non-harassed NGOs.

As if the first re-registration was not enough, a new re-registration was ordered by Presidential Decree No. 2, "On Some Measures on Regulation of Activity of Political Parties, Trade Unions and Other Public Associations," dated 26 January 1999. The decree was "for the purpose of regulation of activity . . . and for improvement of control over it." The re-registration period occurred between 1 February and 1 August 1999, after which any association that had not re-registered was to terminate its activity and liquidate itself. The Republican Commission on Registration, set up solely for this purpose, handled the re-registration. The Commission was made up of 12 individuals representing various ministries, the administration, state committees, and the like. That is to say, no nongovernmental individuals were members of the Commission.[6]

The decree was accompanied by the "Regulation on State Registration (Re-Registration) of Political Parties, Trade Unions and Other Public Associations," which laid out grueling procedures that NGOs (among other groups) were required to follow in order to register or, in this case, to re-register. Included was a long list of specific documents required for submission, such as:

- the graphic representation of the organizational structures of the association, specifying their location;
- the confirmation of the availability of the legal address of the association;
- a detailed description of the symbolism of the association, including the conclusion of the State Committee on Archives and Record Keeping for each type and the image of this symbolism in four copies, sized 10 x 10 cm, as well as the respective decisions of authorized bodies on the approval of the symbolism;
- a certificate of the inspection of the State Tax Committee [to prove that the association owed no back taxes].[7]

Once the complete package of materials was submitted to the registration body, it was forwarded to the Republican Commission, "which shall, within a 5-day period from the time of receipt of the materials, give a conclusion on the possibility of registration (re-registration) of the association and shall forward it to the registration body." This body then reached a final decision based on the Com-

---

[6] *Decree of the President of the Republic of Belarus, No. 2*, Minsk, 26 January 1999: pts 1–3. (Unofficial translation.)

[7] *Regulation on State Registration (Re-Registration) of Political Parties, Trade Unions, and Other Public Associations*, Approved by Decree No. 2 of the President of the Republic of Belarus of 26 January 1999, §4. (Unofficial translation.)

mission's recommendation.[8] Reasons for denial ranged from violation of procedures, noncompliance with the law, failure to submit all documents, and, "if within one year before the re-registration, the registration or another state body has indicated to it in writing and within its competence a violation of the Charter of the association or of the current legislation." The regulation did provide an appeals process in the courts.[9] In general, the re-registration requirement has been viewed as a form of harassment. The official position of Belarusian authorities has been that the re-registration was called to "review" all associations with the intent of not re-registering the ones involved in "illegal activities." However, a more credible approach would have been to review only those organizations in question and not to force all organizations to undergo the rigorous re-registration process.

Of the roughly 2,200 public associations registered pre-1999, some 1,500 applied for re-registration, of which some 1,300 were actually registered. Around 200 were denied registration. However, even with 1,300 registered public associations, only some of which are NGOs, a slightly false picture is painted of the strength of the third sector in Belarus. The actual number of well-organized and well-functioning NGOs in the country is far fewer.

The government's issuance of written "indications" or warnings caused great concern during the re-registration of NGOs. In the first three months of 1999, over 30 warnings were issued, mostly connected with NGO activities during the presidential elections, which the Supreme Soviet of the 13th session had called for on 16 May 1999. Warnings were issued not only for NGOs' involvement in electoral activities but also, for example, for their work in human rights. After receiving several warnings, a NGO could be shut down.

Technically, NGOs have no right to be directly involved in political activities, including the election process. In addition, NGOs have no right of legislative initiative.[10] These two factors combined reduce the impact that NGOs can have on authorities. NGOs try to remain apolitical, but with the current situation in Belarus, this is

---

8   "Regulation on State Registration," §7.

9   "Regulation on State Registration," §11; §16.

10   Tonkacheva, "Sostoianie zakonodatel'stva," p. 11.

impossible for some. Despite the restrictions, numerous NGOs are deeply involved in political matters, especially electoral ones, and are making their voice heard inside and outside of the country. Very often, the state treats all NGOs as political entities, because it fails to make a distinction between them based on their activities. Any entities striving for change, whether they are NGOs or trade unions, are labeled as political.

Many NGOs have difficulty in their relations with local authorities, while others have no relations with local authorities at all. In effect, NGOs in Belarus have no significant impact on local governments. This can be explained by the system of vertical power in which local governments are responsible to higher authorities, and those authorities dictate, albeit not publicly, when the work of NGOs goes against the state interests and therefore must be obstructed. However, in some parts of the country, local authorities silently allow NGOs to exist, and it is rather the central authorities in Minsk who are in charge of crackdowns when they occur.

Besides the official harassment, whether open or subversive, other difficulties face NGOs in Belarus, such as lack of financial means to survive, let alone to pursue projects. Because of the poor and continually declining economic situation in Belarus, there is no source of domestic funding for NGOs. The development of NGOs and their work is also hampered by a lack of information on fund-raising, a lack of information for purposes of networking, and a lack of understanding of what a NGO really is. Further, many NGOs have limited knowledge and experience of the legal situation in which they operate, which sometimes creates obstacles by itself.

The internal functioning of NGOs also presents problems. Some NGOs are run as the country is run—that is, by one dominating figure.[11] This results in a one-sided pursuit of ideals and fails to lend itself to the democratic functioning of the organization. But, with outside training and assistance to a broader number of individuals in NGOs, this problem can be addressed.

Another hindrance is competition and suspicion among NGOs

---

[11]   Vladimir Rovda and Victor Chernov, "The Third Sector of Belarus from a Sociological Perspective," *Analytical Bulletin No. 1: The Executive Bureau of the Assembly of Belarusian Pro-Democratic NGOs* (1998): 18–19.

pursuing similar goals. The inability of some NGOs to build their work in concert with other organizations, in some areas, has been damaging. Nevertheless, NGOs in Belarus are trying to associate among themselves by creating a flat, web-like structure across the country, reaching even small towns and villages. This network will function to coordinate NGOs and help them support one another. For example, one project, partially funded by the Danish Ministry of Foreign Affairs, sought to network all NGOs in Belarus by the end of 1999.

It is important for outside donors to learn the NGO terrain in Belarus better in order to give their support only to genuine nongovernmental organizations. Equally important is the need for individuals working in NGOs to develop communication skills. This means developing a working knowledge of other languages, English in particular, and computer skills. Basic technology skills are an essential prerequisite to effective work. However, without equipment (computers, internet access, copy machines, fax machines, etc.), NGOs will be unable to receive and process information, thus their capacity to have a wide impact will be limited.

Perhaps the greatest obstacle facing NGOs in Belarus is the lack of a nurturing climate in the country for their development. In general, the concept of a NGO and its work is foreign to most people. Without an understanding of the role and purposes of NGOs, both everyday citizens and individuals in positions of power are unlikely to support their work. A shift of mentality must occur for NGOs to become sustainable. The extreme of this lack of understanding is intolerance expressed in threats and hostile acts towards individuals associated with NGOs, a serious hindrance to the functioning of NGOs. Those NGOs that pose no threat to the state, of course, rarely suffer from such difficulties.

Situation of NGOs in the Regions

According to 1999 statistics compiled by United Way-Belarus, roughly 43 percent of the NGOs active in Belarus are located in regions outside of the city of Minsk. This percentage is high enough to suggest that NGOs can make a significant impact in small towns and villages. The activities of these NGOs are just as wide ranging as those of NGOs located in Minsk. However, as stated above, the population's lack of knowledge and understanding about the purposes and work of NGOs impedes their activities and effectiveness.

Each oblast has different centers of coordination for NGOs and there is a lot of competition among these structures. One example of a coordination center is the NGO resource center in each oblast capital. The existence of these resource centers, which promote the work of local NGOs, is a positive development. The resource centers are involved in distributing information, producing bulletins, giving advice, holding roundtables on NGO issues, and developing their own assemblies to better coordinate the work of NGOs in their area. Beyond the oblast capitals, the development of NGOs in the countryside is also encouraging. Many of the members of NGOs in these regions are younger people with an academic background, who are very keen to contribute to the development of civil society. This is a very positive trend, one that will have a significant impact on the future of NGOs in Belarus.

NGOs in the outlying regions often claim to be more effective than groups in Minsk. Because they are not as involved in the politics of the regime being played out in Minsk, there is more time to attend directly to third-sector issues and the direct needs of society. Further, the potential for influence seems greater in the regions, with less competition and in-fighting among NGOs. The success of NGOs in the regions recommends a strategy of focusing greater attention upon them to build democracy in regional structures, and later working toward the urban centers.

Despite NGO successes in the regions, the picture is not all rosy. Individuals working in the NGO sphere throughout Belarus need to be politically sensitized. NGOs often make statements, publish materials, or write articles for the "opposition" press that do not present their information well. At times, they are prone to blowing things out of proportion, distorting facts, and giving information out of context, sometimes unknowingly, which ultimately damages their reputation, not only with the state but also with international interlocutors. NGOs have to learn how to make critical, yet accurate, statements and reports in order to lend more credibility to their message.

Assistance to NGOs

Structures do exist to help NGOs overcome official harassment and difficulties. One such structure is the Assembly of Belarusian Pro-Democratic Nongovernmental Organizations (NGO Assembly). The Assembly held its first congress in February 1997, with around 250 NGOs participating. The second congress was held in November 1998, with some 520 NGOs participating. The congress held in December 2000 hosted 460 NGOs.

The congress is an opportunity for Belarusian NGOs to gather and discuss pressing problems and to adopt resolutions professing their objectives. For example, the 1998 congress passed resolutions on the independence of Belarus, the civic sector, the legal and human rights situation, the mass media, and opposition to fascism in Belarus, in addition to routine matters of organization and strategy.[12] The NGO Assembly can assist in coordinating and networking NGOs across the country. Although the Assembly is open to the press, embassies, and international organizations, there still is a lack of connection between the Assembly and the countries and other donors that might be able to provide assistance.

For its day-to-day functioning, the NGO Assembly has organized a working group, which discusses issues and exchanges information, and an executive bureau, which consults and coordinates. The Assembly coordinates with the regional NGO resource centers, which are located in the major cities of the oblasts. The Assembly also works with non-registered groups that ascribe to its goals and objectives. Recently, however, internal quarreling has caused some NGOs to disassociate from the Assembly.

Certain NGOs are geared specifically to provide practical assistance to other NGOs. One organization worth special mention is United Way-Belarus, which is primarily active in NGO development. It assists NGOs in the government registration process, for example, by providing legal advice. After registration, it contributes to their further development by offering the resources of its Minsk office, including the library, an NGO database, internet connection, and

---

[12]   The texts of these resolutions can be found in *Analytical Bulletin No. 2: The Executive Bureau of the Assembly of Belarusian Pro-Democratic NGOs* (1998).

training opportunities. United Way also gathers statistical information on a number of Belarusian NGOs, including type and geographical distribution, and a directory, including contact information for each organization.

Another local organization, the Support Center for Associations and Foundations (SCAF), maintains a library solely devoted to funding opportunities and agencies. SCAF advises NGOs on places to seek funding, assists in filling out grant applications, and prints a regular newsletter with grant information and other related articles.

As for international assistance, the local office of the United Nations Development Programme (UNDP) assists Belarusian NGOs by coordinating programs among NGOs and holding meetings for NGOs working primarily in the humanitarian sector. In addition, UNDP holds meetings among donor agencies to share information on proposed projects and to coordinate activities in order to avoid overlaps and fill in gaps where they exist.

The United States Agency for International Development (USAID), through the local office of the United States Information Service (USIS), has also been a large supporter of democratic NGOs in Belarus. USAID, in cooperation with the Counterpart Consortium, holds roundtables for the NGO resource centers, with discussion focusing on such topics as networking, seminars, and common problems. In addition, USAID offers a small-grants program, which gives special support for independent media activities.

Since the Advisory and Monitoring Group (AMG) of the Organization for Security and Cooperation in Europe (OSCE) was established in Belarus in early 1998, it has maintained contacts with numerous and varied NGOs. The AMG cooperates particularly closely with NGOs working in the areas of politics, human rights, democratic development, and humanitarian and social issues. For example, the AMG has regular contact with the Belarusian Helsinki Committee and the L. Sapieha Foundation in Minsk and in the regions, two of the more prominent and active organizations in the country. In Minsk, the AMG also works with Charter 97, Spring 96, the Euro-Atlantic Association, the PEN Center, and the Belarusian Association of Journalists. It also maintains good contacts in the oblasts with, for example, the Ecology Union in Vitebsk, and the Society for Human Rights and the Association of Women Lawyers, both in Brest.

Concrete Examples of the Usefulness of Engagement

As stated above, the Belarusian Assembly of Pro-Democratic NGOs has played an important role in the development of the third sector in Belarus. In the opinion of the Assembly, they are "most successful in conducting informational exchange and providing various assistance to Belarusian NGOs." To name just a few examples of its activities, the Assembly publishes an analytical bulletin on a regular basis, organizes roundtables to study the experiences of NGOs in the regions, publishes informational materials that help with the registration process, and trains regional NGOs in fundraising.[13] The Assembly has greatly contributed to the development of NGOs in Belarus, despite its meager office space and minimal funds. If the Assembly had more sophisticated computer and office equipment, more space, and more funds, particularly for printing materials and holding seminars, their impact on NGOs in Belarus would be much greater.

Another organization worth mentioning is Legal Assistance to the Population. This NGO is particularly involved in rendering legal assistance to poor people, whose interests it represents in court. It also publishes a magazine and various bulletins on human rights issues.

In the outlying regions—in Hrodna [Grodno], for example—the organization known as Ratusha is spending what little funds it has on publishing around 15 local newspapers and bulletins. The purpose of these publications is to provide residents of small towns and villages with information in a public format on violations against their fellow citizens. Seeing something in print and knowing it is public information reduces citizens' level of fear, making them more likely to speak out to protect their rights and the rights of others. Printing such information holds officials accountable for their actions and increases the likelihood that they will think twice before committing a violation.

In another region, in Brest, the Belarusian Association of Women Lawyers, a very active local women's organization, is touring small

---

[13]   Vladimir Rovda, "First Experience of the Third Sector in Belarus," *Analytical Bulletin No. 1: The Executive Bureau of the Assembly of Belarusian Pro-Democratic NGOs* (1998): 28.

towns and villages, lecturing on human rights protection and giving free legal advice to citizens. This is done quietly, of course, but interest in the Association's work has been great. Women's groups generally have a strong impact on their constituencies, so that engagement with them is particularly productive and results oriented. For example, the OSCE AMG provided Russian language materials on human rights instruments to the Association's instructor, who within a very short time was requesting significantly larger quantities of the materials for distribution and use.

This last example points to the need in Belarus for more materials written in local languages. Although there are documents, publications, and other materials available in Russian, particularly from international organizations such as the UN and the OSCE, the amount provided does not meet the social and institutional need for them. Belarusian citizens are highly literate and motivated to learn, thus there is a large audience for written material. It cannot be emphasized enough that there is a significant need to provide native-language texts on human rights, rule of law practices, examples of democratic laws, etc., in large numbers. The distribution of such materials is an effective way to influence Belarusian social consciousness. Another example of the hunger for materials was seen at the 2nd Congress of the NGO Assembly, where boxes of OSCE materials were grabbed up literally within minutes of being placed on the table, more quickly than they could be unpacked. With the materials gone, there were numerous requests for additional copies.

The OSCE AMG in Belarus cooperates with NGOs and tries to engage with them in the process of transitioning away from the Soviet past. One such program trains domestic election observers. In 1999, the AMG—with the assistance of the OSCE Office for Democratic Institutions and Human Rights (ODIHR), the U.S. government, and several Western foundations—provided experts and organized a series of seminars to train domestic election observers in the principles of free and fair elections. The seminars were geared toward promoting public awareness of democracy and democratic practice and not to prepare observers for any particular election. Two seminars were held in each region, one for government-nominated participants and one for NGO participants.

The impact of the seminar was markedly different for each group.

The government participants, who included teachers and official trade union members, among others, were less inclined to take an active part, but were open to the information presented. The NGO participants, on the other hand, who represented a wide spectrum of NGOs, were extremely active. They were enthusiastically interested in discussing not only election observation as a method of promoting democracy, but also methods for dealing with the current political situation, building relationships with local authorities, and developing credibility. The seminars were highly valued by the NGOs as a tool for the future to assist them in their goal to reform civil society. Following these seminars, the trained election observers expanded to create a nation-wide network of independent observers, which was active during the parliamentary elections in October 2000.

The OSCE AMG, together with the Belarusian Helsinki Committee, has also organized training seminars for public defenders sponsored by NGOs. According to Belarusian legislation and the judicial system, public defenders are allowed to take an active part in court proceedings on behalf of defendants.

While contributions to the advancement of human rights, democracy, and rule of law are important, the role of NGOs in other spheres of life, such as health and the environment, must not be overlooked. The international community needs to provide resources to NGOs working in these spheres also.

International Exposure

Because of the closed nature of the Belarusian state today, it is extremely important that Belarusian NGOs have exposure not only to other countries and to other ways of democratic life, but also to outside NGOs promoting similar goals. The NGO Assembly, at its first Congress in 1997, adopted an appeal to NGOs, foundations, and other international organizations outside Belarus to assist them in developing democracy in Belarus. Six points in the appeal are particularly illustrative of the type of cooperation sought:

> 1. International organizations and foreign donors should "reconsider carefully the conception of their cooperation with governmental structures in Belarus . . . The Working Group of the Assembly can

provide information on reliable partners";

2. International organizations and foundations should establish offices in Belarus "to get first-hand information and better study Belarusian NGOs' needs and capacities";

3. A constructive dialogue should take place between international organizations and the Working Group of the Assembly;

4. The outside world should be informed about the situation in Belarus and investigate opportunities for cooperation;

5. International foundations should pay primary attention to supporting programs aimed at the organizational development of NGOs; and

6. NGOs from Central and Eastern Europe and the CIS should develop common projects with NGOs in Belarus.[14]

One forum where the exposure of Belarusian NGOs is possible is the OSCE ODIHR Human Dimension Implementation Meeting held in Warsaw. The meeting gathers together government representatives from OSCE participating States, who discuss the current state of affairs in the field of the "human dimension," that is, human rights and fundamental freedoms, democracy, tolerance, and the rule of law. NGOs are allowed to attend and actively participate. However, no regular source of funding is available for NGOs to attend, and NGOs in Belarus do not have financial means to attend such meetings, even if they take place just across the border in Poland.

In 1997, a representative of the Assembly of the Belarusian Pro-Democratic NGOs participated in the meeting. In 1998, the OSCE Advisory and Monitoring Group in Belarus took upon itself to fund 10 NGOs to participate in the meeting. The total cost of funding was only about $1,500 and was well worth the minimal expense. The participation of these NGOs had several positive results: (1) it allowed the official information from the government delegation on the human

---

[14] "Appeal to International Organizations and Foundations," *Analytical Bulletin No. 1: The Executive Bureau of the Assembly of Belarusian Pro-Democratic NGOs* (1997): 5.

rights, judicial, and media situations to be challenged; (2) it provided the Belarusian NGO participants the opportunity to network with dozens of other NGOs from the other OSCE participating States; and (3) it gave smaller Belarusian NGOs with no international connections, like the Soligorsk Center for Social Initiatives, its first opportunity to experience such an international forum. Each of the NGOs made presentations to the working sessions of the meeting. In 1999 and 2000, the AMG continued to support the participation of Belarusian NGOs in this meeting.

Helping members of NGOs to travel outside of Belarus in order to learn about the work of NGOs in other countries is only one means of gaining international exposure. Of equal importance is having agents of outside countries and donor agencies travel to Belarus, or better yet, spend significant time there, to better familiarize themselves with the actual situation on the ground. Without a proper sense of the inner workings of Belarus, it is difficult for outside entities to develop assistance programs that are both appropriate and effective.

The Future of NGOs in Belarus

Despite harassment and other difficulties facing NGOs in Belarus, their numbers are growing. Currently, the highest rate of growth is of NGOs serving the youth sector. If Hrodna is taken as an example, in 1995, there were 7 registered and 10 nonregistered youth NGOs; by 1998, the number had increased to 24 registered and 17 nonregistered youth NGOs. The statistics show that 78 percent of these NGOs are located in the city of Hrodna, with the rest spread throughout the oblast.[15] As can be seen from this, counting the number of groups registered is not necessarily the best way to judge growth.

Overcoming the problems that face NGO development in Belarus requires the following:

> 1. Better legislation is needed to promote the development of NGOs. Legislation must not place restrictions or unreasonable controls on the establishment and functioning of NGOs.

---

[15]   RADA 23, "Information and Resource Support of the Network of Youth NGOs from Grodna Oblast" (1998).

2. Individuals working with NGOs need training in several areas: NGO purposes and goals, operation, task delegation, fundraising, development, communication skills, and promotion.

3. State bodies need education on the purposes of NGOs in order to shift their orientation from one of distrust, which leads to harassment, to one of partnership. NGOs can perform tasks that complement the work of state bodies, even filling gaps, and they can assist the government in its work, for example, by reviewing and commenting on legislation.

4. Government and NGOs need to come together to discuss issues of common concern. Joint meetings could be tried. They have been instituted in other post-Soviet countries and serve to reduce suspicion and tension. Highly controversial issues do not necessarily have to be the topic of such meetings.

5. The government needs to relinquish its suspicion of the international community's willingness to support and promote, especially financially, NGOs in Belarus.

6. As the economic situation in Belarus is not likely to improve in the next few years, foreign funding needs to be strengthened to support the spread of information among NGOs about outside funding agencies and opportunities. According to a survey by the Belarusian Assembly of Pro-Democratic NGOs in 1997, 72 percent of NGO respondents named lack of funding as the greatest obstacle to their work.[16]

7. Funding agencies outside Belarus need to be informed of the situation inside Belarus to recognize the need for funding for the immediate future and to insure that funding is given to truly *nongovernmental* organizations pursuing worthwhile causes.

---

[16] Rovda and Chernov, "The Third Sector of Belarus," p. 20.

Conclusion

Investing in and supporting Belarusian NGOs is the best and most efficient way to have an impact on Belarus. NGOs have an influence on citizens, and on society in general, that officials and politicians, even opposition politicians, do not have. NGOs are dealing with issues of concern to citizens, whether it is the Chernobyl nuclear catastrophe, promoting and protecting the Belarusian language and culture, observing elections, or protecting and promoting human rights. Slowly, more and more people are becoming involved in the NGO movement.

This said, some NGOs cooperate very closely with political parties, trade unions, and the independent media. The political situation in Belarus has pushed groups pursuing democratic reforms into the so-called "opposition." While political parties spend most of their time struggling to exist, trade unions are having an increasing impact on workers, a large sector of the population who are very important to Belarus' successful transformation. Therefore, investment and assistance to the independent trade unions should be pursued.

Engagement in Belarus through NGOs cannot be encouraged enough. Assistance is needed, but not just in the financial sense. Although large sums of money are useful, they are not required, because much can be achieved with very little. Rather, assistance should come in the form of training, networking, and advising on projects and activities—and, of course, general political support. The more outside countries, organizations, foundations, and other groups become engaged in the situation in Belarus—through NGOs, in particular—the greater the chance for a speedy and peaceful transformation to democracy.

18

Caryn Wilde
The Challenge of Using NGOs as a Strategy for Engagement

Since 1996, Western development agencies have watched their relations with the Belarusian government and business sectors steadily deteriorate. President Aliaksandr Lukashenka does not believe that a democratic society and free-market economy, as championed by the West, are in the best interests of the people in his newly independent country. He has made it clear on numerous occasions that foreign entities operating in Belarus will play by his rules or find their progress blocked. He seeks to shield his population from what he believes will be a painful transformation. Checked, but undaunted, Western development agencies have turned their focus toward the nascent third sector—nongovernmental organizations (NGOs), political parties, independent trade unions, and other associations not directly affiliated with the Belarusian government. The West now believes that supporting NGO activity is a viable strategy for accomplishing reform. Unfortunately, this new strategy has created confusion among Belarusians, who are still unclear about the nature of the third sector and its role in society. While their confusion complicates the West's effort to support reformers who earnestly desire democracy and transition to a market economy, it is not a harbinger of failure.

The theory that underlies the activities of the United States Agency for International Development (USAID) is that motivation for democratic participation will first emerge at the community level. By engaging Belarusians in solving social problems of importance to themselves, the U.S. will contribute to the development of a third sector capable and motivated to interact with the government and

business sectors. Since embarking on this strategy, the West has discovered that engaging the Belarusian citizenry through public organizations is nearly as challenging as engaging the government and the
business sector. Reformers and donors have encountered significant
barriers to building civil society in a post-communist country.

This chapter discusses four factors to be considered when
developing a strategy for engagement with Belarusian NGOs. How
the West addresses these factors may influence the success of the
overall reform process. Those four factors influencing a strategy for
engaging Belarusian NGOs are:

1. the absence of a preexisting infrastructure for a third sector,
    and the lack of interest among the Belarusian people to
    support the concept of a third sector;

2. the potency of a Belarusian administration that believes
    only governmental structures should provide services to the
    people, and its ability to obstruct those who would advocate
    otherwise;

3. the likelihood that progress, by Western standards, will be
    slow because many of the philosophies proposed may first
    require acceptance and adaptation to the Belarusian culture;
    and,

4. the importance of "balancing interests," both Belarusian
    and Western.

By no means does this chapter suggest that the situation is
hopeless or that no progress has been made in the past eight years.
Hundreds of NGOs are serving constituencies at this very moment,
and each day new initiatives emerge. Also undaunted, NGOs pursue
the dream of a civil society at their own social, economic, or political
peril. Mikalai [Nikolai] Statkevich, leader of the Social Democratic
Party, when asked about his participation in the seemingly fruitless
autumn 2000 parliamentary elections, said that "he and his candidates
had a chance to hold campaign rallies and work with voters—
something they couldn't have done if they [had] boycott[ed] the
ballot. Moreover, without opposition candidates for [the] government
to harass, no one in the West would have paid attention."[1]

---

[1]   Maura Reynolds, "Belarus Opposition Hopes to Learn from Yugoslavia in
Ousting Dictator," *Los Angeles Times*, Home Edition, 15 October 2000: A-8.

The challenge facing the West is to be alert to and leverage the opportunities it finds present to create programs that meet both its goals and the needs of the Belarusian people. It is a delicate balance that needs to be struck, but it can be accomplished.

Western Research and Analysis

Research conducted by Western experts from 1992 to 1999 recommends a long-term and self-sustainable development strategy based on a partnership between Western donors and local nonprofit leaders. Daniel Siegel and Jenny Yancey, in their 1992 work *The Rebirth of Civil Society: The Development of the Nonprofit Sector in East Central Europe and the Role of Western Assistance*, outlined four priorities for building local capacity:

1. strengthen the capacity of indigenous NGO development and training mechanisms through the development of an intensive 6- to 9-month train-the-trainer program in the West;

2. expand information-sharing and networking activities between NGOs;

3. increase the availability of small grants to be disbursed by a local advisory structure; and,

4. assist in the development of nonprofit legal and fiscal frameworks that support third-sector organizations.

Other recommendations included facilitating East-East and East-West dialogue and networks, encouraging collaborative efforts among donors, gradually shifting resources toward building local nonprofit institutions, increasing the use of Western personnel to work closely with the local organizations, and focusing on critical social issues.[2]

In 1994, Marcel Messing cautioned the West that Belarus had just started on the path to democracy, and for this reason, the West should expect to make a long-term development commitment.[3] He went on to

---

[2] Daniel Siegel and Jenny Yancey, *The Rebirth of Civil Society: The Development of the Nonprofit Sector in East Central Europe and the Role of Western Assistance* (Rockefeller Fund, Inc., 1992).

[3] Marcel Messing and Sergei Stepanov, *The Voluntary Sector in Belarus* (Charities Aid Foundation, July 1994).

say that it would require patience in a process of intercultural learning; and although the Belarusian society looked familiar, it would probably always be different from West European and American societies. Messing reminded the West that Belarusians had little experience with foreign funders, but thought them an inexhaustible source of hard currency. He also noted that although eager to learn from the West, Belarusians frequently asserted that foreigners, by definition, are unable to understand certain aspects of Belarusian society. He wisely predicted the possibility of suspicion on the part of the Belarusian government and people and recommended that donors establish trust by being open about their objectives for involvement in Belarus. Messing warned that local NGOs would be amazingly flexible when it came to adapting their organizational missions to suit funding initiatives, and that conscientious oversight and accountability should be balanced with understanding, as they would need considerable guidance. He recommended that funders gather as much information as possible, understand the context in which Belarusians work, and strive for a neutral position with local organizations to minimize competition among NGOs. Messing also advocated several objectives:

1. establish a center to maintain databases, provide legal advice, technical support, network NGOs, and interact with donors;
2. support projects identified by Belarusians;
3. fund organizations that use volunteers rather than paid staff to reduce the potential for jealousy; and,
4. exercise care not to create financial dependency. (Messing, overly optimistic, incorrectly assumed that NGOs would soon develop the capacity to raise funds locally.)

In 1999, East West Institute (EWI) prepared a comprehensive report on the status of the Belarusian third sector. This report was to set the stage for discussions during the Second Donors' Conference held in Prague.[4] EWI confirmed earlier reports that the Belarusian NGO sector (1) continued to be divided by contradictions in ideology, organizational structure, personal motives, and competition for grants;

---

[4]   Ivanna O. Klympush, Stephen B. Heintz, Oleksandr V. Pavliuk, and Vasil Hudak, *International Organizations and the Development of Civil Society and NGOs in Belarus*, (East West Institute, April 1999).

(2) faced growing impediments from the Belarusian government; and (3) needed to improve public relations as the majority of the people still did not understand the NGOs' activity and the Western assistance they received. It was apparent that the Belarusian government was using the people's confusion to discredit the entire third sector.

EWI's report outlined viable options for future activity and indicated that donors should consider the following nine recommendations:

1. Continue funding programs that promote democracy, but consider adding social projects to their assistance strategy;

2. Maintain continuity by supporting organizations that have achieved a measure of success and are ready to move to the next level of development;

3. Create a micro-grant program that supports grassroots initiative and develops local organizations' managerial capacity to redistribute small grants;

4. Intensify the level of training in order to reach a wider audience;

5. Improve the technical capacity of all forms of communication;

6. Encourage networking and partnering both internally and externally;

7. Open representation offices in Belarus that will raise the profile of the international community, enhance their ability to monitor projects, and help them gain better insight of the over-all situation and future needs;

8. Establish a Belarus Donors' Forum, similar to the coordinating structure that was successful in assisting NGOs in Slovakia; and

9. Initiate small and medium enterprise (SME) development projects to improve the potential for local fund raising.

Over a span of seven years, researchers' recommendations remained essentially the same. Unfortunately, during this same period, the physical environment for NGOs and other third-sector organizations worsened. This might lead one to ask if the West should have reevaluated their initial strategy for engagement much earlier.

Western Strategies for Engagement

Aid to Belarus has come from many countries throughout the world. Assistance ranged from single grants from private foundations to multilateral programs such as the European Union's Technical Assistance for the Commonwealth of Independent States (TACIS) program and the bilateral U.S. Democracy Fund's Small Grants Program. Strategies included humanitarian aid in the form of baby food and medicines or vacations abroad for thousands of children living in the Chernobyl radiation zones. However, the dominant Western strategy for assistance was directed toward restructuring government and state enterprises and private sector development. As the West's relationship with the Belarusian government deteriorated, development agencies shifted their focus to NGOs. They believed humanitarian aid and social programs could have a secondary benefit of maintaining an unofficial connection with Belarusian governmental agencies. By keeping the lines of communication open, the West preserved the possibility to influence.

The countries assisting Belarus each had its own theory about philanthropy, focus, and the development process. However, they shared a fundamental belief in the importance of the rule of law, protection of human rights, an independent media, and a fair election process. Where Europe and the United States differed was in their prediction of how long the transition would take.

In 1989, U.S. policymakers and foreign assistance specialists in the countries of Central and Eastern Europe (CEE) and the Newly Independent States (NIS) envisioned USAID programs as a "jump start" in the process of political and economic reform.[5] Prevailing thought that a quick "in and out" was an appropriate strategy for the United States proved inaccurate. Ten years later, USAID's assessment of the progress of transition to democracy and a market economy revealed significant variation from country to country. One size did not fit all. Social, political, and economic events had created complex challenges for what the United States thought to be a relatively straightforward process.

---

[5]   Information about early USAID program strategies has been taken from interviews and review documents.

The collapse of the Soviet Union had a serious impact on the old systems in Belarus. The United States could not just "send in" capital, technology, and training, for there were no reliable institutional structures, systems, or leaders with whom to interface. The business environment, political order, and social support systems were in flux. The Belarusian people did not seem to have any consensus as to how they saw the future of their newly independent state, or who was going to lead them to wherever they were going. The United States overestimated the institutional capacity of the country—and under-estimated the difficulty involved in reorienting the remnants of the remaining institutions and the implications of the Communist legacy.

An even more complicated challenge, and one that the U.S. had not anticipated, was the resistance to democratic reform of Lukashenka, Belarus' first duly-elected president. His ardent opposition to privatization in preference for a state-controlled economy, his resistance to political reforms that would encourage citizen involvement, and his blatant violations of human rights led the U.S. to take a position of "selective engagement" in Belarus. As the terms of the U.S. Ambassadors David H. Swartz (1992–1994), Kenneth Yalowitz (1994–1997), and Daniel Speckhard (1997–2000) progressed, any illusion of working with the government of Belarus to effect democratization or to develop lucrative markets for American businesses dissipated. Finally, U.S. representatives began to see that for the time being, neither the government nor the business sector holds significant potential for achieving lasting change. The combination of an authoritarian leadership, a citizenry with a low level of civic knowledge and no history of previous civic engagement, and run-away inflation together with plunging monthly incomes forced the U.S. to rethink its assistance strategy.

The 1999–2001 mission of the U.S. in Belarus continues to be the support of reforms needed to establish a democratic society and free market economy. However, the strategy is changing. USAID states that the motivation for democratic participation will first emerge at the community level. Therefore, involving people in community-level efforts to solve problems of importance to them will establish a third sector capable and willing to interact with the government and business sectors.[6] Based on these premises, USAID revised its

6   *USAID Strategy Report, 1999–2002.*

strategy for engagement to include supporting the activities of the NGO sector.

Anticipated outcomes of the proposed, four-year USAID strategy include increasing citizens' awareness of their rights, creating programs that directly affect people's welfare, reaching into small rural communities with training and technology, and improving people's ability to solve problems in their community. USAID hopes to see an increase in the number of people involved in NGOs, improved coordination of the NGO community, and increased donor communication and collaboration. The new strategy includes innovative ways to promote the benefits of private initiative through enterprise development. Successfully helping Belarusians create small businesses would not only improve their economic situation, but also create a foundation for future support of the NGO sector.

USAID recognizes a number of impediments to reaching its goals. The policy of selective engagement curtails U.S. investment and credit guarantees and limits contact with the Belarusian government. Growing controls by the Lukashenka regime are expected to include higher levels of harassment and oppression of NGOs, political parties, independent trade unions, and the free press. Suppression of free speech and overt hostility toward Western democracies (especially the U.S.) reinforces economic policies that seriously limit privatization, entrepreneurship, and foreign investment. Moreover, the Lukashenka government has expanded the money supply, and the economy has many inflationary characteristics.

Western development agencies are committed to the goals of an informed, educated, and engaged Belarusian people. Their strategy to achieve those goals through a partnership with Belarusian NGOs offers the potential for the people to develop the capacity to address societal problems and gives impetus to economic and democratic reforms. However, these strategies will only be effective if they are compatible with Belarusian goals.

Chronology of the Nascent Belarusian NGO Sector

Belarus readiness, or lack thereof, to engage in a partnership with the West for purposes of developing the public organizations that make up the third sector is strongly linked to its past. While political parties, trade unions, and religious organizations are a part of the previous life, NGOs, "true" volunteerism, and philanthropy are not. The Belarusian people's willingness to participate and support these concepts will be dependent on their willingness and capacity to accept a change in mind-set as to how social and organizational life are to continue. What follows is a brief chronology of the development of the Belarusian NGO sector.[7]

Pre-Soviet Period

During the tsarist era, the royal family was responsible for the welfare of the country and its people. Occasionally, wealthy families felt it their duty to assist the destitute population. Depending on the times, the Russian Orthodox Church offered support to the faithful. There are stirring legends about women from prominent families who left the security of their homes to minister to the people. For example, since the twelfth century, Yefrosinia of Polotsk, the daughter of the Prince of Polotsk, has been revered in Belarus as the great enlightener. She was an ardent defender of human rights, political diplomacy, and cultural education.[8] This is not to say that people did not care for one another's needs. Indeed, they did help one another survive during this difficult time. However, there were no formal institutions through which these acts of caring could be sustained.

Soviet Period

Between 1921 and 1991, the few voluntary organizations that existed were sanctioned and fully funded appendages of the Communist party. The party also approved, but did not fund, other organizations that were oriented toward culture and language. Siegel and Yancey report in their 1992 study, "the Communist regime tolerated little space for individuals to participate in private and autonomous groups, viewing such self-organization as suspect and beyond permissible ideological

---

[7]   Caryn M. Wilde, *Leaders of Change: The Belarusian Assembly of Pro-Democratic Non-Governmental Organizations*, A leadership case study prepared for the Hubert H. Humphrey Institute of Public Affairs, University of Minnesota (1999).

[8]   *Belarusian Women As Seen through an Era*, National Report, UNDP, Minsk (1997).

boundaries."[9] *The predisposition for suspicion of this sort of activity is an extremely important factor that Western donors must integrate into their strategies.* Theoretically, there was no need for voluntary organizations, as the state met the needs of the people. This premise has likely been a major impediment to the development of social programs through which the average person could contribute to improving the quality of life.

On 26 April 1986, life was irreversibly altered in the USSR, and most especially in Belarus. The nuclear reactor in Chernobyl, Ukraine, melted down and released a cloud of radioactive material over 70 percent of the territory of Belarus. Belarusians consider the ecological damage and harm visited on the health of the inhabitants as extremely severe and permanent. For the first time, the comprehensive Soviet system appeared unable to meet the needs of the people. Foreign governments, private organizations, and individuals offered their assistance to overcome the effects of the tragedy. Surprisingly, their offers were accepted. Foreign efforts concentrated on medical treatment, the rehabilitation of children, and ecological issues.

Previously, Belarus had been closed to the West, so foreign assistance providers had little knowledge of the country they were now determined to help. For efficiency, partnerships were forged with the local population, and thus, in 1988, voluntary organizations were created. Gennady Grushevoy, a philosophy professor at Belarusian State University, founded one of the first NGOs, Children of Chernobyl.[10] Today, this NGO has numerous international partners, affiliates, and volunteers in every region of Belarus and provides a broad range of social services to thousands of people every year. In 1994, Messing suggested that the Chernobyl disaster had opened Belarus to the West and inspired the formation of a small group of organizations that might serve as a starting point for Western donor engagement. Most would agree his prediction was accurate.

---

[9]   Daniel Siegel and Jenny Yancey. *The Rebirth of Civil Society* (Rockefeller Brothers Fund, Inc., 1992).

[10]   Henadz Hrushevoi [Gennadii Grushevoi] is a member of the ousted Supreme Soviet of the 13th session, one of the visionary leaders in the Belarusian Assembly of Pro-Democratic NGOs, and an active participant in many recent social initiatives.

Independence

In 1992–1993, the West began a cursory investigation of the potential for civil society in Belarus. It was apparent that the newly established state would face serious impediments to meeting the needs of the people. Vital social structures were either broken or had never existed, the economic situation was uncertain, and there were few leaders in the transitional government interested in guiding the development of a civic initiative. It was apparent to the West that the people themselves would have to generate the initiative to address the social problems affecting their lives.

Possessing little or no training, ordinary Belarusian citizens began to create small public organizations around areas of personal interest. Between 1994 and 1996, the number of socially oriented NGOs grew dramatically. Coming to their assistance were several Western organizations.[11] The Soros Foundation was the first Western donor to open an office in Belarus. The Belarusian Soros Foundation (BSF) provided grants, training, and equipment to educational, political, and social projects. BSF and the resource centers of Counterpart International and United Way International brought NGO leaders together for training and encouraged them to network.

In 1995, Counterpart Belarus and 30 local NGOs forged a fledgling Club of NGOs. The Club was successful in providing training and experience in group dynamics. However, when its key Western and Belarusian leaders left for other positions in the NGO sector, the NGOs drifted apart and the Club ceased to exist. Today, Counterpart Belarus, under the direction of local specialists, continues to make a significant contribution to the development of social capital among the Belarusian population.

NGOs faced a steep learning curve in the early years. In addition to forming and successfully navigating the registration process, they learned "by doing" how to comply with state regulations on banking, employment, and record-keeping. Once administrative duties were done, they began the search for Western assistance. They attended courses on the technical aspects of writing grants and tried to develop

---

[11]   Other organizations providing significant assistance during this period were: EURASIA Foundation, National Endowment for Democracy (NED), and Institute for Democracy in Eastern Europe.

an understanding of the Western theory behind philanthropy. If they successfully completed the first stages, they tackled the challenge of opening an office, buying equipment, and training personnel. It was apparent to those working in-country that the less competitive atmosphere during this period gave new organizations the benefit of drawing on the experiences of those more established and helped them to grow without having to fight on their own for every inch of progress. By the end of January 1995, Ministry of Justice records indicated that there were 1,000 registered NGOs. They were largely oriented around activities of family, education, culture, ecology, scientific research, and restructuring the systems of local self-governance. They were not involved in the pursuit of regional or federal power. That tussle was left to the political parties and parliamentarians.

Donor organizations struggled with many of the same logistical obstacles described above, and their learning curve was proving to be equally severe. It is therefore not surprising that Western donors concentrated on the NGOs located in Minsk, the capital city, and the four BSF affiliate offices in the regions. These affiliates would later play an important role in the development of rural civic engagement and in the founding of the Assembly of Pro-Democratic Nongovernmental Organizations.[12]

Post-1996 Referendum

The Referendum of 1996 was a landmark event that changed all of the policymaking structures in Belarus. It eliminated the separation of powers between the executive, judiciary, and parliament; abandoned the rule of law and conventions of human rights; and closed the political forums, arenas, and courts to the general population. Displaced parliamentarians, political leaders, bureaucrats, judges, and lawyers turned to the third sector and the formation of NGOs in order to regain legal status and access to finances to support their work.

The 1994 Act on Public Organizations makes a distinction between public organizations and political parties, trade unions, religious organizations, institutions of local self-government, and organizations founded by the state administration institutions.

[12]   Wilde, *Leaders of Change.*

Unfortunately, following the 1996 Referendum, the administration began to view NGOs as belonging to the same class as political parties, independent trade unions, and movements. Lukashenka linked them all together with one label—the "opposition." This has created confusion for local regulatory agencies, the general population, and donors. It contributed to the politicizing of all public organizations, regardless of mission. Politicization has isolated public organizations from the citizenry and private businesses and undermined a fragile trust that had just started to emerge.

The West reacted to the Referendum by imposing sanctions. One of the most significant sanctions was the West's diversion of funds from projects with the Belarusian government to new initiatives they identified for the third sector. The West believed that the network of NGOs could effectively carry the message of democracy and market economy throughout the country. The goal of advancing principles of democracy, the rule of law, human rights, and strengthening independent media and free trade unions moved to the top of most donors' agenda. This injection of political goals into a "non-political" sector exacerbated an already-blurred demarcation between the organizations within the third sector and altered the composition and mission of many NGOs. All voluntary organizations, whether they wished it or not, became "politicized."

The confusion surrounding the third sector and NGOs has recently been complicated further by the actions of the government of Belarus. According to the Act on Public Organizations, the state has the legislative right to "render assistance to public organizations." It has done so, not by broad-based sector initiative, but by creating what the other public organizations call "government nongovernmental organizations" (GONGOs). These GONGOs enjoy state funding, prime office space, and preferential presidential attention. They are parallel organizations to those initiated by the public. Two organizations that receive this preferential status are the Belarusian Patriotic Youth League and the Belarusian Union of Women. In 1999, Lukashenka "helped" to select the president of the Belarusian Union of Women.[13] While it is a duly-registered NGO whose activity is

---

[13] The Belarusian Union of Women is the renewed version of the Union of Byelorussian Women, which was active during the Soviet era.

financially supported by the administration, it also seeks funding from Western donors. As the Union of Women has affiliates under other names, it is difficult for donors to distinguish which organizations are truly independent women's NGOs.[14]

By the end of 1996, the NGOs realized that coordination, sharing of information, and a general strategy were critical to protecting public organizations from the administration's growing distrust and oppression. In February 1997, the First Congress of the National Assembly of Democratic Belarusian NGOs was convened. The most established Minsk NGOs were joined by a handful of regional NGOs (BSF affiliates) and the newly displaced political leaders. Together they formed the Belarusian Assembly of Pro-Democratic Nongovernmental Organizations. The goals of the Assembly, finalized in September 1997, were to establish cooperation among NGOs, provide information exchange, build a system of mutual assistance and service-rendering, expand the influence of the third sector in Belarusian society, build a collective system for the protection of rights of NGOs, and involve new organizations as members of the Assembly.

The four regional BSF affiliates and an NGO from the Brest region formed a new network, the Regional Resource Centers. These centers provided training, legal advice, access to equipment and other material resources to rural NGOs. They established networks with other Belarusian NGOs and initiated contacts with Western donors. As if to validate the importance of what the NGOs had just accomplished, the Belarusian Soros Foundation finally gave up its long battle with the administration and closed its office in Belarus. This was a significant event in the world of the Belarusian third sector. Aside from losing the spark that ignited a wide array of local initiatives and provided a primary source of funding, the NGOs had to deal with the realization that the administration could successfully attack and seemingly vanquish the powerful Soros Foundation. Although BSF's departure indicated that the nascent NGO sector had

---

[14]   This comment is not to imply that the activities of the Belarusian Union of Women are not worthy of Western donor assistance; but quite the contrary, it is meant to demonstrate that some organizations, with administrative support, are carrying out vital service projects. It is merely important for donors to know with whom they are working, and what their relationship is to the Belarusian government and people.

progressed, the reality of being on its own brought a new crisis of confidence that the sector had to absorb. In 1998, the Assembly was ready to reach out to NGOs in the regions. Information forums, held in each of the six regions, resulted in the creation of the Regional Assemblies of Democratic NGOs and Provincial Assemblies. The infrastructure for a union of NGOs now existed on the national, regional, and local levels. The Second Congress of the National Assembly, convened in November 1998, was attended by NGOs, independent trade unions, and political parties. The Assembly enlarged the national program to include the support of regional mass media, the protection of human rights, the promotion of social spheres, and education. The administration's reaction, when learning of the third sector's pursuit of inter-organizational cooperation and support, was to issue a decree requiring all NGOs, political parties, and independent trade unions to reregister with the Ministry of Justice.

Between 1 February and 1 July 1999, the re-registration of the entire third sector was to take place.[15] The Assembly issued the following statement: "The announced conditions for its implementation showed that authorities were guided not by the will to regulate and facilitate the activities of the civil sector, but quite the opposite, to limit it as much as possible and to get rid of the most active opposition NGOs in a legal way."[16] The call for re-registration was an obvious attempt to weed out those organizations the administration considered troublesome. A less obvious repercussion was to throw the entire third sector into disarray during the period that led up to the expiration of Lukashenka's term as president.[17]

The Assembly, with the assistance of their Western partners, initiated its most ambitious project up to that time. SOS Third Sector was a rescue program designed to counteract the imminent threat of the re-registration. According to the NGO Assembly, only 57 percent

---

[15] It turned out that the state's reregistering bodies could not physically accomplish the process during that period, and the registration was completed in October 1999.

[16] The Assembly of Belarusian Pro-Democratic Non-Governmental Organizations, *Re-Registration 1999 of the Belarusian NGOs* (Minsk, 2000).

[17] The opposition and its Western supporters did not recognize the results of the 1996 Referendum. According to the 1994 Constitution, Lukashenka's term expired in July 1999; according to amendments to the Constitution made as a result of the Referendum, Lukashenka's term was extended until 2001.

of the existing NGOs were re-registered after the state issued its mandate. Of 2,210 NGOs registered in February 1999, only 1,268 remained one year later in February 2000. An analysis of the outcome of the re-registration reveals a counterintuitive result: while the number of registered NGOs plummeted by half, the number of Assembly members more than doubled. The Assembly, founded by 250 organizations, now has a membership of 570. It appears that the Assembly motivated the committed to set aside their differences and form a unified front. Those NGOs that remain are forged with steel and are determined to create a civil society in Belarus.

In March 2000, the administration made another attempt to divide the third sector and to pacify Western and Belarusian human rights advocates. Lukashenka announced the beginning of a series of Public Dialogues with NGOs. The first Dialogue was convened in April 2000. An old quandary—whether to engage or cooperate with the administration—reemerged. The NGOs and their Western supporters still have not reached consensus as to whether the first Public Dialogue was a success or not. The administration claims it as a victory and proof positive that it supports freedom of public expression and activity. The opposition NGOs feel otherwise and view it as yet another form of manipulation.

The Lukashenka administration has not created a fertile climate for the nurturing of public organizations, and this poses a serious threat to the Belarusian-Western partnership that strives to build a civil society. NGOs encounter outright acts of hostility and go about conducting their day-to-day activities as if navigating through a minefield. Re-registration, tax audits, burglary, and loss of office space become mere inconveniences when compared with the threat of bodily injury. The reports of violent acts committed against NGOs are endless, and the perpetrators are unknown and will probably remain so as the police conduct little substantive investigation.

The administration's hostility extends to Western development agencies and creates complications and limitations that are, at times, difficult for their representatives to comprehend, much less cope with. On 12 March 2001, President Lukashenka issued Decree No. 8, "On Certain Measures of Regulation of the Procedure of Receipt and Use of the Foreign Gratuitous Aid."[18] The decree establishes: that "foreign gratuitous aid" is money and goods (property) provide for use and disposal; which entities will be included under the new regulations; that said individuals and entities will secure legal registration from the Department of Humanitarian Activities; and stipulates that aid in cash money is subject to compulsory customs declaration and must be deposited into a Belarusian bank account within five banking days. The decree specifies five spheres of activity for which "foreign gratuitous aid" may be used: (1) liquidation of complications of emergency situations of natural and technological character; (2) conducting scientific research, development, and education; (3) promotion, restoration, and creation of historical culture, wildlife reserves, and rendering medical help; (4) provision of social assistance to needy and socially unprotected citizens; and (5) other purposes upon the decision of the Department for Humanitarian Activities under and coordinated by the President of the Republic of Belarus.

"Foreign gratuitous aid" may not be used for: activities directed at change of the constitutional order of the Republic of Belarus; seizure or overthrow of the State power; encouragement of actions of war or violence; or kindling of social, national, religious and race enmity. "Foreign gratuitous aid" may not be used, in any form, for preparation and holding of elections, referenda, recall of office holders; holding gatherings, meetings, street marches, demonstrations, picketing, strikes; production or dissemination of agitation materials; holding seminars and other forms of agitation and mass work with the population. Violations will be subject to stiff fines and taxation, confiscation of property, liquidation of organizations, and deportation for foreigners. Detailed documentation will be required before approval of activity, during project implementation, and at closure of activity.

"The Decree noticeably complicates and restricts the receipt of foreign gratuitous aid and its use for such kinds of activity as creative work, protection of human rights, enlightenment, propaganda of

---

[18] Translation of Decree No. 8, provided by the Assembly of Pro-Democratic Non-Governmental Organizations.

healthy way of life, youth programs, etc."[19] The initial reaction of foreign organizations currently working in Belarus has been one of disbelief and confusion. A thorough understanding of and respect for the influences that affected and continue to influence the development of the NGO sector is key to the West's strategy for engagement.

Profile of Belarusian NGOs

> "We don't see things as they are, we see them as we are."
> Anaïs Nin

Is a Belarusian NGO—a voluntary organization, the opposition, or a private entrepreneur? For average Belarusian citizens, this is a serious question, and the answer may be crucial to engaging their support and participation. The activities of Belarusian NGOs, political parties, trade unions, and opposition movements appear to be so intermingled that it is difficult to distinguish one from the other.

Belarusians experience NGOs in multiple ways. They may receive the services of an NGO, witness the members of the same NGO protesting in a demonstration, or observe that the NGO leader's economic status has significantly improved. The first experience is a positive one; the second is confusing; and the third is definitely viewed negatively. Combining these contradictory experiences with the mounting warnings from the administration that NGOs are really on the West's payroll, threatening the security of the country, and only in it for personal gain, results in a very confused, suspicious, and jealous population.

If given the opportunity, the NGOs will explain that they are sincere about their service to the citizenry, they are only exercising their constitutional rights and responsibilities, and their work extracts a personal sacrifice that money and travel abroad can never compensate. The founder of the Belarusian Association of Women Lawyers offers an excellent illustration of one NGO leader's selflessness.[20] One of their missions is to raise the legal literacy of and

---

[19] Excerpt taken from "Our Comments," Assembly of Pro-Democratic Non-Governmental Organizations, March 2001.

[20] Galina V. Drebezova is the founder and director of the Belarusian Association of Women Lawyers. Her organization sponsored "Sunday schools" that have taught

provide protection to women and children. She has dedicated her personal and professional expertise to educating women and children on their constitutional rights and responsibilities. She has earned the respect of Western donors, who seek her perspective, fund her programs, and invite her to conferences that provide her with valuable experiences. Her dedication and outspokenness have also earned her the label of opposition leader, consumed valuable time from her private law practice that supports her living, and taken up most of her leisure time that might have been spent with family and friends at her little dacha. In truth, she rarely discusses the current administration or political matters in public, but instead concentrates on teaching others how to live within the laws the administration has created. For Belarusians who do not know her or her NGO personally, there is a tendency to fear or be jealous of her. For those who have been empowered by her, there is admiration and appreciation.

Is a Belarusian NGO a potential partner or an adversary? According to the administration, public organizations and the citizen action they arouse are unnecessary and a threat to the orderly running of the Belarusian government. Although unspoken, the theory seems to be, "If the Belarusian people have a need, the state will fill it, that is, providing the state determines that the need is valid." Accordingly, in 1998, the administration created the Presidential Fund of Programs Support. To date, it is known to have assisted few NGOs. Citizen participation in their governance challenges the authority of those who have already assumed that responsibility and clearly undermines the security of the nation from an administration viewpoint. Therefore, stringent laws and severe punishments await those who form NGOs or participate in public gatherings. Moreover, NGOs and civic activity are supported by the West and that alone makes motive and allegiance suspect. On 20 October 2000, U.S. Ambassador to the OSCE David T. Johnson described the current relationship between the administration and Belarusian NGOs: "In Belarus, state authorities often regard grassroots NGOs . . . as anti-government organizations. As a corollary, the government attempts to limit NGOs' activities. Under current

---

hundreds of Belarusian youth about their rights and responsibilities under Belarusian law. In conjunction with lawyers provided by American Bar Association-Central and Eastern Europe Legal Initiative (ABA-CEELI), the Association introduced the country's first program on domestic violence.

regulations in Belarus, the authorities can close NGOs [for minor discrepancies in their documents or infractions] after two warnings."[21] Clearly, statements of support such as those made by Ambassador Johnson contribute to the administration's reasoning that NGOs are adversaries.

Are Belarusian NGOs friends or foes? During the Soviet era, public organizations were oriented around culture, language, history, and so forth. Tolerated by the ruling bodies, they generally drew little attention from the public or from one another. NGOs that emerged in the late 1980s as a result of the Chernobyl accident, on the other hand, were prestigious organizations because of their contacts and funding from the West; their ability to send children, whose health had been affected by the radiation, on rest-holiday to the West; and their personal access to travel to the West. It was during this time that competition emerged among these organizations. Name-calling, accusations of misappropriation of donor funds, and hints of questionable business practices were common. Their struggle was obvious to in-country Western observers and to the general population. The tenor of the third sector changed again after the 1996 Referendum. With third-sector organizations and activities intertwined with politics and Western donors focusing more attention on them, tensions escalated. On the surface, NGOs were going through the motions of cooperation and sharing; however, secretly, they were forming small cliques that guarded contacts and withheld information. The bright lights in this dark hour were the efforts of the Assembly, the Belarusian Think Tank, and the Regional Resource Centers.

Western development specialists have observed a much higher level of mistrust among Belarusian NGOs than they experience in their own countries. This may be one of the less positive legacies of the Soviet period. Sharing information or contacts with one another, or even with members of their own organization, is skillfully avoided. Information and contacts are power: either you have it or your colleague has it. Rarely is it believed that you both can have power.

---

[21]   Reported at the OSCE Human Dimension Implementation Review meeting in Warsaw, Poland. David T. Johnson, U.S. Ambassador to the OSCE, 20 October 2000. Excerpt from *Belarus Update*, ed. Victor Cole, 3(44) October 2000, International League for Human Rights.

Loss of power means a loss of funding for future projects and the end of a NGO's livelihood.

KGB agents, infiltrators, and GONGOs are also threats to the survival of NGOs. The first group reports to the administration on an NGO's activities; the second creates internal organizational conflict to disrupt the NGO's operation; and the third can potentially purloin limited donor funding. Accusations of an NGO being or harboring any one of the three are common, and whether true or false, are an effective way to blight an NGO's reputation with peers, donors, and the population at large.

Whether or not to cooperate with governmental bodies has been, and remains, a controversial issue among NGOs. The missions of some NGOs, such as monitoring human rights violations or promoting election reform, make it impossible to coordinate with official structures. NGOs engaged in public education and health care find it impossible to carry out their missions without the cooperation of official structures. Yelena Levchenko, manager of a civic education project in Homel, said, "NGOs can assist state institutions by offering new ideas, projects, methodologies, volunteers, or even finances. NGOs can also help care for some of the clients or problems that the state institution is not capable of handling."[22] While the West perceives this kind of cooperation as moving in the right direction for building civil society, many NGOs perceive Levchenko's attitude as collaboration with the enemy. Different needs and realities continue to fuel the heated debate.

Accusing another NGO of personal profit or misuse of funds is a potent tool employed to denigrate a competitor. Such accusations are most often used when the accusing NGO is concerned that the merits of its own proposal are weak. Sometimes, donors use NGOs with whom they have had successful dealings to "counsel" them on the proficiency of other NGOs. This can lead to accusations that the "counselors" have sabotaged a competitor. As few Western donors maintain local offices or even spend much time in Belarus, they can be easily influenced by accusations that can be neither proven nor disproved. Occasionally, donors hire people from the local population

[22]   Yelena Levchenko, "Steps toward Cooperation: NGO Brings Civic Education to Belarusian Schools," *Give & Take: A Journal on Civil Society in Eurasia*, ISAR 3(3) (Fall 2000).

to serve as their representatives. While this may seem to be, on the surface, a reasonable compromise between maintaining an office with Western personnel and having no local presence, it is often unsatisfactory to Belarusian NGOs. They complain of favoritism, kickbacks, and filtering. There are no easy answers to these issues of trust and potential abuse of position. Western donors need information, and if they cannot get it for themselves, they must rely on resource centers or people they have come to trust. On the other hand, the concerns of some NGOs are legitimate, and donors must realize that incidents of manipulation, deception, and fraud have occurred in the past and will likely happen again.

It is difficult to build alliances where there is little trust, and it is even more problematic to build them when the parties are in direct competition for limited resources. There is a tendency for NGOs to pursue similar projects and to request funding for the same type of project repeatedly. It is unclear whether this is because opportunities are limited in the overall environment in Belarus or because Belarusians have been in the NGO business for such a short time that they have not reached their full creative potential. Another reason for repetition in projects is that donors have directed funding to a very narrow sphere of activity, or appear to have directed funding according to certain formulae that the NGOs are eager to reproduce in order to guarantee a grant.

Urban versus rural and established versus new are also two dynamics of competition between organizations. Western assistance began in Minsk, so these urban NGOs have a healthy head-start in making contacts and developing professionalism. While it is understandable that donors want to maximize the effectiveness of their assistance, their tendency to go with NGOs located in larger cities and with proven track records has had the effect of impeding capacity building in the provinces and frustrating the grassroots initiative that is vital to establishing a civil society for the whole of Belarus.

Youth, women, and minorities have also had to work harder to secure funding. Often, their missions and projects are not the focus of donor initiatives, and although their requests are modest, they have not developed a track record to merit support. Donors perceive them to be less professional and riskier prospects. It is heartening to see that this thinking has begun to change. USAID and its service providers,

Winrock International and the Agricultural Cooperative Development International and Volunteers in Overseas Cooperative Assistance (ACDI-VOCA), have supported women's initiatives and found them to be above reproach.[23]

Not all relations or efforts between NGOs have been mistrustful and competitive. Organizations like the Belarusian Association of Think Tanks, the Independent Institute of Socio-Economic and Political Studies, the NGO Regional Resource Centers, and the Assembly continue to train others and share their resources, to urge NGOs to see the benefits of working together, and to promote the growth of the third sector as a whole. Individual NGOs have taken the initiative to model cooperation, and Western development specialists continue to bring NGOs together in the hope that partnerships will develop, despite the NGOs' basic instinct to mistrust most forms of unification.

Two NGOs, the Belarusian Association of Think Tanks and the Independent Institute of Socio-Economic and Political Studies, analyze the impact of social, economic, and political policy and conduct public opinion survey research. As a wide scope of timely information is generally difficult to access in Belarus, third-sector organizations and Western development agencies benefit from the insight these NGOs provide. Through the public opinion surveys they conduct, the Belarusian people are kept abreast of what their peers think about current events.

United Way Belarus (UWB), the first registered Belarusian NGO Resource Center, is representative of the dozen or more resource centers operating throughout Belarus. Its mission, modeled after United Way of America, is to increase the organized capacity of people to care for one another. "United Way Belarus builds capacity by offering technical assistance, training, and access to electronic

---

[23] In 1999, Winrock International and ACDI-VOCA collaborated to deliver the USAID-funded Women's Economic Empowerment program in Ukraine, Moldova, and Belarus. Although only a small portion of the $2.6 million project went to Belarus, today hundreds of Belarusian women from the provinces have received training in leadership and organizational management. As a final phase of the program, the graduates will soon begin micro-community action projects. The success of the Belarusian Women's Economic Empowerment project (BWEE) has led USAID to include Belarus in two new development projects for women.

equipment. In helping Nongovernmental Organizations (NGOs) to function effectively, and [by] coordinating public awareness of their accomplishments, UWB assists in the development of a strong third sector in the Republic of Belarus."[24]

The structure of the Assembly is a beacon of hope that competition and other divisive issues can be overcome. Its membership is open to all, and yearly congresses make decisions through majority vote. Between congresses, a voluntary work group coordinates activities. If one were to find any fault with the Assembly's process, it would be that, in its desire to respect the welfare of all members, sometimes it is nearly paralyzed when it comes to arriving at decisions and enforcing them.

A praiseworthy example of the Assembly's ability to coordinate and cooperate is SOS Third Sector. Involving the volunteer labors of lawyers, consultants, and media, the Assembly crafted this effort to assist hundreds of NGOs throughout Belarus in reregistering. The Assembly maintains that neither the registration agencies nor the NGOs were ready for the re-registration. As discussed earlier, many NGOs did not fulfill the legal requirements and failed the process. The poor quality of legal documents is directly related to the low level of legal literacy of most NGOs. Although SOS Third Sector was not able to save every viable NGO, the Assembly's coordination of Western funding and local expertise saved or improved the odds for many.

The Assembly is not a panacea, and its development has not always been smooth. Internal problems have slowed its progress, and a recent crisis was serious enough to threaten its continued existence. However, the Assembly appears to be learning from its mistakes. In a report published in spring 2000, the Assembly renewed its commitment to the founding principles and added several new initiatives designed to enhance the development of the third sector.

Are Belarusian NGOs—partners or wards? The relationship between NGOs and Western donors is quite complicated. In 1992–1993, when Western development agencies began to assist the emerging voluntary sector in Belarus, they did not appear to understand fully the complexity of Belarusian cultural norms or the influence these norms would have on the change initiative. The West

---

[24] Excerpt from *United Way Belarus Report on Objectives for 1995–1996.*

was also unaware that the country was devoid of an infrastructure vital to establishing and sustaining a voluntary sector. NGO staff and leaders probably did not understand all the ramifications of Western assistance and the full significance of developing social capital and civil society.

Belarusian NGOs' outward demeanor toward Westerners was, and still often is, extremely gracious and in many respects deferential. Deference is perhaps wise when one perceives that another holds the key to the future. Belarusians often try to articulate what they think Westerners want to hear, agree to what they understand is wanted, and avoid discussing just how desperate their situation really is, for fear that it will scare off the donor. This behavior, which can be described as chameleon-like, is nevertheless vital for survival. While Westerners are puzzled by the Belarusians' lack of predisposition to pour out their hearts, Belarusians wonder about Westerners' motives and about how long their interest in Belarus will last.

If the West is to achieve a lasting partnership with Belarusian NGOs, it must understand how their cultural norms influence the processes in which it hopes to engage them. Belarusians have described their national character as having been formed by fairy tales and paternal leadership. As children, Belarusians are told stories of the golden fish, the firebird, and other magical personalities, who, in the blink of an eye, can transform one's situation from poor and helpless to rich and powerful. These magical outcomes require no effort or intelligence on the part of the recipient, just purity of heart.

Whether an effort to leverage history to his advantage or his reality, President Lukashenka refers to himself as *bat'ka,* which means "father" in Belarusian, and is reminiscent of the paternal name that rural people used to refer to the tsar. In the Soviet period, strong leaders promised adults that all would be taken care of equitably and everyone would live contentedly. Once again, this led to the belief that the good life requires little effort or learning on the part of the citizen—just trust in the leaders and diligent performance of their daily tasks.

Now, after the collapse of the Soviet Union and with the Belarusian government's inability or lack of desire to meet all social needs, the people find their security and standard of living dramatically declining. They wait for salvation to come, rather than strive to rebuild it for themselves. Western development agencies compound this emerging crisis by insisting that the people assume responsibility and become involved in their own governance. Unfortunately, the West does not take into consideration that Belarusians simply have little cultural or historical precedent on which to base such behavior.

The concept that life will magically improve or that all will be taken care of by the father clashes with Western expectations and challenges the Belarusian people just when they feel they have neither the time nor expertise to make important decisions for themselves. It should not come as a surprise to the West that its overtures for civic engagement are met with disinterest or resistance. It is hard to be excited about something one does not fully understand and that seems extremely difficult, especially when cultural precedence indicates "the father" will provide.

Belarusians are not a homogenous population. Each of the six regions has a distinct historical experience and, as a result, has different strengths, weaknesses, threats, and opportunities. People's attitudes have a lot to do with the section of the country in which they reside. One example is the attitude toward the Belarusian language. For some, it is the center of Belarus' struggle for identity. For others, it is merely a dialect. When working in Belarus, Westerners need to know when they should use Belarusian and when they should use Russian. Familiarity with the country's history is helpful for making the language distinction and other cultural distinctions. Belarusians from western Belarus have a longer history with Europe, having for many years been part of Poland or the Lithuania Duchy. They cherish the Belarusian language as a defining component of their national character. They experienced the Russian Empire and the Soviet Union to a different degree than eastern Belarus. Belarusians from eastern Belarus, on the other hand, tend to identify more with Russia, as they have been a part of Russia culturally for much longer. The operational word here is "tend," for one may find all viewpoints anywhere in Belarus.

Drakokhrust and Furman write about the "Belarusian consciousness" when analyzing the proposed Belarusian-Russian unification.[25] The insight they offer also provides a partial explanation of the challenges with which the West struggles as it advocates democratization through civic engagement. If the Belarusian consciousness of sovereignty is more akin to their experience as the Belarusian Soviet Socialist Republic (BSSR) than the fleeting People's Belarusian Republic of 1918, it is understandable that the Western model of an independent nation might not be a match. The phenomenal development of the individual and the country that Belarus experienced during the Soviet period makes a poor comparison to the low quality of life they find themselves leading ten years after the "transition" to democracy and a market economy.

Toward the end of 1998, the rising development curve of NGOs seemed to stall. This could be attributed to the lingering effects of the 1996 Referendum, or to the fact that donors have focused almost exclusively on the rule of law, human rights, and an independent media. Social projects, which many NGOs feel would reach deep into the population and benefit millions, were superseded by politically oriented projects that appear to benefit only an elite few.

In the last year or two, Belarusian NGOs have started to articulate how they see their relationship with the West and the nature of their expectations. On 14 November 1998, the Assembly held the Second Congress of Pro-Democratic NGOs. In attendance were 520 NGOs out of an estimated 3,000 registered and unregistered organizations. This author organized an anonymous survey distributed to participants.[26] The survey was designed to elicit the NGOs' assessment of the previous four years of public activity and their relationship with Western donors.

In the survey results, the NGOs indicated their motivation for creating an NGO was to meet a need that the government or other organizations were not meeting. Their most critical needs were financing, equipment, a strong professional third sector, foreign contacts, and information. Only 50 percent of the respondents had received donor assistance, and the rest reported that self-financing was

[25]   Drakokhurst and Furman, "Belarus and Russia: The Game of Virtual Integration," Chapter 9 within this volume.

[26]   Data taken from *Survey for Participants of the 2nd Assembly of Belarusian Pro-Democratic NGOs*, conducted by Caryn M. Wilde, Minsk, Belarus, 14 November 1998.

the main source of operating funds. Nearly half of those who had received training or equipment indicated that they frequently shared these tools with other NGOs. In response to questions rating communication between NGOs and donors, only 33 percent rated it above average. To improve the situation, they suggested that donors should establish local offices and Belarusians should be included in strategic planning. The most frequent unsolicited comment by NGOs was that donors do not understand them or their situation and that this gap leads to policies that are incompatible with developing a viable third sector with healthy NGOs. On 25 January 1999, a coalition of leading NGOs, politicians, and former members of the Belarusian government wrote an open letter to USAID to express concerns about relations between the NGOs and donors. "During 1998, various emissaries and diplomats traveling to Belarus have offered various opinions and evaluations about the activities of the Belarusian Third Sector which have in part obscured and confused the unfolding political, economic, and social situation."[27] Candidly, they said that the draft report presented at the First Donor Conference held in November 1997 in Brussels was "superficial and contained biased analysis," and resulted in a decrease in the quantity and quality of foreign aid to the Belarusian third sector. Further, the report had fueled the spreading of false information about NGOs and political parties and bolstered Lukashenka's campaign to discredit public organizations in Belarus. This was a daring step for the Belarusian organizations, admittedly financially dependent on the letter's recipient. It is interesting to note, however, that, according to discussions with some of the authors, it apparently drew little reaction from USAID. What remains unknown is why USAID did not react. One possible explanation is that USAID was put in the same puzzling situation that the NGOs have been in for the past eight years. The NGOs likely asked USAID to do something that it did not know how to do, and the request simply went against all the strategies and systems commonly understood within the agency. Perhaps, in the NGOs' request, there is an opportunity for the powerful Westerners to

---

[27]   Excerpt from, *Open Letter to United States Agency for International Development, January, 15, 1999.* This letter was also published in a leading newspaper in Kyiv, Ukraine.

change themselves in order to find a middle ground that works for both sides.

Strategies for Future Engagement of Belarusian NGOs

If there is one recommendation that this chapter might contribute to future strategies for engagement of Belarusian NGOs, it is to "balance the interests." There is merit in the West's plan to partner with Belarusian reformers, to reach out to the citizenry and motivate them, and to establish a democratic society and a free market economy. There is also merit in the belief that participation will come from the community and that a grassroots initiative will spread, building awareness and trust in civil society institutions as an alternative to autocratic governance. But, the West can only get what it wants if the Belarusians get what they want.

Western development agencies can achieve a balance of interests by:

1. Investing the time and resources to gain a genuine understanding of the Belarusian people and the environment in which they live;

2. Respecting the Belarusian culture, including attitudes, values, goals, and practices;

3. Forming a bona fide partnership that assists rather than acts, and shares both responsibility and the decision-making process;

4. Dedicating ample Western human resources to mentor, cheerlead, and referee;

5. Allowing adequate time (i.e., no limits) for change and anchoring to occur;

6. Adapting programs to local conditions;

7. Keeping expectations high, but attainable; and

8. Respecting themselves by providing responsible stewardship over the financial resources dedicated to the endeavor.

Western development agencies are being challenged to listen to their Belarusian partners, to be willing to rethink their assumptions, and to adjust their strategies to reflect the interests of the partnership.

"Empowerment is a process that people forge themselves as they come to develop their individual and collective capacity for effective action."[28]

---

[28]   Harry Boyte, et al., *Creating the Commonwealth. Public Policy and the Philosophy of Public Work* (Kettering Foundation, 1999). Boyte co-directs the Center for Democracy and Citizenship at the Humphrey Institute, University of Minnesota.

Appendix
The Text of Charter '97[*]

Мы, грамадзяне Рэспублікі Беларусь, заяўляем, што дзеяньні цяперашніх уладаў скіраваныя на зьнішчэньне неад'емных правоў і свабодаў чалавека. У краіне асноўны закон - Канстытуцыя. Беларускаму народу адмоўлена ў праве выбіраць сваіх прадстаўнікоў ва ўладныя структуры. Вядуцца сыстэматычныя наступы на свабоду слова, на права грамадзянаў ведаць сапраўдны стан справаў у краіне. Разбураецца нацыянальная культура і школа, выцясьняецца беларуская мова. Штодзённае павыцэньне коштаў і галечы заробак ставяць на мяжу выжываньня сотні тысячаў семьяў. Напярэдадні XXI стагоддзя ў цэнтры Эўропы ўсталяваўся дыктатарскі рэжым. 10 мільёнаў чалавек аказаліся ва ўладзе самавольства.

Мы верым, што нашая Радзіма вартая свабоды і росквіту. Мы верым, што менавіта такой яе зробяць нашыя сумесныя намаганьні. Нас натхняе прыклад свабодных народаў, якія прайшлі гэты шлях раней за нас. Мы памятаем, як гурт мужных чэскіх і славацкіх праваабаронцаў падпісаў "Хартыю-77", што абвесьціла барацьбу з таталітарызмам у сваёй краіне, і як праз некалькі год ад чырвонай дыктатуры ва Усходняй Эўропе не засталося й сьледу. Людзі ў гэтых краінах атрымалі магчымасьць свабодна будаваць сваё жыцьцё і дасягаць дабрабыту.

Мы ня можам мірыцца з самавольствам, зьневажаньнем законаў, злачынствамі супраць свайго народу й асобнага чалавека. Мы будзем салідарныя з кожным, хто змагаецца за свае правы, дамагаецца свабоды й дабрабыту для сябе і сваёй сямы.

Мы прытрымліваемся розных лаітычных поглядаў і рэлігійных веравызваньняў, але нас аб'ядноўвае любоў да свабоды й Бацькаўшчыны. Падмуркам нашай падрыхтаванасьці да сумесных дзеяньняў па

[*] Taken from the Charter '97 Website: <http://www.charter97.org>.

вызваленьню беларускага народу стане павага да поглядаў і веры адзін аднога. Нашая салідарнасьць пераможа гвалт і бессаромны падман. Усе, хто стаў на шлях барацьбы за свае правы і чалавечую годнасьць, павінны быць упэўненыя ў агульнай падтрымцы.

Мы спадзяемся на разуменьне з боку сусьветнай грамадзкасьці і салідарнасьць усіх сілаў, якія бачаць небясьпеку фармаваньня новай карычневай імпэрыі на постсавецкай прасторы. Асколак таталітарызму павінен быць вырваны зь цела Эўропы.

Мы, грамадзяне Беларусі, заяўляем сёньня пра сваю адказнасьць за лёс краіны, за будучыню нашых дзяцей. Мы зробім Беларусь свабоднай, незалежнай, квітнеючай эўрапейскай краінай, дзе абароненыя правы чалавека, дзе няма палітзняволеных, дзе ўсе маюць вартыя ўмовы для жыцьця.

Мы заклікаем усіх грамадзянаў Беларусі далучыцца да нашай Хартыі, каб разам змагацца за свае павы й свабоды, за аднаўленьне дэмакратыі і законнасьці ў нашай краіне.

Жыве свабодная Беларусь!

Адамовіч Славамір	Голубеў Валяньцін
Андрэяў Віктар	Ганчар Віктар
Бяляцкі Алесь	Грыб Мечыслаў
Бабкоў Ігар	Грыцкевіч Анатоль
Багданкевіч Станіслаў	Сіўчык Мічаслаў
Бандарэнка Зьміцер	Скочка Яўген
Барадач Уладзімір	Статкевіч Мікалай
Барадулін Рыгор	Саснао Аляксандар
Баршчэўскі Лявон	Тарас Валяньцін
Букчын Сямён	Трыгубовіч Валяньціна
Бураўкін Генадзь	Трусаў Алег
Бухвостаў Аляксандар	Тычына Міхась
Быкаў Васіль	Гразнова Людміла
Быкаў Генадзь	Грушавы Генадзь
Васількоў Віталь	Гусак Станіслаў
Вашкевіч Аляксандар	Данэйка Павал
Вільман Віктар	Дашчук Віктар
Волкаў Уладзімір	Дабравольскі Аляксандар
Вольскі Лявон	Домаш Сямён
Вячорка Вінцук	Дрэбязава Галіна
Гавін Тадэўуш	Дударава Надзея
Гілевіч Ніл	Ялфімаў Віктар

Жаляпаў Хрыстафор
Жук Павал
Журакоўскі Валеры
Захаранка Юры
Знавец Павал
Івашкевіч Віктар
Іпатава Вольга
Камоцкая Кася
Каравайчык Іван
Карназыцкі Павал
Карпенка Генадзь
Кацора Уладзімір
Кобаса Міраслаў
Казлоўскі Павал
Карняенка Віктар
Кароль Аляксей
Фадзеяў Валеры
Фрыдлянд Міхась
Халезін Мікалай
Халіп Уладзімір
Хашчавацкі Юры
Хадыка Юры
Чарнао Віктар
Чыгір Міхаіл
Шалкевіч Віктар
Караткевіч Вольга
Костка Валеры
Лаўроўская Ірына
Лябедзька Анатоль
Ліцьвіна Жанна
Марыніч Міхась
Маркевіч Мікалай
Марачкін Алесь
Марцэлеў Сяргей
Мацкевіч Уладзімір
Мілінкевіч Аляксандар
Міндлін Лявон
Міцкевіч Марыя
Нісьцюк Уладзімір
Агурцоў Яўген

Арлоў Уладзімір
Астроўскі Алесь
Пастухоў Міхась
Паганяйля Гары
Патупа Аляксандар
Процька Тацяна
Роўда Уладзімір
Саверчанка Ян
Саньнікаў Андрэй
Севярынец Павал
Сівуха Валеры
Шарэцкі Сямён
Шатернік Аляксандар
Шарамет Павал
Шэрман Карлас
Шлындзікаў Васіль
Шушкевіч Станіслаў
Шчукін Валеры
Юрына Галіна
Якаўлеўскі Раман

We, the citizens of the Republic of Belarus declare that the actions of today's authorities are aimed at elimination of inalienable human rights and freedoms. The Constitution -the basic law of the country - has been violated. The Belarusian people is denied the right to elect its representatives to offices. There are systematic attacks against freedom of speech, against the right of citizens to know the real state of affairs in the country. National culture and school are being destroyed, the Belarusian language is being ousted. Hundreds of thousands of families are on the brink of survival due to the daily rise in prices and miserable salaries. On the eve of the 21 century a dictatorship has been established in the center of Europe. 10 million people have found themselves in the grip of despotism.

We believe that our homeland is worthy of freedom and prosperity. We are convinced that these goals can be achieved through our joint efforts. We are inspired by the example of free peoples that have chosen this way before us. We remember the group of courageous Czech and Slovak human rights activists that signed "Charter 77" declaring struggle against totalitarism in their country. Several years later Eastern Europe got rid of the red dictatorship. The peoples of these countries gained the possibility to develop freely and to work for their well-being.

We cannot reconcile ourselves to despotism, violation of laws, crimes against the people and individuals. We will be in solidarity with everyone who fights for one's rights, seeks freedom and well-being for oneself and one's family.

We are of different political views and faiths but we are united by the love of freedom and our homeland. The basis of our readiness for joint actions to liberate Belarusian people will be respect to the views and faiths of each other. Our solidarity will overcome violence and shameless lies. All who have chosen to fight for human dignity and rights shall be confident in common support.

We count on the understanding of international community and solidarity of all forces that are aware of the danger of the emergence of a new brown empire in the post-Soviet space. The thorn of totalitarism must be removed from the body of Europe.

We, the citizens of Belarus declare today our responsibility for the destiny of the country, for the future of our children. We will make Belarus a free, sovereign and prosperous European country, where human rights are protected, where there are no political prisoners and everyone can live in dignity.

We call upon all citizens of Belarus to join our Charter in order to fight together for our rights and freedoms, to restore democracy and rule of law in our country.

LONG LIVE FREE BELARUS!

Adamovich, Slavomir
Andreev, Victor
Belyatsky, Ales
Bobkov, Igor
Bogdankevich, Stanislav
Bondarenko, Dmitry
Borodach, Vladimir
Borodulin, Rygor
Borshchevsky, Lyavon
Bukchin, Semyon
Bukhvostov, Alexander
Buravkin, Guennady
Bykov, Guennady
Bykov, Vasil
Chernov, Victor
Chigir, Mikhail
Daneiko, Pavel
Dashuk, Victor
Dobrovolsky, Alexander
Domash, Semyon
Drebezova, Galina
Dudareva, Nadezhda
Fadeev, Valery
Fridland, Mikhail
Gavin, Tadeush
Golubev, Valentin
Gonchar, Victor
Grib, Mechislav
Gritskevich, Anatoly
Grushevoy, Guennady
Gryaznova, Ludmila
Guilevich, Nil

Gusak, Stanislav
Ipatova, Olga
Ivashkevich, Victor
Kamotskaya, Kasya
Karavaichik, Ivan
Karnazytsky, Pavel
Karpenko, Guennady
Katsora, Vladimir
Khalezin, Nikolai
Khalip, Vladimir
Khashchevatsky, Yuri
Khodyko, Yuri
Kobasa, Miroslav
Korneenko, Victor
Korol, Alexei
Korotkevich, Olga
Kostka, Valery
Kozlovsky, Pavel
Lavrovskaya, Irina
Lebedko, Anatoly
Litvina, Zhanna
Marinich, Mikhail
Markevich, Nikolai
Marochkin, Ales
Martselev, Serguei
Matskevich, Vladimir
Milinkevich, Alexander
Mindlin, Leonid
Mitskevich, Maria
Nistyuk, Vladimir
Ogurtsov, Yevgueny
Ostrovsky, Ales

Pastukhov, Mikhail
Pogonyailo, Garry
Potupa, Alexander
Protko, Tatyana
Rovdo, Vladimir
Sannikov, Andrei
Saverchenko, Ivan
Severinets, Pavel
Shalkevich, Victor
Sharetsky, Semyon
Shaternik, Alexander
Shchukin, Valery
Sheremet, Pavel
Sherman, Carlos
Shlyndikov, Vassily
Shushkevich, Stanislav
Sivchik, Vyacheslav
Sivukha, Valery
Skochko, Yevgueny
Sosnov, Alexander
Statkevich, Nikolai
Taras, Valentin
Tikhinya, Valery
Tregubovich, Valentina
Trusov, Oleg
Tychina, Mikhas
Vashkevich, Alexander
Vasilkov, Vitaly
Vilman, Victor
Volkov, Vladimir
Volsky, Lyavon
Vyachorka, Vintsuk
Yakovlevsky, Roman
Yelfimov, Victor
Yurina, Galina
Zakharenko, Yuri
Zhelyapov, Christofor
Zhuk, Pavel
Zhurakovsky, Valery
Znavets, Pavel

Index*

ABM (Antiballistic Missile) Treaty
(1972), 267
Abramava, Volha [*Rus.* Olga
Abramova], 388
Abramovich, Aliaksandr [*Rus.* Alek-
sandr], 102
Act on Public Organizations (1994), 440,
441
Adamkus, Valdas
on Belarusian-Russian integration, 337
on relations with Belarus and Russia,
322, 325
Aiatskov, Dmitrii, 246
Alternative Labor Exchange, 71
Antanovich, Ivan [*Rus.* Antonovich],
196, 207, 338, 376
Anti-Corruption Committee, 84
Antonchyk, Siarhei [*Rus.* Sergei Anton-
chik], 63–64, 71
Aragona, Giancarlo, 376
Aushev, Ruslan, 228, 246

Bahdankevich, Stanislaŭ [*Rus.* Stanislav
Bogdankevich], 58, 65, 95, 335, 385
Baltic Energy Bridge, 178
Bandarenka, Zmitser (Dzmitri) [*Rus.*
Dmitrii Bondarenko], 62, 63
Barshcheŭski, Liavon [*Rus.* Lev
Barshchevskii], 62, 384
Barysaŭ [*Rus.* Borisov], 61
Baublis, Victor, 331
BelaPAN, 58, 366
Belarus
background of, 6–8
border issues, 185–88, 194, 202–203,
207–208, 324, 338, 339, 340
EU funds for border crossing, 330
coat of arms, Pahoniia, 99

demographic characteristics
age, influence of, 33, 43, 46
community of, in Lithuania, 332–33
education and social status, 32, 43,
47, 158–59
language use, 30, 32, 43, 48, 94–95,
368–69
national identity, 29–32, 263, 323
in Poland, 351–52
religious beliefs, 31–32, 43, 47
as destabilizing force, 395
development compared to neighboring
countries, 78
economy. *See* Belarusian economy
education and youth exchange
programs with Lithuania, 332–33
energy consumption, 169. *See also*
energy policy
foreign policy. *See* Belarusian foreign
policy
foreign trade. *See* Belarusian foreign
trade
historical influences on internal and
foreign policies, 322–25, 366–67
geographic location, importance of,
163, 171, 173, 193, 226, 260–62
independence, declaration of (1991),
60, 369
international organizations, role of,
366–92
"Lukashenka phenomenon," 77–108.
See also Lukashenka, Aliaksandr
national holidays, 66
national symbols, 56, 61, 94–95, 99,
367
NATO and, 303–305, 314
impact of NATO enlargement on
Belarus, 105–106, 220–21, 223,
260, 262, 266, 338, 398